*for Cony*

*fu Michi*

*Хорошего пути.*

**Athol Yates** (Антон Ятис) researched and wrote the first edition of this book. He has had a long fascination with Russian politics, history and language and has travelled extensively throughout Russia as a student, journalist, and researcher. He has an engineering degree, a Graduate Diploma in Soviet Studies, and a Masters in Public Policy. He studied Russian at Melbourne University, Moscow's Patrice Lumumba University, and Hungary's Egar Teachers' Institute. He is currently a policy analyst specialising in industry, defence and infrastructure policy in Canberra, Australia.

**Nicholas Zvegintzov** (Николас Звегинцов) researched and updated the second edition of this book. Born in England, he learned about Russia and travelling from his immigrant father. He has a degree from Oxford University in Psychology and Philosophy, and has studied Russian at Moscow State University. He lives in New York City and is a software consultant and writer, helping in the management and modification of existing software. He practises long-distance travel on the New York City Subway, the Moscow Metro, the London Underground and, of course, the BAM. Contact him at ✉ zvegint@attglobal.net.

**Siberian BAM Guide – rail, rivers and road**
First edition October 1995
This second edition September 2001

**Publisher**
Trailblazer Publications
The Old Manse, Tower Rd, Hindhead, Surrey, GU26 6SU, UK
Fax (+44) 01428-607571
Email: info@trailblazer-guides.com
www.trailblazer-guides.com

**British Library Cataloguing in Publication Data**
A catalogue record for this book is available from the British Library

**ISBN 1-873756-18-6**

**Editor:** Anna Jacomb-Hood
**Editorial consultant**: Rashit Yahin
**Series editor:** Patricia Major
**Typesetting:** Anna Udagawa and Bryn Thomas
**Cartography:** Athol Yates, Bryn Thomas & Nick Hill
**Layout**: Anna Jacomb-Hood
**Index:** Jane Thomas

Every effort has been made by the authors and publisher to ensure that the
information contained herein is as accurate and up to date as possible. They are,
however, unable to accept responsibility for any inconvenience, loss or injury sustained by anyone as a result of the advice and information given in this guide.

Printed and bound by Kelso Graphics (☎ 01573-223214), Scotland

# SIBERIAN
# BAM GUIDE
### RAIL, RIVERS & ROAD

## Путеводитель по району БАМ
### железные и автомобильные дороги, реки
#### Включает БАМ, реку Лена, Колымскую трассу

## ATHOL YATES &
## NICHOLAS ZVEGINTZOV

# TRAILBLAZER PUBLICATIONS

## Other contributors

**Photographs** Tatyana Pozar-Burgar is fascinated with both photography and Russia. Determined to capture the country on film, she has travelled Russia extensively over the last eight years accumulating a vast collection of photographs on the richness of Russian culture and ancestry. She studied Russian at Melbourne and Moscow universities. Tatyana has a strong interest in Indian arts and toured and danced throughout India in 1997 with the Natya Sudha Dance Company. Recently Tatyana has started writing a cultural and historical Slovenian cuisine book.

**Editorial Consultant** Rashit Yahin takes enormous pleasure in revealing the natural treasures of the BAM Zone and the North Baikal region to both Russians and Westerners. In many ways, Rashit symbolises the tragedy of the Soviet era and, in particular, the delusion under which the BAM builders toiled. Rashit was born in a prison camp, the son of an imprisoned and exiled Tatar mullah. He was discriminated against as a child of an 'enemy of the working class' but, against all odds, he obtained an engineering degree and went to work in Moscow at the BAM planning organisation, BAMProek. Rashit arrived in Severobaikalsk with the first BAM builders in 1974 and worked there until being dismissed for signing a letter of complaint about working conditions which was sent to the Minister of Railways. He was later re-employed as a tunnel labourer. He is a Master of chess, a prominent activist in the Eastern Siberian environmental movement and speaks excellent English. He is currently Director of BAMTour Co, in Severobaikalsk.

**Editor, Jacinta Nelligan** Without her meticulous editing, moral support and indulgent patience, the first edition of this book would have been just a jumble of words.

**Editorial Consultant, Marina Aleksandrovna Kuzmina** Marina is one of the Russian Far East's foremost experts on gulags, Japanese prisoners of war and the history of the BAM. She has written three books on these subjects in Russian. She is currently the Secretary of the Japanese-Russian Friendship Society's Komsomolsk-na-Amure Branch, Chairperson of Memorial, which is a group representing those who suffered during the years of Stalinist repression, and is active in local politics.

**Contributor, Paul Geldhof** (✉ paul.geldhof@laposte.net) Paul earns his living in micro-electronics design but manages nevertheless to go travelling every now and again. Fascinated by Russia and the Russians since his first trip in 1992, he has been back four times and in total has spent more than a year in the country, especially in Eastern Siberia and the Russian Far East.

**Russian language editors** Vera Gordonova, Ilya Karachevtsev and Inna Karachevtseva: Thanks for your help.

## Acknowledgements

**From Athol Yates**: Ilya and Inna Karachevtsev, John Sloan, Elena Vvedenskaya, Marion Mitcham.

**From Nicholas Zvegintzov**: Pasha Nelunova and Denis Alyonushkin of the Yakutsk Internet Café, Arsen Karlovich Antonyan of the Diana Children's Camp, Don Croner and Elliot Mainzer for information on the source of the Lena, Marina Grigorieva and Galina Zhuravlova of Alfa Tour, Judith Marx Golub of Software Management Network, Vyacheslav Ipatiev of TourService Center Ltd, Tim Littler, Peter Hedderly, and Marina Linke of GW Travel Limited, Evgeny Maryasov of the School of Tourism-Ecology Education, Vladimir Ivanovich Natresenyuk, Mayor of Verkhnezeisk, the New York Public Library, Nadezhda Konstantinovna Nizova of Nadezhda Ltd, Mikhail Radokhleb of Nata-Tour Co Ltd, Anatoli Semilet of Tourist Club Kedr, Alexander F Shelopugin of Dersu Uzala Tourist Centre, Anatoli Stepanovich Stativa of PNILZ, Leonid Mikhailovich Yadrov of Tynda School-Youth Centre for Tourism and Excursions; Viktoriya Alexeeva, Ivan Averichev, Nikolai and Zoya Bęlski, Ray Bengen, Natalya Vitalevna Chernetsova, Yuri Nikolaevich Kokovin, Afanasi Nikolaevich Maksimov, Elena Maslennikova, Leslie McAllister, Pat Ormsby, Vasili Klimovich Pavlov, Vladimir and Tatyana Shestakov, Hafis Yahin, Athol Yates, Anna Zvegintzov.

# CONTENTS

# 6  Contents

## PART 3: BAM MAINLINE ROUTES
(Описание пути по магистрали)

## PART 4: BAM BRANCH LINE ROUTES
(Описание путей по веткам)

## PART 5: REPUBLIC OF SAKHA

## Appendices (Приложения)

**Route maps**

# INTRODUCTION
## (Введение)

East of the great Siberian plain rise formidable mountain barriers stretching more than 3,000km to the Pacific and the Arctic oceans. This is the Russian north-east – famous for political exiles, pristine environment, indigenous villages, cold war secrets and communist dreams. The region contains the world's largest contiguous forest and fertile wilderness. At the same time it is the site of the largest single civil engineering project of the post-war world – the 3400km BAM railway and its visionary cities. It is Russia's last frontier.

In many ways, it is a region of secrets. First, it is dauntingly inaccessible. Jumbled mountain ridges with thickly wooded valleys and flanks scored with rock slides can only be travelled where rivers have dug their twisting canyons. Along the rivers, trappers, merchants and exiles travelled by boat in the summer and by sled in the winter. Settlers built trading posts and then towns and then cities by the rivers. Yet beyond the rivers the mountains kept their secrets.

Second, the region was politically closed. Throughout the Soviet era all foreigners and most Russians were banned from the entire area. Behind the barrier were gulags, military installations and sophisticated defence industries. Many residents have never met a Westerner.

Third, the region is something of a vacation secret for adventure travellers from the rest of Russia. Parties travel to the north-east for days in the train with packs, tents, kayaks, and floats to run the wild and almost endless rivers, or in winter to ski across inaccessible passes and sauna in hot springs with ice in their hair. But tourists in the usual sense are few and far between. You can travel all over the railways, rivers and roads of the north-east and never see a Western traveller.

The traditional highways of the region are the great rivers – the Yenisei, the Lena and the Amur. The Russian settlements of the 17th century, now cities – Irkutsk, Yakutsk, and Khabarovsk – are built on these rivers. The great road across the continent, which was paralleled in 1897 by the Trans-Siberian railway, leapfrogged between the rivers to reach the Pacific at Vladivostok by the easiest path.

The Soviet state, with its boundless enthusiasm and abundant free labour, dreamed of opening up direct pathways through the north-east mountains, links between the cities, access to gold, diamonds, coal and timber. In 1933 the government published plans for a new railway, the BAM or Baikal-Amur Mainline, to branch off from the Trans-Siberian at Taishet in eastern Siberia, head north of Lake Baikal and cross the mountains to the Pacific harbour of Sovetskaya Gavan, 900km north of Vladivostok. In 1937, the AYaAD, the Amur Yakutsk Highway, was completed due south from Yakutsk to Bolshoi Never on the Trans-Siberian, crossing two major chains of mountains and many rivers. Construction of the BAM continued until Stalin's death in 1953, when most of the project was shelved.

In 1974 under Brezhnev the BAM was revived as a national priority and was made a Komsomol shock project, with the participation of the entire USSR. The 'golden spike', completing the main line, was hammered in 1984 and the entire line was opened to all traffic by 1990. The route crosses three major mountain ranges and threads through the watersheds of all three major rivers. For most of the route, the railway is the only land access – roads are at best rugged, at worst non-existent.

Along the way, architects and construction brigades from all over the USSR created three new cities and over 100 new settlements. The BAM towns form a brilliant string of imaginative designs, boldly sited, vigorously built and filled with interesting buildings. The string of bold railway stations is a delight. It should be as famous in the wilds as the Moscow Metro is in the city!

This guide opens the Russian north-east to the visitor. It is not only a guide to travel but a handbook to this rarely visited region. It recognises that it is the culture, daily life and environment of people that is most interesting, rather than dry history and monuments. For this reason, the book emphasises the human aspects of the region, profiling a range of people, discussing the post-Soviet Russian culture and describing the daily life of the inhabitants and the towns.

Come and share the secrets of this fascinating region. Good journey! Счастливого пути!

### The Nanai 'Venus'

The Nanai 'Venus', featured in the part headings of this book, is a 5-6,000-year-old pottery image found in 1965 in the Nanai village of Kondon, 5km from the BAM railway (see p166). One of the most exciting archaeological finds in the Russian Far East, it establishes the characteristics of the earliest inhabitants. Along the Lena and Amur rivers and the BAM railway you can still see the soft oval face, broad cheekbones, arched eyes, long thin nose, slender chin, and small pouting lips of this ancient portrait.

# PART 1: PLANNING YOUR TRIP
## Планирование путешествия

## Introduction
### Введение

This chapter explains what you need to know when setting off for Russia, and for north-east Russia in particular.

Russia as a whole has little tourist culture and the north-east has none whatever. This means that you are unlikely to be shuttled in private buses, shepherded by English-speaking guides, served group meals or herded into folkloric museums. Instead, you will travel with ordinary Russians going about their regular lives – business people on business trips, workers on jobs, soldiers on travel orders, families going to visit their relatives, school parties, even bums. You will be granted the ordinary courtesy and camaraderie of the traveller, but nobody will offer you, or even know how to offer you, the special consideration of a tourist or the obsequious service of a rich customer. (Equally you are unlikely to be cheated or tempted with tourist scams). But this means that you will be expected to know what you are doing and what you want to do, or at least to be able to ask for directions.

Thus the purpose of this chapter and the next is to inform you how to get into Russia, how to travel, how to find a bite to eat and a place to sleep, how to get where you want to go and see what you want to see, and how to share life with a rugged, buoyant and warm-hearted people.

## Getting information
### Как получить информацию

The maxim 'You get out what you put in' is just as true for travelling as it is for anything else. For this reason, it is advisable to read as widely as possible about Russia and its north-east before travelling.

This guide provides the detail for the traveller – the routes through the region, the cities and towns and villages, how to travel, where to stay, the wilderness and mountains and wild rivers and how to experience them, as well as the history and character of the people. Other resources – such as travel guides and other books, documentary and fiction films, and travellers' tales on the web and elsewhere – are listed in Appendix E (p355).

Russia is a centralised, industrialised country. In the north-east you will find the same towns, government buildings, schools, highways, railways, police, food-stores, hotels, markets and pharmacies that you will find in other parts of Russia. The way of life is European, though the longitudes range from that of Thailand on the west to that of Japan in the east. Knowledge of life in Russia will prepare you for the north-east. Yet the people have a frontier character – physically tough, active, self-reliant, outgoing and humorous – contrasting with the cautious and sometimes melancholy people of western Russia. Many are from families that faced the worst that society could throw at them – confiscation, exile and imprisonment – and they survived and prospered.

English-language books about the north-east include a few travel guides, regional histories, economic studies, chronicles of the *gulags*, and the glossy albums, communist propaganda hero-constructor novels, and technical books about building the BAM.

The best sources of information are in the region. The section Travel Agents (see pp17-19) lists agents in most major centres of the region; besides making local and tour arrangements for you, they can put you in touch with local people and with other travellers. Several of the agents have websites and email.

While it won't help you when preparing for a trip, once you are over there it's worthwhile going to libraries and bookshops and asking for maps or other information on your particular areas of interest. Sometimes, tucked away on the shelves, are maps of trekking routes in the mountains, fishing guides and other rare finds. Another source of information once you are over there is local (Russian) papers which provide information on upcoming public celebrations, museum displays as well as interesting things to see and do.

Learn as much as you can. On the other hand, don't believe everything you read. The Russian north-east is a long way from most media and is correspondingly mythologised.

Remember that only bad news sells and that most of the media coverage of Russia as a whole is negative. (Typical of this tendency to exaggerate was the so-called 'Food Crisis' in 1991 and the 1994/5 'Crime Wave'). Misinformation (дезинформация) is especially rife about the north-east. Remember that Komsomolsk-na-Amure is nearly three times as far from Moscow as it is from Tokyo. Several documentary and TV crews have asked the writers of this guide to help them film 'the real horrors'. Moscow sources (including travel agents) told us that the north-east is full of criminals, that there is famine, and the trains don't run. Maybe they are genuinely afraid, remembering how long Moscow has been banishing its rejects to the farthest corners of the country.

None of this is true, though perhaps the north-easterners don't wholeheartedly contradict their reputation.

# Getting there
## Как доехать

## TO RUSSIA (До России)

Since the end of the Soviet system independent travel is legal and feasible in Russia. There are no prohibited areas any more except military and secure sites. Provided you have a visa, you can enter and leave Russia by any passenger port of entry (as it says on your visa – 'Через пограничные пункты, открытые для рассажирского движения'). Effectively, any airport with international flights, any place where a railway or a main highway crosses the border, and any port at which foreign ships dock is a legal port of entry. Therefore you have a wide choice of routes to approach Russia.

From Moscow you can take a plane direct to Irkutsk, Yakutsk, Komsomolsk-na-Amure and Khabarovsk. Khabarovsk has the largest airport in the Russian Far East and has international flights from Japan, China and other countries. Remember that in Khabarovsk you are seven time-zones away from Moscow and only five time-zones (and an International Date Line) from Alaska and six time-zones from California.

Ports include Vladivostok (ferry from Japan) and Vanino (ferry from Sakhalin) on the Pacific coast, Nikolaevsk-na-Amure at the mouth of the Amur river, and Tiksi near the mouth of the Lena river.

Foreign rail links are from Mongolia (the Trans-Mongolian), China (the Trans-Manchurian), and North Korea.

So you can enter Russia anywhere and then travel to the north-east.

## THE VISA (Виза)

A Russian visa is essential. In the Soviet days, a visa was issued for a specific route at a specific time. The state travel monopoly, Intourist, provided a visa for as many days as accommodation was booked. The hotel at which you stayed and the transport that you used would check your authorisation and report your presence.

Those days are gone and now you can get a visa for as many days as requested. A visa is issued against an invitation from a licensed Russian organisation or from a private person who has registered your intended visit with the authorities. You must attach the invitation to your visa application and present it with the appropriate fee to the Russian consulate. In practice, however, the consulates prefer to cut through the bureaucracy by dealing with a visa service, an organisation with an arm in Russia that issues invitations and an arm in your country that presents your application to the consulate (and charges you a fee). The consulate will supply a list of such visa services. If a travel agent gets you your visa, it may operate such a visa service or use one.

Until 1999, a Russian visa listed your itinerary (Маршрут следования (в пункты)). This is no longer the case.

The old system and the new co-exist uneasily over the question of towns listed on your invitation. Though no towns are listed on your visa, Russia is still insisting that they must be listed on the invitation. A visa service will gladly type any destinations that you request on your invitation. Nobody really knows if you are forbidden to visit other places. The important thing is that some hotels and some police forces think that this is so, and particularly so in places that see few visitors or that have a history of security concerns.

If you find yourself in a town not listed on your invitation, and the hotel or police or the railway challenge you on it, the matter is usually solved in an accommodating way. In our experience you will not be deported or imprisoned or made to sleep in the waiting room. You should not argue, but promise to leave tomorrow, and plead that you are in transit or had to make an emergency stop or that the consulate in your country assured you it was all in order. At worst you may have to pay a fine, of the order of US$10.

Certain places have specific visa regulations or have a bad reputation for visa hassles. The Republic of Sakha (Yakutiya) requires the names of the towns you wish to visit on your Russian invitation. Therefore if you intend to visit Yakutsk or one of the Sakha gold or diamond towns, have them listed on your invitation ahead of time. (For more on this see pp230). In addition, one of the editors had a huge hassle with the railway police at Vanino because the town was not listed, so list it if you intend to stay there or to take the ferry to Sakhalin.

A one-entry/one-exit visa is valid for a period of 30 days from entry. A multiple-entry visa is valid for one year. A stay of more than three months (13 days in Sakha) requires a doctor's certificate of freedom from HIV.

As Russian visa rules and regulations change all the time, you should contact your local consulate, travel agent or visa service for the latest information.

## TO THE NORTH-EAST AND THE BAM
(До северо-востока и до БАМа)

Besides the international connections just listed, there are direct flights from Moscow to Yakutsk, Magadan, Khabarovsk, and Irkutsk, roughly forming the four corners of the north-east. Many towns and even small settlements in the north-east have air services if you are willing to change and possibly wait around.

The best connections are by railway. There is a direct train from Moscow every day to either Lena or Tynda on the BAM. This train branches off from the Trans-Siberian at Taishet. The BAM runs from Taishet to the Pacific north of and roughly parallel to the eastern end of the Trans-Siberian. From Tynda there is a daily train to Komsomolsk-na-Amure and from Komsomolsk-na-Amure a daily train to Vanino. For information about this route see the sections starting on p61.

There are three south-north branch lines that link the Trans-Siberian to the BAM (see pp206-224). In addition, you can reach the BAM by taking the hydrofoil from Irkutsk down the Angara to Bratsk (see p70), from Irkutsk up Lake Baikal (see p88), and also down the Amur river from Khabarovsk to Komsomolsk-na-Amure (see pp224-228).

The roads of the north-east range from rugged to non-existent. There is no paved road across the Russian Far East, let alone the north-east. Crossing the Far East by four-wheel drive, motor cycle, or pedal cycle has spawned a small literature of travellers tales (p356, Appendix E). However, there are highways, and some of them have bus services. The most important highways, not paralleled by railways, link Yakutsk – the AYaAD Highway to the south (see pp272-278) and the Kolyma Highway to the east (see pp279-290).

# Itineraries
## Маршруты

A straight trip from Moscow over the BAM to the Pacific takes $8^{1}/_{2}$ days; $5^{1}/_{2}$ days from Moscow to Tynda direct, a day-time stopover at Tynda, two days to Komsomolsk-na-Amure and one night to Vanino.

Most tours of the BAM start or end at either Khabarovsk or Irkutsk, where there are direct Trans-Siberian trains from Moscow in the west and Vladivostok in the east and a good air service.

### SIX-DAY TOUR OF THE BAM

This route takes you from Khabarovsk to Irkutsk, through the BAM highlights, with only minimal stops.
**Day 1**  Take the hydrofoil or a shared taxi from Khabarovsk to Komsomolsk-na-Amure. Arrive in the afternoon. (If you take the train, you arrive in the evening). Leave in the evening on the Komsomolsk-na-Amure–Tynda train.
**Day 2**  Pass through the Dusse-Alin tunnel early in the morning. Stop at Novy Urgal and Urgal-1. Change time-zone early afternoon. Stop at Fevralsk early afternoon and Verkhnezeisk after midnight.

**Day 3** Arrive Tynda in the morning. Leave on the Tynda–Moscow train in the afternoon. Reach Yuktali by evening and Khani after midnight.

**Day 4** Cross the Udokan range by night and reach Novaya Chara early in the morning, pass the Leprindo lakes and the Kodar tunnel. Change time zone. Stop at Taksimo late morning. Cross the Severomuisk pass after midday. Stop at Novy Uoyan in the afternoon and arrive at Severobaikalsk by evening. At Severobaikalsk you can stay overnight and take the hydrofoil down Lake Baikal to Irkutsk in one day.

Alternatively continue on the BAM. Head into the Baikal mountains and pass through the Baikal Mountain Tunnel late in the evening.

**Day 5** Cross the Lena river during the night and stop at Korshunikha-Angarskaya early in the morning. Cross the Bratsk dam in the middle of the day. Arrive at Taishet on the Trans-Siberian in the evening. According to the timetable you can catch the west-east Trans-Siberian express 'Rossiya' with 11 minutes to spare.

**Day 6** Arrive at Irkutsk early in the morning. From here you can catch a direct train to Moscow, Vladivostok, Ulaanbaatar, or Beijing.

## Stops on the BAM

There are many excursions and side-trips that can be added to the main trip, for one to six days, for example:

● **Severobaikalsk** Swimming, sailing, canoeing, cruising on Lake Baikal; fishing and ice-fishing; seal-watching and seal-hunts; visit hot springs and spas; climb and hike; visit gulag sites in the mountains; trek with horses or reindeer; float trips; white-water river running on the Lena.

● **Taksimo** Run the Parama Rapids, long-distance rafting.

● **Kuanda** Fishing, mountain and glacier climbing, hiking and swimming on the lakes.

● **Novaya Chara** Visit the sand dunes, hiking and mountaineering, expedition to the Marble Canyon Gulag.

● **Yuktali** Visit Ust-Nyukzha, ancient town, ethnographical museum, and reindeer breeding farm; river camping.

● **Tynda** Indigenous village, long-distance river trips.

● **Fevralsk** Rafting, hot springs, gold mining.

● **Komsomolsk-na-Amure** War and repression memorials; the aircraft factory and museum; the Pivan BAM tunnel; rafting, floating, and white-water; extreme skiing; the Komsomolsk Nature Reserve; indigenous villages; hydrofoil down the Amur river to the ocean; cruising to the Shantar islands.

● **Vanino and Sovetskaya Gavan** Tour the Pacific coast and the 1930s anti-Japanese fortifications; see spawning fish runs (August and September); wilderness safari. Another option is to catch the ferry to Sakhalin Island.

## TOUR OF THE LENA AND YAKUTSK

A trip down the 4,400km Lena river, using available transport and allowing minimal stops, takes 11 days. (It could take longer, depending on connections). Upstream against the current the entire journey takes four more days.

Here is a sample, starting from Irkutsk.

**Day 1** Bus, Irkutsk–Zhigalovo. Stay overnight.

**Day 2** Hydrofoil, Zhigalovo–Ust-Kut, Osetrovo River Station. Stay overnight.

**Day 3** In the morning take the river steamer from Ust-Kut, Osetrovo River Station downstream to Yakutsk.

**Day 4** Early in the morning stop at Kirensk. Late at night stop at Vizirny.

**Day 5** Stop at Vitim in the middle of the night, and Peledui early in the morning. Major stop at Lensk in the afternoon. Stop on demand at many small villages through the evening and night.

**Day 6** Major stop at Olekminsk in the morning.
Stop on demand at many small villages through the evening and night.

**Day 7** Afternoon, pass through the Lena Pillars.
Arrive Yakutsk late in the evening.

**Days 8-11** Take the river steamer downstream from Yakutsk to the Lena delta and the Arctic Ocean port of Tiksi.

### Stops on the Lena and around Yakutsk

Excursions and side-trips on the Lena and around Yakutsk, for one to six days, include:

● **The source of the Lena** Boat in from Lake Baikal, climb the Baikal Range and camp at the source of the Lena.

● **White water on the Lena** Face Class 3 rapids in the first 150km of the Lena.

● **Kachug to Verkholensk** Expedition to the Paleolithic and Neolithic petroglyphs and rock drawings.

● **Ust-Kut and Lena** Explore the busiest port on the river and stay at the famous spa.

● **Kirensk** Old wooden-built river town.

● **Lensk** Trip to the diamond town of Mirny.

In and around Yakutsk there are many possible trips:

● Tour the old and new city, the Regional Museum and the Permafrost Institute.

● Take the river trip to the Druzhba Historical Park, with original Russian and Evenk buildings on the site of the first settlement.

● De luxe cruise down the Lena to the ocean with picnics, barbecues, sing-songs, fish feasts, visits to native villages, and visit the International Biological Station for bird-watching in the delta park preserve.

● De luxe cruise to the Lenskie Stolby ('Lena Pillars').

● Residential visit to the Bakaldyn Evenk ethnographic complex – stay in a nomad tent or an indigenous log building, trek with reindeer and ski or canoe, squirrel hunt, Evenk ceremonies.

● Take the hydrofoil down to the mouth of the Aldan river and up to the gold and coal region of Khandyga.

● Take the river steamer down to the mouth of the Vilyui river and up to the diamond regions beyond Nyurba.

● Visit the 'pole of cold' between Tomtor and Oimyakon with the northern hemisphere's lowest winter temperature – -71°C.

## ALONG THE AYAAD AND AYAM FROM YAKUTSK TO TYNDA

From Yakutsk you can return on the AYaAD highway and the AYaM railway due south to join the main line of the BAM at Tynda:

**Day 1**  Leave Yakutsk by bus or shared taxi. Cross the Lena river by ferry or ice-road. Arrive Aldan.

**Day 2**  Bus Aldan–Neryungri. Train Neryungri–Tynda.

Excursions and side-trips along the way include the gold mines and gold factories of Aldan, the Vasilevka gulag, the gigantic open-pit coal-mine at Neryungri, rafting and canoeing on the Iengra river and the precipitous crossing of the Stanovoi range.

# Travel arrangements
### Подготовка к путешествию

Regardless of what travel agents say, it is possible, although sometimes difficult, to book train tickets and hotels by yourself. In the north-east you are almost always assured of a seat on any train (though not necessarily a coupé), and you can always find a hotel bed even if you have to try a couple of hotels.

You may make your major travel plans with an external agent but, given the general ignorance of the north-east, if you want local arrangements or a specialised tour you should make arrangements with an agent in the region.

Agents are listed in the Getting assistance sections under each town. All the agents listed have experience helping incoming visitors as well as organising outgoing travel for local people. Some of the agents have special experience with either business travel or adventure expeditions.

Follow these guidelines in assessing a local agent:

● Ask for their government issued, international tourist operations licence number.

● While they may be experts and can organise everything in their own town, how will they, and with whom will they, organise activities in other towns?

● Can they issue visa invitations?

● Can you pay only a deposit and the rest once you arrive?

● Do they have a hard currency bank account so you can electronically transfer money?

● Most important of all, be explicit about the services you want and suggest a price. See Costs p19.

## TRAVEL AGENTS (Агентства)

The following agents are also discussed in the Getting assistance sections of their respective towns. In some cases more details can be found there.

### Severobaikalsk (Северобайкальск)

BAMTour is the best-known company organising tours on the BAM and in the north Lake Baikal region. Director Rashit Yahin is one of the oldest residents in Severobaikalsk, having worked on the railway in the early 1970s, and is Editorial Consultant on this guide. Contact Rashit Yahin at BAMTour Company, 671717 Severobaikalsk, ul. Oktyabrya 16-2, ☎/🖹 +7 30139 21560, 🖳 rashit.yahin@usa.net (671717 Северобайкальск, ул. Октября, 16-2, БАМТУР, Яхин Рашит).

The School of Tourism-Ecology Education organises outdoor events for local students and for groups and individuals from outside Severobaikalsk. It has accommodation in Severobaikalsk and at Slyudanski Lakes (Слюданские озера), 15km south. It can organise excursions and transportation for individuals and groups, and supply maps, camping equipment, canoes and floats. Contact Evgeny Maryasov at the School of Tourism-Ecology Education, per. Shkolny 11, ☎ +7 30139 2-03-23, 🖳 davan@burnet.ru (671717 Бурятия, г. Северобайкальск, Пер. Школьный, 11, Муниципальная школа туристско-экологического образования, Марясов Евгений).

### Tynda (Тында)

Nadezhda Ltd, owned by the energetic Nadezhda Konstantinovna Nizova, is licensed to organise travel for residents and tourism for visitors. It can set up local excursions and long-distance travel on the BAM. Contact Nadezhda Ltd, Nadezhda Konstantinovna Nizova, General Director, 676080, Russia, g. Tynda, Amurskaya Oblast, ul. Festivalnaya 1, (☎ +7 41656 2-05-93, 🖹 +7 41656 2-13-58, telex: 288126 DWC SU, 🖳 td_nadejda@amur.ru (676080, Россия, Амурская область, г. Тында, ул. Фестивальная, 1, Торговый Дом «Надежда», Низова Надежда Константиновна, Генеральный директор).

The Tynda School-Youth Centre for Tourism and Excursions organises outdoor events for local students and can organise excursions for groups and individuals from outside. Leonid Mikhailovich Yadrov is Director. Contact him at Detsko-yunoshcheski tsentr turizma i ekskursi, Festivalnaya 7, ☎ 2-72-33 (676080, Россия, Амурская область, г. Тында, ул. Фестивальная, 7, Децко-юнощеский центр туризма и экскурсий, Ядров Леонид Михаилович, Директор).

### Komsomolsk-na-Amure (Комсомольск-на-Амуре)

Nata-Tour Co Ltd, run by Mikhail Radokhleb, organises adventure tours, including white-water rafting and river floating, expeditions into the *taiga* on foot and by vehicle, train tours as well as gulag and POW camp tours. Radokhleb was educated as a railway engineer; his hobby was outside sports, especially rafting. His office, with phone/fax, copier, maps, photos, brochures and Internet access, is on the ground floor of Voskhod Hotel. Contact him at Nata-Tour Co Ltd, pr. Pervostroitelei 31, Hotel Voskhod, Room 104, Komsomolsk-na-Amure, 681010 Russia, ☎/🖹 +7 42172 3-03-32, 🖳 natatour@kmscom.ru, www.amur.rusnet.ru/natatour (681010, Россия, г. Комсомольск-на-Амуре, пр. Первостроителей, 31, Гостиница «Восход», 104, «Ната-Тур», Радохлеб Михаил).

Dersu Uzala Tourist Centre, run by Alexander F Shelopugin, organises specialised tours (business, archaeological, geological) and adventure tours (hunting, fishing, climbing, rafting, skiing), plus trips for young people and for foreigners. Contact him at ul. Sevastopolskaya, House 12, Office 16, Komsomolsk-na-Amure, Russia 681000 ☎/🖹 +7-42172 47088, 🖳 shel@kmscom.ru (681000, Россия, г. Комсомольск-на-Амуре, ул.Севастопольская, дом 12, оф. 16, Туристический центр 'Дерсу Узала', Шелопугин Александр Ф.).

### Yakutsk (Якутск)

TourService Center Ltd, under general director Vyacheslav Ipatiev, offers tours including trekking, cultural/indigenous, sport-fishing, birdwatching and river cruises along the Lena river. It also organises business visits for Russians and foreigners, and holidays for Russians. TourService Center Ltd also maintains a useful website, 🖳 www.yakutiatravel.com. Contact the company at 5, ul. Oktyabrskaya, Yakutsk, Russia 677000, ☎ +7 4112 25 11 44, 🖹 +7 4112 25 08 97, 🖳 tours@online.ru (677000 Якутск, ул. Октябрьская, 5, Компания «ТурСервис Центр»).

### Neryungri (Нерюнгри)

Alfa Tour, under its director, Galina Zhuravlova, organises business and holiday travel for Neryungri, and specialised activities for outsiders – river runs, hunting, geological, scientific, and trading. Contact Alfa Tour Agency, pr. Lenina 6, 678922, Neryungri, (☎/🖹 +7-41147-43058, ☎ +7-41147-64210, 🖳 juravlev@yakutugol.ru (678922 Россия, Республика Саха (Якутия), г. Нерюнгри, Пр. Ленина, 6, «Дом книги», Туристическая фирма «Альфа-Тур», Журавлева Галина).

## Travel agents outside Russia

● **UK – The Russia Experience** (☎ 020-8566 8846, 🖹 020-8566 8843, 🖳 info@trans-siberian.co.uk, 🖳 www.trans-siberian.co.uk), Research House, Fraser Rd, Perivale, Middlesex UB6 7AQ.

● **UK – Regent Holidays** (☎ 0117-921 1711; 🖹 0117-925 4866, 🖳 regent@ regent-holidays.co.uk, 🖳 www.regent-holidays.co.uk), 15 John St, Bristol BS1 2HR.

● **Australia – Passport Travel** (☎ 03-9867 3888, 🖹 03-9867 1055), Suite 11, 401 St Kilda Rd, Melbourne, Victoria, 3004. Incorporates Russian Passport 🖳 www.russia-rail.com.

### Luxury tours

● **UK – GW Travel** (☎ 0161-928 9410, 🖹 0161-941 6101, 🖳 mail@gwtravel.co.uk, 🖳 www.gwtravel.co.uk), 6 Old Market Place, Altrincham, Cheshire WA14 4NP, organises luxury train travel throughout Russia, with first-class catering and sleeping accommodation (including a shower coach), with trains often hauled by steam locomotives. Watch for their occasional itineraries taking in the BAM.

# Travelling conditions
## Условия путешествия

## COSTS (Цены)

There is little price stability in Russia and giving absolute prices is difficult. Therefore the following should be considered as a guideline only. All prices are given in US dollars. Since the inflation that started in 1998, the rouble has been undervalued, making costs low for foreigners, especially since the ruling (generally but not universally followed) that train, plane and hotel costs must be the same for foreign as for Russian customers.

Basically, the BAM Zone is cheaper for travellers than the big cities in European Russia as there is no tourist culture. This means that accommodation can be organised for as little as $5 a night at railway hostels to $30 a night, being the cheapest accommodation in Komsomolsk-na-Amure. Because of the varying value of the rouble, absolute costs for hotels given in this guide are approximate, though the relative costs of hotels in a group are a reliable guideline.

Budget for about $10 a meal in restaurants with no alcohol and $4 in a canteen. A taxi around a small town costs about $2.

If you organise local services, typical costs are $30 a day for an interpreter, $30-50 a day for a guide, $2 a litre for petrol, $10 a day for catamaran or kayak hire, $30 a day for motor-boat hire and driver excluding petrol, $50 a day for car hire and driver excluding petrol and $10 a day for homestay excluding meals. If you get a local company to organise a special programme, budget for $100 a day. Remember that communication costs quickly add up when faxing Russia.

## MONEY, TRAVELLERS' CHEQUES AND CREDIT CARDS (Деньги и т. д.)

Russia's currency is the rouble (рубль), which consists of 100 kopecks (100 копейк). Because of massive inflation of the early 1990s, the rouble was divided by 1,000 in 1997; old and new notes circulate side by side with similar designs. Notes with Lenin's head or the old Soviet Union national symbols on them have been superseded and are not legal tender.

US dollars are freely exchangeable by both Russians and foreigners at banks and currency exchange points (Обмен валюты), therefore there is no black market rate. The exchange rate is a moving target due to inflation. Russians commonly use US dollars as their bank account.

US cash is the best method of carrying hard currency in Russia. Travellers' cheques are difficult to cash except in Moscow and St Petersburg, and credit cards are hardly accepted in the north-east. It is hard to get cash advances from your credit card in the north-east and if you can you will be charged a hefty commission.

It is best to carry and accept only crisp and unmarked US dollar bills of the latest design (American banknotes have recently been redesigned). This is because there are always rumours in Russia about forged US notes and many banks will turn down notes that are not in excellent condition and not of the latest design. Many Russians mistakenly believe that the old notes are not legal tender any more because of the Russian government's practice of replacing old currency with new notes and then outlawing the old currency within a few months.

In spite of using US dollars as a banking currency, and in spite of the fact that this guide quotes prices in US dollars (to allow for inflation), you will make all public payments – tickets, hotels, restaurants, stores – in roubles. Only for private deals (for example, homestays) are US dollars appropriate.

Keep your money in a moneybelt or similar on your body at all times. You should also carry a wallet with a small amount of Russian and hard currency in it as your normal source of money. As well as enabling you to get to your money quickly, the wallet can be lost and you won't lose too much.

## WHEN TO GO (Когда путешествовать)

The decision about when to go depends on a number of factors, notably the weather and your interests. The average temperature table (p21) gives you some ideas of the temperatures of towns in the north-east and compares them with Moscow and St Petersburg.

Summers are hot. For general sightseeing, the best time to visit is from June to August. (You should discount the pessimistic proverb: 'Июнь ещё не лето, Июль уже не лето' – 'June not yet summer, July no longer summer').

Travel is particularly difficult in autumn (October to December) and spring (April to May) when the rivers are neither navigable nor frozen, and when the roads are particularly slick. At these seasons railway travel is reliable and air travel is relatively reliable, but road travel is almost impossible.

● **Trekking** It is best to go after June when the deadly bush tick has gone (see Health p23).

● **Fishing** For the best times to fish and when to see the fish spawning, see p343.

❑ **Average temperature table °C**

| Location (elevation) | Jan | Feb | Mar | Apr | May | June | July | Aug | Sep | Oct | Nov | Dec |
|---|---|---|---|---|---|---|---|---|---|---|---|---|
| St Petersburg (4m) | -5 | -1 | 1 | 7 | 14 | 19 | 22 | 19 | 14 | 7 | 1 | -3 |
| Moscow (156m) | -9 | -6 | 0 | 10 | 19 | 21 | 23 | 22 | 16 | 9 | 2 | -5 |
| Irkutsk (468m) | -18 | -14 | -6 | 2 | 11 | 19 | 21 | 19 | 11 | 3 | -16 | -16 |
| Kirensk (256m) | -27 | -22 | -11 | -2 | 7 | 15 | 19 | 15 | 7 | -2 | -15 | -25 |
| Aldan (680m) | -27 | -24 | -16 | -6 | 3 | 13 | 17 | 13 | 6 | -6 | -20 | -27 |
| Bomnak (357m) | -32 | -24 | -14 | -1 | 8 | 15 | 18 | 15 | 7 | -3 | -20 | -30 |
| Yakutsk (100m) | -42 | -35 | -22 | -7 | -5 | 15 | 18 | 15 | 6 | -7 | -28 | -40 |
| Khabarovsk (86m) | -23 | -17 | -9 | 3 | 10 | 17 | 20 | 20 | 13 | 4 | 8 | -19 |
| Komsomolsk-na-Amure (60m) | -26 | -9 | -3 | 5 | 12 | 21 | 23 | 10 | 18 | 0 | -9 | -18 |
| Nikolaevsk-na-Amure (46m) | -27 | -20 | -12 | -3 | 7 | 11 | 17 | 17 | 11 | 2 | -10 | -20 |
| Kholmsk (28m) | -10 | -8 | -4 | 2 | 7 | 11 | 16 | 18 | 14 | 8 | 0 | -6 |
| Oimyakon (740m) | -50 | -44 | -32 | -15 | 2 | 11 | 15 | 10 | 2 | -15 | -26 | -47 |
| Okhotsk (Magadan) (6m) | -25 | -20 | -14 | -6 | 1 | 6 | 12 | 13 | 8 | -2 | -15 | -21 |

*World summary of climatology*, Elsevier Scientific Publishing Co, Amsterdam, 1977.

● **Birdwatching**  Refer to the book, *A Field Guide to Birds of the USSR*, listed on p356, Appendix E.
● **Seal watching**  It is best to go in May (see Severobaikalsk, p92).
● **Rafting**  It is best to go in July or August (see pp110-115). The river water is surprisingly warm (at least 15°C) since the rivers are fed by summer rains not by thawed run-off.

Another factor to consider is the availability of fresh food. This is particularly important if you are a vegetarian. Although food is available all year round, the end of summer is the only time when there are plenty of fresh vegetables. Collecting indigenous berries, nuts and mushrooms is an enjoyable experience and a table in the Wild food section of Appendix B lists when these ripen.

## HEALTH (Злоровье)

Medical treatment is readily available in Russia at the polyclinic (Поликлиника) and sometimes at the railway station (Медпункт – Medpunkt). The standard Russian hospital is considerably less well-equipped and supplied than those in the West. However, most doctors are just as competent, so if you land in a hospital for stitches or need an x-ray, don't be too concerned. Because of the shortage of medical equipment, hospitals are forced to reuse syringes so it is best to take a few for yourself. If you need an operation, contact your embassy and arrange for evacuation to a Western country.

You should take out medical and travel insurance. A high level of insurance (similar to Western Europe) is advisable to allow you to recover the cost of Western medical services in Russia, and international evacuation.

Many Western medicines are available in pharmacies (Аптека – Apteka), but take your own prescription drugs if you rely on them. Some people believe that if you are going to be in Russia for more than a few weeks you should take vitamin tablets as it is difficult to get a balanced meal most of the year.

There are no mandatory vaccinations for travelling in the north-east or anywhere else in Russia. It is recommended that you have tetanus and hepatitis inoculations, and take precautions against typhoid and diphtheria. You should check with your local doctor or travellers' medical centre for the latest requirements.

It is safe to drink water from the tap in most towns except Yakutsk and Khabarovsk. If in doubt, ask 'Is it safe to drink from the tap?' («Можно ли пить воду из крана?» – 'Mozhno li pit vodu iz krana?'). If not, drink bottled water or from the hot water samovar. On trains and boats don't drink from the tap but drink from the hot water samovar or hot water tap provided.

❑ **The Ixodes tick (Клещи)**
The Ixodes ticks are the most serious health threat in the north-east. These aggressive creatures appear from the start of spring to late June and cause fever, excruciating headache, vomiting and central nervous system disorders. Victims die or remain crippled for life with their neck, arm and leg muscles paralysed. The condition was called Kozhevnikov epilepsy until the 1930s when it was found to be inflicted by a bite of the Ixodes tick carrying the encephalitis virus, which is in the

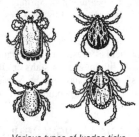
*Various types of Ixodes ticks*

blood of wild animals. The disease is called Russian Spring Fever.

While it is possible to get inoculations against the tick, it is much better to do as locals do and simply avoid going into taiga before June. The tick is not present in the BAM Zone towns at this time.

There are several varieties of ticks including grey, black, and black with a red stripe around their belly. The ticks prefer valleys in taiga, broad-leaved forest, and cleared tracts of forest. The ticks position themselves in bushes, waiting for warm-blooded creatures to walk by and then drop onto them. They then crawl imperceptibly under the skin, leaving only the tail end of their abdomens sticking out, giving them the appearance of a black cucumber seed on your skin. To pull one out without breaking off its head is impossible. The only reliable way of getting rid of them is to pour paraffin or salt onto the skin and they will crawl out.

If you do have to go in the taiga in the dangerous months, you should wear protective clothing and consider a course of inoculations. The Russian protective clothing consists of a woven singlet of thick weave that ensures that your outer protective garment stays about 1cm from your skin. The outer garment is a poloneck jumper with a hood and long sleeves made of light-weight material impervious to insects. You should always wear long trousers and tuck them into your socks or put a rubber band around your trouser legs to prevent ticks from crawling up. As an added precaution, you should spray your clothing with insect repellent. It is essential that, after returning from the taiga, you check every inch of your body for ticks, particularly warm skin creases, and get someone to check your hair, back and other parts you can't see.

Inoculations are inconvenient, as the serum is difficult to obtain outside Europe. The immune globulin serum is made by a Viennese company, Immuno, and one dose will provide protection for up to four weeks while two shots, two weeks apart will provide protection for a longer time. There is a Russian serum but it is difficult to find. The Russian vaccine involves three injections with a gap of a few days between each and another shot after six months, with an annual booster for year-round protection.

If you get bitten, it is essential that you get medical help immediately as treatment can save your life.

This encephalitis tick should not to be confused with either the tick-borne Siberian typhus or Japanese encephalitis, neither of which occur in the BAM Zone but nearby in the lower areas of the Russian Far East and Amur regions.

At the beginning of spring, some people will suffer bloody noses and headaches caused by the forest blooming. After a day or so, the problem disappears.

A moderate degree of physical fitness is needed in Russia. Russians, particularly easterners, are vigorous and self-reliant, and nobody will help you with luggage or stairs or climbing into a bunk unless you specifically ask. As there has been no consideration for the disabled in Russia, mobility-challenged people should consider carefully before travelling in this region.

## RUSSIAN LANGUAGE (Русский язык)

As the north-east is rarely visited by foreigners, there are few English or German speakers and even fewer tourist facilities. This makes some Russian language essential.

Russian uses the Cyrillic alphabet of 33 letters. It can be quickly mastered. If you take the time to do this, you can read timetables and signs, and you will find navigating around much easier and more enjoyable.

The Russian language guide (Appendix C) defines the alphabet, basic phrases and vocabulary useful on the railway and other transport. A short Russian-language course plus this book should make it possible to travel the north-east without help. If you have no Russian-language knowledge at all, it is recommended that you join an organised tour.

## ELECTRICITY (Электричество)

The electricity supply in Russia is 220 volt AC, 50Hz and a standard European two-pronged plug is used. Adaptors should be purchased before you leave home as they cannot be easily bought in Russia.

# What to take
Что брать

Prepare for your trip well in advance and avoid last-minute packing. This will ensure that you enjoy your trip without worrying about buying things you forgot to bring. The following ideas may help you decide what to take. As the supply of personal items is extremely unpredictable, it is recommended that you take everything you need (see p26 for checklist).

A backpack or soft suitcase is preferable to a hard suitcase as they are easier to carry on and off trains and buses. If you do take a case, carry two small ones rather than one big one, and bring a two-wheeled trolley to move them around. Wheels built into suitcases are of limited use as the stations and pavements in Russia are rough. Carry a small day pack for day trips. Do not carry excess luggage as there are no porters and excess luggage on flights is expensive.

On the train you will find it comfortable to take slip-on scuffs.

A heavy-duty water bottle that will withstand boiling water from the train's samovar is vital. When cooled, this water becomes your drinking water for the next day.

Carry a spare set of passport photos in case you need another visa. Also take a photocopy of your visa and the important pages of your passport and keep them separate from your passport. Also copy other valuable documents, such as credit cards and travellers' cheques, before you leave and give the copies to someone whom you can notify if you lose them.

Bring all the clothes you are likely to need and do not rely on buying any when you arrive.

Bring the batteries on which your camera or other equipment depend. Don't rely on finding them in stores. Bring slide film if that is what you use; it is not sold in Russia.

The best sort of gifts to take are souvenirs from your country such as US flags or kangaroo stick pins, baseball caps, T-shirts, glossy picture books, maps, or travel videos. Pens, calculators and digital watches with your company's logo emblazoned on them are essential if you are travelling on business. The days are gone when Russians wanted jeans or runners as nowadays these can be bought in Russia.

You should always carry around a pack of good-quality unopened biscuits or chocolates, which you can buy in Russia, as your contribution if you are invited to share a meal.

Take plastic bags as they are not provided in shops or markets.

A pen and paper are always useful and a good way of carrying them is to buy a pocket-sized notebook and staple or glue to its cover a plastic sheath that can hold a pen.

Bring a small medical kit. It should include several syringes, Band-Aids, antiseptic, headache tablets, antiseptic gauze, personal medication and insect repellent.

Women should bring whatever sanitary products they like to use.

Bring contraceptives if you expect to need them.

If you play a musical instrument that is portable, take it along, as playing is a good way of making friends.

It is prohibited to take antiques, old art works and medals out of Russia. If you are buying new paintings, make sure you get an official receipt stating that the goods can be exported and the year of their production. This also applies to samovars.

Russians dress up to travel (at least when leaving and arriving – they change into casual clothes on the train or boat). You should be able to wash, fold and iron your own clothes; most hotels have facilities for this.

Also the *dezhurnaya* (дежурная, hotel floor attendant) will often do this for you for a small extra fee.

The north-east summer weather is pleasant, so light clothing is normally adequate. During May and September sharp changes in temperature occur and warmer clothing is needed. A raincoat, umbrella, and overcoat are essential for these months. During winter, extra warm clothing is essential as temperatures go as low as -40°C. It is recommended that you take lined boots, padded full-length skiing jacket, thermal underwear, a woollen hat, woollen pants (jeans are not warm enough), and thick gloves.

---

### ❏ What to take checklist

| | |
|---|---|
| Two-pin electricity adaptor | passport |
| 2.5m length of rope for clothes line | photocopies of visa & passport |
| alarm clock | plastic bags |
| anti-tinea cream | pocket dictionary |
| baby powder | pocket knife |
| books & magazines | pocket mirror |
| business cards | resealable containers |
| camera film & batteries | sanitary items |
| can & bottle opener | sewing kit |
| contact lens solution | shaver |
| contraceptives | slip-on scuffs |
| curry & other spices | soap, shampoo & comb |
| diary | souvenirs |
| electric immersion coil | spare set of passport photos |
| guidebooks & maps | strong plastic cup |
| hat, gloves & scarf | suitcase trolley |
| heavy-duty water bottle | sun glasses |
| knife, fork & spoon | sunscreen |
| laundry detergent | tampons |
| lip chapstick | tea, coffee, sugar, milk, salt |
| medical kit & medications | tissues |
| money belt | toilet paper |
| mosquito repellent | toothpaste |
| nail clippers | universal sink/bath plug |
| paper, envelopes & pens | vitamin tablets |

For camping, fishing and hunting, bring the following: (They are also available from hunters' stores and outfitters in Russia).

anorak or waterproof cape
gutting knife with sheath and whetstone
hat with mosquito net
hooded sweatshirt
sleeping bag and pad
wading boots and short socks for them

# PART 2: EN ROUTE
По дороге

## Train travel
Железнодорожный транспорт

Trains, where they exist, are the cheapest and most reliable mode of transportation. They are least affected by the weather and ticket prices are less than (in ascending order) buses and planes.

## TYPES OF TRAINS

The major classes of trains are fast, passenger, suburban and *firmenny* trains.

**Fast trains** (скорый поезд) are long-distance express trains stopping only at the largest stations. These trains are typically up to 24 carriages long. In the BAM Zone, the trains don't deserve the title 'fast'. For example, the average speed of the Tynda to Severobaikalsk 'fast' train is just 47km/h.

**Passenger trains** (пассажирский поезд) are also inter-city trains but they normally only go a few hundred kilometres, stopping regularly for locals to get on and off. The average speed of the passenger train on the Tynda to Severobaikalsk section is 41km/h.

**Suburban trains** (пригородный поезд) are normally electric suburban trains in European Russia. However, in the BAM Zone they refer to trains that travel up to 300km or four hours, connecting a big town with the surrounding villages. Suburban trains normally consist of a diesel locomotive and one or two *obshchi* carriages.

**Firmenny trains** (фирменный поезд) are fast trains leased to private companies. This allows the railways to charge a higher ticket charge than the government permits. Some of the long-distance trains on the BAM and the Trans-Siberian are firmenny. This seems to make no difference to the train except possibly to the price. For firmenny trains, buy tickets at the station just like other rail tickets.

## LIFE ON A PASSENGER TRAIN

### The crew

A passenger train has a Train Captain (Начальник поезда), who has an office somewhere in the middle of the train, one or two Mechanics (Механик), a restaurant or buffet-car crew, sometimes a small detachment of police and on every passenger carriage a pair of conductors, *provodniki*. The passenger crew is recruited from the same location and works together throughout the entire round trip of the train. (The locomotive drivers work for a single shift, stay over at a railway hostel and drive another train on the next working day.) Naturally, a strong social system develops on the train. Married couples sometimes work on the same train. When a train on one leg passes the same train on the opposite leg, the crew members hang out of the doors to exchange greetings, news and packages. On a Moscow to Tynda train the first edition of this guide caused great excitement because it contained a picture of a *provodnitsa* who was working the train.

Life in your carriage is dominated by the conductor, called the provodnik (проводник) if male or provodnitsa (проводница) if female. There are normally two provodniki on each carriage, on alternating shifts. They share a sleeping cabin at the end of the carriage and next to it they have a small office with the carriage's electrical and musical controls. They usually keep the toilet next to their compartment for themselves.

Their job is to ensure that the carriage is clean, everyone has tickets and that no problems occur. The provodnik is your guardian. When you get on the train (s)he takes your ticket and assigns you your place; (s)he keeps your ticket until you are about to get off, when (s)he gives it back and announces your stop. The provodnik keeps interlopers out of the carriage. If you go into a neighbouring carriage you may be challenged; if, for example, you want to look out of a corridor window on the opposite side, ask permission of the provodnik of that carriage. At least once a day, the provodnik sweeps all the cabins and mops the corridor. The most zealous provodniki will put down a mat in the carriage's entrance so that no-one tramps dirt or snow through their carriage.

At stations the provodnik opens the carriage door, sees passengers off and on, watches the carriage door, gathers in passengers at the end of a long stop and flags the driver that the carriage is clear to leave.

Marina Yakovlevna Savchuk, *provodnitsa* on the Tynda–Kislovodsk train, signs her photo in the first edition of the BAM Guide. (Photo © Nicholas Zvegintzov)

Sergei, a student provodnik on the Tynda to Komsomolsk-na-Amure train.
(Photo © Nicholas Zvegintzov)

During the summer holidays, the provodniki are supplemented by students performing their work-study or 'praktikum'. For obvious reasons, the boy students and girl students are assigned to separate trains.

## Life as a passenger

Life as a passenger is also a social scene. It is always polite and prudent, and often rewarding, to introduce yourself and meet your fellow travellers and share where you are going and why. You will meet people on business, military under travel orders, families going to see relatives, very occasionally groups travelling for camping or hunting, but almost never a tourist in the Western sense.

It is always polite to stow away your own belongings neatly in the area assigned to you (under your bunk if you are below or on the roof shelf if you are above), to keep your bedding neat and not to clutter the window table. It is polite to share your food and drink, but it is also polite to yield the table and the compartment to a group if they are preparing to eat together.

Be accommodating about lights-out. Russians sleep long hours while travelling. If you're wakeful and want to watch the scenery, go in the corridor.

Wear comfortable clothes – a tracksuit, slippers, even a bathrobe are acceptable, but not bare feet in the corridor. Russians are formal when leaving on journeys or arriving and will change out of street clothes the moment they settle into the compartment and change back before getting off. It is polite for males to leave the compartment while females or families are changing or preparing for bed.

Get up first and go to the toilet before breakfast and well before the end of the trip to beat the rush. Remember the toilet is locked just before the train arrives at a station and will not be opened until you are moving again.

If the toilet door is locked you can still wash your utensils at the water tap near the samovar – but don't splash the floor.

If you have any problems, such as wanting to move to another berth, go to the provodnik and if the matter is not resolved to your satisfaction, to the Train Captain.

## Eating

Most trains have a restaurant car, which normally has just one entree and one main course. Two-thirds of the dining car contains seats while the remainder is occupied by a kitchen, pantry, scullery and refrigerators. There are twelve 4-seat tables together with a table for the supervisor who is also the cashier. Unfortunately, though the restaurant car might be able to offer hot food cooked in a real kitchen, it sometimes seems to serve as the club-car of the train staff, with passengers not welcome. A railway catering supervisor offers this hint: restaurant cars run by women are more accommodating than those run by men.

Trackside bustle at Suluk, a small town east of the Dusse-Alin Tunnel. On the left produce is being unloaded for the town store. (Photo © Nicholas Zvegintzov)

On the BAM, there are also some newer carriages that consist of a buffet selling processed food and four coupé compartments.

In practice most people bring their own food or buy it from station vendors at long stops. Some stops, for example, Vikhorevka, Novy Uoyan and Komsomolsk-na-Amure, are blessed with vendors who bring excellent and varied foods.

## PASSENGER CARRIAGES

There are four types of carriage for passengers – obshchi, platskartny, coupé and SV.

### Obshchi

Obshchi (общий – 'general') is the lowest class of carriage and it is an old platskartny carriage with no bedding. Up to 87 people can be crammed into a carriage and there is no seat numbering. They are normally dirty, stuffy and hell if you have to sleep in them overnight. They are okay to travel on for a few hours but, without any padding, they get uncomfortable quickly. These carriages are normally only attached to passenger trains and used by workmen or fishermen.

### Platskartny

Platskartny (платцкартный) is the most common type of carriage in Russia but not the most pleasant. It is a sleeping carriage that has two tiers of berths in open compartments on one side of the corridor with a row of berths arranged lengthways down the other side. It accommodates 58 passengers. Mattresses and pillows are supplied. By an ingenious mechanism, the aisle berths can be lifted up and down to make aisle seats and tables. These carriages are noisy, stuffy and lack security. Avoid getting the berth next to the toilet otherwise you get the banging door next to your head which vibrates your bunk as well. It is not recommended to travel in platskartny unless you sleep well and have

Wagon curtain on the BAM.
(Photo © Nicholas Zvegintzov)

nothing valuable on you. However, they are fine for daytime journeys.

## Coupé

Coupé (купейный) carriages are the most enjoyable way to travel as they offer privacy, security and comfort. A coupé carriage consists of eight or nine 4-bunk enclosed cabins. As you will be sharing the cabin with Russians, there is plenty of opportunity to practice your hand signals or test a phrase book. There are two types of coupé, an older type which has 36 berths and normally has white laminex and the new one which has 32 berths, brown laminex and more padding.

The 4-berth coupé compartments are separated from the corridor by a sliding door that can be locked from the inside. The conductor has a key that can open this lock from the outside. As an additional safety device, there is a flick-down lock high up on the inside of the door that cannot be opened from the outside. Some people go to the trouble of jamming a cork in this lock to ensure that no-one can open it by devious means from the outside.

The two top bunks can be put up during the day to give you more head room. Under the bottom two bunks are luggage spaces which are secure as they can't be reached unless you get off the bunk. The corridor has a false ceiling which makes space for a luggage shelf accessible from the top bunks. Each bunk has a pull-down shelf and some light hooks. At the corridor end there are also high hooks for hanging clothes. At the end of each bed is a reading lamp and the 2- or 3-way switch near the door controls the main cabin lights. The loudspeaker volume knob is usually above the window. There is a bottle opener under the table. If the table is in the way, you can fold it up.

Although the bunks are well-padded, a mattress and pillow are supplied. You will need to hire a linen set that includes two sheets, a pillow case and small towel. These are either laundered cotton, which must be returned at the end of your trip, or throwaway paper. The hire charge is about $1.

In winter, blankets are supplied; during summer you have to ask for them. In winter the windows are locked and the heater is turned way up which ironically means that you swelter under just sheets. To make matters worse, the windows can only be opened with a special key. The only ventilation is a roof vent which can be turned on and off.

There are advantages and disadvantages to sleeping in the upper bunk. While this berth allows you to go to bed when you want and gives you more privacy, it is hotter, difficult to climb up to and much brighter being closer to the main cabin light. The lower berths are in general preferred and sometimes a ticket-seller will say apologetically 'Only upper berths'. If you have been assigned a lower berth and an upper berth has been assigned to a pregnant woman or a parent with a baby or toddler or an old person, it is polite to offer to swap.

The worst compartment is the last one, with berth Nos 33 to 36. This one is closest to the smelly toilet, over the wheels which gives you a rough ride and is closest to the banging corridor door. The compartment with berth Nos 13 to 16 gives the best ride. You cannot reserve a particular berth unless you tell a very good story to the booking staff.

## SV
SV (СВ – спальный вагон – 'sleeping carriage') are sometimes called *myagky* (мягкий – 'soft') carriages. These cars have nine 2-berth compartments, each containing a 2-tier set of berths or two berths on the same level. These carriages are used on the Trans-Siberian but not on the BAM.

## Stolypin carriages
In addition, there is the 'Stolypin carriage' (столыпинский вагон) for prisoners, often described in gulag literature. If you find yourself assigned to a compartment with shuttered windows and barred doors, and occupied by up to 16 others, you are in for extreme adventure travel.

## Layout of the carriage
When you enter the train, you step into the carriage's vestibule. This is a narrow platform with four doors – one each side to the open, one to the link with the next car and one into the carriage itself. This is the only smoking area.

If you start at the provodnik's end, going through the door into the carriage itself will take you past a toilet (usually reserved by the provodniki), the on-duty provodnik's office, the provodnik's living compartment and the hot water urn or samovar (самовар). You can use this water for tea, coffee, soup and dehydrated Chinese noodles. Some samovars have a flat top, which means that you can cook a meal on them. Most samovars are electric, but there are a few coal ones left. A temperature gauge on the side of the samovar indicates the temperature; only use the water when it is in the red band. Although there is a drinking water tap near the samovar, a better source of drinking water is to pour the samovar water into a heavy-duty canteen at night and in the morning it will be cool enough to drink. If the water is not hot in your samovar, try the next carriage and if all else fails, go to the restaurant car and ask them.

The compartments run the length of the carriage off the corridor. In the corridor, there are seats that you can flip down. The train timetable is posted on the wall of the corridor. (Sometimes the provodnik has extra copies of the timetable to distribute.)

At the end of the corridor there is another toilet, open for passengers, and a rubbish bin. Unfortunately environmental awareness has yet to

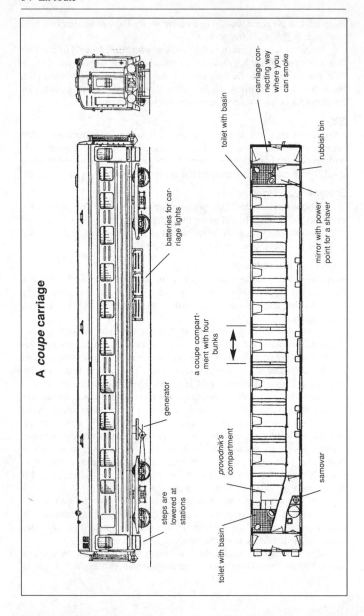

**A *coupe* carriage**

batteries for carriage lights

generator

steps are lowered at stations

a coupe compartment with four bunks

toilet with basin

carriage connecting way where you can smoke

rubbish bin

mirror with power point for a shaver

*provodnik's* compartment

samovar

toilet with basin.

reach most of the provodniki as they normally empty the bin by throwing the rubbish out of the train as it is moving.

Beyond is the vestibule at the other end of the carriage.

The toilet can range from clean to noisome, depending on the zeal of the provodniki. It has hot and cold water. The water is replenished by station staff at each major stop. Turn the water on by pushing up the lever just behind the spout. Bring your own toilet paper and soap and an all-purpose drain-plug.

There are no showers on the train. To shower, either fill the basin and slosh the water over yourself with a mug, or carry a short hose and attach it to the spigot (this is what the provodniki do). Don't worry about splashing water around, as there is a drain in the floor. (If the toilet is sopping wet, it may be because of this process.)

There is a 220V AC electric power point in or near the toilet designed for shavers («220 В ДЛЯ БРИТЬЯ») but it runs off an alternator and must be turned on by the provodnik. It has enough power to charge a laptop. Along the corridor there may be 110V single-phase outlets that may also drive your laptop.

The carriage windows on the corridors and inside the compartments can be opened, but are often sealed against the winter («ЗАКРЫТО НА ЗИМУ» stencilled on them). The provodnik can open them with a key and standing here in the fresh breeze is briskly refreshing.

## BUYING RAILWAY TICKETS

Booking railway tickets in Russia is easier today than at any time in the past. Booking and printing a ticket is computerised and supply is now greater than demand due to the increase in the cost of tickets. Despite the price rise, overnight rail tickets are still cheaper than in the Western world and train is still the cheapest way to travel, followed by bus and plane.

A Russian train ticket specifies the passenger's name, the train, the date of travel, the origin and destination stations, the number of travellers, the carriage number, the place number or numbers and the price.

There are three ways to get a ticket:
● By queuing at a ticket window, *kassa* (касса).
● By applying to the Train Captain (Начальник поезда) when the train is in the station.
● Through an agent. (The agent will use one of these two methods to get the ticket.)

There are always ticket windows in the railway station. A few cities (eg Tynda and Khabarovsk) have additional satellite railway booking offices.

To help you buy your own tickets, the table on p36 shows, side by side in English and Russian, the key phrases for asking information about tick-

## ❏ Train information and ticket-buying table

Please help me. I don't speak Russian. Please read the question I point to and write the answer.

Будте любезны, помогите мне. Я не говорю по-русски. прочтите вопросы на которые я укажу, и напишите ответ.

MT = Moscow Time
* = Circle your choice
Q = question/A = answer

МВ = Московское Время
* = Я показал свой выбор
Воп. = вопрос/Отв. = ответ

### Information

**Q.** When is the next train with spare SV* coupé* platskartny* tickets to ..........................?
**A.** It departs at ....... : ....... (MT) and is Train No. ........

**Q.** Are there SV* coupé* platskartny* tickets to ........................... on Train No. ..........?
**A.** Yes No

**Q.** When does the train depart and arrive?
**A.** It departs at ....... : ........ and arrives ........ at ........ : ........ (MT).

**Q.** How much is a SV* coupé* platskartny* ticket?
**A.** It costs ............ roubles.

**Q.** Which ticket window should I go to?
**A.** Ticket window No. ............

**Q.** What platform does train No. ............ leave from?
**A.** Platform No. ............

### Информация

**Воп.** Когда следующий поезд со свободными местами (СВ* купе* плацкарт*) до .................?
**Отв.** Поезд отправляется в ...:...(МВ) и номер у поезда ........

**Воп.** Есть свободные места (СВ *купе* плацкарт*) до ............. в поезде номер ..........?
**Отв.** Да Нет

**Воп.** Когда поезд отправляется и прибывает?
**Отв.** Поезд отправляется в .... :.... и прибывает в ....... : ....... (МВ).

**Воп.** Сколько стоит билет в СВ* купе* плацкарт*?
**Отв.** Билет стоит ...... рублей.

**Воп.** К какой кассе мне подойти?
**Отв.** Касса номер ...........

**Воп.** С какой платформы отправляется поезд номер .......?
**Отв.** Платформа номер ..........

### Buying tickets

**Q.** May I buy ...... SV* coupé* platskartny* tickets to ..................... on Train No. ........departing on ........? (Use DD/MM/YY format, eg 31/12/00.)
**A.** Yes, it costs ............ roubles.
**A.** No.

**Q.** Why can't I buy a ticket?
**A.** There is no train.
**A.** The train is fully booked.
**A.** You have to buy a ticket at window No. ...............
**A.** You can only buy a ticket ....... hours before the train arrives.

Thank you for your help.

### Покупка билетов

**Воп.** Можно купить .. (СВ* купе* плацкарт*) билет до .................. на поезд номер ........... который отправляется до ............?
**Отв.** Да. билет стоит ...... рублей.
**Отв.** Нет.

**Воп.** Почему я не могу купить билет?
**Отв.** Нет поезда.
**Отв.** Нет мест.
**Отв.** Вы должны купить билет в кассе номер...........
**Отв.** Вы можете купить билет за ... часов до прибытия поезда.

Большое спасибо за помощь.

ets and for booking tickets. With this table you can communicate your requirements to the ticket-seller and the ticket-seller can write answers. In Appendix C there is also an English-Russian dictionary of words and phrases used in booking and timetables.

## Buying a ticket from a ticket window
**Step 1: Which train?** The first step is to find out which train you want to go on. Check the timetable, which will be displayed in the booking hall. It will state the train's number, the time of departure and on which days of the week it travels.

Things to remember:
● The train number indicates which way it is heading. If the number is even it means that it is going to the east, if odd to the west towards Moscow.

● The time quoted on timetables is invariably Moscow time (московское время). Times in the north-east range from +5 to +8 hours from Moscow time (time-zones are indicated in the guidebook sections of this guide). The clock in the booking hall is normally set to Moscow time. In rare cases where timetables are written in local time it will state this at the top of the timetable (местное время).

● Many trains depart every day. Some run on odd number days – 1st, 3rd, 5th, etc – (Неч. – нечетным числам) and some on even days – 2nd, 4th, 6th etc – (Чет. — четным числам). In addition, a few trains run only in summer or winter.

Write down the train number, date of departure, the class of ticket and your destination. If you don't speak Russian, write this information on the booking table above. Have ready the passport and visa of every person for whom you are buying a ticket.

**Step 2: Which window?** Railway ticket windows are almost the last environment in which the tourist can join in the traditional Russian activity of strategic queuing.

The ticket-windows, known as kassa (касса), are located side by side in the booking hall. Each has its own queue. The only precaution is to avoid the Stationmaster's window (Начальник вокзала) and the advance ticket window, which do not sell current tickets. The question 'Tickets?' ('Bilety?' – «Билеты?») to the window or to people nearby ought to avert this danger. In some stations there are several sorts of ticket windows for different types of passengers, but not in the north-east.

Each window is signed with its hours of service, in a 24-hour clock; 'круглосуточная' means 'open 24 hours'. On the other hand, 'перерыв' is a break, when the ticket-window will be closed. In addition, some ticket-windows close for 15 minutes every hour for 'a technical break'. Before queuing, check the opening and closing times of all the windows.

If there are several people in your party, one person should wait in each queue. If you are alone, it may be better to queue up at a closed kassa which will open in an hour than to wait in a long line where the kassa might close before you get to the head of the queue. (Ticket windows are in general reliable about opening at the promised time.)

Queues look shapeless but they have a strict linear order. When joining a queue you should ask 'Who is last?' ('Kto posledny?' – «Кто последний?») and establish who you are behind and then who you are ahead of. In addition, the person in front of or behind you may ask you to hold their place for a while; it is polite to do this. You can do the same thing; just the word 'Please', pronounced 'pazhalsta' with a gesture to the door and your watch should be enough to get the idea across.

The queue forms from the right; interlopers attempt to break in from the left. These are usually people trying to change or cancel a ticket, drunks and people with tall stories. It is the job of the front-queuers to repel interlopers ('This poor old grandmother has been queuing for two hours and you dare to break in? Shame!'), but Russians are accommodating and long-suffering. Those changing a ticket have a special priority because they may be releasing reservations; unfortunately changing a ticket seems to take at least four times as long as buying one.

There are two railway divisions that run the north-east railways (including the BAM). The western one, the East Siberian Railway (Восточно-сибирская ж. д.), is efficient, with printed timetables and quick queues. The eastern one, The Far Eastern Railway (Дальневосточная ж. д.), is less so. The worst queues are at Komsomolsk-na-Amure, which has three long-distance trains per day, and Vanino, which has one; allow several hours queuing time at these locations.

**Step 3: Buying the ticket**  When you get to the window, tell the ticket-seller the train number, date of departure, class of ticket, number of tickets and destination, and pass in the travellers' documents. If you don't speak Russian, give the ticket-seller the filled-in booking table above. Good luck!

**Buying a ticket from the Train Captain**
This method is legal and is not a bribe. The Train Captain has authority to sell you a ticket and to write it and take your money.

To accomplish this you locate the Train Captain when the train has arrived in the station. She will have an office somewhere in the middle of the train. You tell her where you want to go and what class of ticket you want and make some explanation of why you failed to book a ticket at the station (usually the queue was too long or your Russian was not good enough). She has discretion to sell you a ticket if she can identify for you a free place in a carriage.

This manoeuvre is naturally easier if the train is making a 20-minute stop than if it is making a two-minute stop, but correspondingly the Train Captain may accommodate you in either case.

## What do the tickets look like?

By far the commonest type of ticket is the computer-printed ticket on salmon stock, pictured here.

If you buy a ticket from a Train Captain or from a very small station, you may receive the old-style long paper ticket with all the classes of berths printed on it. The ticket-seller cuts off the options you have not paid for, writes in the destination, your train, compartment and berth numbers and then dates it with a hole punch.

## Ticket prices

Ticket prices are made up of three components: a booking fee, the class of ticket and the distance to be travelled. The booking fee is about $2. The cheapest class of ticket is obshchi, followed by platskartny, coupé and SV, with each class being about $1\frac{1}{2}$ to 2 times the cost of the previous class. The cost per kilometre reduces with distance.

The cost for 24 hours of travel, including a coupé, is $30-40, depending on the speed of the train.

## Booking tickets in advance

You can buy a ticket for most trains up to 40 days in advance from all stations.

## CHANGING YOUR TICKET

It is possible to change your ticket but it is best to get it right the first time and avoid the hassles. If you want to change the date of travel before the scheduled time of your ticket, you can do this by paying the booking fee again. If you don't want to travel and you return your ticket 24 hours ahead of departure, you get a full refund minus the booking fee. If you return it between six and 24 hours from departure, you lose 50 per cent of the ticket price if it was a platskartny berth or 18 per cent if it was a coupé. If you are late and miss your train by less than three hours, you lose everything if you had a platskartny ticket or about 50 per cent if it was a coupé ticket. If you arrive at the station more than three hours after the train has left, you will have to fill in some forms that are sent off to the central booking office for a decision.

Ticket changes have priority in the Russian queuing environment. To make a change you can argue your way into the front of a queue. Unfortunately, changes seem to take four times as long as new ticket issues and your heart may sink if many changers push into a queue ahead of you.

## IF YOU CAN'T GET A TICKET

There are three main reasons why you can't get a ticket: you didn't get in the queue soon enough, there are no berths, or because tickets are only sold a few hours before the train arrives. (The third case happened more often before computerisation, but it still occurs at small stations. It results in a mad scramble to get tickets in the one or two hours before the train arrives.)

In these cases you should try to buy a ticket on the train (see Buying a ticket from the Train Captain, p38). The Train Captain can often find a place for you, even if it is not in the class that you prefer (be flexible). However, occasionally the train will be completed booked out, notably in holiday seasons.

You could always try to travel free, known as travelling like a rabbit (как кролик) but you will find it hard to evade the provodniki, though we have sometimes seen it done between a suburban station and the centre of town.

## GETTING OFF IN THE MIDDLE OF NOWHERE

Officially trains only stop at scheduled stops. However, in the BAM Zone where there are only a few trains a day, trains will stop for people to get on and off at unscheduled stops. You will see this particularly in summer as hiking groups get off in the middle of nowhere. To get off somewhere special, your best bet is to talk directly with the driver, although the Train Captain or your provodnik might organise it on your behalf. If you are lucky, the driver will invite you into the cab so that you can get off quickly.

# Other methods of transport
## Другие виды транспорта

### ROAD TRANSPORT (Дорожный транспорт)

The roads of the north-east are not good. Few are hard-surfaced (the exceptions are the paved roads connecting Bratsk to Irkutsk and Komsomolsk-na-Amure to Khabarovsk), and some large towns (Severobaikalsk and Vanino, for example) are not connected by roads at all. The roads are most passable in summer and in winter, with conditions very bad in fall and spring (and Yakutsk unreachable across the river). In winter roads appear along frozen rivers and lakes.

Nevertheless, long-distance buses run regular schedules in the north-east and long-distance trucking is a significant supply line.

Buses load at the bus station (автовокзал), where you can find tickets and schedules. Fares are in general higher than on the trains; however there is no special higher fare for foreigners. Buses are important on routes where the railway does not go – particularly The Republic of Sakha (Yakutiya) and the Magadan region.

In addition it is possible to hitch rides on trucks, either by waving from the highway or by visiting a truck base (автобаза).

There are no car rental companies in the north-east.

### AIR TRANSPORT (Воздушный транспорт)

In Soviet times Russia's national air company, Aeroflot, provided frequent service at subsidised rates. The break-up of Aeroflot into many small regional companies that had neither sufficient training, employees, nor spare parts resulted in a number of crashes. However, the biggest problem was that most flights never took off due to a lack of fuel and aircraft. The mid-1990s rationalisation of air companies and the tightening of safety standards has resulted in the number of scheduled flights being reduced but these are now much more likely to depart and, having departed, to arrive. While fuel supplies are still a problem, the greater impediment to flying is the weather. Fog, smoke, wind, snow storms and howling rains can delay planes for several days or more. Another problem with local internal flights, eg Bodaibo to Chara, as opposed to long-distance flights, eg Moscow to Komsomolsk-na-Amure, is that they are virtually impossible to book outside Russia.

Nevertheless, air travel is an important regional link and for many communities in the far north-east at many times of year, the only link.

Find schedules and fares at the air booking office in town (usually the former Aeroflot agency) or at the local airport (Аэропорт).

In the past, hiring a helicopter was reasonably cheap but nowadays the going rate is about $500-800 an hour. The standard helicopter for rental is the MI-8 and these are owned by the military, Aeroflot and specialist organisations. Generally, the military pilots are less experienced at mountain flying than civilian crews and the most experienced crews work for the rescue organisations KSS (КСС – Контрольно-спасательная служба) or KSO (КСО – Контрольно-спасательный отряд), or forestry protection rangers (Лес охрана). Remember there are various grades of pilots, with the highest grade being permitted to land on unprepared sites. So, before you hire, check their credentials.

## RIVER TRANSPORT (Водный транспорт)

Water transport is a vital transportation and freight link during the summer months. Excluding small boats, the passenger vessels that ply Russia's rivers and lakes are hydrofoils, river steamers and cruise ships. While hydrofoils travel far faster than river steamers, steamers are a more elegant way of travelling and an excellent way to meet Russians. There are also freight barges, especially on the Lena river.

Find schedules and fares at the river station (Речной вокзал) in towns on the Amur and Lena rivers, or at the harbour on Lake Baikal.

### Hydrofoils

Hydrofoils look futuristic with sleek lines and bubble windows. They have powerful engines and run at high speed (60kph including stops). They only travel during daylight due to the danger of hitting an unseen object. You can either doze in the stuffy comfortable cabins, which have the feel of long-distance buses, or look out of the windows (or, on some models, stand on the open gallery) and watch the endless serpentines of the giant river unfold. Hydrofoils travel extensively along the Amur river and the Lena river, and on Lake Baikal from Severobaikalsk to Irkutsk.

There is no common word in Russian for a hydrofoil. A Russian will always refer to them by their specific type and if that is not known call it a raketa. Hydrofoils come in different sizes and flavours:

● **Meteor (Метеор)** The largest one of the family, which seats passengers in three sections – front, middle and rear. There are large expanses of window in each section, which provide good viewing if you pull aside the

The space-age looking *Meteor* hydrofoil, going under the Khabarovsk bridges over the Amur. (Photo © Nicholas Zvegintzov).

dainty curtain. The front section is popular because it allows you to see the entire river ahead through the wrap-around window. The bridge is reached via attic-like steps from this area. The middle section contains the majority of seats and a small kiosk, which provides hot water, beer and candy. Between the middle and rear section is an open-air walkway. As you descend the walkway to the rear section you pass two toilets on the right and the crew's room on the left. The rear section is closest to the engines; it is the warmest and the noisiest. There is another open-air section at the rear, but you'll mainly breathe exhaust fumes there.

● **Voskhod (Восход)** Like a small Meteor, but narrower and with only two sections. The front section is much the same as that on a Meteor. There is no open-air section.

● **Raketa (Ракета)** Yet one size smaller, with only one section to seat passengers. It does not have a wrap-around window at the front, but you can get into the open air at the rear.

● **Polesye (Полесье)** Roughly equivalent in size to a Raketa. There is no open-air section, nor is there any forward or rear view, as the front is taken up by the bridge and the rear by the engine.

● **Zarya (Заря)** Not technically a hydrofoil as it does not have underwater wings, but it does have water-jet propulsion. It is a flat-bottomed vessel used on stretches of shallow water (like Ust-Kut to Zhigalovo) and it is useful in serving smaller settlements, as it will run right up to the riverbank. As the exit is through the front, there is no need for any gangway or port installations to be provided. A Zarya goes at less than half the speed of a proper hydrofoil, because of its construction and of the many stops. The interior (a single saloon) is more like that of a local bus.

## River steamers

A river steamer (пароход or теплоход) is a working boat for passengers, contrasted with a cruise ship, which is for entertainment and for foreign tourists (see p45). On river steamers you will mix with an extreme variety of travellers and visit fascinating remote scenes, besides experiencing an elegant way of travelling. There are now few left, but there are river steamers on several routes on the Lena river (see Travelling the Lena river, p241).

As you may expect with ships built in the Soviet era, the working ships offer a rich class structure. On the *Krasnoyarsk* between Ust-Kut and Yakutsk the classes are as follows:

● **1st**  Two-person room with a large window and a washbasin; forward on the 1st deck.
● **2nd soft**  Four-person room with a large window and a washbasin; on the 1st deck.
● **2nd hard**  Four-person room with a large window and a washbasin; on the 2nd deck.
● **3rd**  Six- or eight-person room on the 3rd deck in the bowels of the ship; dark, crowded and claustrophobic with only a porthole to give you a glimpse of the outside world from just above the water line.
● **Steerage**  Sleep on your luggage on the lower gangways.

Second hard seems to be the best compromise between price and comfort and is even slightly better than second soft in that it offers more privacy – on the upper deck people are constantly passing in front of your window, whereas only the crew use the lower deck walkway.

Services on board this ship include a shower ($0.50), a restaurant served by an excellent kitchen, a small shop with limited food and sweets, a modest bar of beer and vodka supplied by the crew, evening videos in the 1st deck lounge ($0.50), taps with boiling water for tea or noodles (a convenient by-product of a steam-powered vehicle), promenades up the rocky shore at the longer stops (sometimes with *shashlik* and ice creams), stops off-shore at tiny stockaded villages, and as much fresh river air, gossip, flirtation, meditation, reading, writing, arm-wrestling, draughts and tranquil relaxation as you can stand.

Life on board is pretty much as on a Russian train. There is a provodnitsa for each class of travel, who will check your ticket, rent you a set of sheets ($5 for as long as you need it), clean your cabin once a day and

The Lena river steamer, *Krasnoyarsk,* moored in Kirensk. (Photo © Paul Geldhof).

vainly attempt to police the class structure. As the scenery slides by even slower than on a train, there is ample time for reading and talking and a stop is always a big event with everyone out on the deck to watch, to the point that the ship noticeably leans to one side. Once, on a hot day and four hours ahead of schedule in Vitim, we stopped for two hours to give people a chance for a swim in the river.

## Cruise ships
Cruise ships are set up for Russian holidaymakers and Western tourists. The river cruise ship *Demyan Bedny* (Демян Бедный) operates out of Yakutsk on the Lena river (see Yakutsk p240), and occasionally cruise ships operate on the Amur river. These ships are comfortable by anyone's standards, with all cabins having private facilities. The food in the restaurant is of the kind you find in a good Russian restaurant, the service is charming and friendly, and there is a bar, lounge, movie theatre and sauna.

## Freight barges
Most of the traffic on the Lena and Amur rivers is freight. Freight ships may also take passengers. You would have to inquire locally about freight ships willing to take you. Bear in mind that they are slower than the passenger ships and that you would not have the same level of comfort. They might be cheaper, though.

# Around a town
## Путешествие по городу

The maps and descriptions in the guidebook sections of this guide, plus the Towns section in Appendix B, are your best guide to finding your way around any north-east town. The guidebook descriptions have sections Orientation, Getting around, Where to stay, Where to eat, Getting assistance and What to see. The following pages have general information on these topics.

## ORIENTATION

Most towns of the north-east are small and compact, with hotels, stations, government buildings, stores and sights within a compact area. The maps in this guide should enable you to find most things. Hotel staff are a great resource and will often make calls all around town to locate someone or something for you. This is often more effective than looking in the town directory (справочное) which is likely to be out of date. If you still have trouble finding something, you can always go to the police station where they invariably have a large map of the town and surrounding region on the wall.

On the other hand, if you want to visit a particular place, don't give up after being told by several people that they have never heard of it. Often locals have only been in the area for a few years and many have a poor regional knowledge. And even if someone tells you exactly how to get somewhere, keep asking until you get independent confirmation of it.

Finding toilets is always hard in Russia. In big towns there is the occasional public toilet but your best bet is any large public building such as a cinema, museum, or restaurant. You will normally have to pay a few roubles to enter a public toilet, or pay the museum entry fee. In small towns, there is normally a toilet near the station and that's about all. So the best advice is to go just before you get off the train and always use a toilet when you find one.

## GETTING AROUND

Towns too large to conveniently walk across have public transportation – mostly buses, but also trams in Komsomolsk-na-Amure and trolley-buses in Khabarovsk (though no underground systems). The cities have extensive networks and even commuter buses. Public transit offers a cheap way of getting around as well as giving you a tour of the town. If you get on the wrong bus, don't worry, as it will eventually return to where you got on. The guide notes important routes and the source of transport maps. Fares are collected by the driver or by a conductor and are commonly less than $0.50.

Taxis, often clustered by the railway or bus station, usually charge $2-3 for a trip around town (ask the price before getting in). In addition, taxi-drivers invariably know where all the hotels and other lodgings are, which are open and what their rates are; this is usually a useful and reliable service.

Finally, you can stand on the kerb with your right arm raised at 45° and your palm facing traffic (many statues of Lenin have this position); some people advise holding a small bill between the fingers. This is the universal sign for seeking a private ride and also has a standard fare, usually less than $3, and is effective, respectable and safe if you use common sense (eg don't ride in a car with three drunks). If the driver accepts you, (s)he will take you where you want to go.

## WHERE TO STAY

There is a hotel in virtually all but the smallest towns in the BAM Zone.

Hotels are shabby but almost always clean and secure. Most important, the bed-linen and towels, though threadbare, are clean and laundered. There is a 24-hour reception and in larger hotels there will be a forbidding dezhurnaya (дежурная) or floor attendant who will supply you with flasks of hot water and tea and is the guardian of room keys. These functionaries create security by keeping strangers and loiterers out of the hotel. The reception desk will store luggage for you, sometimes for a small fee.

Accommodation ranges from a private toilet and bathroom, a private washroom with showers down the hall, a washroom shared with one other room, or toilets and showers down the hall. Most rooms have two, three or four beds per room. If you are travelling alone you will not be asked to share with a stranger unless there is an extraordinary and unlikely pressure on hotel space. The best hotel rooms are called *lyuks* (люкс) and most hotels have at least one such room. Lyuks is a relative term and it just means that it is the best of all the rooms in that one hotel.

A few large towns (for example, Komsomolsk-na-Amure and Bratsk) have giant tourist-business hotels. In the Soviet period you would have been forced to stay there. Nowadays they are grim, alienating and often half abandoned and you have the luxury of not staying there.

The most common hotel in the north-east is the local Russian one owned by the municipality which has 20-40 rooms. These are busy and welcoming and may have a cafeteria or a restaurant. Here you will meet business people and military on travel orders.

There are also private hotels, either owned by individuals or spun off from colleges and institutes. These are usually the cheapest and here you will meet budget travellers, students and Chinese traders.

The Locomotive Brigade Hostels (Дом отдыха Локомотивной бригады) are spaced a four-hour rail journey apart on the railway. They are used by railway crews who have finished their shift and are staying overnight between work-shifts. They are open to the public, though if there is also a municipal hotel in the town you may be referred to it. They often have a canteen attached which is open 24 hours a day.

Other accommodation options include holiday homes (Дом отдыха) such as those at Severobaikalsk and Cape Kotelnikovski hot springs and sanatoria (саниторий) such as those at Kuldur, Ust-Kut and Neryungri. These are like small hotels well away from the town with a number of single, double and triple rooms with communal facilities. They normally have a canteen, sauna, pool and various forms of medical treatments.

The roughest kind of accommodation is in small towns and villages that have no hotel. Here you can stay in the municipal building, possovet (посёлковый совет), which will contain a room with a bed but often no running water.

A good way to experience Russian life is to stay with a family in a homestay. This is still rare in the BAM Zone but can be organised if you ask the company you are dealing with. To minimise the clash of cultures, you should remember the following when living with a Russian family.
● You should organise a time each day for your meals.
● Be prepared to pay your family for additional services such as organising theatre tickets, sightseeing and ordering taxis. Ask beforehand how much it will cost before agreeing to it and set an upper limit on how much you want to pay.
● Be prepared to supplement the household's food shopping when you visit the markets. Buy fruit or goods that they normally do not have.

Under the Soviet system hotels shared responsibility for keeping track of travellers. Therefore sometimes reception staff will still worry over your documents. Since Russian visas no longer show an approved itinerary, there is nothing for them to worry over, but this will not necessarily satisfy them. They will not refuse you accommodation, but in the worst case you can promise to visit the police station in the morning, or simply proceed on your journey. The old tourist hotels and the municipal hotels are the worst worriers, with private hotels much less concerned.

You hardly need to book accommodation in advance, except possibly for your first night in Russia. The best way to book is simply to send a telegram to the hotel. While this does not guarantee you a bed, as hotels rarely reply to confirm or decline your request, it will increase your chances.

## Laundry and cleaning
There are no coin-operated laundrettes in Russia and laundry and dry-cleaning establishments are only found in large cities, take days and are

hard to locate. However, Russians dress up to travel and most hotels have facilities for washing and ironing your own clothes. You can do it yourself, or ask the dezhurnaya or the receptionist if they know someone who could do it for you.

## EATING

### Where to eat

There are three main places to eat in Russia – canteens, cafés/bars and restaurants. The variety and presentation of food is less than in the Western world, but the food is almost always made from scratch in the kitchen.

**Canteens (столовая)** This is a basic serve-yourself eating place located in stations, highway stops, around towns and in railway hostels. They normally serve three meals a day but close quite early except for the 24-hour ones in railway hostels. If the town is small, canteens may be the only place where you can buy hot food. Usually the food is basic but tasty, with Russian salad (винегрет), soups, a meat or fish course, puddings, *kompot*, tea and, of course, bread. An almost universal dish is braised chicken thighs and legs, called for historical reasons 'Bush's legs' (ножки Буша). A hostel or hotel cafeteria will cook requests for you, within the limit of their supplies, such as fried eggs (глазунья – *glazunya*) or *bliny* (блины). An excellent meal can be had for $3.

Shashlik seller in Komsomolsk-na-Amure. (Photo © Nicholas Zvegintzov).

A great vegetarian food is sea cabbage or *morskaya kapusta* (морская капуста). This is seaweed cut into thin strips in a little oil. It can be eaten straight out of the tin or as a salad. It is common in shops as the Russians don't particularly like it.

**Cafés (кафе) and bars (бар)**  These are small sit-down places for quiet eating, often with a speciality menu such as pelmeni. Alcohol is sometimes available.

**Restaurants (ресторан)**  These establishments seem to serve the same bland dishes throughout the country. People don't come here for the food but the alcohol and the loud band.

**Other places**  Food is also available from roadside shashlik braziers, pie-sellers, *kvas* barrels and ice-cream stands. Most shopping centres have snack-bars tucked away inside. Grandmothers sell home-cooked dishes at long stops on the trains. And a bakery (булочная) often sells cooked foods such as *pirozhki* (пирожки).

### What to eat
Nowadays, almost all Western foods, from herbal tea to Mars Bars, are available in towns. While this provides a good security net, Russian food will be cheaper and shopping for it is an educational experience. The food in the north-east is about twice the cost of that in Moscow and about $1\frac{1}{2}$ times that of Irkutsk and Khabarovsk. The reason for this is that wages are higher than the rest of the country due to the hardship allowances and because food has to be freighted in.

Russian food that is commonly available all year-round includes kolbasa, cheese, bread, pickled vegetables, preserved fruit, tins of jam, jars of cooked kasha, macaroni, rice, milk, butter, cream, dehydrated Chinese noodles, frozen fish, slabs of meat, *salo*, eggs, tinned meat, biscuits and dried fruit.

Many travellers carry dehydrated oriental noodles in a polystyrene bowl which can be instantly reconstituted with hot water from the train's samovar. Note that the flavouring sachet often contains monosodium glutamate.

Wilted vegetables can be obtained for most of the year, supplemented by locally grown fresh vegetables in late summer.

## Vegetarians

Being a vegetarian in Russia is not easy. Russians like plenty of grease and salt and meat is served with nearly every meal. In a cafeteria you will find salads, possibly a vegetable or low-meat *borscht* (борщ) soup (borscht is basically a vegetable soup and chunks of meat are added), a fish soup, potatoes and other vegetables and fruit and kompot. When dining out, inform your host in advance if you are vegetarian or have another dietary requirement (many Russians believe that vegetarian simply means that you will not eat solid lumps of red meat). If you are afraid of not eating a balanced diet, bring some supplies and vitamin tablets.

## Shopping

Shopping in Russia is much easier than it used to be. Competition has eliminated most queues and laborious methods of paying. When you enter a store or a market, watch what the other shoppers are doing and copy them.

## WHAT TO SEE

Details on local tourist sights and excursions are located under each town or city. Generally large cities have theatres, museums and concert halls, while in small towns civic life revolves around the House of Culture (Dom kultury). Things to do around town include dancing and drinking in restaurants to ear-splitting music, watching sports events and the poolside scene at indoor swimming pools. Also watch out for special events and parades on national and regional public holidays.

Outdoor and group activities have suffered since the collapse of the Soviet Union. This is because many clubs, such as those involved in climbing, rafting, walking, chess, stamp collecting, flying, parachuting and painting, were sponsored by the trade union movement or the military and these have had their government funding stopped. The demise of the young communist organisations, Komsomol and Pioneers, has similarly reduced the opportunity for outdoor activities for children. However, the Russians' traditional support for the education and development of their children survives, with summer camps and activity centres for young people organised by the local school systems (see the Getting assistance sections in the route descriptions).

At home there is television and talking around the kitchen table.

Locals entertain themselves by going to the *banya* or to the *dacha* on weekends and by doing outdoor activities such as fishing, gardening, picnicking, or berry and mushroom picking. If you get asked, go along with the Russians on these outings as it's always interesting.

## POST AND TELECOMMUNICATIONS

Mail, telephones, telegrams and faxes are normally available at the post office. Post offices are divided into two main sections, occasionally located in separate buildings. The first is the postal office, where you send postal items and telegrams, and the second is the intercity and international telephone exchange.

### Mail

The postal section of the post office has three main counters – normal for letters and postcards, banderoli (бандероли) for books and documents, and posylki (посылки) for other items. The normal section also serves as the poste restante (востребование). Unfortunately, the three sections are also occasionally in different buildings, such as at Komsomolsk-na-Amure.

Be aware that the postal service is unreliable and often items that are valuable never leave the country. To increase the chance of your mail making it, send everything by registered post (заказной). While it is technically possible to mail books and other things, it is recommended that you don't do this. It is both time consuming and frustrating. To export a book, you need to pay a tax based on the book's cost. Remember when you send parcels, don't seal them before going to the Post Office as they need to be examined.

Airmail letters normally take three to six weeks between the Western world and north-east Russia. If you send material by land and sea mail, allow three to six months.

### Telephones

Telephoning from the north-east can be a challenge. Before trying to make a call, you may ask advice or even help from locals. The hotel staff, at least in smaller hotels, will sometimes throw themselves into the challenge.

Local calls are free, sometimes even at public phones on the street. Therefore most hotels will lend you a phone to make local calls, or will sometimes have a public phone just inside the front door. (On the other hand, some hotels may have no phone service at all, or have had it cut off for not paying the bill.)

Even local calls can be complicated because of parallel telephone systems. The Russian Ministry of Railways operates one of the world's largest private telephone networks with over a million lines. Of these, 60 per cent are located in railway stations and offices, 30 per cent in railway employees' homes, and 10 per cent in commercial establishments. In larger towns, there is a combination of railway and civil phones, but in many BAM towns there are only railway phones. Although there are connections between the civil and railway phone systems, this is extremely difficult to organise and it is often necessary to call the main railway telephone switchboard in Tynda or Moscow to get such a connection. Therefore, even to make a local call, you have to ensure that the phone you are using and the phone you are calling are on the same network.

For making an intercity or international call the easiest method, if you can arrange it, is to use a private telephone, either by direct dialling or by booking a call with the operator. Some hotels, particularly those

> ❏ **Emergencies**
> To get assistance by phone, dial the following numbers. If you don't speak Russian, get help from a Russian.
> 01  Fire
> 02  Police
> 03  Ambulance
> 07  Long-distance telephone connections
> 09  Directory assistance

that regularly host Chinese traders, may have an intercity and international phone, as well as a procedure for making calls and charging for them (ask at the reception desk).

If these methods fail, the telephone section of the post office is called *Peregovorny punkt* (Переговорный пункт). Even if you don't want to make a call, you should visit one of these chaotic places to hear tens of Russians in individual phone booths yelling to overcome the poor line quality and each other's shouting.

To make a call, you need to fill in a form stating the town, phone number, name of the receiving party and the length of time you want to talk for. You then pay for the call and wait until your name and telephone booth number is called over the loudspeaker. As soon as you pick up the phone in the booth, your time starts. The operator will tell you over the phone when there is 30 seconds left. If your call can't get through, you get a refund. A typical wait is from 15 minutes to one hour but if you want it to be put through quicker, you can pay a premium for a quick *srochny* (срочный) call. Frequently in the north-east it will be impossible to get an international line so you may have to make several trips to the Peregovorny punkt. In some places, there are intercity direct-dial pay phones (междугородный автомат) which can instantly connect you with other cities in Russia. These take tokens that you buy from the cashier. Due to a strange twist of logic, these automatic phones are about twice as expensive as booking a call with the cashier. In Komsomolsk-na-Amure and Bratsk, there are credit card international phones in the biggest hotels which provide instant but incredibly expensive communication. For example, a call from Komsomolsk-na-Amure to New York will cost $15 a minute.

Direct dialling into the north-east from abroad is usually not a problem providing you are calling a normal phone number. It is virtually impossible to call a number on the Russia railway phone system; you have to call the railway operator, who will then redirect your call to the railway phone network.

If you are making an international call, remember that the time in the north-east is from GMT +8 at Severobaikalsk to GMT +11 in Magadan. Thus Severobaikalsk is five hours later than Moscow, eight hours later than London, 13 hours later than New York and one hour earlier than Tokyo.

## Telegrams and faxes

Telegrams are the easiest way to communicate internationally as any post office will send them. They are also relatively cheap. Unlike telexes, which only a few post offices can send, telegrams are sent to the address of the recipients via their country's national post office. They normally are delivered a day or two after they are sent. Telegrams are commonly used within Russia to book accommodation and meetings.

Most large post offices have a public fax machine.

## Email and internet

Most north-east towns have email providers (ask the agents in the Getting assistance sections). Yakutsk has good internet connections (see the Yakutsk Getting around section, p235).

# Security and police
### Безопасность и милиция

Being a Westerner you instantly attract attention and envy in Russia. For a very small group of Russians, this can mean an opportunity for their quick gain and your quick loss. Fortunately the north-east is considerably safer than Moscow and probably safer than most Western cities. Common sense is the best safeguard and here are a few rules.

● Minimise the things you carry around.

● Dress down and blend in with Russians.

● Carry money and documents next to your body in a moneybelt, never in a bag.

● Carry a wallet with enough money in it for the day and nothing else so if you lose this 'sacrificial' wallet, it does not matter.

● Be discreet and don't draw attention to yourself by talking loudly in English or carrying a camera around your neck.

Ironically, dressing like a Western adventure tourist may get you iden-tified as homeless (бездомный) or 'lacking definite residence' (БОМЖ – без определённого местожительства). In general, Russians dress up to travel (though they may change out of their good clothes for a long sojourn in a *coupé*). Homeless travellers wear jeans and sneakers and old sweaters and windbreakers, and carry shapeless shoulder-bags – just like many Westerners.

## TYPES OF POLICE

Regardless of horror stories of corrupt police, they are your best bet for getting reliable information. The vast majority of police are honest and trustworthy with foreigners. As all police officers have to do military service before they enter the force, the youngest officers are 21 and have proved themselves to be reliable and trustworthy.

The police identity card is the standard red vinyl flip-open card carried by all Russians so unless you read Russian, flashing an identity card means nothing.

Police come in many guises, including civilian police, railway police, highway police and railway property guards and it is useful to know their areas of responsibility, as they are reluctant, if not prohibited, to work outside them. It is often hard to distinguish between the types of police as they mostly wear either a military uniform or the civilian police blue uniform, a blue peaked cap with a red band, black baton, short-range radio and pistol.

● **Civilian police (Милиция)** These are your average police officers who are responsible for curtailing common crime. Most street police teams consist of one plain clothes officer and one in uniform.

● **Railway police (Железнодорожная милиция)** These police, also known as transport police (Транспортная милиция), wear the normal police uniform but are employed by the Ministry of Railways. There is a railway police officer at every railway station and they will sometimes travel on trains. If a problem does occur on a train, the Train Captain can radio the next station and the railway police will be ready to storm aboard.

A typical small BAM town, such as Verkhnezeisk, has a complement of 13 civilian police and eight railway police.

● **Highway police, GIBDD (ГИБДД -- Государственная инспекция безопасности дорожного движения)** These police man control traffic intersections along major roads. Drivers show them enormous respect as they can levy hefty fines or confiscate your car. When they point their black-and-white striped baton at your car, you must pull over. The officer will eventually stroll over and demand your driver's licence and passport. They are experts at finding something wrong with your documents or car, but a bribe can get you on your way with the minimum of inconvenience. During the day, they will normally wear a pistol and baton but at night, particularly at the more remote posts, they will carry automatic pistols.

● **Railway property guards (Военнизированная охрана)** These paramilitary officers guard freight yards and other railway property. They normally wear army uniforms, carry machine pistols and occasionally patrol with German shepherd dogs. Most are ex-soldiers, many of whom have fought in Afghanistan or returned from Germany.

● **Railway troops (Железнодорожная войска по строительству и восстановлению)**  While the vast majority of troops within the Railway Forces for the Construction and Maintenance of Railways are involved in building railways, a small percentage guard the ends of bridges and tunnels. This means that they are often based in the middle of nowhere and have a profoundly boring job. Despite the fact that they are not part of the Ministry of Defence, their uniform is identical to that of normal soldiers except they have their own railway insignia. The current government policy is to replace the bridge-guarding soldiers with civilian guards.

● **Military police (Патруль)**  These soldiers wander the streets and stations looking for military personnel on unauthorised leave. There is always one officer and at least one enlisted man. They wear a large badge or red armband emblazoned with the word «Патруль», and carry a pistol, baton and radio. Most of these police are normal soldiers rostered to this duty but full-time military police are identified by an arm patch with a 'K' meaning Commandant Corps on it.

● **FSK police (ФСК)**  These police are part of the old KGB which has been renamed FSK (Federal Counter-Intelligence Service – Федеральная Служба Контразведки). The FSK investigates crimes against the state and across administrative borders. These police are most often encountered if you are caught photographing something that they consider inappropriate such as a railway bridge.

● **Border guards (Пограничник)**  While these guards wear the Russian military uniform, they are actually part of the Ministry of Internal Affairs. Probably the only time you will meet them will be as you enter and leave the country. They have their own navy, airforce and ground troops, and wear a green band around their peaked caps.

● **Cossacks (Казаки)**  These self-appointed, volunteer, paramilitary soldiers should be avoided. The Cossacks first explored Siberia and their descendants feel that by wearing the old Cossack uniform, consisting of a Russian military uniform with a yellow stripe down the trousers and a yellow hat band around a peaked cap, they are recapturing their true heritage, which entitles them to respect. As most of the Cossacks are louts, the average Russian eyes them warily. The Cossacks were banned during Soviet times, but have now returned.

An uneasy truce exists between the regular police and the Cossacks. They are not allowed to carry guns but carry truncheons and long whips. Cossacks believe in the three principles of common ownership, military service in support of the state and regional autonomy. These principles made them ideal tools for the Tsar in conquering new land and guarding borders but have little relevance today. Thankfully there are only a few Cossacks in the north-east as their power base is in the Don region in southern European Russia.

## THE PASSPORT BUREAU

The Passport Bureau (Паспортный бюро) is an office at the local police station that deals with passports and residence registration both for Russians and foreigners. Sometimes a jittery hotel will send you here if they are worried about your visa but this should result only in a wait in the waiting-room and a brief interview (see The visa, p11).

## CRIME ON THE RAILWAYS

There are many stories of crimes on railways. The majority are exaggerations, distortions, or complete fabrications. The most outrageous story in recent years has been the so-called Sleeping Gas Incident on the Moscow—St Petersburg train. This story involved an entire carriage being put to sleep by sleeping gas and everyone being robbed. After a week of international media coverage, the Russian journalist who wrote the story admitted that it was fictitious but she still maintained that she did lose her purse when she was asleep.

Having said this, crime does exist on railways and a few simple precautions will substantially reduce your chances of being a victim. These include locking the cabin from the inside when you are asleep by the normal lock and the flick-down lock, putting valuables under the sleeping bench which means that they can't be reached without lifting your bed, dressing on trains like a Russian (but not a homeless person), not displaying cameras, talking softly and always carrying your valuables on your body.

Some people feel the need to chain and padlock their bags but this is excessive. It is a good idea to always leave someone in the cabin to look after the luggage. If everyone has to leave, ask the conductor to lock your cabin. Although valuables can be left in a small safe that is located in the chief conductor's cabin, this is not recommended.

If there is a problem, first go to your provodnik who will call the head conductor, who in turn will notify the police if it is warranted.

# Customs and manners

Russia and its people are significantly different in attitude and customs to Westerners. Being receptive and noticing their behaviour can save you a great deal of misunderstanding and offence. It is often said that the Russians are rude and abrupt. This may be true in business spheres but in personal matters they are probably more open and willing to please than Westerners.

Simple courtesy will often go a long way and if you are not sure of the appropriateness of your actions, ask.

A common problem is what to take as a present for the host when visiting a Russian house. Flowers are ideal, indeed almost obligatory, to a female host, as is a bottle of alcoholic drink for a male host. What kind of drink to take? Usually, something stronger than 30 per cent proof.

Alcoholic beverages are usually drunk neat and in the 'bottoms up' style. If you mix your vodka with juice or water, Russians may find it strange and call it 'a spoilt drink'. Moreover, if you are a man it will be appreciated if you drink it straight and straight down. A strong opinion some Russians have is that if you make a toast but do not drink it all in one gulp, then you are not sincere. So, if you propose in your toast something like, 'for the well-being of the host' or 'to Russia', make sure that you drink it to the end.

To minimise vodka damage, eat butter or fat before you drink, as this will line your stomach with a protective layer, which will slow the rate of alcohol absorption. Always follow vodka with a water or fruit juice chaser and something to eat. It is not advisable to sip vodka but gulp it down quickly without leaving it in your mouth. In addition, don't mix alcoholic drinks.

You do not have to drink, even if your hosts press you. Some Russians do not drink and that is quite acceptable. Some suggest drinking toasts in water or mineral water 'because that looks like vodka'. It may be wise not to start on a sequence of toasts with vodka and then have to quit in the middle.

The legal drinking age in Russia is 18 years old.

It is customary in Russia to show respect for older people and this means that when travelling on public transport, it is the accepted norm to give your seats up to elderly people, women and small children. People may make disapproving remarks if you do not. In addition, it is polite to use a person's first and patronymic name if they are older than you. The

---

### ❏ Women travellers

Women should be aware that the unwritten rules between the sexes are not the same as in the West.

A young woman who has travelled extensively in Russia advises:'Men hold doors, pull out chairs, hold coats and offer to carry bags for women. It is easier just to go along with this. If you refuse, their male pride may be injured. They are also likely to be quite effusive and pay you many compliments, of which you can usually discount at least 85 per cent. Men usually expect to pay for drinks/meals/tickets etc and may get very offended if you try to or insist on paying your share. And finally, do not invite a single man out for a drink/dinner/walk unless you know each other well, or are prepared for him to assume that your feelings for him are stronger than they actually are and make what may be an unwanted move. This is a serious point. Although foreigners are exempt from some of the social rules, they are not exempt from the one that says 'Single woman invites single man = she wants it now'. This attitude is probably relaxing among younger people (under the age of 30ish) but it's worth bearing in mind.'

patronymic name is the modified version of the person's father's name. For example, if your name is Anton and your father's name is Alexander, your full formal name with the patronymic would be Anton Alexandrovich. The additional suffix to make the first name into a patronymic for men is '-ovich', and for women is '-ovna'.

Another difference between Westerners and Russians is that Russians usually don't greet strangers by saying the Russian equivalent of 'How are you?' which is *Kak dela?*. A Russian when asked such a question may think that you are genuinely interested in how they are and they may start to tell you about their fortunes and misfortunes! In Russia the most common way of greeting people is by saying *Zdravstvuite* which means 'be healthy'. Men usually greet each other by a handshake.

Another custom in Russia is to take off your hat and shoes when entering a house. It is believed that the custom originates from the traditions of old Russia, when it was necessary for a warrior to take his helmet and armour off in order to show the host of the house that he trusted him and did not consider him an enemy.

You should also remember that Russian society is heterogeneous. Westerners often call everyone who lives in the territory of the former Soviet Union a Russian. However, there are about 120 nations and nationalities inhabiting Russia and an equal number of languages are spoken. Some nationalities may take offence if you call them Russian while others may feel honoured.

Russians are in general reliable and punctual. You may doubt this having suffered with a cashier or an official who is not at their job at the posted times, but this mirrors a dichotomy between the public and the private spheres. As Russian public facilities are often slovenly and dirty while private houses are clean, so public behaviour may be careless and inconsiderate but private behaviour is not. If a taxi-driver says 'I will be at your door at 7am to take you to the station', or an acquaintance or contact says 'I will meet you on the platform at the door of the third wagon of the Moscow train tomorrow at 00.30', expect them to fulfil their promise to the letter and on the dot. You should be equally exact and punctual.

## Tips and bribes

Tipping is not normally done as a reward for good service, but is more of an ostentatious display of wealth or as a bribe. If you want to show your gratitude, give a small gift such as a stick pin, baseball cap, pen, or a bottle of liquor.

Bribes, known as vzyatka (взятка), are common in Russia but unless you are well versed in Russian and the Russian ways, don't attempt them. If you are travelling with a Russian let them do it. A better approach for foreigners is to be patient and go through the official channels and if a bribe is expected, let the Russian initiate it. In the north-east where foreigners are rare, being asked for a bribe is incredibly rare. However, an appropriate response to someone's assistance in getting a railway ticket, a tour of a closed museum, or a reserved room in a hotel, is a small gift.

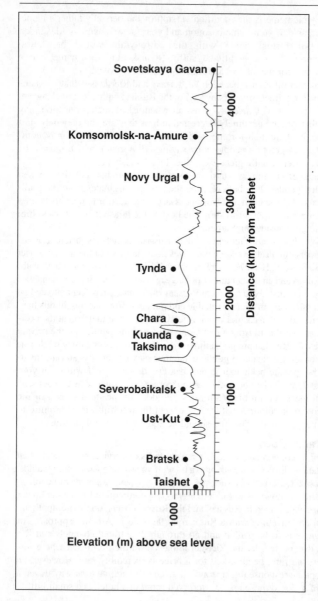

Ups and downs of the BAM main line: The BAM main line plotted from west to east (Taishet to Sovetskaya Gavan) with the elevation in metres above sea level.

# PART 3: MAINLINE ROUTES
## Описание пути по магистрали

## Taishet–Bratsk
### Тайшет–Братск

### THE ROUTE (See Route Map 1, p366)

On your right as you leave Taishet, first you see a large railway maintenance and shunting area, then the Trans-Siberian disappears as it curves
off to the south-east.

The route crosses from the
Biryusa river to the Chuna river (both
flow north to join the Angara river)
and then to the Bratsk Reservoir on
the Angara river. The terrain is low
(1,000m hills) past meadows and
small creeks. In summer you will see
haymakers with scythes and rakes and
motor-cycles with side-cars and tents.
Some scythe in mosquito masks, others stripped to the waist.

> ❑ **Route description legend**
> In the route descriptions, the
> following signs indicate the
> size of locations:
>
> ⊠   **Station only**
>
> 🏭   **Town**
>
> 🏚   **Village**

This part of the BAM was built
between 1937 and 1947, with station buildings in Siberian gingerbread,
painted pale blue and pale green and decorated with diamond panels.

The time is Moscow time +5 hours.

### 🏭 TAISHET (Тайшет) 0km

This town, with its population of 70,000, straddles the junction of the
BAM and the Trans-Siberian railways. From Taishet, the BAM heads
north and east around the northern end of Lake Baikal; the Trans-Siberian
heads south and east around the southern end. From Lake Baikal they both
head roughly parallel to the Pacific coast.

### Orientation

Taishet is a small town; you can
explore it in a few hours. The main
street, ul. Transportnaya (ул.
Транспортная), runs parallel to the
railway on the north side. The town is
divided into a new settlement on the

> ❑ **Taishet (Тайшет)**
> Area code ☎ 395-63
> 665000 Irkutsk Oblast, Taishet
> (665000 Иркутская
> область, г. Тайшет)

northern side, where the station, apartment blocks and administrative centre are located and the old part on the southern side.

## History

Taishet was founded with the arrival of the Trans-Siberian. It contains at least one stunning piece of 19th-century architecture, one of the massive brick water-towers, with windows and turrets, built with the Trans-Siberian. The water tower stands opposite the station and is now disused, since the town has a modern water plant on the Biryusa river. This is possibly the last pre-revolutionary building that you will see along the BAM, since the BAM was built to open up uninhabited land.

Taishet is famous in gulag literature as it was a transit camp for Stalin-era prisoners heading east and west. In addition Taishet was a major camp of Ozerlag, the gulag complex that built the Taishet–Bratsk section of the BAM. The building of this section started in earnest following the end of the Great Patriotic War and at the height of construction there were over 300 camps dotted along the 350km stretch from Taishet to Bratsk with a total population of 100,000 prisoners. In *The Gulag Archipelago* Solzhenitsyn wrote, 'And Taishet, with its factory for creosoting railroad ties (where, they say, creosote penetrates the skin and bones and its vapours fill the lungs – and that is death).' The factory that makes the ties, or railway sleepers, still operates.

Some residents proudly recall the visit of Tsar Nicholas II, others the Stalin-era camps!

## Getting there and away

Trains on both the Trans-Siberian and BAM railways stop here.

The timetable (Расписания) in the station has three sections – west (toward Moscow on the Trans-Siberian), east (toward Vladivostok along the Trans-Siberian), and north (along the BAM). A printed timetable, which is sometimes available from the ticket window, simplifies this to just west and east.

From the west on the Trans-Siberian, trains arrive from Moscow ($72^{1}/_{4}$ hours), Ekaterinburg ($43^{1}/_{4}$ hours), Novosibirsk (22 hours) and Krasnoyarsk ($7^{3}/_{4}$ hours). From the east on the Trans-Siberian, they arrive from Irkutsk (11 hours 35 minutes), Chita ($30^{3}/_{4}$ hours), Khabarovsk (74 hours) and Vladivostok ($87^{1}/_{2}$ hours). From the east on the BAM, trains arrive from Bratsk ($6^{1}/_{2}$ hours), Ust-Ilimsk (15 hours), Ust-Kut ($16^{1}/_{4}$ hours), Severobaikalsk (22 hours) and Tynda (44 hours). On a minor branch line from the south-west trains arrive from Sayanskaya (6 hours 10 minutes).

On the Trans-Siberian there are roughly six mainline trains a day (taking into account trains that run daily, on alternate days, and on certain days of the week). From the west and continuing on the BAM mainline

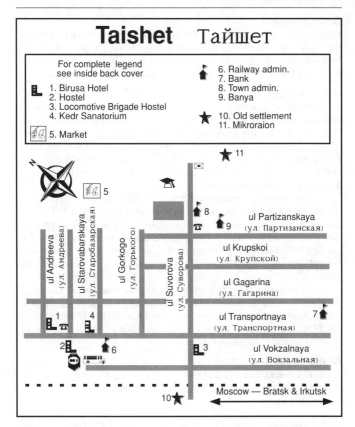

# Taishet   Тайшет

For complete legend
see inside back cover

1. Birusa Hotel
2. Hostel
3. Locomotive Brigade Hostel
4. Kedr Sanatorium
5. Market

6. Railway admin.
7. Bank
8. Town admin.
9. Banya

10. Old settlement
11. Mikroraion

ul Andreeva (ул. Андреева)
ul Starovabarskaya (ул. Старобазарская)
ul Gorkogo (ул. Горького)
ul Suvorova (ул. Суворова)
ul Partizanskaya (ул. Партизанская)
ul Krupskoi (ул. Крупской)
ul Gagarina (ул. Гагарина)
ul Transportnaya (ул. Транспортная)
ul Vokzalnaya (ул. Вокзальная)

Moscow — Bratsk & Irkutsk

there are a Moscow–Tynda train (via Kazan) and a Moscow–Lena train on
alternate days, a Krasnoyarsk–Severobaikalsk train every other day and a
Kislovodsk–Tynda train twice a week. In addition there are three trains a
day that arrive from Irkutsk in the east on the Trans-Siberian, reverse
direction, and leave to the east on the BAM (one to Gidrostroitel and two
to Ust-Ilimsk), providing a circuitous south-north link. These trains are
attractive options for BAM travel because they leave Taishet largely
empty. The mainline trains from the west are liable to be jammed with
people who have spent three days and nights in their berths.

Taishet is located on the M53 Moscow–Irkutsk highway.

Planes arrive at Taishet from Bratsk, Irkutsk and Krasnoyarsk.

## Getting around

Buses operate along the main street (ul. Transportnaya) and out to the old town and to the new district (*mikroraion*) out of town a little way. If you have several hours to spend, you can take a pleasant 25- to 30-minute car trip to the Biryusa river where dachas are located.

## Where to stay

The default accommodation in town is the municipal *Hotel Biryusa*, opposite the railway station. It is a four-storey building with 60 rooms. Prices are $20 for foreigners. All rooms have toilets and showers. Hotel Biryusa is at ul. Transportnaya, ☎ 303-18 (ул. Транспортная, Гостиница «Бирюса»). Another option is the *hostel* (☎ 524-23) at the station. It has rooms with three and seven beds; it is clean but does not have showers. It costs $6 a bed.

The three-storey *Locomotive Brigade Hostel* for locomotive drivers is another option. It has twin and triple rooms from $5 per person. The hostel is on ul. Suvorova, ☎ 526-76 (ул. Суворова, Дом отдыха Локомотивной бригады,). To get permission to stay there, you need to ask the chief of the locomotive repair shop, phone ☎ 5-36-22 (home) or ☎ 5-32-08 (work). It also contains a 24-hour cafeteria, which is open to the public.

The best accommodation in town is the *Kedr Sanatorium*, which has full accommodation, meals, health rooms, saunas and a 25m by 5m swimming pool. Accommodation costs $12-20 per person. Ask permission to stay there from the Chief Doctor (☎ 5-38-21), Sanatori Profilaktori Kedr, ul. Starobazarnaya (ул. Старобазарная, Санаторий Профилакторий «Кедр»).

## Where to eat

There is a *restaurant* in the station. A 24-hour *canteen* operates in the Locomotive Brigade Hostel. The new main *market* is located three blocks north of the station.

## SOSNOVYE RODNIKI (Сосновые Родники) 129km

The station's name, which translates as 'pinewood springs', is different from the town which is called Oktyabrski (Октябрьский).

The town is located on the right bank of the Chuna river and its main industry is lumber. Timber is floated down the 1,203km Chuna river, which is called the Uda river in its upper course and loaded into railway wagons at Sosnovye Rodniki. The river freezes in late October or early November and is ice-free in late April or early May.

## CHUNA (Чуна) 142km

Chuna was another major gulag camp centre and its camps included 119 Wood Processing Plants, 104 Deportation Camps and brick-making works.

❑ **Gulag Camp No 410, Vikhorevka – a prisoner's account**
'It was daytime when we arrived in Vikhorevka ... When I saw the prison building from the outside, I was surprised to see how gloomy a place could be made
to be. This squat, grey, one-storey concrete building, located on the perimeter of
the settlement, was surrounded by an old, grey wooden fence and an off-limits
zone with watchtowers. The walls, floors and the ceilings of the prison were cast
with cement and iron bars into a cold block. This indestructible reinforced-con-
crete vault was built in the wintertime. Thus, in order to make the concrete hard-
en as quickly as possible, salt had been added to it. The result, however, was that
the floors, walls and ceiling were constantly wet. With a creak of the door and
a squeak of the hinges, I was locked into my cell of 15 square metres. I was at
home. Directly opposite the door was a window under which stood a large plank
bed for eight persons. It was made of thick wooden blocks held together by iron
clamps that were spaced some 30 to 40cm apart from one another. Ice glimmered in the indentations in the floor. The window was also covered with a
thick layer of ice. Drops of water clung to the ceiling; water trickled down the
wall.' (From *A World Apart* by Gustav Herling)

## VIKHOREVKA (Вихоревка) 269km

Vikhorevka is 35km south-west of Bratsk. It has a population of 35,000
and was officially founded in 1957, despite gulag camps operating there
since the mid-1940s.

The town is now the headquarters of the Taishet–Lena administration
of the East Siberian Railway. On the platform is a fine steam locomotive
as a memorial 'To the First Builders of the BAM from Grateful
Successors'.

A little further along the line, on the right at the equipment yards, is
another fine steam locomotive, rusting away and high on an upthrust
plinth an elektrichka (a suburban electric railway car). Vikhorevka was the
site of the prison hospital for the camps located along the entire length of
the Taishet–Bratsk railway.

## MORGUDON (Моргудон) 283km

Morgudon is the junction of the BAM and a spur line to the centre of
Bratsk. Only suburban trains stop here so you have to get off at Anzebi to
change for the suburban train. The 20km spur line was completed in 1971.

The stations on the line are: Morgudon (Моргудон), Bagulnaya
(Багульная) 7km, Bratsk Porozhski (Братск Порожский) 17km and
Port Novobratsk (Порт Новобратск) 20km.

## ANZEBI (Анзёби) 292km

This is the best BAM station to change trains for the suburban train that
goes to the centre of Bratsk. The adjacent settlement on the Vikhorevka

river is called Chekanovski (Чекановский) after A L Chekanovski, a
famous explorer of central Siberia (1833-76). Chekanovski was born in
the Ukraine, but was a Pole by nationality. He took part in the Polish
Uprising of 1863-65 and for his troubles was exiled to Siberia. However,
the Russian Geographic Society appreciated his geographical training and
commissioned him to conduct geographic surveys of the Irkutsk region in
1869-71. He later explored the upper Lena and Olensk rivers and a number of towns in the region have statues and memorial plaques to him.

### 🚉 GALACHINSKI (Галачинский) 303km

Only suburban trains stop at the small station.

### 🚉 BRATSKOE MORE (Братское Море) 314km

Only suburban trains stop at this small station. See Bratsk (p67) for more
information. The train winds through the suburbs, with industrial plants
on the horizon, and then makes an S-bend, south over a low ridge and
north around a small inlet of the reservoir. On a hill above the cutting,
there is an active green and gold Orthodox church.

### 🚉🚉🚉 PADUNSKIE POROGI (Падунские Пороги) 325km

This station services the suburbs of Padun (Падун) and Energetik
(Энергетик) on the west bank of the Bratsk dam. See Bratsk (p68) for
more information. The railway and the road cross the Bratsk dam.

### 🚉🚉🚉 GIDROSTROITEL (Гидростроитель) 339km

This station services the residential area of Gidrostroitel which is also
known as Osinovka (Осиновка) on the east bank of the Bratsk dam. See
Bratsk (p68) for more information.

# Bratsk–Ust-Kut
## Братск–Усть-Кут

## THE ROUTE (Route Map 1, p366)

The train loops through low hills around the watershed of the Bratsk Sea and then crosses the Ilim river at the upper end of the Ilimsk reservoir, which is formed by a dam lower down the Angara river at Ust-Ilimsk. From here the route crosses several more small watersheds through gradually higher hills (up to 300m) and drops down to the Lena river at Ust-Kut. You have now crossed from the watershed of one of the Arctic-flowing rivers of Siberia, the Yenisei, to the other, the Lena.

The time is Moscow time +5 hours.

## BRATSK (Братск)

Bratsk is not one town but a ring of connected settlements around the man-made Bratsk Sea (Братское море), which is a large reservoir created by the Bratsk dam. The setting is impressive, with the man-made challenging the natural. The settlements ring the hilltops around the dam – or what would be the hilltops but for the immense lake lapping at their feet. The dam straddles a 4km valley, burying the former Padun Rapids. Below the dam the Angara river threads northward through the hills, only to be backed up again by the Ust-Ilimsk Dam.

> ❑ **Bratsk (Братск)**
> Area code ☎ 39531 (Bratsk)
> Irkutsk Oblast, Bratsk
> (Иркутская область, г. Братск)
> Postal codes: Bratsk More 665707, Padun 665701, Energetik 665709

Bratsk is fascinating, principally as an example of what not to do when you are creating a gigantic industrial complex in the middle of the taiga. Despite being in the top ten most polluted cities in Russia, Bratsk is still awe-inspiring considering the achievement of constructing a modern city of 280,000, a giant dam and massive industrial complexes in just two decades.

### Orientation

The settlements of Bratsk are arranged in a rough semicircle at the northern end of the Bratsk Sea. Clockwise from the southern end is the suburb of Porozhski (Порожский) and the administrative centre of Bratsk at Tsentralny (Центральный). Both can be reached by a suburban electric train from the BAM station of Anzebi, which is 12km away.

The Taiga and Bratsk hotels are at Tsentralny.

The suburbs of Padun (Падун) and Energetik (Энергетик) are 25km north, at the left side of the dam, served by the mainline station Padunskie Porogi. (The station's name derives from the Padun Rapids, which existed before the dam was built.) Energetik has Hotel Turist and Hotel Instituta Energetika. It contains the most attractive part of Bratsk as it has a pleasant promenade, with an old log watchtower and the city's only working church. You can also walk along the abutment of the dam wall but not the wall itself. Bratsk airport is a 40-minute drive north of Energetik. GSK-Bratsk Hydro-electric Construction Conglomerate (Братск ГСК-Гидроэлектрический Строительный Комплекс), which is the biggest construction enterprise in eastern Siberia, is located in Padun. In addition, the town has several health sanatoria for armed forces personnel but why they would be located in such a polluted place is still a military secret.

Gidrostroitel (Гидростроитель) and Osinovka (Осиновка) are on the right side of the dam and are served by the mainline station of Gidrostroitel.

## History

The Bratsk area with its rich agricultural lands was an important staging area for exploring and colonising Eastern Siberia and the Russian Far East. The word Bratsk comes from the Russian words *Bratskie lyudi* (Братские люди) which was given to the local indigenous people, the Buryats. 'Lyudi' means 'people'. 'Bratskie' is either a mispronunciation of 'Buryat' or it means 'fraternal', although this may be a false but politically-correct derivation. Old Bratsk was founded as a fort in 1631 but has long since disappeared under the giant Bratsk Sea.

As well as being an excellent farming region, the area provided much of the industrial base essential to propelling development in eastern Siberia in the late 1890s. In 1895 the Nikolaevsk pig iron works began operation on the Dolonovka river, not far from Bratsk. The works built steamers that sailed on the Angara, produced equipment for the gold fields on the Lena and manufactured rails for the Trans-Siberian railway. They were closed in 1899 when Irkutsk was connected to Moscow by the Trans-Siberian and cheaper iron could be shipped in.

In 1954 the decision was taken to build the Bratsk hydro-electric station and it rapidly became a gem in the nation's industrialisation crown. The reservoir is one of the largest in the world, being 169.3 cubic kilometres in volume with a surface area of 5,470 square kilometres. Within seven years of the start of the dam's construction, electricity was being generated and, in conjunction with the nearby Ust-Ilimsk hydro-electric station, the region now generates a mammoth 4.5% of the nation's electricity. To utilise this enormous amount of power, large industrial complexes were simultaneously built. These include the LPK Bratsk Timber Complex (ЛПК-Лесопромышленный Комплекс) (1965) and BRAZ Bratsk

**Bratsk & Surrounding Area**

Airport / Аэропорт

Angara River / Река Ангара

Energetik / Энергетик

Padunskie Porogi / Падунские Пороги

Osinovka / Осиновка

Padun / Падун

DAM / Дамба

N

Gidrostroitel / Гидростроитель

Tsentralny / Центральный

Bratsk Sea / Братское море

Anzebi / Анзёби

Porozhski / Порожский

Aluminium Complex (БРАЗ-Братский Алюминиевый завод) (1966).

The planning and construction of Bratsk has been a series of errors but considering that the city arose out of virgin taiga, it is hardly surprising. One of the first major mistakes was the underestimation of the speed in which the reservoir would fill. In all, 249 settlements had to be moved and most villagers had to shift to their new towns before they were completed. In addition, the rising water quickly submerged the forests in the Bratsk and Ilimsk basin before they could be harvested, which was a massive waste. The flooding resulted in a major downturn in agricultural production as the best farming land was in the submerged valleys. The novel *Farewell to Matyora*, by Valentin Rasputin, tells of the flooding of the Ust-Ilimsk region and the resulting social problems of the resettled villagers.

Another major planning error was the vast under-utilisation of the dam's energy. Although on the drawing board the planned industrial complexes would consume all the electricity, in reality the plants were simply too big and complex to operate continuously at full capacity and therefore couldn't reach their theoretical energy consumption. For example, the paper and pulp mill has enormous problems obtaining the seven million cubic metres of raw materials it needs annually. Even the Soviet media acknowledged the complex's problems and in 1971 the industrial journal *Sotsialisticheskaya Industriya* stated that 'there had been serious negligence in the building of the complex'.

However, the greatest problem is air pollution. The belching of the industrial smokestacks regularly blackens the skies over Bratsk and poisons the water. When the wind blows across town, the smell from the paper and pulp plant is dreadful. The biggest threat to life comes from the fertiliser factory. Every year there are accidental releases of nitrogen gas and the clouds float over the city. The city administration's solution was to install loud speakers on poles, which advise you to stay indoors when an accident has occurred. This problem is compounded by the fact that despite the city plan showing industrial and residential zones, there is virtually no green belt between them. As might be expected, Bratsk has an active environmental movement.

### Getting there and away
Stopping at Anzebi (for Tsentralny), Padunskie Porogi and Gidrostroitel there are a Moscow–Tynda train (via Kazan) and a Moscow–Lena train on alternate days, a Krasnoyarsk–Severobaikalsk train every other day and a Kislovodsk–Tynda train twice a week. In addition there are three trains a day that arrive from Irkutsk in the east on the Trans-Siberian, reverse direction, and leave to the east on the BAM (one to Gidrostroitel and two to Ust-Ilimsk). These trains are attractive options for BAM travel because they leave Taishet largely empty (see Taishet, p63).

There are daily buses to Ust-Ilimsk in the north-east. To reach Bratsk by car from the west, you must first go to the town of Tulun (Тулун) which is 180km south of Bratsk on the M53 Moscow–Irkutsk highway.

The airport is 8km north of Padunskie Porogi. There are flights to Irkutsk, Moscow (once a week), St Petersburg, Chelyabinsk, Rostov and Ekaterinburg. The Aeroflot office (8.00-19.00) is at ul. Deputatskaya 17.

On Sunday, Wednesday and Friday from Bratsk (Monday, Thursday and Saturday return) there is a Meteor hydrofoil up the Bratsk reservoir and then on the Angara to Irkutsk ($10), stopping at 16 places en route. It loads in Bratsk at Port Novobratsk (bus from Tsentralny (Центральный)) and in Irkutsk at the River Station (*rechnoi vokzal*, речной вокзал), downstream from the Irkutsk dam on the right bank of the Angara.

### Getting around
Local buses serve each of the residential areas, with hourly buses between Tsentralny and Energetik (bus No 118) and between Energetik and Gidrostroitel. The main bus station is at Tsentralny on ul. Yuzhnaya, next to the suburban train station. In Energetik, most buses pass Hotel Turist. The local buses do not stop at the Padunskie Porogi railway station; to get

a bus, walk up the bank to the road and across to a bus shelter at the inter-section (or take a taxi).

## Where to stay

There are two hotels in Tsentralny. *Hotel Taiga* is a medium-quality Intourist hotel, four blocks from the bus station, with a restaurant on the first floor and café on the ground floor. It is expensive at $50 for a single and $60 for double rooms with private facilities. Hotel Taiga is at ul. Mira 35, ☎ 44-39-79 (ул. Мира, 35, Гостиница «Тайга»). *Hotel Bratsk* is very basic, has a restaurant and costs $24-46 for a single room. Hotel Bratsk is at ul. Deputatskaya 32, ☎ 43-84-36 (ул. Депутатская, 32, Гостиница «Братск»).

There are two hotels in Energetik, both a five-minute taxi ride from the Padunskie Porogi railway station. *Hotel Turist* is the old tourist hotel, a dispiriting, deserted block. It has a restaurant. It is nearly as expensive as Hotel Taiga, starting at $30. Hotel Turist is at Energetik, ul. Naumyshina 28, ☎ 37-87-43 (ул. Наумышина, 28, Гостиница «Турист Энергетик»). The *Hotel of the Bratsk Industrial Institute* occupies a floor in Dormitory 1. The rooms have the common dormitory configuration of two adjoining rooms sharing a bathroom and shower. The staff are friendly and cheerful, though apologetic for the simple furnishings and the price is $5. Contact Gostinitsa Instituta Energetika, 665709 Bratsk-9, Studencheskaya 8, Obshchezhitie 1, ☎ 37-72-88 (665709 Братск-9, Студенческая, 8, Общежитие 1, Гостиница Института Энергетика).

There is also a *hotel* at the airport.

## Getting assistance

Bratsk Intourist is located on the second floor of Hotel Taiga, ☎ 41-39-79.

## What to see

Bratsk Intourist offers two-hour tours of Bratsk for $20.

Any visit to Bratsk would not be complete without seeing the 50th Anniversary of Great October Revolution Bratsk Hydro-electric Station, BGES (БГЭС-Братская Гидроэлектрическая Станция). The dam consists of a 506m concrete wall with 3.5km of earth walls on its left and right. The complex generates 4500 MW via 18 turbines. The BAM line runs along the top of the dam and gives an excellent view of the Bratsk reservoir on one side and the Angara river on the other. The road runs below the railway. You can also walk on the promenade along the embank-ment up to the guard-house at the edge of the dam but not on the dam wall itself. The easiest way to reach the dam is to take any bus marked Gidrostroitel (Гидростроитель) and get off at the GIBDD (Highway Police) post where the embankment meets the dam itself. You enter the powerhouse by walking down the steps from the top of the dam. It is well worth a visit and Intourist Bratsk provides a two-hour tour for $45. The

Rechushka station on the BAM

Bratsk Hydro-electric Station is also the subject of a poem cycle by the famous poet Evgeni Yevtushenko (Евгений Евтушенко).

On the outskirts of Bratsk at Angara Village is an open-air ethno-graphic museum containing an Evenki camp, a watchtower, a fort from Bratsk's early years and several houses of past generations. It is open in summer from 10.00 to 17.00 except Mondays. Intourist Bratsk provides tours to the museum for $40, but you can organise a visit yourself by hir-ing a taxi for the day.

Besides the hydrofoil to Irkutsk, there are local ferries that travel to dacha villages and nearby settlements. Visiting one of these places makes a pleasant day trip. Boats leave from the piers at Gidrostroitel and Port Novobratsk between late May and the end of September.

## ☒ RECHUSHKA (Речушка) 438km

On the right, the first of many station buildings in the grand BAM style, a tiny three-room station with a central atrium and a proud portico at the top of ceremonial flight of steps.

## ☖ VIDIM (Видим) 463km

Vidim is located on the Vidim river, which is one of the many rivers that flow into Bratsk Sea. Its population of 6,600 is mainly involved in the timber industry. A good road connects Vidim with Zayarsk on the Bratsk reservoir and Zheleznogorsk-Ilimski.

## 🚂 SREDNEILIMSKAYA (Среднеилимская) 546km

The train comes out of woods and runs down the left bank of what appears to be a narrow lake, with a huge collection of dachas on the other side and one large building inside a fence (a children's camp). This lake is in fact an upper arm of the Ust-Ilimsk reservoir (Усть-Ильимское водохранилище), on the Ilim river. Then the train crosses a girdered bridge and stops briefly at Sredneilimskaya. The dacha village and the working village of Suvoro-Angarski (Суворо-Ангарский) were built since 1974 to replace the drowned villages of Shestakovo (Шестаково) and Berezova (Березова).

The train continues on up the Korshunikha creek, passes below the tailings and the approaches of the open-cast mine (on the right), travels through a short tunnel to cut off a bend of the creek and then pulls into Korshunikha-Angarskaya.

## 🚂 KORSHUNIKHA-ANGARSKAYA (Коршуниха-Ангарская) 554km
### Zheleznogorsk-Ilimski (Железногорск-Илимский)

Although the railway station is called Korshunikha-Angarskaya, the surrounding town is known as Zheleznogorsk-Ilimski (Железногорск-Илимский), literally 'Irontown-on-the-Ilim'. The station gets its name from the creek that the town is above, the Korshunikha. The station is in a narrow valley with industrial buildings and steep cliffs on the other side and settling ponds in the bottom, and the mine down the hill.

Zheleznogorsk is on the sides of the valley, out of sight of the industrial workings. Despite being a mining town, it is one of the cleanest towns on the BAM and has a lot to offer travellers. The settlement was founded in 1948 when ore deposits, ostensibly iron, were discovered. As well as processing local ore, the works also concentrate ore from the Rudnogorsk deposit, 125km north-east of Zheleznogorsk-Ilimski. It became a city in 1963 and is now the administrative centre of Nizhneilimski Raion with a population of 33,000. A good road connects Zheleznogorsk with Vidim and Ust-Kut.

Zheleznogorsk is a classic company town. One of the writers of this guide was sent to the police for not having Zheleznogorsk on his visa, was shadowed by a plainclothes policeman and given one day to get out of town ('This is not a tourist town').

> ❑ **Zheleznogorsk-Ilimski**
> **(Железногорск- Илимский)**
> Area code ☎ 39566
> 665680, Irkutsk Oblast,
> Nizhneilimski Raion,
> Zheleznogorsk-Ilimski
> (665680, Иркутская область,
> Нижнеилимский район, г.
> Железногорск-Илимский)

## Orientation

Zheleznogorsk is built on one face of a steep valley. The streets are built level and parallel across the slope. The main boulevard heads up from the station, crossing the streets at an angle. Five hundred metres up the hill the boulevard widens into a plaza where the House of Culture faces the hotel. A little further up, on the right, is the Regional Museum. At the end of the boulevard is Yangel Square (Площадь Янгела), a grand plaza with the post office, telephone office, stores and municipal buildings. From the plaza steps run down the hillside to the War Memorial, the stadium and, one block away, the Dolphin pool-house with a 50m swimming pool.

## Where to stay

The municipal *Hotel Magnetit* is a busy hotel with pleasant staff and a surly manager. Many rooms have both toilet and shower. Costs are $16 for a single room. The hotel is a 15-minute walk uphill from the station. Hotel Magnetit, ☎ 214-60 (director), ☎ 217-58 (reception), ▤ 226-05 (Гостиница Магнетит).

## Where to eat

There is a restaurant in *Hotel Magnetit* on the ground floor open for lunch and dinner, and a buffet on the second floor, open 9.00-21.00 daily.

## What to see

A 15-minute walk up the main street from the hotel will bring you to Yangel Square (Площадь Янгела) where you will find the post office, Mayor's office, three museums and a monument to aircraft and spacecraft designer Mikhail Yangel. The museums consist of a local regional museum, a museum to Mikhail Yangel's life and work and a museum of Japan Friendship. For the past 15 years, Zheleznogorsk has had a sister-city relationship with the Japanese city of Sakata and both cities have hosted many sister-city cultural and sporting groups.

Mikhail Yangel (1911-71) is a Soviet success story – the child of peasants who became one of Russia's greatest rocket scientists. His work was instrumental in putting the world's first astronaut, Yuri Gagarin, into space in 1961. During his life and immediately after his death, his achievements were unknown as they were a state secret and it has been only in the last 15 years that their publication has made him into a local celebrity.

He was born in the village of Zyryanovo (Зыряново), a 90-minute bus ride from Zheleznogorsk, where there is a house-museum containing much of his family's original furniture and many of his personal belongings, including the suitcases taken on his trip to the USA in 1935.

Two blocks down the main boulevard is the Regional Museum, displaying furniture and tools of the early European settlers, icons from destroyed churches and a haunting painting of a drowned village, with all its activities, seen through the grey water of the reservoir.

# Zheleznogorsk-Ilimski
## (Железногорск-Илимский)

**⚡** Magnetit Hotel & Restaurant
**↑** Town Administration
**★** Korshunov Iron Mining Co

For complete  legend see inside back cover

**🏛** 1. Yangel & Japanese Friendship Museums
**🏛** 2. Regional Museum
**🌿** 3. War & Historical Memorials
**⬭** 4. Stadium & Pool-house

STEPS

Vidim

Ust-Kut

Note: The station is called Korshunikha-Angarskaya (Коршуниха-Ангарская).

Bratsk — Severobaikalsk

Down the steps from Yangel Square is the Great Patriotic War Memorial and a metal pylon topped with an onion dome and an orthodox cross, commemorating the first European settlement in 1655 and the two villages and 36 hamlets flooded by the reservoir. 'Native region, your memory will not be drowned' (Край родной память о тебе не утонет). The museums open Tuesday to Sunday, 9.00-17.00, closed 13.00-14.00.

## Getting assistance

Zheleznogorsk is home to one of eastern Siberia's most active adventure clubs, the Tourist Club Kedr (Туристический клуб «Кедр»).

The club organises expeditions for local young people, and a summer festival and games at a meadow site above the Ust-Ilimsk reservoir. The club is well-known throughout the region, particularly in the Lake Baikal area. Members hold many climbing records and have discovered a number of glaciers and climbing routes to peaks. Their members are willing guides for rafting, biking, mountaineering and trekking trips in summer, and skiing in winter. It is possible to explore caves all year-round but it is best to visit them in winter when the cave temperature is warmer than outside. Guides charge $10-40 a day. The club also manufactures rucksacks and inflatable rafts, using imported fabric, which are excellent and reasonably priced. Most equipment can also be hired for $5 a day. The club can also organise homestay.

Contact Anatoli Semilet at Kvartal 6A, House 4, Apartment 35, home phone via Zheleznogorsk ☎ +7-39566-2-19-73, home phone via Moscow ☎ +7-095-430-46-22, work phone via Moscow ☎ +7-095-242-91-05, 📄 +7-39566-2-26-05, 💻 ovo@uilimsk.irtel.ru (665680, г. Железногорск, квартал 6А, дом 4, квартира 35, Семилет Анатолий).

## 🚉 KHREBTOVAYA (Хребтовая) 575km

The railway climbs the Korshunikha creek to Khrebtovaya, the junction of the BAM and the branch line to Ust-Ilimsk. For information on this line, see Khrebtovaya–Ust-Ilimsk (p206).

Within 20km the train crosses the watershed and starts down the Kuta, a tributary of the Lena. You will see narrow meadows by the river and traditional Siberian settlements, with log or plank houses, and sometimes with planked inner courtyards separating the house from the insulated shelters for pigs and chickens and from the summer kitchen. The Kuta broadens above its confluence with the Lena. On a peninsula on the opposite side of the river the large institutional and residential buildings in their own grounds are the Ust-Kut Sanatorium.

# Ust-Kut–Severobaikalsk
## Усть-Кут–Северобайкальск

### THE ROUTE (see Route Map 1, p366)

From Lena to Komsomolsk-na-Amure, more than 3,000km, is the section of the BAM built between 1974 and 1989. All of the route and most of the settlements are entirely new.

The route crosses three major mountain ranges and threads through the watersheds of all three major waterways of Siberia and the Far East, the Yenisei, the Lena and the Amur. Apart from the settlements clustering around the railway, the BAM takes you through the largest fertile wilderness in the world. For most of the route, the roads are at best rugged, at worst non-existent.

From Lena, the railway crosses a low range of hills to the Kirenga, a tributary of the Lena. It crosses the Kirenga's swampy meadows, then heads into the rugged Baikal Range, famous for its scenic beauty, passes through the 6.7km Baikal Mountain Tunnel and winds down to the north end of Lake Baikal.

The time is Moscow time +5 hours.

## UST-KUT (Усть-Кут) 715km

Ust-Kut is one of the most vibrant towns on the BAM, as it is a major rail and river terminal for the Lena and the Republic of Sakha (Yakutiya).

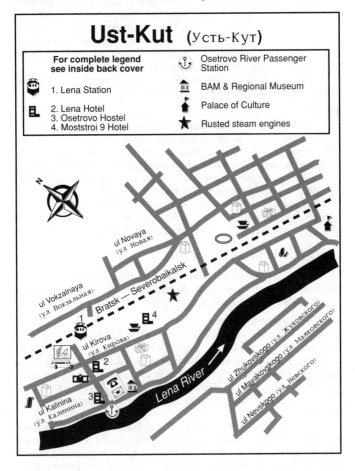

# Ust-Kut (Усть-Кут)

**For complete legend see inside back cover**

1. Lena Station

2. Lena Hotel
3. Osetrovo Hostel
4. Moststroi 9 Hotel

⚓ Osetrovo River Passenger Station

🏛 BAM & Regional Museum

Palace of Culture

★ Rusted steam engines

ul Novaya (ул Новая)

ul Vokzalnaya (ул Вокзальная)

Bratsk — Severobaikalsk

ul Kirova (ул Кирова)

ul Kalinina (ул Калинина)

Lena River

ul Zhukovskogo (ул Жуковского)

ul Mayakovskogo (ул Маяковского)

ul Nevskogo (ул Невского)

## Orientation

❏ **UST-KUT (Усть-Кут)**
Area code ☎ 395-65
665780, Irkutskaya Oblast, Ust-Kut
(665780 Иркутская область, г. Усть-Кут)

Ust-Kut is 40km long and lies at the junction of the mighty 4,400km Lena river and the 408km Kuta river. The town sits astride the BAM, which runs parallel with the Lena river. Present day Ust-Kut was created in 1954 by amalgamating several settlements. From west to east they are Kirzavod (Кирзавод), Ust-Kut, Lena (Лена), Rechniki (Речники), Rechniki-2 (Речники-2), Geologists (Геологи), Neftebaza (Нефтебаза – 'Oil Terminal') and Yakurim (Якурим). This amalgamation causes confusion with travellers as the main passenger station in not Ust-Kut but Lena. A short walk from Lena station will bring you to the Lena River Passenger Station, known as Osetrovo.

The freight port is located near Ust-Kut station. In the late 1980s, this port shipped 80 per cent of all cargo for the Sakha region.

## History

Ust-Kut was founded by the famous explorer Yerofei Khabarov in 1631 and it rapidly became an important trading port as it supplied most of eastern Siberia with food and equipment until the 20th century. Rich deposits of salt were discovered nearby which were exploited until the beginning of the revolution. Several pre-revolutionary exiles found themselves in Ust-Kut, including Leon Trotsky in 1902 (he escaped).

Rail traffic first reached Lena in 1958 when a temporary railway was laid across the Bratsk reservoir. The town now has a population of 70,000 and has one of the nation's few river transport institutes.

## 🚂 LENA (Лена) 722km

This is the main passenger station, rather than Ust-Kut, as travellers for the river vessels that travel to the Republic of Sakha depart from nearby Osetrovo River Passenger Station.

### Getting there and away

From the west there are a Moscow–Lena train and a Moscow–Tynda train (via Kazan) on alternate days, a Krasnoyarsk–Severobaikalsk train every other day, and a Kislovodsk–Tynda train twice a week. The last three also go east on the BAM. There is also a daily local train east to Vikhorevka.

The town has air links with Irkutsk, Bodaibo, Yakutsk, Chita, Kirensk, Lensk, Mirny, Olekminsk, Kirenga, Mama and many other smaller settlements.

A good road connects Ust-Kut with Novaya Igirma and Khrebtovaya.

From late May to September, it is possible to go by regular passenger boat down the Lena to Yakutsk (four days, nine hours) and by hydrofoil both down and up the Lena. Tickets are bought at the Osetrovo River

## ❑ Khabarov: the celebrated killer

While Yerofei Khabarov (Ерофей Хабаров) may have been one of Siberia's greatest explorers and was even honoured with the city of Khabarovsk being named after him, he was also one of Russia's most brutal conquerors. His exploits ranged over the whole territory of far-eastern Russia covered by this guide.

Khabarov arrived in Ust-Kut in 1631 from European Russia with a small fortune from his early trading ventures. He initially started farming, then founded a salt works, before branching out into corn wholesaling. However, due to his hot temper, heavy-handedness and brutal treatment of peasants, in 1641, all his enterprises were appropriated by the State.

He moved down the Lena river to Kirensk and started farming again. A group of peasants were sent from Yakutsk to settle in this region a few years later, which Khabarov tried to discourage with violence. Frustrated by the peasants' encroachment, Khabarov sailed to Yakutsk, collected 150 mercenaries and unexpectedly appeared before the governor to ask for permission to sail to the Amur river. Confronted with so many soldiers, the Governor was only too pleased to get rid of the troublemaker and Khabarov's force sailed further down the Lena river in March 1649 to the Olekma river then onwards to the Amur river. He returned to Yakutsk in May 1650 with few spoils but news that there was grain in the Amur valley and it could be transported to Yakutsk in just two weeks at a significantly cheaper cost than grain from European Russia.

Later that year he returned to the Amur river with a larger group of mercenaries, cannons and provisions and decimated many indigenous Daurian villages. Even among the callous Russian explorers, Khabarov's deeds were considered barbaric. Khabarov took thousands of prisoners yet few lived, and he administered punishment as a weapon of fear not justice. His treatment of women was particularly offensive. He built up harems at each stop but when he and his Cossacks moved on, they simply abandoned or executed the women as more were to be found in the next settlement.

The taking of tribute, women and provisions from the Amur region infuriated the Chinese rulers and when Khabarov was camping on the site of present-day Khabarovsk, a Chinese army attacked. The Chinese lost and, ironically, the captured provisions allowed Khabarov and his men to winter in comfort.

As soon as word of Khabarov's conquest of the Amur valley reached Yakutsk and the rest of Russia, hundreds of volunteers flocked to him. As these men were attracted by spoils and owed no allegiance to Khabarov, they resented his harsh and arbitrary treatment. Within a short time, his force rebelled and imprisoned him. He was eventually transported to Moscow not as a hero conqueror but as a deposed despot.

In Moscow, the Tsar confiscated his property and sentenced him to death. However, Khabarov was able to convince the Tsar that his conquests were in the best interests of the state and that they had opened up the unknown riches of the Amur. Pragmatism won the Tsar over and he restored Khabarov's property and made him a nobleman or *boyar* with control over several villages in the Ilimsk region. He retired to this area, which is now under the Ust-Ilimsk reservoir.

Passenger Station, ul. Kalinina 8, ☎ 2-63-97 (dispatcher), 2-65-06 (chief), 🖹 2-07-28 and 2-15-00 (attention: Osetrovo River Port), ☎ 2-32-53 (general), (ул. Калинина, 8, Речной вокзал Осетрово).

## Travelling the Lena river

The mighty Lena river (река Лена) is the second biggest river in water volume in Russia (after the Yenisei), yet it is virtually unknown outside Russia. The 4,400km river starts in the mountains to the west of Lake Baikal and snakes through north-eastern Siberia until it floods into the Laptevykh Sea (Море Лаптевых) in the Arctic Ocean. Since the mid-1600s, the river has been the lifeline to the capital of north-eastern Siberia, Yakutsk, supplying it with grain, salt, guns and adventurers. It was from here that the exploration, conquest and eventual colonisation of eastern Siberia and the Russian Far East were launched.

The Lena is a godsend for travellers as it is one of the most interesting ways of exploring hidden corners of Russia. As few foreigners have ever travelled these routes, you are guaranteed an extraordinary insight into the lives of river villages, both Russian and indigenous. In addition, the complete lack of Intourist's presence, except in Yakutsk, means that the price of tickets and accommodation is reasonable.

For information on travelling the Lena, see Sakha and Yakutsk via the Lena River and AYaM (pp229-278).

## Getting around

The main bus station is in front of Lena station. Bus No 1 goes to Ust-Kut; bus No 2 to Kirpichny Zavod mikroraion (and passes the Ust-Kut Sanatorium); bus No 3 to Neftebaza mikroraion; bus No 4 to the hospital complex near Rechniki mikroraion; bus No 6 to the other side of the Lena river; bus No 101 to the airport; and bus No 102 to Yakurim mikroraion.

## Where to stay

The most expensive hotel in town is the new 9-storey 220-bed *Lena Hotel*. It is opposite the railway station and the prices are single from $60, bed in twin $40. All rooms have full facilities. There is an air-ticket counter in the lobby of the Lena hotel.

The best value accommodation is *Hotel Moststroi-9*, ul. Kirova 85-A, ☎ 2-07-66 (ул. Кирова, 85-А, Гостиница Мостстрои-9). Although its name means the Hotel of Bridge Constructors Unit No 9, you don't have to be a builder to stay there. It is a 15-minute walk from Lena station or two stops on any bus heading east. The hotel is well-hidden at the back of a compound, so you will have to ask around. Prices are $20 single and $18 for a bed in a twin room. The rooms have full facilities and are well-kept.

*Osetrovo River Passenger Station* also has a few rooms including five 4-person bedrooms, ☎ 214-80.

---

(**Opposite**)  **Top:** Shunter drivers work between the scheduled passenger and freight trains. If you ask, they may give you a ride – or at least tell a good story. (Photo © Tatyana Pozar-Burgar).  **Bottom:** The Kolyma Highway climbing the steep Vostochnaya river toward Kyubeme. Many bridges are washed out east of here. (Photo © Paul Geldhof).

## Where to eat
There is a small **buffet** on the ground floor of the office section of the building housing Hotel Moststroi-9. There is a **restaurant** in Lena Hotel. There is a **market** between the post office and Lena Hotel and there are several **food shops**. From some of the **kiosks** in front of the railway station you can get hot snacks and shashlik.

## Getting assistance
Irkutsktourist Travel Company, located in Lena Hotel, can book rail and boat tickets and arrange excursions. Its main business is organising travel for Russians and it has been operating for more than 10 years. The Director is Elvira Musatova, ☎ 21-880, 🖹 20-729 or 21-500 (att: Irkutsktourist), (ул. Кирова, 88, Иркутсктурист).

Foreign currency can be changed at the bank on ul. Kirova, across the street from Lena Hotel.

## What to see
The Regional Museum (closed Sunday and Monday) contains information on the BAM railway and the region. It is near the Osetrovo River Passenger Station. Also worth a visit is the Palace of Culture, 500m east along ul. Kirova. It is a white and dark green building built in the Stalinist style, but wholly of wood. It is also possible to tour the river fleet shipyard known as REB, which was founded in the 17th century. To get there take bus No 6 to the other side of the river.

Another option is to visit the balneological-pelotherapeutic mud spa at Ust-Kut Sanatorium (Санаторий Усть-Кут), renowned throughout Russia. The spa uses diluted sodium chloride brine containing bromine and silt mud from Lake Ust-Kutskoe. The baths are used to treat muscular, gynaecological and peripheral nervous system disorders. The spa is 3km from Ust-Kut and the easiest way to get there is to take bus No 2 (along the ul. Kirova from the Lena station towards the west) until you see a footbridge across the river. Cross the bridge. At the end is a wooden gate with the word 'KURORT' (КУРОРТ), meaning 'spa', on it. ☎ 2-32-92.

Another interesting sight is the Ust-Kut freight port. Bus No 1 goes to the freight port and onwards to Lena station.

## 🏠 LENA-VOSTOCHNAYA (Лена-Восточная) 736km

On the west bank of the Lena is the station Lena-Vostochnaya which is the official start of the BAM railway.

---

**(Opposite)** Orthodox, Old Believers, Communists, Buddhists, Shamanists can all be found in the BAM and Lena region – and even missionary cults such as these Hare Krishna devotees. (Photo © Tatyana Pozar-Burgar).

After leaving Lena-Vostochnaya, the train passes over the first bridge built after Brezhnev announced that the BAM was to be built. The 418m bridge was completed in 1975.

## 🏛 ZVEZDNAYA (Звёздная) 786km

In February 1974, construction work started on Zvezdny settlement. The town became famous throughout the USSR as the first of several hundred new towns to spring up in the path of the BAM. It was named after the cosmonaut settlement of Zvezdny near Moscow but commemorates terrestrial rather than cosmic pioneers. There is a memorial board in the town listing the 14 male and two female Komsomol youths who were the 'first' pioneers to arrive at the future town site located on the banks of the Tayura river. In reality, Zvezdny was built on the site of an old village called Tayura.

Zvezdny today is a combination of rustic wooden cottages, new concrete buildings and an impressive railway station. The town has shrunk considerably since the 1970s as the promised new industry which justified its construction never materialised.

## 🏛 KIRENGA (Киренга) 890km

Kirenga is a small railway settlement with the nearest town being Magistralny (Магистральный) which is 12km to the east. There are regular buses between the two places. Magistralny is a sizeable town of 10,000 on the Kirenga river and its main industry is timber. The river port is called Klyuchi – 'springs' – (Ключи) but since the construction of the BAM, few craft ply the river. A one-hour drive to the north will bring you to the small town of Kazachinskoe (Казачинское), the capital of the *raion*. This isolated town was founded in 1776 and its inhabitants' main occupations are farming, hunting and fishing. Until the arrival of the BAM, with its large influx of workers, expeditions used to visit Kazachinskoe to study ancient Russian dialects, which had been preserved by descendants of early settlers.

There is a *Locomotive Brigade Hostel* with a canteen.

As you cross over the Kirenga river, notice the road bridge alongside. This 391m bridge was opened in October 1998 as part of the modernisation of a temporary road running along the BAM. Both the road and the new bridge are important to the development of the nearby Kovykta gas-condensate deposit.

## 🏛 ULKAN (Улькан) 931km

This town of 10,000 is located on the Ulkan river, a tributary of the Kirenga. The BAM town of Ulkan was sponsored by the Crimean Regional Komsomol Party, which is reflected in road names such as Crimea Street. About 1km from Ulkan is the ancient village of Yukhta

(Юхта) which is surrounded by two smaller villages called Tarasova (Тарасова) and Munok (Мунок). A total of 51 men, virtually the entire able-bodied male population of the three villages, departed to fight in the Great Patriotic War. Sadly not one returned and consequently the villages have become virtual ghost towns. The war memorial in Yukhta lists the names of those who died.

Between Ulkan and Kunerma are several hot-water springs, which are regarded as having great healing power. There are no tourist facilities.

## KUNERMA (Кунерма) 983km

Kunerma is a nice place to visit on a day trip from Severobaikalsk, as to get here you pass through scenic mountains. The town is also attractive as it consists of a number of wooden two-storey apartment blocks, a recently refurbished station and a single shopping complex. Only 700 people live here and it provides an interesting insight into small town life. It is also a popular fishing destination as there is a well-stocked lake nearby.

As well as the daily trains from Tynda to Moscow, suburban trains terminate here from Severobaikalsk. There are three suburban services to Severobaikalsk daily. There is no accommodation in the town.

The train grinds up an alpine valley between stony mountains, where the wooded taiga gives way to tundra. You may see scarves of cloud hanging below the 2,000m peaks and in summer runnels of water foaming down their flanks.

## DELBICHINDA (Дельбичинда) 1,005km

Delbichinda is the last station before the 6.7km Baikal Mountain Tunnel (Байкальский тоннель). The line makes an abrupt left U-bend and enters the tunnel. This tunnel was the easiest of all the BAM tunnels to build and took only three years and eight months to complete. It was opened on 1 October 1984. Between 1979 and 1984 trains ran over the mountains on a dangerous 15km bypass, whose remains can be seen about 5km from the western entrance of the tunnel on the right side. About 500m to the right of the Baikal Mountain Tunnel entrance is another rail line going into a tunnel. This was an exploration tunnel and extends for less than 100m. To visit the exploration tunnel and the bypass, you need to get off at Delbichinda and walk about 10km.

## DABAN (Дабан) 1,015km

As soon as you emerge from the eastern tunnel entrance, you pass the tunnel guard-tower and the barracks and come to the station of Daban. The stop, at 1,500m above sea level, is a popular starting point for hikers and cross-country skiers. The only building at this stop is the station and there is no accommodation here.

As you descend from the mountain, you will see the Goudzhekit river on your left and, after a few kilometres, a solitary red brick chimney in a large field. This is all that remains of the town that was constructed for the 3,000 workers who built the tunnel. Eliminating all traces of construction and returning the area to its natural condition was an important element in the BAM's environmental policy. A further 3km from the tunnel on the left side is the military camp that supplies guards for the tunnel entrances. Between Daban and Goudzhekit, you cross the signless border separating the Irkutsk oblast (Иркутская область) and the Buryatiya Republic (Республика Бурятия).

### 🏨 GOUDZHEKIT (Гоуджекит) 1,029km

This town was once a holiday resort and, although its trade has died with the economy, it still has its attractions, including hot springs, a swimming pool and a small, basic *hotel*.

### 🏨 TYYA (Тыя) 1,043km

The Goudzhekit creek joins the Tyya river. On most rail maps this stop is called a rail siding or is simply not mentioned. However, near the station is the medium-sized town of Solnechny (Солнечный). Near the town is a 340m down hill ski run with a tow and ski rental. Three suburban trains a day stop at Tyya. Just outside Tyya on the left is a disused shooting range beside a small house on a lake. In the Soviet era, these ranges were financed by the Ministry of Defence as a way of maintaining military skills among citizens.

The train emerges from the narrow Tyya valley and makes an immense counter-clockwise circle around the first settlement of Severobaikalsk. On your right you glimpse the northern end of Lake Baikal and on your left the grand boulevard of new Severobaikalsk, the westernmost of the new BAM towns. You draw up beside the cathedral arch of the station.

# Severobaikalsk
## Северобайкальск

Severobaikalsk is a prosperous and resourceful town, ringed by rugged roadless 2000+m mountains and facing the north end of Lake Baikal, the world's deepest, purest and ecologically most diverse freshwater lake.

It is an unrivalled base for outdoor adventure. You can explore bays, islands, mountains, hot springs, nature preserves, indigenous villages and gulags; swim, sail, canoe and cruise in the summer; ski, skate and ride the ice in winter; hike, trek and mountaineer; photograph the unique birds and seals; and catch and taste the native fish. It is probably the most popular destination on the BAM, yet fewer than 200 Western tourists a year visit.

## ORIENTATION

The new town of Severobaikalsk, designed by Leningrad architects, is built on a plateau above the lake along both sides of the wide Leningradski Prospekt, from the soaring station building to the town square, with the government building, the House of Culture and the markets. The temporary settlement of substantial wood buildings is behind a greenbelt higher up the hill, with an embryo suburban development of single family houses beyond.

Below the railway line and towards the lake is an area of large homes and, below the cliff on the lakeside, a marina of two-storey dachas with boat docks.

## HISTORY

The history of Severobaikalsk provides a fascinating insight into the way that BAM towns have changed with the railway's fortune and post-Soviet economic collapse.

Severobaikalsk has a population of 35,000 and grew out of the virgin taiga with the arrival of the BAM constructors. The city was planned by the Leningrad Zonal Research Institute of Experimental Planning which is blamed by most inhabitants for the town's badly designed apartment blocks and lack of suitable housing.

At first glance the apartment blocks look like standard Russian ones, but a closer look reveals that they don't have balconies. For Russians, balconies are invaluable, as they are a storage area and giant refrigerator in the winter. The reason for this massive oversight was that the buildings were designed for the hot climates of Central Asia by the Leningrad Institute and simply transplanted to Severobaikalsk. While northern Russian building designs could have been used, only the Central Asian ones were earthquake resistant, which was essential for the seismically unstable north Baikal area.

The best years of the town were in the late 1970s and early 1980s when the town was being sponsored by Leningrad's Komsomol. In these years, the town had access to many restricted goods, but when the BAM arrived most of the workers with their privileges moved on. Leningrad's sponsorship finally ended in 1984 and today the only remnant of the original constructors is a detachment of the LenBAMstroi (Leningrad BAM Construction) organisation. Since the slowdown of construction work on the BAM in the early 1990s, LenBAMstroi's 600 workers have had little to do and are on unpaid leave for months at a time.

While most organisations, like LenBAMstroi and the Severobaikalsk City Council, wait for non-eventuating money and work from Moscow, a few

❑ **SEVEROBAIKALSK**
(Северобайкальск)
Area code ☎ 30139
671717 Republic of Buryatiya,
Severobaikalsk
(671717 Республика Бурятия,
г. Северобайкальск)
Moscow time +5 hours

locals have tried to develop new industries and inspire optimism. Unfortunately residual Soviet-era centralised control and secrecy limit the success of such projects.

One such attempt was the international 1990 Expertise Conference, held in Severobaikalsk. Participants included the Californian Earth Institute, UNESCO, Moscow-based Russian government and scientific officials, and a handful of local representatives. The conference's aim was to develop an economic and environmental strategic plan for the Lake Baikal region. Despite recommendations being made, the conference report was never released in Russia. However, the report was freely available in the USA and Rashit Yahin, head of BAMTour and local environmental activist, obtained a copy. He translated it back into Russian and organised its publication in Severobaikalsk, creating a political storm. The reason the report was never released in Russia was because its main recommendation – to list Lake Baikal on the World Heritage Register – was unacceptable to local authorities. This would have entailed establishing a ring of national parks around the lake, which would restrict industry, tourism and town development. Lake Baikal was finally accepted onto the World Heritage Register in 1996 except for five already built-up lakeside areas, of which Severobaikalsk is one.

The town is stark but following the 1994 programme of street-scaping and tree planting, it should be attractive in a few years. (Why it has taken so long for the City Council to plant trees is a mystery.)

## GETTING THERE AND AWAY

From the west there are a Moscow–Tynda train (via Kazan) and a Krasnoyarsk–Severobaikalsk train on alternate days and a Kislovodsk–Tynda train twice a week. The two Tynda trains also go west on the BAM, every other day and twice a week respectively.

Three local trains per day run west beyond the Baikal Mountain Tunnel, one as far as Kirenga. Three local trains per day run east to Novy Uoyan, Kichera, and one as far as Novaya Chara.

The airport (☎ 51-899) is at Nizhneangarsk (50 minutes by bus). It has flights six times a week to Ulan-Ude (Улан-Удэ), the capital of Buryatiya and three times a week to Irkutsk.

The road connections of Severobaikalsk are not good. The only paved roads are to Kichera to the north-east and to the farming village of Baikalskoe in the south. From February to April, it is safe to drive down the frozen Lake Baikal to Sakhyurta or Listvyanka (for Irkutsk) and Ust-

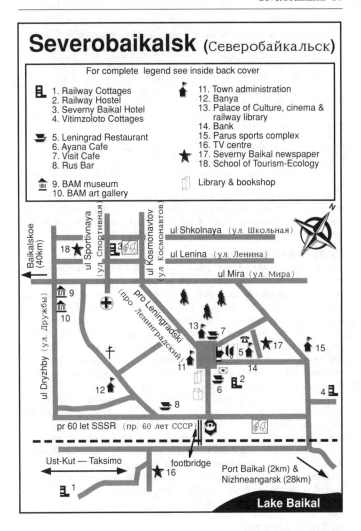

# Severobaikalsk (Северобайкальск)

For complete legend see inside back cover

1. Railway Cottages
2. Railway Hostel
3. Severny Baikal Hotel
4. Vitimzoloto Cottages

5. Leningrad Restaurant
6. Ayana Cafe
7. Visit Cafe
8. Rus Bar

9. BAM museum
10. BAM art gallery

11. Town administration
12. Banya
13. Palace of Culture, cinema & railway library
14. Bank
15. Parus sports complex
16. TV centre
17. Severny Baikal newspaper
18. School of Tourism-Ecology

Library & bookshop

ul Shkolnaya (ул. Школьная)
ul Lenina (ул. Ленина)
ul Mira (ул. Мира)
ul Sportivnaya (ул. Спортивная)
ul Kosmonavtov (ул. Космонавтов)
Baikalskoe (40km)
ul Dryzhby (ул. Дружбы)
pro Leningradski (про. Ленинградский)
pr 60 let SSSR (пр. 60 лет СССР)
Ust-Kut — Taksimo
footbridge
Port Baikal (2km) & Nizhneangarsk (28km)
Lake Baikal

Barguzin (for Ulan-Ude; two days in the summer, but only eight hours in the winter.) The ice road is not an official *zimnik* (winter road) and there are no commercial services on it, but it is almost always possible to share a ride.

❏ **Hydrofoil timetable between Irkutsk and Nizhneangarsk**

| From Irkutsk | | Place | From Nizhneangarsk | | Distance |
|---|---|---|---|---|---|
| Arrive | Depart | (local time) | Depart | Arrive | (km) |
| | 07.50 | Irkutsk (Иркутск) | | 19.00 | 683 |
| 09.00 | 09.20 | Port Baikal (Порт Байкал) | 17.50 | 17.30 | 628 |
| 09.30 | 09.40 | Listvyanka (Листвянка) | 17.20 | 17.10 | 621 |
| 13.30 | 13.40 | Cape Bazarnaya | 13.20 | 13.10 | 403 |
| | | (Бухта Базарная) | | | |
| 19.50 | 20.00 | Severobaikalsk | 07.00 | 06.40 | 18 |
| | | (Северобайкальск) | | | |
| 20.20 | - | Nizhneangarsk | 06.20 | - | 0 |
| | | (Нижнеангарск) | | | |

From 15 June to 15 September, a hydrofoil runs three times a week between Nizhneangarsk, stopping at Severobaikalsk and Port Baikal (for Irkutsk). The hydrofoil docks at the Severobaikalsk port, which is 2km east of town by taxi or by bus No 1. (☎ 51-904).

## Hydrofoils on Lake Baikal

The Kometa hydrofoil that plies Lake Baikal is an interesting ride because, although it has only one official stop on the lake, it will stop anywhere en route for any local or traveller who prearranges it. For this reason when you are travelling on the hydrofoil, you will observe motor boats meeting your vessel and transferring mail, food or passengers. For many isolated communities and individual hunters, the hydrofoil is their only link with the rest of the world. The one official stop on the trip is halfway down the lake at Cape Bazarnaya (бухта Базарная) which is on the mainland near Olkhon Island (остров Ольхон). There are basic cabins for rent, a camping site and a canteen at this stop.

Tickets for the hydrofoil cannot be booked in advance and have to be bought on board. So it is a good idea to get to the pier early and stand in the queue. There is only one hydrofoil and, as it takes the whole day to travel the length of the lake, departures from Severobaikalsk are every second day. The hydrofoil docks in Irkutsk at the Hydrofoil Pier above the Angara Dam, 5km from Irkutsk (bus No 16 from pl. Kirova).

Although the trip down the lake is long, be grateful that there is a hydrofoil; before its introduction in 1986, the boat trip between Irkutsk and Severobaikalsk took five days.

## GETTING AROUND

Everything in Severobaikalsk is within walking distance, with the exception of the port from which the hydrofoil departs. To get to the port, take bus No 1 from the central bus station in front of the railway station. Bus No 3 goes past the BAM museum and near the Severny Baikal Hotel.

## WHERE TO STAY

There is a wide range of accommodation in Severobaikalsk. The best places are the four *guest cottages* owned by the railway. Each has two bathrooms, toilet, sitting room, kitchen and three bedrooms. It is possible to rent them per room or the entire house. They can be reached by a 10-minute walk from the station and they have an excellent view of the coast. They have their own hot-water systems which means that you aren't inconvenienced by the summer maintenance shut-down of the town's hot-water system. The railway cottages are located near ul. Sibirskaya (ул. Сибирская). The cost is $15 a night per person. Book via BAMTour (see p90).

The *Vitim Zoloto Gold Company Guest Cottages* are also good, but they are farther out of town. This complex consists of three cottages, with 16 beds altogether, a sauna, pool and canteen. Contact Viktor & Evgeniya Kuznetsov at Guest Cottages, Vitim Zoloto ☎ 23-912 (home) (Дом отдыха, Витим Золото, Кузнецов Виктор и Евгения). Accommodation is $20 a night per person, or $30 with full board.

The *School of Tourism-Ecology Education* (see Getting assistance, p90) has five 4- to 6-bed rooms in summer and three 5-bed rooms in winter, with a common hall and a kitchen, at $10 a night. Contact Evgeny Maryasov at School of Tourism-Ecology Education, per. Shkolny-11, ☎ 2-03-23, 🖳 davan@burnet.ru (671717 Бурятия, г. Северобайкальск, Пер. Школьный-11, Муниципальная школа туристско-экологического образования, Марясов Евгений).

There is a *Railway Hostel* in the centre of town. It is shown on the map but is difficult to find. It can't be reached from ul. Leningradski as its only entrance is from the courtyard on the other side of the building.

The worst accommodation is the municipal *Severny Baikal Hotel*, which is in the old settlement and can be reached on bus No 3 from the station. The bus trip takes 20 minutes. The hotel has no hot water or showers and only squat toilets; $8 per night per person. ☎ 77-12 (Гостиница «Северный Байкал»).

BAMTour (see p90) can organise *homestay* or *apartment rental*.

## WHERE TO EAT

Severobaikalsk has a surprising number of good restaurants and cafés, including the *Leningrad Restaurant* (which prides itself on once having served a US ambassador) and the *Rus bar* (which brews its own beer on the premises) – both in the evening. Other good places to eat include the *Ayana* and *Visit cafés* and *Bar Tikhonov i Synovya* ('Tikhonov and sons') in the Palace of Culture. Above the Visit café is a small *bar/restaurant*, which deserves a special tourist award for the best rest-rooms on the BAM. The *canteen* in the station offers the cheapest meals in town. The specialities of the region are, of course, the freshwater fish of Lake Baikal. Look for the 25cm omul (омуль), whose delicate white flesh is equally good baked, braised, salted, or smoked. Eat with your fingers! Watch for bones!

## GETTING ASSISTANCE

BAMTour is the best-known company organising tours on the BAM and in the north Lake Baikal region. Director Rashit Yahin is one of the longest-standing residents in Severobaikalsk, having worked on the railway in the early 1970s and is Editorial Consultant on this guide. Contact Rashit Yahin at BAMTour Company, 671717 Severobaikalsk, ul. Oktyabrya 16-2, ☎/📠 +7 30139 21560, 🖳 rashit.yahin@usa.net (671717 Северобайкальск, ул. Октября, 16-2, БАМТУР, Яхин Рашит).

The School of Tourism-Ecology Education organises outdoor events for local students and for groups and individuals from outside Severobaikalsk. It has accommodation in Severobaikalsk and at Slyudanski Lakes (Слюданские озера), 15km south. It can organise excursions and transportation for individuals and groups, and supply maps, camping equipment, canoes and floats. Contact Evgeny Maryasov at School of Tourism-Ecology Education, per. Shkolny 11, ☎ +7 30139 2-03-23, 🖳 davan@burnet.ru (671717 Бурятия, г. Северобайкальск, Пер. Школьный, 11, Муниципальная школа туристско-экологического образования, Марясов Евгений).

The Khozyain tourist company organises vacations and operates the skiing and hot-springs resort at Solnechny. Contact Khozyain at Viktor Grigorevich Marinichev, pr. Leningradski 5-43, ☎ 232-79, 📠 245-12 (пр. Ленинградский, 5-43, «Хозяин», Мариничев Виктор Григорьевич).

## WHAT TO SEE

### BAM Museum and Gallery

The museum has a display on the first BAM explorers to this region and a railway model showing the stretch with the four Mysoviye tunnels between Severobaikalsk and Nizhneangarsk. It also has information on the Decembrists exiled to this area in the 1820s, but lacks any reference to the region's Stalin-era gulags. It also has a small exhibition of Buryat traditional costumes and jewellery, and celebrations of the 250th anniversary of Buddhism in the Buryat republic in 1991. BAM Museum (☎ 2-16-63) is at ul. Mira 2 (ул. Мира 2). The museum is open from 10.00 to 18.00, but not on Mondays.

BAM Art Gallery, ul. Druzhba (ул. Дружба), around the corner from the museum, contains a good range of work by local artists.

### Art and culture

Without doubt, Severobaikalsk is the most active cultural centre on the BAM and most activity is focused around the excellent Palace of Culture.

This delightful building has a small indoor garden and a large hall, and is always putting on theatrical and musical performances. If it is a national holiday, you can be guaranteed that something worth seeing will be on.

The town also boasts six well-known painters and poets, and one composer. For aspiring artists, there is also an art school. The school and the Palace of Culture staff are only too pleased to show anyone around their facilities.

# Exploring North Baikal
## Окрестности Северного Байкала

Lake Baikal is one of the wonders of the world. The northern end of the lake, ringed by rugged roadless 2000m+ mountains, is more magical and remote than the south end – a world-class resource for the nature-lover, the contemplative and the outdoorsman. Severobaikalsk and Nizhneangarsk are the only towns. Beyond are the wilderness mountains, with their waterfalls, glaciers and hot springs, the untrampled shoreline of points and coves, and the ever-changing face of the deep, pure lake.

Explorations in North Baikal can take you to bays, islands, mountains, hot springs, nature preserves, indigenous villages and gulags; to swimming, sailing, canoeing, sunbathing and cruising in summer; to skiing, skating and riding the ice in winter; to hiking, trekking and mountaineering. Excursions can be tailored for every physique, from active outdoors adventure to tranquil enjoyment of the scenery and the wildlife.

## ORIENTATION

Severobaikalsk is near the northern end of Lake Baikal. The BAM enters on the west down the small Tyya river, crosses the northern end of the lake and leaves up the Upper Angara river. On the west and the east, the lake is closely penned between two ranges, the Baikal Range (Байкальский хребет) and the Barguzin Range (Баргузинский хребет).

Excursions are described in the following sections:
● On Lake Baikal
● Between Severobaikalsk and Nizhneangarsk
● North of Lake Baikal
● North-western coast of Lake Baikal
● North-eastern coast of Lake Baikal

Much of the land around Lake Baikal is included in game reserves (заказник) and nature preserves (заповедник). Check with excursion organisers for up-to-date information on fees and permits.

## On Lake Baikal

Lake Baikal (озеро Байкал), 636km long, is the world's deepest fresh-water lake (1,637m). (Its floor is slowly sinking due to seismic movement.) Its water is pure and extremely clear. It nurtures abundant water species, three-quarters are unique to the lake, including the Baikal *nerpa* (нерпа), the freshwater seal and the *golomyanka*, which bears live young.

In summer, Baikal's surface waters are warm and offer excellent swimming. The views from the lake are spectacular at all seasons.

## Travelling on the lake

In the summer months, a commercial hydrofoil service travels the entire Lake three times a week, picking up and letting off passengers by pre-arrangement at tiny settlements and camp-sites around the lake (see Hydrofoils on Lake Baikal, p88).

The Severobaikalsk Yacht Club possesses 30 boats including five 6-person yachts. Sailing is an excellent way of travelling around the north end of Lake Baikal, enabling you to stop in at villages and hot springs. The Severobaikalsk regatta occurs at the end of July and several children's sailing camps are run during the sailing season from June to October. Contact Georgi Ekimok, Director, at ul. 60 let SSSR, dom 14, kv 125, ☎ 2-45-56 (ул.60 лет СССР д 14 кв 125, Екимок Георгий).

You can also hire canoes and catamarans. For day-trips across the lake, for cruises, or for fishing trips, you can charter launches and cabin cruisers (катер – ie 'cutter'). These are built locally and offer simple coupé-style accommodation, washing facilities and kitchens, and come with a crew (usually the owner and his family). A small launch will cost about $45 per day, a cabin cruiser $100 per day. For hiring and chartering, contact one of the tourist agents listed under Getting assistance, p90.

---

❑ **Seal watching**

The Baikal seal or *nerpa* (Байкальская нерпа) is in danger and is already virtually extinct in the southern part of Lake Baikal. The main killers are not hunters but pollution and starvation from diminishing fishing stocks. The population of nerpa in northern Baikal is stable despite 3,000 being hunted each year.

Although there are no regular trips offering *nerpa* seal watching, it is possible to organise it from Severobaikalsk. The best time to see seals is towards late May and early June when the ice has virtually all gone and the seals bask on the ice that remains in protected bays. During summer they live mostly near Bolshoi Ushkani Island (Остров Большой Ушканий), about 250km from Severobaikalsk. As you may need several days to travel to this isolated area and view the seals, a recommended program is to travel on the hydrofoil to the Ayaya Lodge (which is only 15km from the island) and stay there.

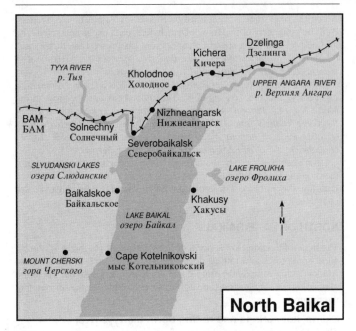

From December to April the lake is frozen and forms a winter road for cars and trucks. The ice is smooth and level and has a delicate green colour. During this season, you can go ice fishing or cross-country skiing across it. The hot springs of the region are a special resource in the winter; lolling in the hot water with your hair frozen solid is a unique experience.

## BETWEEN SEVEROBAIKALSK AND NIZHNEANGARSK

This trip is scenic as both the road and railway run along the northern shores of Lake Baikal. The road is paved and is excellent for bicycle riding.

When the BAM was being built, a temporary railway line ran beside the road linking the towns, but due to the problems of landslides, snow avalanches and pollution the line was relocated several hundred metres inland. This decision required the digging of four tunnels and the building of several rock shields on this 28km stretch. The Mysoviye Tunnels (Мысовые тоннели – 'Cape Tunnels') consist of four tunnels with lengths from east to west of 1.5km, 2km, 0.5km and 2km. They were built by Tunnel Detachment No 16, which today is still located in Nizhneangarsk. Work started in 1978 and finished in 1989.

Along the road route is what must be Russia's most artistic bus shelters. Built by volunteers of the Tunnel Detachment, each one is decorated with mosaic tiles and has a specific theme. From east to west the themes are: *Glory to the tunnel builders, Lake Baikal is the most precious asset in Siberia, Take care of nature* and *Let the sun always shine*.

At the second bus shelter from Severobaikalsk is an underground mining vehicle mounted on a plinth. The monument has the inscription: *MoAZ No. 143, 25 tonne underground tractor used on the construction of the Cape Tunnels from 1975-82. The No 2 Tunnel was opened on 16 October 1982 in honour of 20 years of defence of the USSR. Tunnel Detachment No 16 of BAM Tunnel Construction Enterprise.*

Between the last bus shelter and Nizhneangarsk is the only monument on the BAM dedicated to the small number of tunnellers who died building the railway. For more on the town of Nizhneangarsk, see pp100-101.

## NORTH OF LAKE BAIKAL

The major attractions to the north of Lake Baikal are, to the west, the ski area, hot springs and rafting down the Tyya river, and, to the east, the Akukan gulag camp and rafting down the Upper Angara river. There are also serious mountaineering and adventure routes through the surrounding mountains.

### Skiing, hot springs and rafting down the Tyya river
The BAM, heading westwards up the Tyya river, gives convenient access to:

● The ski area near Solnechny (Солнечный) – near the town is a 500m downhill ski run with a tow and ski rental.
● The hot springs at Goudzhekit (Гоуджекит), which has a small, basic hotel.
● Rafting and float trips down the Tyya river to Lake Baikal.

### Akukan Gulag (Акукан ГУЛаг)
The highlight of a visit to North Baikal is the Akukan Gulag. The camp operated in the late 1930s, mining mica, which was used as electrical insulation. It was closed just prior to the Great Patriotic War when a man-made substitute for mica was found. The camp is located in the Akukan valley alongside the Akukan Stream.

Today, the remnants of those terrible years are plainly visible and consist of several collapsed wooden and stone buildings, towers and barbed wire fences. Four hundred metres further up the valley on the left are three mine shafts where mica veins can still be seen. The shafts are buttressed with wooden logs but are unsafe to enter. Winches and overhead ore buckets litter the area.

The hike to the camp and back takes about four hours from Kholodnoe village or railway station. From the railway station, you walk

## ❏ Seal hunting

Permission for hunting in northern Baikal is granted to only 30 to 40 hunters each year, the majority of whom are indigenous people with a 65 seal quota. For many, seals are an important source of food and money as the meat is salted for winter, and seal blubber and pelts sold to the state. The only buyer of seal products is the seal collective in Baikalskoe village and due to low prices and a small market, there does not appear to be a black market. The state pays only $0.60/kg for seal blubber and meat and $15 for pelts which means an average seal is worth only $30. Many of the hunters are also fishery inspectors which ensures that unknown vessels are quickly spotted and unlicensed hunters arrested.

*Nerpa* hunting requires considerable patience and one seal a day is considered a successful day. Hunting is only permitted after seal breeding from 20 April until the disappearance of the ice in June. Seals bask in the sun while sleeping on the ice and as the ice melts they become restricted to protected bays. Hunters cruise the open lake looking for bays with ice and to enable them to get as close as possible without disturbing the mammals, the hunters wear white coats and hats, and put a white sheet over the front of the motor boat. Hunters use only 22-calibre rifles which means that they must approach within 40m of the seals. Boats are normally brought to within 200m of the seals before the motor is turned off and then paddled the last 160m. Once the seals are within range, the hunter whistles which makes the seals raise their head, thereby offering a clean target. Unless a seal is shot in the head and killed outright, the wounded seal will slip into the water and disappear. Unfortunately, it appears that about 50 per cent of the seals shot are wounded and most injured *nerpas* probably die from their head wounds.

Accompanying seal hunters is an emotionally draining experience, particularly when later that day you are presented with a lump of boiled black seal meat and expected to eat it as a way of sharing the hunter's good fortune. If you do eat this meat, consume only a small amount as it is very rich and unless you eat it with bread, you are likely to bring it up. Seal hunting by foreigners is strictly prohibited.

The unique Baikal nerpa seal

along a tarred road for about one hour towards Kichera. This route takes you over the Kholodnaya river and up a long hill until you reach the 42km marker on the hill's summit. A further 200m past a long stretch of white highway protection barriers is an overgrown dirt logging track off to the left. After about one hour of walking along this track you pass under power lines and after another hour the track changes into a walking path that winds up the Akukan valley. The path beside the Akukan stream is easy to follow and there are logs and planks washed down from the camp laid over the stream and muddy parts of the path to aid you. The path leads directly to the camp.

The walk up the valley is fairly strenuous so you should plan to have your lunch at the camp before returning. The best time to visit the camp is in July and August after the Ixodes tick has disappeared. Only very fit cross-country skiers should attempt this route in winter.

### Floating down the Upper Angara (Верхняя Ангара)

The Upper Angara provides a leisurely float-trip on catamaran rafts with river camping. Take the BAM eastward to Kyukhelbekerskaya (Кюхельбекерская), the last stop on the train before it heads into Severomuisk mountain. From there, make a 2km portage to the river and a 2-day float-trip to the railway crossing near Novy Uoyan (Новый Уоян), with a side excursion to the Evenk village at Uoyan. Continue with a two-day float trip and a side expedition to Dzelinga (Дзелинга) for the hot springs (see pp102-104). Possibly continue with a further two-day float trip to Lake Baikal.

### Mountaineering and trekking

The Lake Baikal ranges and the Stanovoe plateau (Становое нагорье) north and east of the lake have some of the highest and most rugged peaks of the Russian east.

There are several clubs that can provide adventure guides, including the Severobaikalsk Adventure Club (contact through BAMTour) and Tourist Club Kedr (Туристический клуб «Кедр») based in Zheleznogorsk (see pp75-76, Korshunikha-Angarskaya).

Take note that Russian outdoorspeople are used to extreme conditions, heavy loads and long trips.

## NORTH-WESTERN COAST OF LAKE BAIKAL

This is a popular wilderness recreation area as it contains the beautiful Baikal Mountain range, crystal clear lakes and pristine wilderness. You can start from the old Russian fishing village of Baikalskoe, the Cape Kotelnikovski hot springs resort, or the Bolshoi Cheremshany lodge.

---

(**Opposite**)  **Top:** The omul, native to Lake Baikal, is equally good baked, braised, salted, or smoked. These are smoked.  **Bottom:** A vodka or two to pass the time on a journey home for these fireman who are returning from a summer training camp. (Photos © Tatyana Pozar-Burgar).  **Overleaf:** In March and April unofficial highways cross the ice of Lake Baikal. These cars are detouring a place where a truck sank early in the season. (Photo © Nicholas Zvegintzov).

## 🏘 Baikalskoe (Байкальское)

This village is connected to Severobaikalsk by an excellent 40km highway, which is also good for bike riding. About 15km from Severobaikalsk you will get an excellent view of the large Onakarshanskaya Bay (Онакаршанская бухта). This place is sacred for the indigenous Buryats and was consecrated by a Lama from a monastery near Ulan-Ude in 1992. At the top of the hill is a viewing area with a tree to which strips of clothing are tied and under which gifts are laid. The gifts, which include cigarettes, vodka, bullets and money, symbolise gratitude for the beautiful places on earth such as this bay.

From this place you also see the fourth largest of the 24 islands in Lake Baikal, Bigakhan Island (остров Бигахан). This remote island had one notable visitor in the early 1980s when Brezhnev had a secret picnic there. So as to ensure that the General Secretary of the Communist Party had a completely relaxing time undisturbed by noise, his overzealous staff ordered the closure of Severobaikalsk and Nizhneangarsk ports, as well as a ban on all motorboats!

A further 10km towards Baikalskoe, you pass the Slyudanski lakes (Слюданские озера), two small lakes above the shoreline of Lake Baikal, where the Severobaikalsk School of Tourism-Ecology Education has accommodation at its 'Echo' tour-base.

Baikalskoe is an ancient Russian village, previously called Kharemika (Харемика), which contains the only seal-hunting and seal-pelt collective in north Baikal. This collective buys seal meat and skins from mainly indigenous hunters and makes seal-skin hats and boots. You can visit the collective's seal-clothing workshop, which is near the pier.

Before the arrival of Russians in the 1600s, the cliff near the town was used for sacrifices by the Evenk people. Archaeologists have found numerous pots and other artefacts here, which can now be seen in the Irkutsk ethnographical museum. A polar fox farm is located about 1km further on from the town

A bus runs three times a day between Severobaikalsk and Baikalskoe.

## Cape Kotelnikovski Hot Spring Resort (мыс Котельниковский)

This tourist base is one of the best kept secrets in north Baikal. It was built by BAM tunnel workers as a *holiday resort*. It consists of excellent accommodation for 16 people (two single, one double and four triple rooms), a canteen, sauna and outdoor and indoor pools heated by 86°C hot spring water. It is used by hikers, tourists sailing the lakes, or people wanting a day away from Severobaikalsk. To stay here costs $10 per person per

---

**(Opposite)  Top:** Boys will be boys. Slingshots as the train passes by.  **Bottom:** Near Fevralsk along the Selemdzha river a rusting yet still functional steam gold dredger still proudly carries Lenin's head. (Photos © Tatyana Pozar-Burgar).

❑ **Gulag buildings**

Camps prior to the Second World War were very rudimentary, with the typical camp consisting of the prisoner zone surrounded by a fence of wooden planks and wire, and perimeter guard towers. Guard barracks and offices were made of timber but prisoners often slept in freezing tents unless there was plenty of nearby wood.

No bedding was provided so prisoners slept in their own clothes, fearing to take anything off in case it was stolen. Wooden prisoner barracks had a metal stove but when it worked, it would only radiate heat for five to six metres. Often there was no fuel for the stoves despite the abundance of wood in Siberia. This was because the prisoners had to meet their work quotas before wood could be collected. In addition, the collection of wood depended on the whim of the guards who often were too lazy to accompany the prisoners.

Following the end of the Second World War, barbed-wire fences around the camp zones were strengthened and enlarged, iron bars were put into the windows of the barracks, visits to neighbouring barracks were forbidden, the prisoners' rights to correspond with their families were restricted, the number of guards increased, and inmates were ordered always to have their numbers attached to their garments. These changes were caused by the influx of POWs and anti-Soviet partisans who could not be intimidated as easily as the pre-war peasant inmates. Their hatred of the Soviet power united them against the camp authorities. The non-Russians took their anti-Soviet hatred out on the ethnic Russian prisoners which eventually led to these two groups being segregated.

The post-war prisoners organised numerous protests and strikes, and there were several mass breakouts. Although hundreds were shot during these actions, the actions did result in a general improvement in food and conditions throughout Soviet camps.

night, or to just swim in the pools costs $1. If you intend to stay and require food, it is worth booking by telephone radio through BAMTour. In summer the springs can be reached by motor boat from Baikalskoe ($50 return boat hire) and in winter by car over the frozen lake.

## Mount Cherski (гора Черского)

The highest peak in the range is Mount Cherski (гора Черского) at 2,588m. The lands surrounding the mountain are among the most beautiful around the lake. Here one can enjoy the emerald Gitara Lake, waterfall cascades, glaciers and snow-covered peaks. Mount Cherski is the most difficult mountain in the region and there are glaciers at its foot. The best time to climb is from mid-July to August and no attempt has been made to climb it in winter. It takes four days to cover the 80km to Mount Cherski, starting and returning to Cape Kotelnikovski. Extra days and special equipment are needed to scale the peak.

### Bolshoi Cheremshany Lodge (Болшой Черемшаный Лодж)

One hundred and forty kilometres south of Severobaikalsk is a remote, well-appointed *lodge*, which can be a base for seal watching or trekking in the Baikal Mountain Range. Situated on 65,000 hectares with a 50km shoreline, the lodge consists of two buildings with a kitchen, a recreation room and five bedrooms with beds for 10 people. The lodge is maintained by two hunters/fishermen and observing their lifestyle is one of the most interesting aspects of staying at the lodge.

The easiest way to get to the lodge is to take the hydrofoil from either Irkutsk or Severobaikalsk and arrange for one of the hunters to meet the hydrofoil at sea. Another way is to take a boat from Severobaikalsk (six hours) or from the other side of the lake at Ust-Barguzin (Усть-Баргазин) (five hours) which can be reached from Ulan-Ude.

### Sources of the Lena river

The Lena river rises on the west shore of Lake Baikal about 200km south of Severobaikalsk. The easiest way to get to the source is via Cape Pokoiniki (мыс Покойники) or Cape Sharshlai (мыс Шаршлай), nearly level with Ushkanaya Island (остров Ушканая). To get there you can either hire a boat from Severobaikalsk or arrange for a local with a dinghy to meet the hydrofoil that plies between Severobaikalsk and Irkutsk. The walk up the east escarpment of the Baikal Range is steep but no special equipment is needed. The distance is 10km as the crow flies but may be 40km by foot. For more on the upper reaches of the Lena see p245.

## NORTH-EASTERN COAST OF LAKE BAIKAL

The north-east of Lake Baikal is a popular wilderness recreation area as it contains the beautiful Barguzin Mountain range, crystal clear lakes and pristine wilderness. Attractions on the east shore are Lake Frolikha and the Khakusy hot springs. Both places may be reached by long hikes from the north end of Lake Baikal, or by launch. During winter you can cross-country ski the 50km across the frozen Lake Baikal. You will need to sleep on the lake one night before getting to the camp.

Much further down (250km) is Ust-Barguzin (Усть-Баргузин) and the wide valley of the Barguzin river, best approached by road from Ulan-Ude or by hydrofoil from the southern end of the lake.

## Lake Frolikha (озеро Фролиха)

This small mountain lake is an easy three- to four-day hike from Nizhneangarsk, or a two-hour trip by launch, landing at either Frolikha Bay (губа Фролиха) or Ayaya Bay (губа Аяя) and following a 7km trail. Most travellers camp overnight on the lake. A 15km hike brings you to Khakusy.

## Khakusy (Хакусы)

At Khakusy there is a hot-springs resort, with springs, bath-house, conservatory, lodge, dining room and cottages. Accommodation, with meals and therapeutic baths, is $17 a day in summer. Reach Khakusy by launch; land at the jetty and walk 500m through the sandy woods. Or hike 15km from Lake Frolikha. For reservations (in Nizhneangarsk) phone ☎ 51-421 or 51-719.

# Severobaikalsk–Novaya Chara
## Северобайкальск–Новая Чара

## THE ROUTE (see Route Map 2, p367)

The line leaves Lake Baikal up the broad valley of the Upper Angara and heads into a wilderness of mountain ranges, creeks, lakes and taiga. Three hundred and twenty kilometres to the east the railway takes spirals and hairpins across the Severomuisk mountain range while the planned tunnel is still being built. The line runs down the Muya valley to the gold-mining town of Taksimo, crosses the Vitim river, climbs the Syulban creek to a short tunnel through the Kodar range, threads between the two tranquil Leprindo Lakes and crosses the broad valley of the Chara. Along most of the route there is only a vestigial road, the washed-out remains of the road built during construction of the railway line.

The time is Moscow time +5 hours until the crossing of the Vitim river at Shivery. Beyond that it is Moscow time +6 hours.

### SEVEROBAIKALSK (Северобайкальск) 1,064km

For information on Severobaikalsk, see pp84-91.

### NIZHNEANGARSK (Нижнеангарск) 1,104km

## Orientation

Nizhneangarsk is the Russian equivalent of a low density, sprawling suburb. It is wedged on a 20km strip between Lake Baikal and steep mountains, with each end bounded by the Nizhneangarsk railway station. The Nizhneangarsk station is not actually 20km long but consists of two stations Nizhneangarsk 1 (closest to Severobaikalsk) and Nizhneangarsk 2.

Nizhneangarsk's large man-made harbour and the town's centre are at Nizhneangarsk 1 station while the airport is located at Nizhneangarsk 2. Strangely the largest station is remote Nizhneangarsk 2 and it is the only stop in Nizhneangarsk for long-distance trains.

## History

Prior to the BAM, the 2,000 residents of Nizhneangarsk were mostly fishermen. Following the start of the BAM, the town rapidly expanded and now boasts 10,000 citizens, the headquarters of the BAM Tunnel Construction organisation (БАМТоннелСтрой) and the seat of the regional government. Despite being the regional power, Nizhneangarsk is smaller than neighbouring Severobaikalsk.

The modern history of the town provides an interesting insight into the enormous planning problems of such a gigantic project as the BAM. In the early 1970s, Nizhneangarsk was selected as the centre of the western end of the BAM and it was anticipated that about 75,000 people would live there. At that time, Severobaikalsk was regarded as the site of just a small workers' town. However, after the construction of a few large buildings, it became apparent that the marshy ground was not at all suitable.

This problem is illustrated by the town's hospital, which now lies abandoned as it sinks slowly into the ground. The hospital was built in 1976 and closed in 1993 when further repairs became impossible. The hospital is now housed in what was the town's hotel, next to the City Council building. The marshy ground has meant that no building can be more than two storeys high and that all are restricted to the narrow strip of suitable land along the railway wedged between the marsh and the mountains. As a result, the site of the headquarters of the western end of the BAM was transferred to Severobaikalsk. However, this was after the building of the Nizhneangarsk airport, which also serves as Severobaikalsk's airport.

Another inadequately researched planning decision was the construction of the large Nizhneangarsk port and pier complex. This vastly underutilised facility was designed to receive BAM building materials in the mid-1970s so that the work could commence on the section east of Nizhneangarsk before the BAM reached Nizhneangarsk from the west. However, the work on the western section of the BAM progressed much faster than anticipated and the rails arrived at the same time as the port was completed. The railway connected to the Trans-Siberian offered a year-round service for shipping material, cheaper than an Irkutsk–Nizhneangarsk ferry. Consequently, the port was never used for what it was intended for and today it just serves a small fishing fleet and the hydrofoil that plies the Nizhneangarsk–Severobaikalsk–Irkutsk route.

## Getting there and away

See Getting there and away in the Severobaikalsk section, p86.

☐ **NIZHNEANGARSK
(Нижнеангарск)**
Republic of Buryatiya,
  Nizhneangarsk
(Республика Бурятия, г.
  Нижнеангарск)

## Getting around

It takes a couple of hours to walk from one end of the town to the other so a better way is to catch the local bus as it runs from Severobaikalsk through Nizhneangarsk 1 to the airport. About 10 minutes on foot further eastward is the Nizhneangarsk 2 station.

## Where to stay

Since the town's hotel has been taken over by the hospital, there is limited accommodation in the town. The only options are the *BAM Tunnel Construction guest cottages* for visiting dignitaries and the very basic *BAM Tunnel Construction Organisation hostel* for visiting workers. However, the best option is to stay in Severobaikalsk where there is a much wider range of accommodation.

## Where to eat

The town has two *canteens* (shown on the map, p103).

## What to see

The town is pleasant to stroll around with its mainly wooden buildings. Despite most of the town being built since the mid-1970s, Nizhneangarsk is one of the few BAM towns which is not dominated by five-storey concrete flats and prefabricated buildings. Even the two-storey City Council building is wooden. An architectural oddity is the wooden boat rental and water rescue station on the lake's edge. The fish-processing factory is worth a visit as it is an eye opener to Russian methods and working conditions. The plant makes delicious smoked and salted omul.

## 🏠 KHOLODNY (Холодный) 1,120km

A 20-minute walk down the tarred road is a village of indigenous Evenk people from the Baikal area. The village is trying to keep its traditional way of life alive with *tchums* (similar to Mongolian yurts), hunting, reindeer raising, fishing and animal husbandry. A small museum in the school displays traditional Evenk utensils and religious items.

## 🏠 KICHERA (Кичера) 1,141km

Kichera is a BAM railway town with a population of 3,000. It was built by the Estonian Young Communist Party and its architecture is notably Baltic influenced. The Kichera river runs through the town and along the railway.

## ☒ DZELINGA (Дзелинга) 1,171km

The tiny station was built in 1996 to serve the resort being built by the rail-

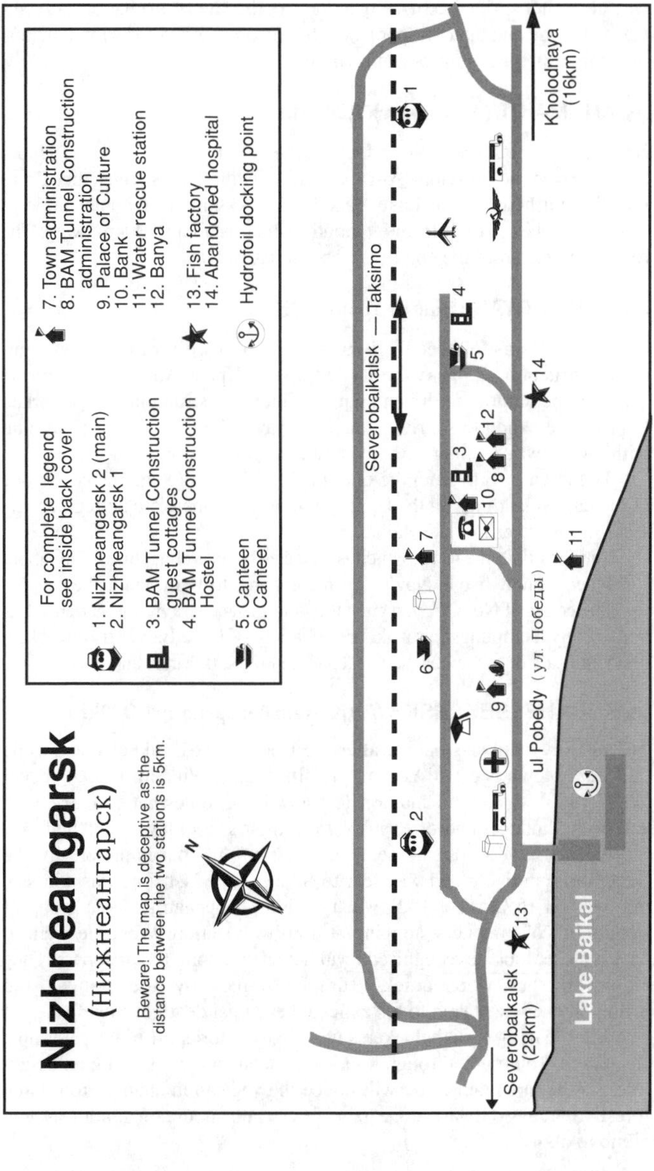

# Nizhneangarsk
(Нижнеангарск)

Beware! The map is deceptive as the distance between the two stations is 5km.

For complete legend
see inside back cover

1. Nizhneangarsk 2 (main)
2. Nizhneangarsk 1

3. BAM Tunnel Construction
   guest cottages
4. BAM Tunnel Construction
   Hostel

5. Canteen
6. Canteen

7. Town administration
8. BAM Tunnel Construction
   administration
9. Palace of Culture
10. Bank
11. Water rescue station
12. Banya

13. Fish factory
14. Abandoned hospital

Hydrofoil docking point

N

Lake Baikal

Severobaikalsk — Taksimo

ul Pobedy (ул Победы)

Kholodnaya
(16km)

Severobaikalsk
(28km)

way at the hot springs 2km away in the woods. The *resort* has several cottages, a lodge and open-air pools. Highly recommended for winter swims; in summer the mosquitoes can be fierce.

## ANAMAKIT (Анамакит) 1,242km

Between Anamakit and Novy Uoyan, the BAM crosses over the Upper Angara river (р. Верхняя Ангара) which is the largest river that flows into the northern end of Lake Baikal. This 438km river is navigable in motor launches 270km from its mouth, which is about 100km away. The river is frozen from the end of October to early May.

## NOVY UOYAN (Новый Уоян) 1,257km

Novy Uoyan was founded in 1976 as a support base for railway and tunnel construction. Goods were hauled up the Upper Angara river during summer and autumn or driven up it in winter. Construction teams worked in primitive conditions, driving their railway in both directions to join up with the railway coming from the east and west.

The town is 7km from the old village of Uoyan (Уоян) which is one of the largest landings on the Upper Angara river. There are no regular services on the river to Lake Baikal.

Latvians built the town, which is reflected in its architecture. Only about 6,000 people now live in Novy Uoyan compared to 10,000 in its heyday.

The cooks of Novy Uoyan greet the long-distance trains with a rich selection – bliny, dumplings, pirozhki and a variety of Lake Baikal fish, smoked, dried and salted, as well as the usual ice creams, soft drinks and beer.

## KYUKHELBEKERSKAYA (Кюхельбекерская) 1,330km

The railway station is named after the Decembrist Kyukhelbeker, while the nearby town is called Yanchukan (Янчукан). Wilhelm Kyukhelbeker (1797-1856) was a kind and hopeless idealist, a somewhat eccentric poet and critic, and a friend of Pushkin from their schooldays. Kyukhelbeker received a severe prison sentence due to his participation in the Decembrist uprising and was sent to Siberia. The last time Pushkin saw him was on 15 October 1827 when Pushkin happened to see a group of troikas full of prisoners stopping at a railway station. When he went to have a closer look he recognised Kyukhelbeker among the prisoners. They embraced, but were quickly dragged apart by the police, and Kyukhelbeker was taken to his exile and eventual death in Siberia.

After leaving Kyukhelbekerskaya, the train forks off to the right up a side creek. You travel through a series of steep valleys as you gain height to cross the mountains. You will notice the vegetation change from larch forest to scraggy dwarf stone pine forest and mountain tundra as you climb to above 1,200m.

⊠ **OSYPNOI (Осыпной) 1,385km**

The stop is the western escarpment base for the tunnellers who are building the 15.7km Severomuisk Tunnel. The nearby workers' settlement is called Tonnelny (Тоннельный) and is destined for demolition once the tunnel is finished.

## CROSSING THE SEVEROMUISK RANGE

The train now crosses the Severomuisk ('North Muya') Range (Северомуйский хребет), where peaks rise to 2,500m and are snow-capped year-round. The design calls for a tunnel, which is still being built. Meanwhile trains take a bypass over a 1,200m pass. The bypass crossing, which is an engineering feat in itself, takes two hours and is famous as a scenic experience.

Try to schedule your journey so that you cross by day (for example, on the westward long-distance trains). There are spectacular views of both scenery and engineering on both sides of the train.

### Severomuisk Tunnel (Северомуйский тоннель)

The Severomuisk Tunnel is the only BAM tunnel not yet complete. Eventually, it will be 15.7km long, making it the fourth longest railway tunnel in the world.

When work started on the tunnel in 1978 it was estimated that it would be finished by 1984. In December 1997 the service tunnel from each end met; in April 2001 the train tunnels met. The tunnel finishing, track laying and signal equipment installation should be completed in 2002.

The slower than expected rate of construction is due to the horrendous geological structure of the Severomuisk Range. These mountains contain four major fault lines and are located in a highly seismic area which experiences 400 tremors a year on average. The entire tunnel is lined with seismic sensors.

However, the biggest dangers faced by the tunnellers are the range's numerous underground lakes and rivers. After just a few metres of drilling, the tunnellers encountered streams of water and the epic of water drainage began. The further the tunnel went, the more water entered it. The subterranean water is at pressures up to 35 atmospheres, which means that water is always breaking through the tunnel walls. The huge granite fault lines offer a conduit for underground rivers and they must be approached very carefully.

The decision to build the tunnel was fundamentally wrong, according to Vladimir Ignatovich, chief geologist for the Buryat Geological Production Association (Buryatgeologia), which surveyed the original BAM line. 'Back when the route was being surveyed, we warned the designers at Novosibirsk's Siberian State Transport Design Institute and the Leningrad State Subway Design Institute about the highly complex conditions in the BAM's Buryatiya sector. ... We felt it would be better to bypass it from the south with minimal excavation work. However, the shortest path was chosen, a 15km tunnel.'

The tunnel is actually two tunnels – a small service tunnel wide enough for a truck and the main two-track rail tunnel. The service tunnel is drilled parallel and ahead of the main tunnel which provides a warning of impending difficulties for the main drilling crews as well as a safety passage if one of the tunnels floods or collapses.

When the sheer difficulty of constructing the tunnel was recognised, international tunnel experts were invited from Germany, France, Japan, USA and Finland. Unfortunately the unique situation of the Severomuisk Tunnel meant that Western experience was of limited value. Consequently, the Soviet builders were forced to develop new technology including a method of pumping liquid nitrogen into the rocks, which freezes the water and temporarily stops water seepage. The tunnel would then be coated with concrete which would permanently seal out the water. Along both sides of the tunnel are drainage channels which, when the tunnel is completed, will drain all the water by gravitation, eliminating the need for costly pumping.

## The Severomuisk Bypass

When it became obvious that the Severomuisk tunnel would not be finished on time, a temporary above-ground bypass was built across the mountains. This 28km bypass was completed in 1987 and designed to last only until 1992 when the tunnel was expected to be complete. The gradient was extremely steep, being a 40m change in altitude for every kilometre. It was so dangerous that rolling stock was restricted to 15km/h and only freight traffic was allowed. A 1987 report in *Sotsialisticheskaya Industriya* described the bypass's condition: 'Two or three electric locomotives pull the cars. The grades and the drops are so steep that, when the cars are heading down hill, the drivers literally ride on the locomotives' running boards so they'll be able to jump off in time if there's an accident.'

Once it became apparent that the 1992 completion date would not be met, a second bypass was built. This 54km bypass contains two short tunnels and was completed in 1989. This is the current bypass and although it is safe for light-weight passenger trains, there are regular derailments of the heavily laden goods trains.

The bypass line climbs up the right side of the creek, leaving below the new track to the tunnel. At Osypnoi, the line makes a huge hairpin to the right, crossing above the tunnel portal. Then the bypass enters a tunnel whose sole purpose is to reverse the train; watch for the exit portal 30m from the entry portal. The train passes a small halt, Pereval (Перевал – 'Pass'). Look back on the left of the train to see four levels of the track.

## ❑ Severomuisk Tunnel Disaster

'It happened towards morning. Kozhemyakin's brigade of tunnellers was preparing to turn over the work face to the next shift. They had done more than their norm. The next day was to have been their day off, so everybody was in excellent spirits. And then disaster struck. The granite wall in front of the face, which had seemed stronger than anything on earth, suddenly shuddered. An alarming rumble came from deep within the mountain and then everything began to thunder. The forbidding wall of rock toppled and with enormous force, a torrent of water carrying sand and rocks poured into the face. The drilling unit, which weighed many tonnes, was instantly hurled back dozens of metres as if it were a piece of fluff. The lights went out. Only the lamps on the tunnellers' hard hats glimmered faintly through the spray of water and the thick fog rising from the thermal springs. The hot roaring mass rushed swiftly through the tunnel, sweeping up everything in its path', Vladimir Aslanbekovich Vessolov. *Pravda*, 28 February 1983, reporting on an event in September 1979.

What had happened on that morning in September 1979 was that the drilling team had hit an unexpected fault line containing a 140m deep underground lake. The reservoir contained a massive 12,000 cubic metres of water, sand and rocks. The water surged into the gallery in just a matter of seconds, drowning several miners. Had most of the miners not escaped to the service tunnel, then the death toll would have been significantly higher.

The disaster highlighted the inadequate geological work to date and so extensive surveys were carried out. To drain the underground lake, another tunnel was dug under the existing tunnel and the water was pumped out.

Eighteen months after the disaster, on 10 October 1981, work recommenced on the tunnel which now was narrower as the need for a second track was dropped.

The typical Soviet and now post-communist Russian obsession with secrecy has meant that the death toll from this disaster has never been published. While some Western commentators claim that several hundred workers died, probably only between four and 10 tunnellers died. There are no memorials to those who died in Severomuisk.

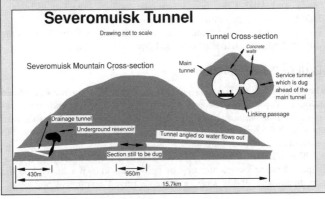

The highest point on the bypass is over a bald shoulder of scree. On the left of the train you will see the access road crossing a lower point in the ridge (too narrow and steep to allow a railway crossing). Look out on your left to an S-bend ahead of you and, beyond a shoulder, you can see the Muya river valley far below (to which you are headed). The train takes a tight left turn around the ridge and a long right hairpin up and down a mountain creek and another tight left turn around the next shoulder. Look ahead on the right of the train to see four more levels below you.

After another small hairpin and a tunnel, you come around a shoulder and see ahead a wide loop to the right on which the train crosses 20m above the tunnel portal and through the engineering yards. The train crosses the access roads and rails and stops at Kazankan station, the end of the bypass.

## 🚉 KAZANKAN (Казанкан) 1,400km

Below this station in the woods is Severomuisk (Северомуйск), the eastern escarpment base for the tunnellers. This has to be one of the most depressing towns in the BAM Zone. It is a sad collection of ramshackle buildings, non-existent roads and despair. It was founded in April 1977 as a temporary settlement for the miners of the Severomuisk Tunnel. It was expected that by 1984, the original completion date for the tunnel, the town would be demolished and the area restored to its original condition. The only people expected to remain in the area are a small number of maintenance workers and the tunnel's military guard.

Although the tunnel is a long way from being completed, many of the miners have left.

The tunnel's entrance is 10km from the station and, while it is possible to walk up to the entrance, it is impossible to enter unless you are on an organised visit. Severomuisk has an airport with irregular flights to Tynda and Ulan-Ude, and a canteen and a hostel run by the BAMTonnelstroi, the tunnel construction organisation.

After Kazankan the train takes two more hairpin turns down to the Muya valley and resumes its eastward direction.

## 🚉 ULGI (Ульги) 1,422km

The stop is named after *ulgi*, which is a general term for Buryatiyan indigenous epic folk songs and folktales. The folk songs, known as *baatryn ulgers* or *baatarlag tuul*, tell the adventures of valiant heroes who battle with the forces of evil and the songs range from several hundred to several thousand lines long.

The folk tales, known as *iavgan ulgers* or *urtu*, are usually short heroic tales. Epic folksongs are sung by performers known as *ulgerch* to the accompaniment of the *khur*, a bowed stringed instrument and of the *tovshuur*, a plucked stringed instrument. Nowadays, ulgi are also recited without musical instruments.

## 🏭 MUYAKAN (Муякан)

The station derives it name from both the Muyakan river and also the nearby 120km Muyakan Range. From Muyakan to Taksimo the route is scenic as you travel along the valleys of the Muyakan and then the Muya rivers with the Verkhneangarski Range (Верхнеангарский хребет) on the left and the Yuzhno-amurski Range (Южно-амурский хребет) on the right. Unfortunately, evening fogs are common in the valleys so the best time to travel through it is in the morning. The Muya river is rich in fish including *taimen*, grayling, *tugun* and whitefish.

## 🏭 TAKSIMO (Таксимо) 1,484km

Taksimo's history dates back to the late Tsarist times when its isolation made it a safe base camp for bandits. After the 1917 socialist revolution, this same isolation attracted White Army soldiers, priests and others who fled the persecution of the communists. Modern Taksimo was built by the Belarussians and Latvians although it is difficult to see their influences. The town has a population of about 14,000 and is the capital of the 28,000 strong Muiski Raion.

### Orientation

Taksimo is on the Muya river just above where it meets the Vitim river. The Vitim river rises deep in the mountains east of Lake Baikal and traces a huge semi-circle through deep mountains until it joins the Lena at Vitim. For more on the lower Vitim river see Vitim, pp252-255.

Taksimo is at the end of the electrified section of the BAM and electric locomotives are changed here for diesel ones.

The major industries of the region are railways, gold-mining and forestry. Sand is also exported and this is noticeable beside the railway just east of the town. The soil is poor for agriculture so most household vegetable plots have a thick layer of rich swamp moss, which is an ideal growing medium, laid over the sandy soil.

South of Taksimo is a huge asbestos reserve known as the Molodezhnaya deposit. Access to this resource was one of the many justifications for building the BAM in the early 1970s, but the market for asbestos rapidly contracted as the health effects became known. Consequently the 41km branch line to the deposit has yet to be started and probably never will be.

❏ **TAKSIMO (Таксимо)**
Republic of Buryatiya,
  Muiski Raion, Taksimo
(Республика Бурятия,
  Муйский район, п.
Таксимо)

Despite this, a team of eight was still working on the plans for the future mine as late as 1994. Incidentally the proposed mining town is to be called Korchagin after the main communist hero in Nikolai Ostrovsky's socialist realist novel, *How the steel was tempered*.

## Getting there and away
There is a Moscow–Tynda train (via Kazan) every other day and a Kislovodsk–Tynda train twice a week. There is a local train every day from Severobaikalsk in the west and Novaya Chara in the east.

Planes arrive from Ulan-Ude, Bratsk, Nizhneangarsk, Yakutsk and Bagdarin, which is halfway to Ulan-Ude.

Technically it is possible during summer to go by boat down the Vitim river to Bodaibo and then to the Lena river. However, fluctuating water levels and two difficult rapids prevent regular services, and nowadays only rafters travel this route.

It is possible to drive to Bodaibo but you will have to get a lift or hire a car, as there are no regular bus services from Taksimo. Despite what some Russian books say, the 125km road to Bodaibo is just a dirt track. The best place to find a lift is at the railway station as Bodaibo gold-mining company buses often meet trains and take the workers to the gold fields.

## Getting around
Like most BAM towns, Taksimo has two parts – the older temporary settlement away from the railway station and the permanent modern settle-

In front of Taksimo station is a Tupolev ANT-4 on a plinth. This was one of the original planes that conducted the aerial surveys for the BAM in the 1930s. The plane crashed nearby into Lake Barencharoe (озеро Баренчарое). Its wreckage was discovered in the 1970s and restored voluntarily by the railway builders. (Photo © Nicholas Zvegintzov).

**Taksimo** (Таксимо)

For complete legend
see inside back cover

1. Railway Hotel

2. Canteen
3. Mozaika restaurant

4. SMP-607
5. Town administration
6. Palace of Culture

7. Aircraft monument

Lake
Barencharoe

Ust-Muya, Bargalino,
Parama Rapids

ment around the station. A bus travels between the two settlements on the
way to the airport, which is 1.5km from the station.

### Where to stay

The only hotel in town is the *ATCh Railway Hotel* (☎ 56-81), ul.
Sovetskaya 11 (ул. Советская, 11, Гостиница АТЧ).

### Where to eat

The only restaurant is the expensive *Mozaika* (Мозаика ресторан)
which is in the TOTs shopping complex. There is also a *canteen* near the
hotel and a *buffet* in the station.

## AROUND TAKSIMO

### Gold-mining

If you are interested in gold mining, there are a number of operations you
could visit. The town is the headquarters of Vitim Zoloto, one of the region's
biggest gold producers. All the operations involve surface mining, mostly
using the simple technique of bulldozing the top 10 metres of soil into giant

washing trays, hosing away the dirt and rock, and extracting the gold once it settles on the tray's bottom. Environmentally-disastrous mercury leaching was discontinued about 10 years ago according to company officials.

The best places to see gold mining are at Irakinda (Иракинда), 60km south by a poor road, or at Kalakan (Калакан), 120km south up the Vitim river to its junction with the Kalakan river. There is no road to Kalakan but you can drive there down the Vitim when it is frozen. To organise a visit to one of these sites, contact Vitim Zoloto on ☎ 54-249 or ☎ 826 (railway).

## Parama Rapids and the surrounding towns

One of the most interesting places around Taksimo is the Parama Rapids (Парама пороги) on the Vitim, and its nearby towns of Ust-Muya, Muya, Bargalino and Nelyaty. These can be reached from Taksimo or Kuanda.

The Parama Rapids on the Vitim river are among Russia's best rafting rapids. They are only suitable for experienced rafters and before the collapse of the Soviet Union about eight groups a year would raft down them. Nowadays the lack of government sports assistance makes the trip to the rapids prohibitively expensive for ordinary Russians and consequently no one has travelled down them since the late 1980s, according to the region's only ranger.

The rapids are formed when the Vitim river narrows from 1km in flood to just 150m. It takes about 10 minutes to descend the rapids and about two hours to walk up them. The rapids are dangerous and it is only safe to travel down them when the water is at a certain level. Even the indigenous people are wary of the river, calling it *Ugryum Reka*, which means 'grim river'.

Until recently, barges and log rafts floated down the rapids and while most traversed it safely, a disaster occurred in 1989 when a captain ignored the advice of the pilot that the water level was too high. The tug lost its two 150-tonne barges which blocked the rapids for other vessels for the rest of the season. The obstacles were eventually removed by waiting until the winter freezing of the rapids, drilling holes through the ice and packing explosives around the barge. The exploded remains were small enough to be washed downstream in the thaw.

The rapids are shaped like an elongated S and halfway down them is a large flat-topped rock. According to local legend, this was where two escaped prisoners from Chara's Marble Canyon gulag were finally caught by the guards in 1946. They had travelled 240km without food and were found exhausted asleep on the rock. Rather than taking them back to camp for execution, they were shot in their sleep and their corpses left as a

**(Opposite)** This giant heroic sculpture in Tynda was built with welded stainless steel by workers of the BAM Bridge Building organisation Moststroi-10. (Photo © Tatyana Pozar-Burgar).

warning. One local claims that his mother remembers seeing the skeletons in the early 1950s.

To inspect the rapids, you need to beach your craft at an obvious place on the right about 500m from the start of the rapids. From here, there is a walking track that cuts off a bend in the river, which means that after about 25-minutes' walking, you arrive at the centre of the rapids.

In the centre of the river near where you beach is a large rock, which is the old measuring stick used to indicate when it was safe to travel the rapids. If the rock is exposed, log rafts can safely traverse the rapids without breaking up. If the water level is above the rock but less than 2.5m above it, it is safe for motor launches and rafts. Above this, it is highly dangerous for any crossing.

The current measuring stick is now located at the ranger's house at Ust-Parama. It measures the total depth of the river. A 14m level equates to water just submerging the rock, which means that a 16.5m water level is safe for rafters. The best time of the year to find the rapids at below 16.5m is in the second half of July. In August the water level will usually fall below 16.5m about twice but it could be any time in the month. You are guaranteed a safe water level from mid-September but the water is then too cold for rafting.

If you want to travel the rapids in style, the only sort of motorised boats that can safely traverse them are the T-63 boats which are 18m by 3.5m with a 0.8m draft and can carry four people, and the KC-100 which can carry 10 people. Despite what boastful locals may say, normal dinghies with outboard motors cannot safely cross the rapids.

You can get to the Parama Rapids from Taksimo and Kuanda. The trip from Taksimo involves driving on a reasonable dirt road to the Muya river (1 hour 40 minutes) and taking a motor boat down the Muya river, to the Vitim river, past Bargalino and Ust-Parama, to the rapids (two hours). The trip from Kuanda involves going 8km north by road to the river and taking a motor boat down the 90km Kuanda river to the Vitim river (three hours). This junction is just upstream of Nelyaty and opposite Bargalino. Remember that coming back against the current takes twice as long.

## Long-distance rafting on the Vitim river system

The Parama Rapids is one of three rapids in the region which make up one of the most challenging rafting routes in eastern Siberia. The 840km route

(Opposite) Top: The Chara valley, looking north. In the foreground are the Chara sand dunes. Beyond is the Sredni Sakukan river valley. Marble Canyon with its gulag is in a side canyon. Bottom: West portal of the 15.7 km Severomuisk tunnel (see p107). Work started in 1978, and in April 2001 the west and east train tunnels met. (Photo © Nicholas Zvegintzov).

starts near the little village of Uakit (Уакит). The easiest way to get to Uakit is to fly from Ulan-Ude to Bagdarin (Багдарин), then onwards to Uakit in a light plane. From Uakit, you take a motorboat 100km down the Uakit river until it joins the Tsipa river (p. Ципа). Assemble your rafts here. The first set of rapids is 50km away. After another 170km, you reach the Vitim river. After a further 160km you arrive at the Parama Rapids and a further 120km downstream are the Uronski Rapids (Уронский пороги). These are even larger than the Parama Rapids. After another 240km you finally reach Bodaibo.

## Organising a trip

A trip to this region requires local knowledge and co-ordination and the best person to do this is the pleasant Chief of the Regional Administration, Viktor Serkin, or his assistant, Yuri Dmitriya. Viktor is responsible for the Muyaski Raion, which comprises Ust-Muya, Muya and Bargalino. For further details contact Viktor Serkin, Chief of Administration, 671414, Muyaski Raion, Selo Ust-Muya, ☎ 1-80 (work), ☎ 1-41 (home) (671414 Муяский район, село Усть-Муя, Главадмистратор, Виктор Серкин).

Viktor Stepanovich Ryzhni, who runs the BAM Turist Adventure Centre for Children, can also assist in organising the trip from Kuanda. For more information on the centre, see Kuanda, pp118-119.

## Towns near the Parama Rapids

To get to the Parama Rapids you need to go through the nearby towns of Ust-Muya, Muya, Bargalino and Nelyaty. There is a reasonable dirt road between Ust-Muya and Muya (6km) and onwards to Bargalino (6km).

Ust-Muya (Усть-Муя) is the newest of the three villages as it was founded in 1947 to supply logs to the gold mines in Bodaibo. Large log rafts took four days to float the 500km downriver to Bodaibo. Many exiled nationalities, notably the Volga Germans, resettled here after horrendous voyages, which took them through the prison towns of Norilsk and Bodaibo far in the north. The town underwent a boom during the years of BAM construction as wood was again in great demand. In those days, the town even boasted a runway where IL-14 planes would occasionally land. In the early 1980s, 400 timber workers laboured in the town. Today only 60 timber jobs remain. Of today's remaining workforce of 300, 200 of these work in Taksimo. As daily commuting is impractical due to the distance and poor road condition, the workers live in Taksimo hostels for 15 or 20 days before returning to Ust-Muya for a similar number of days off. A ferry connects the southern bank Taksimo road to Ust-Muya and it is large enough to take two big trucks or four cars.

Muya (Муя) was founded in Tsarist times and is 3km from the junction of the Vitim and Muya rivers. In the 19th century it was a major staging post for the barges that were floated down the Vitim from Romanovka

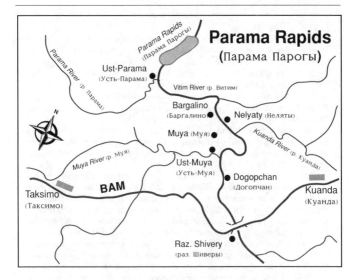

near the Trans-Siberian to Bodaibo. Today there are about 100 houses in the town with the main occupations being hunting and fishing.

Bargalino is worth seeing as it is a living ghost town. The town was founded in the 1800s and once boasted a 1km long street of wooden Siberian houses. However, the disappearance of rural jobs has created a mass exodus to the cities. Today there are just 12 occupied houses in Bargalino.

Nelyaty (Неляты) is on the eastern bank of the Vitim. There is a bad dirt road that connects the town to Kuanda. Nelyaty does not have telephones but the town can be contacted via a radio telephone from Taksimo at 15.00 daily. Like the inhabitants of Muya, the main occupation in Nelyaty is hunting, notably for squirrels, sables, hares, foxes, otters, and occasionally for goats and bears.

### SHIVERY (Шиверы) 1,548km

Between Taksimo and Shivery you pass over the 560m-long Vitim river bridge. This is a popular fishing spot and there is a small village on the western bank. The actual stop of Shivery is about 1km from the bridge. Beside the new bridge is an older one, which was built quickly in order to meet the official opening date of the BAM in 1984. The river is the border between the Republic of Buryatiya and the Amur Oblast. The border

❑ **The ranger**

Siberia has been a destination of forced exile for centuries and it is rare to find someone who is happy to live in self-exile. However, the Parama park ranger and his wife, Petr Ivanovich Saukov and Roza Alexandrovna, are happy on their own. Petr, born in 1924, worked for decades in Moscow as a nuclear physicist and once he retired, sought a place of quiet reflection. He chose the area at the junction of the Parama and Vitim Rivers which was the site of Ust-Paramsk village (Усть-Парамск). Today nothing remains of the town except the Saukovs' house.

The local logging collective, Muyaski Leskhoz (Муяский Лесхоз), pays him a small wage, which supplements his pension, to observe what and who travels past the junction. He reports any suspicious activity via radio to Ust-Muya and Taksimo.

Meeting Petr and Roza is invaluable, not only for their local knowledge but also to gain an insight into the life of isolated Russians. They are proud to show off their self-built house with its enormous larder full of preserved fruits and vegetables, underground cellar kept cool in the summer months by ice cut from the Vitim River in winter, and their garden with the traditional vegetables plus the more exotic vegetables such as kholrabi, swedes and capsicums. If you are lucky enough to be invited to lunch, you will eat in the outdoor kitchen which is the traditional eating place for rural Russians. Few locals now maintain this tradition but the experience of eating freshly caught fish, pickled vegetables and baked bread in the wooden-floored open kitchen while overlooking the river is truly memorable. They also have a small detached cottage of four beds and you may stay here if your trip is organised in advance.

also designates a time-zone change. In Buryatiya the time difference is five hours later than in Moscow while in Amur Oblast it is six hours.

## ⊠ GORBACHEVSKAYA (Горбачевская) 1,576km

This stop is not named after Mikhail Gorbachev, but after the Decembrist, Ivan Ivanovich Gorbachevski (1800-69). The revolutionary Gorbachevski came from the Ukrainian nobility and inherited a small estate upon the death of his mother. However, he refused it and gave it to the peasants for their use, completely and without compensation. At the end of 1823 he was accepted into the Society of United Slavs. He soon became one of its most active figures and carried on revolutionary propaganda among soldiers and officers. An advocate of executing the royal family, Gorbachevski counted himself among those who would make an attempt on the life of Alexander I. During the uprising of the Chernigov Regiment in 1825, he tried to rouse the neighbouring military units and was arrested. In 1826 he was sentenced hard labour for life, which he served in the Siberian cities of Chita and Petrovski Zabaikalski, which is where he died. He wrote a book, *Memoirs*, which is a valuable source for studying the history of the Decembrists.

## 🏠 KUANDA (Куанда) 1,577km

Kuanda is famous in Soviet propaganda as it was here in September 1984 that the celebration of the BAM's completion was held. The actual golden spike joining the east and west sections of the BAM was hammered in about 15km to the east at Balbukhta (Балбухта) but as there were no facilities there, the celebration was moved to Kuanda.

In anticipation of the completion ceremony, Kuanda was built as a model town. Interestingly, Western media were not invited to the opening, which, in retrospect, was an error of judgement. For, although the BAM was not as complete as claimed, the exclusion meant that the project is not well-known in the West despite being one of the 20th century's greatest engineering achievements.

Walking down the main street of Kuanda provides a fascinating insight into the minds of the Soviet elite and how they wished their towns to look. The main street consists of attractive two-storey wooden houses with each pair of houses having a shared wall. Around each house is a medium-sized garden and a picket fence facing the tarred street. Most unusually, there are a number of benches along the side of the road where locals sit and talk. There are even raised roadside garbage collection platforms, which is a godsend. In most towns that still have garbage services (many Russian towns have cut this service to save money), the garbage truck honks its horn when it stops to accept rubbish. Locals are expected to bring out their garbage and throw it into the back of the truck. As most Russian garbage trucks are tip trucks, throwing rubbish high enough is difficult for many people. Occasionally the truck driver and his assistant will help but most of the time they just sit in their cabs. The raised platforms in Kuanda allow people to stand at a level from which it is easy to tip rubbish in.

However, as soon as you walk off the main street, you see the reality of a Russian town. In this sense Kuanda is the same as the other BAM towns with its potholed roads, rotting rubbish piles, concrete apartment blocks, perpetually half-built buildings and a general perception of a community lacking pride. As in other towns, strolling a little further away will bring you to the temporary settlement built for the builders of Kuanda.

The Uzbek Young Communist Party sponsored Kuanda and you can see Uzbek influence in some of the town's houses, the railway station and in the excellent internal courtyard of the hotel. However, it is not the buildings that attract travellers but the region's excellent outdoor activities including mountaineering, trekking, fishing, and animal and birdwatching.

### Getting there and away

There is a Moscow–Tynda train (via Kazan) every other day and a Kislovodsk–Tynda train twice a week and some local trains. The closest airport is at Novaya Chara.

## Where to stay

There are two hotels in town. The ***Locomotive Brigade Hotel*** (☎ 2-51), (Дом отдыха Локомотивной бригады) has 40 basic rooms and charges about $5 per person per night. You will be impressed with the internal courtyard with its fountains but unfortunately the rooms are not up to the same standard.

The second, ***NGCh Hotel*** (☎ 241), (Гостиница НГЧ-3), is virtually next door to the Locomotive Brigade Hotel and consists of a floor of a multi-storey building. It costs the same as the other hotel for Russians but foreigners have to pay three times the price.

## Where to eat

The only *canteen* is in the Locomotive Brigade Hotel. It is managed by Alexandrovna Lubov who will proudly show you her book of foreign recipes. If you give her advance warning of your visit she will try to cook your national dish according to this book, which will be a challenge considering the lack of ingredients. She is also pleased to learn new recipes so if you are vegetarian you can work together on preparing a feast.

## Getting assistance

The BAM Turist Centre for Children (Дорожная станция юник туристов БАМ) provides outdoor activities such as camping, skiing, rafting and mountaineering trips, survival classes and physical fitness camps during school holidays. The Centre has established a permanent camp-site near the Kodar volcanoes where groups stay for up to 18 days with as many as 30 in a group. During the school year, the Centre co-ordinates a range of classes along the BAM such as navigation and photography. Foreign school and sports groups are welcome to use the facilities of the Centre.

The Centre can also provide guides and camping equipment. Director Viktor Stepanovich Ryzhi is writing a book on mountain climbing in the region and guides and advises serious mountain-climbers. Contact BAM Turist Centre for Children, 675161 Kalarski Raion, Station Kuanda, ul. Marta 8, kv 1-4, (☎ 4-41) (674161 Каларский район, ст. Куанда, ул. Марта 8, кв 1-4, Дорожная станция юник туристов БАМ, Виктор Степанович Рыжий).

## What to see

About the only noteworthy thing to see in town is the sculpture on the station's platform. It symbolises the joining of the BAM and consists of two giant pillars with one connecting rail on which 'Kuanda' is etched. From the outer sides of each pillar protrude dozens of rails with names of other BAM stations etched on them.

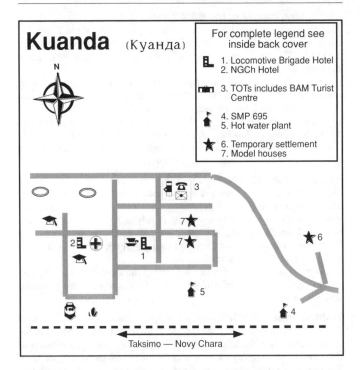

# Kuanda (Куанда)

For complete legend see inside back cover

1. Locomotive Brigade Hotel
2. NGCh Hotel

3. TOTs includes BAM Turist Centre

4. SMP 695
5. Hot water plant

6. Temporary settlement
7. Model houses

N

3

7

2 1

7

6

5

1

4

Taksimo — Novy Chara

Fishing is described below. Rafting on the Vitim and the Parama rapids was described under Taksimo (see pp112-14). Walking to the Marble Canyon Gulag is described on pp128-30. Mountain and glacier climbing in the Kodar range is described on p121.

There are a number of extinct volcanoes to explore about 70km south of Lake Leprindo. The only way to get there is by helicopter, or a minimum of three days' boating and walking to get to the closest volcano and eight days to the largest one. The area is stunning with water courses flowing down lava tubes and the craters are very distinct due to the lack of erosion. Aku volcano is the largest with an 800m-diameter crater, while Chepe, which means 'gap' in Sakhan, is 750m high and has a 150m-deep crater. Other volcanoes include the Syni and Gora-Zarod.

You can make a day trip motor boating or driving up the Kuanda river to its source which is a small hot water spring. In winter, it is beautiful with clouds of steam rising above the snow but in summer it is dull.

## The fishing capital of the BAM Zone

Kuanda is often referred to as the fishing capital of the BAM Zone. The town is surrounded by over 30 large lakes including the beautiful Lake Leprindo. These contain several unique fish as well as rare ones such as the carnivorous taimen.

Since the collapse of the Russian economy and the exodus of many people from the country to the city, fish stocks have actually increased in Siberian waterways. Several years ago, the vast majority of fish were sold to Kuanda's Co-operative PEPO for sale in the rest of Russia. However, PEPO has since collapsed and today little fish is exported outside the region. In addition, the scaling down of industrial enterprises has resulted in less environmentally damaging pollution.

**Types of fish**  Locally available fish include the large taimen, karas, shchuka, som, omul, elits, nolim and soroga. In addition there is the unique targun (таргун) which is tastier than the omul. Targun normally grow up to 20cm long and from about 20 July to 10 September they start to move down the Kuanda river to the Vitim. Special drag-nets are used to catch them. You do not cook them but simply sprinkle salt on them and in about 30 minutes they are ready to eat.

Permission is not needed to catch any of the local fish providing you do not catch over 50kg of fish with a net. However, there are particular seasons for each fish.

**Fishing trips**  Day fishing-trip options include taking the train to Shivery and fishing on the banks of the Vitim river, or going by car to the Kuanda river. It is recommended that serious fishermen go upstream of the Vitim river bridge by motorboat or by motorboat along Kuanda river. For those who want to be guaranteed to catch a taimen, which grow up to 2m and weigh 80kg, you need to travel 160km up the Vitim to the Tsipa river, then travel another 160km to just below the first set of rapids. The actual travelling will take three days upstream and two days downstream.

Even if you are not interested in fishing, the trip up the Vitim and Tsipa is still worthwhile as you will inevitably see many animals including bears, wild goats and deer.

**Finding a good fishing guide**  Despite the fact that most Siberians fish, it is difficult to find a truly knowledgeable fisherman who can take you to proven fishing spots for a range of fish. The best guides are members of the Fisherman's Union, which is a group of professional and fanatical fishermen. The Union is very small with just three members in Kuanda, four in Nelyaty and five in Chara. Most have several prepared camps which maximises your fishing time. Contact Ivan Innokentevich Byankin, who will put you in touch with other members of the union, at

674161 Kuanda, ul. Druzhba Narodov 8, ☎ 4-45 (Rail) (674161 Каларский район, ст. Куанда, ул. Дружба Народов, 8, Иван Иннокентьевич Бянкин).

To give fishermen some idea of the cost, Ivan Innokentevich priced a three-day fishing trip at $170 which includes $30 a day for a fisherman guide, $20 for renting the boat and motor, and $20 a day for fuel.

## Mountain and glacier climbing in the Kodar Mountain range

The 200km-long Kodar Mountain Range is one of the natural and historical highlights of the BAM Zone. For those interested in the dark side of Soviet history, one of the country's best preserved gulag camps, called Marble Canyon, is in this range. For the adventurer, the range also contains some of the most difficult to climb mountains and glaciers in Russia. The Marble Canyon camp is described under Novaya Chara.

The highest peak in the range is Mount BAM at 3,072m with the nearby town of Novaya Chara just 700m above sea level. Up to 1,500m on the northern slopes and 1,700m on the southern are deciduous forest and stunted birch trees. This gradually gives way to thickets of Japanese stone pines and scraggy birches as you approach the tree line. Above this are barren alpine summits and mountain tundra.

To the south of the Kodar mountains is the Chara Valley which is the coldest in the region. Its January temperatures can go as low as -49°C. A temperature inversion ensures that the air remains cold despite the cloudless sky and lack of wind. This results in a strange atmospheric condition in which the higher you go, the warmer it gets. For example, when you set off for a mountaineering trip it may be -40°C in Novaya Chara, but only -25°C at the top of Mount BAM.

The main climbing mountains are around Chara. Some are exceptionally hard to climb, reflected in names such as Fang and Tower and their difficulty attracted the 1989, 1990 and 1991 USSR Mountaineering Championships. Foreign groups have also climbed them in the past. As well as being difficult, their attraction for alpinists is that they are easy to get to, being only about 25km from Novaya Chara station or airport.

There are at least 40 glaciers in the region and new ones are being found every few years. Their total area is 15 square kilometres and they include stationary mountain glaciers and valley glaciers moving at between three and six metres a year.

The main climbing period is from 1 June to 15 September. Snow climbing is also possible from 1 February to 31 March and in November but it is not recommended outside these times.

The best place to obtain information about the routes is from Viktor Stepanovich Ryzhi, who runs the BAM Turist Centre for Children (see pp118-119).

❏ **A Siberian fishing tale**
Fishermen around the world like to tell stories of the giant fish that got away but in this tale it didn't. 'Back in 1985, I was fishing on the Chara River, about 30km from Old Chara. I pulled out my net one morning to discover a hole torn in it. Knowing that this was done by a big taimen, I returned that evening with a stronger net. Again in the morning, the net had a hole in it so again I had to go back home and get my largest net. The next morning it also had a rip in it! So I went back to the village and asked my neighbour for his strongest net. That evening I waited in my boat beside the net and when I saw that something was tangled in the net, I picked up my axe and tried to bash it. Unfortunately the thrashing of the taimen nearly overturned my boat and while I was preventing myself from being thrown out, I lost my axe. However I was able to drag the entangled taimen into my boat after an hour and rode it like a bucking horse, stabbing it with a knife as it thrashed around the half-submerged boat. It weighed 90kg and was 2.2m long! From just its head, I made two pails of fish soup!' – Mikhail Stepanovich, father of the Fisherman's Union member, Ivan Innokentevich Byankin. A more popular way of subduing a taimen is to shoot it when it gets tangled in the net.

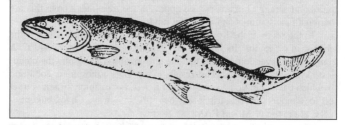

If you are intending to climb to the top of a mountain, remember the Russian practice of swapping the letter left on the summit with one of yours. These letters each contain two parts. The first you send to the person who left it there and the second you send to the national association of Russian mountain-climbers as proof that you made it.

## ⊠ BALBUKHTA (Балбухта) 1,615km

From Kuanda, the railroad labours up the Syulban river (р. Сюльбан).

The Balbukhta railway siding is the spot where on 24 September 1984 the golden spike joining the eastern and western sections of the BAM was hammered in. There is a monument of sleepers and rails built in an A-shape about 400m to the left and east of the station. The left side of the 'A' lists the names of stations from Ust-Kut to Balbukhta while the right side lists them from Tynda.

There are gold deposits nearby which will eventually be developed.

The train squeals around a tight S-bend to gain height.

❏ **Camping out when it is -50°C**

For Russian fishing enthusiasts, the season is not important. Winter fishing involves drilling a hole in the ice and building a tent over it. Sleeping bags are obviously very important. Above -15°C, bird feather bags known as *pukhovy spalni meshok* (пуховый спальный мешок) are okay, however below -5°C, the 15kg camel skin bags known as *verblyuzhi spalni meshok* (верблюжий спальный мешок) are essential. When sleeping out in the middle of winter, most fishermen use the fire and tent arrangement illustrated. The fire in this configuration will last all night and the open tent prevents condensation while providing reflected heat. This sort of heat is much better than direct heat as a larger expanse is heated, allowing several people to benefit from the one fire.

**Key**
1. Roof support
2. Reflecting sheet
3. Side sheets to stop wind.
4. Log to protect your feet from direct heat.
5. Three-log fire which will burn all night.

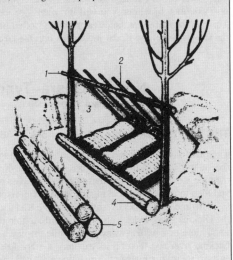

⊠ **KODAR (Кодар) 1,664km**

This stop consists of a small station that provides the guard for the 1.94km Kodar Tunnel (Кодарский тоннель). This tunnel goes through the Kodar mountains and separates the Lake Leprindo district from the Chara plains. The roof collapsed during the early stages of the tunnelling killing a worker. These revealed inadequate geological surveys and, after several months of frenzied research, work resumed and the tunnel was completed on time.

The remains of the Kodar gulag camp are about 10km from this station and the camp is described under Novaya Chara.

### ⊠ LEPRINDO (Леприндо) 1,683km

Emerging from the tunnel you see to your left the beautiful 12km-long Small Leprindo Lake (Озеро Малое Леприндо) and a few miles later you pass over a small bridge and to your right is the 22km-long Big Leprindo Lake (Озеро Большое Леприндо). Behind them are 2,900m peaks.

The lakes are popular fishing spots and the train will usually stop somewhere along this stretch to let fishermen on and off. The lakes are well-stocked with *sik*, *rolets*, *karus* and a unique red meat fish called the *kholetsk dovachan* (холец довачан). In addition, the lakes contain a unique variety of edible waternut called the *chilim* or *ro-gulnik* (чилим, ро-гульник). In winter, you will invariably see ice fishing on the lakes. This is a beautiful area and waterfalls can often be seen tumbling down the steep sides of the Kodar mountains into the lakes.


# Novaya Chara–Tynda
## Новая Чара–Тында

### THE ROUTE (see Route Maps 2 and 3, pp367-8)

The line follows the Chara valley for 50km, edging up the south wall of the valley. Then, as the Chara turns north through the Kodar mountains, the train works its way up a narrow creek to a pass over the Udokan range and then to a shelf overlooking the deep Khani river valley.

The line then works its way down to the Khani and to its junction with the Olekma. The Olekma also heads north, to join the Chara and then the Lena more than 400km away. Meanwhile the line heads south-east up the Olekma river and then up its tributary the Nyukzha. It continues south-east over a rolling plateau to come down a small creek to the railroad and road junction of Tynda. The time is Moscow time +6 hours.

### 🚂 NOVAYA CHARA (Новая Чара) 1,734km

Novaya Chara is the administrative capital of the Kalarski Raion (Каларский район) and has a population of about 15,000. It was founded as a major BAM station and the vast majority of its citizens work for the railway. The handsome railway station with aluminium cathedral roof was sponsored by Kazakhstan.

The original village of Chara, also known as Staraya Chara (Старая Чара), is 18km away to the north on the Chara river. The 851km long Chara river originates on the southern slopes of the Kodar Range, and flows along the Chara Depression before emptying into the Olekma river. It is navigable from the Olekma river 416km upstream. It is fed by rain, snow, glaciers and subterranean sources. High water is from May to September. The Chara freezes over in October and the ice breaks up in May.

The Chara valley lies between the Kodar mountains on the north-west and the Udokan mountains on the south-east.

In 1998 work started on a 70-km railway line from Novaya Chara to the Chineiski ore deposit, which contains some of the world's richest vanadium ores, plus iron and titanium.

Local attractions include the Kodar mountains, the Marble Canyon Gulag, the mysterious Chara Sand Dunes and the BAM museum.

## Getting there and away
There is a Moscow–Tynda train (via Kazan) every other day and a Kislovodsk–Tynda train twice a week. There is one local train per day west to Severobaikalsk and one east to Tynda.

There are daily flights to Chita. The airport is about 1km north of Old Chara. There are buses three times a day between Novaya Chara (stopping at the station), Staraya Chara and the airport.

## Where to stay
The only place to stay in town is *Hotel Kodar* (☎ 4-65), (Гостиница «Кодар») opposite the station. It is a cheerful busy hotel with mountain views. It is basic but has a hairdresser and café on the ground floor. Foreigners are charged $20 a night.

## Where to eat
The best choice is the station's upstairs *canteen*. The hotel also has a *café*.

## What to see
Within town the only place of interest is the BAM museum. Its focus is, of course, on the heroic building of the BAM, including a golden spike and a golden rail anchor from the ceremony completing the BAM. It also has a collection on the indigenous people and the early years of collectivisation, archaeological finds from the Chara Sand Dunes, memorabilia from the gulag camps, and photographs of a recent exploration of the Marble Canyon gulag.

It is open every day except Monday from 10.00-17.00, lunch break from 13.00-14.00. Director V Astrakhantseva-Nadelyaeva, BAM Museum, PO Box 51, 674159, Novaya Chara, ☎ 3-89, (674159 Новая Чара, А-Я 51, Музей, Дириктор В. Астраханцева-Наделяева).

You may also come across someone selling a lilac-coloured rock with black streaks in it called *charoit*. This semi-precious gemstone is found only in the Chara Valley and Muya Mountain Range.

For those botanically inclined, a five-minute walk to the east along the BAM will bring you to a clump of Chozeniya trees. These trees are restricted to Lake Baikal with this one exception. How they got here and survive is still a mystery. From here and from the train, you can see two 200m-high hillocks to the north which the locals laughingly call *babagrud* (бабагрудь), meaning 'breasts', for obvious reasons.

## EXCURSIONS IN THE REGION

### Staraya Chara (Старая Чара)

Despite its name meaning Old Chara, Staraya Chara is relatively young. It was founded in 1933 when the Soviet government's collectivisation policy forced the migrating Evenk to settle down to grow vegetables and raise livestock. As well as bringing the indigenous people under state control, this enabled teachers to instigate a successful literacy programme, which was a major state objective in the late 1920s and 1930s. Unfortunately the collectivisation was not a success as agriculture is unsuitable in most of the Chara basin which is affected by summer frosts and has large tracts of waterlogged land. Of the six original collective farms, the only remaining one is the Charski Sovkhoz which consists of 1,200 dairy cows and is 10km north of Staraya Chara. About 300 of the town's population of just 3,000 are Evenk. There is an Evenk museum.

While you can walk the 18km between Novaya Chara and Staraya Chara, a more comfortable trip is on the bus three times a day between Novaya Chara (stopping at the station), Staraya Chara and the airport. The trip takes 20 minutes.

---

❏ **Kodar and Udokan and the treasure**

The Soviet propaganda machine was always searching for stories to demonstrate the successes of communism to the proletariat and it hit a winner when it enlisted an ancient Evenk (indigenous people) legend to glorify the Soviet discovery of the giant Udokan mineral deposit. The Evenk legend tells the tale of two giants, Kodar and Udokan, who were wandering through the region when they stumbled across a fabulous treasure. Despite being great friends, greed made them quarrel. They decided the only way to determine who owned the treasure was through trial by arms. So they both drew their bows and each fired a deadly accurate arrow simultaneously. Where both giants fell, high mountains rose to hide the valuable cache from low-life bandits and treasure seekers.

The treasure remained hidden until 1948 when the Soviet geologist Yelizaveta Burova and her team of 'dedicated, communist, and self-sacrificing' Moscow geologists discovered it. The implication was that these people, backed by the Soviet Union's technology and scientific methodology, were morally worthy when all else had failed.

Information on the discovery can be seen in Novaya Chara's BAM museum. Incidentally, Yelizaveta Burova was killed nearby in a flying-boat crash on the Vitim river.

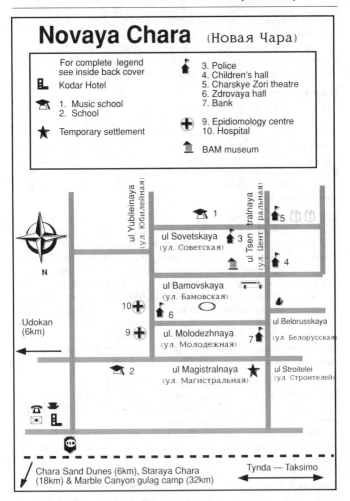

# Novaya Chara (Новая Чара)

For complete legend
see inside back cover

**L** Kodar Hotel

1. Music school
2. School

★ Temporary settlement

3. Police
4. Children's hall
5. Charskye Zori theatre
6. Zdrovaya hall
7. Bank

9. Epidiomology centre
10. Hospital

BAM museum

ul Yubileinaya (ул. юбилейная)

ul Sovetskaya (ул. Советская)

ul Bamovskaya (ул. Бамовская)

ul. Molodezhnaya (ул. Молодежная)

ul Magistralnaya (ул. Магистральная)

ul Tsentralnaya (ул. Центральная)

ul Belorusskaya (ул. Белорусская)

ul Stroitelei (ул. Строителей)

Udokan (6km)

N

Chara Sand Dunes (6km), Staraya Chara
(18km) & Marble Canyon gulag camp (32km)

Tynda — Taksimo

## Chara sand dunes (Чарские пески)

An enjoyable half-day trip is to the Sahara-like 6km-long Chara sand
dunes. How these dunes were created in the midst of 600m thick permafrost is still a mystery. The dunes were an important site for the indigenous people as a large number of stone arrows, axes, and daily utensils

from past millennia have been found there. These are on display in St
Petersburg's Russian Museum of Ethnology and Novaya Chara's museum. The dunes are about 4km south-west of Staraya Chara and 6km north-
west of Novaya Chara. You can see the dunes from the train on the north
side as you approach Novaya Chara from the west.

## Udokan copper mines
One of the main justifications for building the BAM was access to the
nearby massive 1.2 billion-tonne Udokan copper-ore deposit. This
makes it one of the largest copper deposits in the world. After several
decades of setbacks, economic downturns and procrastination, work on
the $100 million, 70km line finally started in October 1998. The line
will also go to the nearby Chineiski deposit which contains some of the
world's richest vanadium ores. Vanadium is used to make heavy-duty,
cold-resistant rails.

## Lake Zapod day hike
A scenic lake with a great view of the mountains is located to the north-
west of Staraya Chara. Lake Zapod (Озеро Запод) also known as Lake
Otkatkyel (озеро Откаткёль) is about 30km from Novaya Chara. Its
name, meaning 'stack of hay', describes the view of the nearby mountain
of the same name. If you climb to the top of the mountain you will be
rewarded by an awe inspiring view of the Kodar mountains which look as
if they have risen sheer out of the ground. Before descending to the lake,
have a look around for a freaky rock pillar that has a distinctive male pro-
file. The easiest way to get to the lake is by road to the indigenous village
called Kyust-Kemda (Кюсть-Кемда) to the north of Staraya Chara, and
then walking the last 6km.

## Marble Canyon Gulag (Мраморное ущелье ГУЛаг)
This camp is probably the best-preserved Stalin-era prisoner camp in
Eastern Siberia. It lies at the end of a magnificent hike, but is a sad and
sinister destination for slave labourers.

The camp operated from 1949 to 1951 and was the biggest of the 10
camps in the Kodar mountains that mined uranium for the Soviet atomic-
bomb project. The camp and mine are real, but it is doubtful if it was anything but a 'Potemkin' or mock source of uranium, since there is no feasible way to bring uranium ore out to be processed. The guards' buildings
and towers are extremely well preserved. You will notice that there are no
prisoner barracks. This was because prisoners slept in canvas tents, as
wood was in short supply, as it had to be carried up the mountains. There
are also slag heaps and one accessible tunnel. In the tunnel there are res-
pirators which were discarded when the camp was closed. The background radiation is now no higher than normal but as a precaution you

should not enter the mine without a mask nor camp on top of the slag heaps. At the top of the canyon there are two graves. One is for an engineer N Azarovoi and another for a prison guard (a friend of the guard campaigned to have this home-made memorial erected).

There are many rumours about the size of the camps with estimates ranging up to 10,000. However, the opening of Moscow's archives has revealed that the number was probably closer to 2,000. The one fact that no-one knows is the number of deaths. The records do not indicate this and, as yet, no cemetery has been discovered.

**Getting there**  There are three main options to reach the gulag. It is advisable to get a copy of the map of the Kodar mountains around Chara including the Marble Canyon camp before embarking on any of these routes.

## Option 1: Walking from Staraya Chara

**Day 1**  Travel from Staraya Chara to the winter hut (зимовье) which is the start of the glacier-gouged Sredni Sakukan river valley (р. Средный Сакукан). Make sure you stay north of the river so you do not have to cross it later on.

**Day 2**  Walk to a the collapsed hut (развалины) halfway up the valley.

**Day 3**: Walk to the creek opposite Marble Canyon, which is a side canyon on the west side. There is a collapsed hut here.

**Day 4**: Climb the very steep lip of Marble Canyon. Some way up the canyon you will find a cluster of comfortable buildings. This is not the gulag but was built about 20 years ago by Irkutsk University climatology students. Continue up the canyon almost to its head; you will find the fences, towers and shafts of the gulag. After lunch walk out of the canyon up the valley until you reach the meteorological station.

**Day 5**  Based at the meteorological station, you can make an easy day return trip to Mount BAM. You walk through the mountain pass called Three Policemen (перевал Три жандарма) which is between two glaciers. From here it is a 1km climb to the base of Mount BAM and back. You have to walk over a glacier but as it is gently sloping, you do not need special equipment. The view of Mount BAM is spectacular.

**Day 6**  The hardest day. Walk down the valley towards Marble Canyon but before you reach it, turn left down the Baltiski river (р. Балтийский). Walk up the creek to the easy Baltiski pass (перевал Балтийский) and down the other side to the Byurokan river (р. Бюрокан).

**Day 7**  Walk down the Byurokan to its junction with the Verkhni Sakukan (р. Верхний Сакукан). You can make a day trip from here to the small Verkhni Sakukan Gulag camp.

**Day 8**  Cross the Verkhni Sakukan river, which is easily waded, to the BAM stop of Sakukan (Сакукан). Catch the train back to Novaya Chara.

## Option 2: Helicopter from Staraya Chara

**Day 1**  Fly by helicopter from Staraya Chara to the meteorological station. This is a 30-minute trip. Walk to the entrance of Marble Canyon to inspect the graves. Return to the meteorological station and stay overnight.

**Day 2**  Fly by helicopter to the gulag camp. In the evening return to Staraya Chara.

Some helicopter pilots will fly up Marble Canyon all the way to the gulag, then turn and return. This trip (though we have made it and survived) appears to leave little margin for safety, since the head of the canyon is barely 50m across.

## Option 3: Quick but economical visit from Staraya Chara

**Day 1**  Travel by tracked vehicle (like a tank but no gun and used for exploration work) halfway up the Sredni Sakukan river valley. Walk from here to the meteorological station, which is a five-hour hike.

**Day 2**  Walk to the Marble Canyon and return to the meteorological station.

**Day 3**  Return by foot to the base of the Sredni Sakukan river valley.

**Day 4**  Return by foot to Staraya Chara.

**Notes**  The bridge that crossed the Sredni Sakukan river in front of the Marble Canyon collapsed in 1992. To cross the river you may be able to walk across its remnants or walk up the valley to a narrower crossing point. It is worth finding out the water level before you depart from Novaya Chara for you may need inflatable rafts to cross the river after heavy rains.

It may be possible to travel the 20km to the base of the Sredni Sakukan river valley in a 4WD vehicle depending upon the weather.

The Sredni Sakukan river valley route is accessible from June to December but snow starts to fall in September. The route is totally impassable in April and May due to heavy snow falls.

A gun should always be carried because of bears, particularly just after they have risen from hibernation.

The cost of hiring a helicopter for a round trip over two days will be at least $1,000, hiring a vehicle to the base of the Sredni Sakukan river valley at least $50, and the daily cost of a guide at least $30.

Only attempt these trips with a guide who has been there before.

## Verkhni Sakukan Gulag (Верхний Сакукан ГУЛаг)

Verkhni Sakukan Gulag operated for only one year until it was decided that the uranium ore at Marble Canyon was a better prospect. It is near the junction of the Byurokan river and the Verkhni Sakukan river. Make your camp near the river junction and make a day return trip to the gulag, which is about 2km away and 600m up the mountains. To get to the river junction, you go by train to the Sakukan BAM stop and walk on a rough track for about 20km alongside the Verkhni Sakukan river. A minimum of three days is required for this trip.

## Kodar Station Gulag

This gulag does not appear to have a proper name so it has been called the Kodar Station Gulag, as it is about 10km from the station. This gulag is the smallest of the three camps and consists of two tunnels, two shafts and a few collapsed wooden buildings. It was only a small exploratory camp and does not even have a barbed wire fence around it. Getting there involves going on a dirt road to an Evenk reindeer herding camp. This is an interesting place to have lunch if it can be organised. About 3km away is the camp, in the valley near the junction of the Khadatkand and Syulban rivers (р. Хадатканд и Сюльбан). The background radiation is higher here than at the other camps so don't go into the tunnels without a respirator.

It is best to visit the camp in winter or late summer as rain turns the road to the Evenk camp into a quagmire. While the trip can be made in one day, it would be better to spend the night at the Evenk camp.

## KEMEN (Кемен) 1,755km

Near this station is the deepest permafrost on the BAM. Here the soil is frozen down to a depth of 600m.

About 5km to the west of this stop are the hot springs at Luktur (Луктур). The springs are near the railway line and can also be reached by the road from Novaya Chara, which runs beside the railway. A small lodge is being built here by Novaya Chara's SMP 577 construction group. The water gurgles out of the ground at 60°C so you need to fill up the bath tubs and wait for them to cool before getting in.

## IKABYA (Икабья) 1,772km

Ikabya was sponsored by the Georgian Komsomol Youth Organisation on the Bolshoi Ikabya river (р. Большой Икабья). The handsome two-storey station is faced with mixed marbles.

About 10km to the east is the Evenk village of Chapo-ologo (Чапо-олого). The village has about 250 Evenks and they manage a polar fox farm. Twenty kilometres from the village are famous hot springs on the shore of the Arbakhalir river (р. Арбахалир) but you can only reach them by the river or frozen winter river road. They are known as Charski Iztochnik (Чарский Источник). You can see Chapo-ologo on the banks of the snaking Bolshoi Ikabya river north of the train as you leave Ikabya. A short distance further on, you cross over the eight span bridge across the Ikabya river which is one of the longest bridges on the BAM's central section.

Leaving Ikabya, you start your ascent of the Udokan Range. The railroad creeps up the foothills, leaving meadows and settlements below and revealing the peaks and the entrance of the Chara river canyon across the valley. Then the railroad turns up a creek through more and more wild and scrubby forest. The train labours up long slow ascents, sometimes taking a hairpin to gain height.

## OLONGGO (Олонгго) 1,851km

Between Olonggo and Khani is the highest point along the BAM railway, 1,310m above sea level. The point is marked by a 2m long and 2m high white monument of a giant rail on the right. It also marks the triple border between the Republic of Sakha (Yakutiya), Amurskaya Oblast and Chitinskaya Oblast. The intersection is along the Khani Valley, which the train now drops down into.

The railroad breaks over a high shelf over a huge valley of the Khani river below. Look ahead on the right at the bright pool in the river and the scar of the railroad going around it, and behind at the deep valley where the river rises. The train descends the scarp gradually, sometimes with scoops up a creek to lose height. Soon the walls close in and the river foams over rough gravel. Ahead is the Stanovoi Range, which extends for 700km, with large coalbeds along its entire length. At the north-east end of the range is Neryungri, site of one of the world's largest coal mines. (This town is described in The AYaM: Tynda–Neryungri–Aldan–Yakutsk, p266-71.)

## KHANI (Хани) 1,879km

Khani is the only BAM town in the Republic of Sakha (Yakutiya), although it is hardly linked to the rest of Sakha. Unlike the rest of Sakha, you do not need a visa to stop here. It is situated in a picturesque valley with snow-capped peaks surrounding it. Khani is also called Luninskaya (Лунинская) after Decembrist Mikhail Sergeevich Lunin (Михаил Сергеевич Лунин), 1787-1845, portrayed on a plaque in the station as a dashing young Guards officer. Trains normally stop here for between five and 40 minutes while the locomotives are changed. In this time, you can quickly run around town.

The police station and post office are both at the station. The only accommodation is the ***Locomotive Brigade Hostel*** (☎ 2-87, Дом отдыха Локомотивной бригады), two blocks up the main street.

Outside town, the only noteworthy place to visit is a geologist's tunnel 6km east of the station that was dug to get information on the region's geology before the BAM was built.

Goods are sometimes carted from Khani by a 199km road to the northern geological exploratory town of Torgo (Торго). Torgo is in the centre of a massive iron ore deposit.

## 🏚 OLEKMA (Олёкма) 1,934km

Olekma is named after the Olekma river, but the station is about 35km from the river. When the BAM was being constructed, barges were towed up the 1,435km-long river from the Lena river to a landing on the Olekma and carted overland to the station. From Olekma to Larba, the BAM climbs the Olekma river and then the Nyukzha. This route is scenic and passes what in Russian is called rock rivers. These are the remains of rock slides with the dirt washed away. The boulders can be up to 2m across and the rivers can be up to 500m wide.

## ⊠ IMANGRAKAN (Имангракан) 1,976km

Imangrakan is at the junction of the Imangra and Olekma rivers.

## 🏚 TAS-YURYAKH (Тас-Юрях) 2,008km

Tas-Yuryakh is at the junction of the Tas-Yuryakh and Olekma rivers. Between Tas-Yuryakh and Yuktali stations you pass over the Olekma river. About 5km further on, you see a small town at the junction of the Yuktali and Olekma rivers. This is the indigenous village of Ust-Nyukzha (Усть-Нюкжа) described under Yuktali.

## 🏚 YUKTALI (Юктали) 2,028km

Yuktali is a small BAM town that has a *Locomotive Brigade Hostel* (☎ 3-38), (Дом отдыха Локомотивной бригады). This is a good place to stay so that you can visit Ust-Nyukzha without rushing. Ust-Nyukzha is an ancient town and has an excellent ethnographical museum and a *sovkhoz* reindeer-breeding farm; it is frequently visited by Russian groups. BAM Kino Studios has made several films on the community.

After Yuktali, you cross the river twice, and turn up the Nyukzha river. The train rides for several hours up the valley on the right bank, great serpents of flat clear river over gravel, between 1,600m peaks. There are no roads, no farms and nobody on the river.

## ⊠ TALUMA (Талума) 2,042km

At this halt a rough roadway takes off across the Stanovoi plateau towards Chulman (Чульман).

## 🏚 CHILCHI (Чильчи) 2,137km

The town is named after the Chilchi river, which is an Evenk name. The town has a *Locomotive Brigade Hostel*, (☎ 2-74), (Дом отдыха Локомотивной бригады).

## 🚉 LOPCHA (Лопча) 2,185km

Lopcha is a timber town with a Russian forestry camp and North Korean sawmill. Interestingly, the town once had a Russian club which studied the Juche philosophy developed by the now dead Great Leader and President Kim Il Sung of the Democratic Peoples Republic of Korea (DPRK), commonly known as North Korea. These clubs exist all over the world and are normally written off as left-wing loony groups.

So what is Juche? According to *A Sightseeing Guide to Korea*, published in the DPRK in 1991, 'In a nutshell, the Juche idea means that the masters of the revolution and construction are the masses of the people and that they are also the motive force of the revolution and construction. In other words, one is responsible for one's own destiny and one also has the capacity to shape one's own destiny. The Juche idea is the guiding idea of the Korean revolution evolved by President Kim Il Sung. The Workers' Party of Korea and the Government of the Republic lead the revolution and construction, guided by the Juche idea.' Impressive!

## 🚉 LARBA (Ларба) 2,232km

Gold is mined here. About 30km upstream on the Nyukzha river is the tributary Urkima river. This is the location of a remote Evenk village called Ust-Urkima (Усть-Уркима). The railway heads east on the Larba creek and crosses a rolling plateau, the divide between the Lena river and the Amur river watersheds.

## 🚉 KHOROGOCHI (Хорогочи) 2,284km

The town has a ***Locomotive Brigade Hostel*** ☎ 2-31, (Дом отдыха Локомотивной бригады). The railway descends toward Tynda along the Getkan (Геткан) creek.

## 🚉 KUVYKTA (Кувыкта) 2,334km

There is a reasonable quality road running from here to Tynda. The famous Moldovan poet Zhanna Ayarzhevkaya (Жанна Аяржевкая) lives here. She came here when the BAM was being built and remained. Another notable visitor was the cosmonaut Valentin Vitalevich Lebedev. These visits by Soviet celebrities were common as they 'demonstrated' that the BAM was being built by everyone in the Soviet Union. The locals of Kuvykta were so pleased with his visit that there is a small space museum in town dedicated to his exploits. Valentin Vitalevich was twice awarded the Hero of the USSR medal for his long duration space flights. His longest was in 1982 when he lived in space for 211 days, nine hours, four minutes and 32 seconds. His first flight was in Soyuz 13.

# Tynda–Novy Urgal
## Тында–Новый Ургал

## THE ROUTE (see Route Maps 3 and 4, pp368-9)

At Tynda, the line is on the watershed of the Amur river, which forms part of the border between Russia and China before turning north to reach the Pacific. In this stretch, the BAM heads south-east through a wide natural depression in the mountains at 300-450m above sea-level, crossing the fan of rivers that feed the Amur – the Gilyui near Tynda, the Zeya at Verkhnezeisk, the Selemdzha at Fevralsk, and the Bureya near Novy Urgal, crossing a sequence of majestic green passes between them. (The BAM finally crosses the Amur itself at Komsomolsk-na-Amure.)

The time is Moscow time +6 hours until the border of Khabarovski Krai at Ulma. Beyond it is Moscow time +7 hours.

## TYNDA (Тында) 2,364km

Tynda is a modern city in deep wilderness. It was the headquarters of the BAM Railroad until 1996 and it is still a major railroading town. It sits at the junction of the four sections of the BAM: eastern BAM, western BAM, AYaM and Little BAM. It is the third largest town on the BAM with a population of 70,000. The main street, Krasnaya Presnya, is lined with 16-storey buildings, which is very unusual for Siberia. Tynda's attractions include the BAM museum, a nearby Evenk village, an excellent Russian banya and a base for wilderness trekking and rafting.

### Orientation

Tynda was built at the intersection of two routes – the south-north route (the AYaM railway and the AYaAD M-56 highway between the Trans-Siberian and Yakutsk) and the west-east BAM railway. The centre of Tynda is built on a rise to the north of the small Tynda river, backing up to a small hill that is preserved as parkland. Tynda was built by the Moscow region and the main street is named Krasnaya Presnya (ул. Красная Пресня) after a Moscow avenue. The uphill (north) side of Krasnaya Presnya is lined with stores and schools, with four 16-storey blocks behind them, backing onto the wide pedestrian Moscow Boulevard (Бульвар Московский). Terraced above Krasnaya Presnya, ingeniously linked by archways and steps, are government buildings and the House of Culture.

The M-56 highway crosses the city west of the downtown area, separating it from the old settlement. The railway and the station are on the south side of the river, linked to the town by a direct footbridge and by the highway bridge. The railway station is a landmark with a tall tower and has a tent-like roof with an internal gallery with shops, a café, and a business centre, from which you can make long-distance telephone calls.

## History

Tynda was the village of Tyndinsky when the south-north Amur Yakutsk Highway was cut through the mountains in the 1920s. It was first joined to the Trans-Siberian in 1937 via the Little BAM. In 1942 the line was pulled up and shipped to the Battle of Stalingrad. Workers started re-laying the line in 1973 and the new Little BAM reached Tynda in 1975.

The early years of Tynda were a litany of poor engineering with constant water and heating shortages, inadequate housing, buildings subsiding into the permafrost and power interruptions. The situation now is vastly improved with the construction of a centralised heating system consolidating the town's 38 separate heating boilers in 1977. Air pollution was also a big problem due to the coal-fired power station, but this closed when the supply of electricity arrived from Zeya, 225km away. Fogs are common in the morning but disappear within a few hours of sunrise.

The architecture of the new city of Tynda is bold and self-confident and uses the sloping site ingeniously. Tynda has a sister-city relationship with Wenatchee, Washington, in the USA. In the early 1990s, an exchange programme for the children of these two cities started.

## Getting there and away

Tynda is a major railroading centre, with trains in all directions.

To the west along the BAM there is a Moscow–Tynda train (via Kazan) every other day and a Kislovodsk–Tynda train twice a week and local trains to Novaya Chara. These trains include through carriages from Neryungri in the north.

To the east there is a daily train along the BAM to Komsomolsk-na-Amure (37 hours). This train has a small buffet carriage with several coupé compartments, a full coupé carriage, a platskartny carriage, an obshchi carriage and a freight wagon. When booking for this train, try to avoid days on which the Moscow or Kislovodsk train arrives from the west. On those days the small eastbound train is liable to be jammed with people who have already spent five days and nights in their berths.

To the north via the AYaM railway there is a daily train to and from Neryungri. For more on the AYaM railway, see The AYaM: Tynda–Neryungri–Aldan–Yakutsk, pp262-78.

To the south via the AYaM railway, Tynda, the Little BAM and west on the Trans-Siberian, there is a train every other day

☐ **TYNDA (Тында)**
Area code ☎ 41656
Amurskaya Oblast, Tynda, 676080
(676080, Амурская область, г. Тында)
Moscow time +6 hours

from Neryungri via Tynda to Novosibirsk. On the south and east on the Trans-Siberian, there is a train every day from Neryungri via Tynda to Khabarovsk and a train every other day from Neryungri to Blagoveshchensk. For details about southern trains, see Bamovskaya–Tynda (The Little BAM), pp207-10.

Buses run along the Amur Yakutsk Highway northwards to Neryungri and southwards to Solovevsk (Соловьевск), Urkan (Уркан) and Bolshoi Never (Большой Невер) on the Trans-Siberian, following a slightly different route than the Little BAM.

There are flights from the Amurskaya Oblast capital of Blagoveshchensk. There is a railway ticket office in the main street, which saves you walking to the station. There is also an Aeroflot office on the main street, but it is hard to find as it is around the side of a building.

## Getting around
The drive from the station to town is about 2km via the highway bridge. However, you can easily walk from the station to the centre of the town directly over a footbridge. Otherwise bus No 5 runs regularly from the station down the main street of town. Be aware that the telephone and post parts of the post office are at different ends of the town. At the east end of ul. Krasnaya Presnya is a small Orthodox church adapted from a social club; a larger church is planned for the centre of town.

## Where to stay
*Hotel Yunost*, ul. Krasnaya Presnya, ☎ 23-1-60 (ул. Красная Пресня, гостиница «Юность») is a crumbling municipal multi-storey 1970s hotel with small rooms many of which have basins and toilets attached. Prices used to be exorbitant ($60) when the hotel catered mainly to railway business, but the Yunost is now competitive and houses the local market traders, with prices down to $10. Make sure you establish the price in advance. Attached in a two-storey annexe are a bar and a restaurant.

The private *Hotel Nadezhda* (usually called 'Pioneer'), ul. Festivalnaya 1, ☎ 2-05-93, 🖹 2-13-58 (ул. Фестивальная, 1, гостиница «Надежда»), is just behind Hotel Yunost. The hotel is in the Pioneer building (Пионер), so-called because it was the first brick building in town, owned by the extremely helpful Nadezhda Konstantinovna Nizova (see Getting assistance, p138). Her company, Nadezhda Ltd, is at the west end of the Pioneer building on the ground floor, and the hotel is on the third floor up the stairs. It has 2-, 3-, and 4-bed rooms, clean and pleasant, with shared toilet and shower. The hotel has its own hot water supply for times when the city hot water is turned off. There is a communal kitchen with sink, ranges, and refrigerator, and the hotel will make breakfast and other meals on request. A single is $10. Because Krasnaya Presnya curves around the contour of the hill, the Pioneer building is not on it, but behind trees and an office building, in front of the open-air market.

The best accommodation is in ***Orbita Railway Hotel,*** ul. Nadezhdy, ☎ 33-64 (ул. Надежды, гостиница «Орбита»), which is where senior railway officials stay when they visit Tynda. Although in principle open to the public, you will need permission from the Manager of the Tynda Railway Branch (Начальник Тындинсково отделения Дальневосточной железной дороги).

The Orbita is a small mansion surrounded by gardens about 15 minutes walk from the city's bus station. The rooms are large, and there are several suites. The restaurant is excellent and there are several places for meetings. Well worth the $16 per person per night. To get to the hotel from the railway station, go over the highway bridge towards the centre of town and, rather than turning up Krasnaya Presnya at the city's bus station, keep going straight ahead for another 500m. Turn left up ul. Nadezhdy and take the left fork at its end. You then pass into the hotel's grounds, which are surrounded by a large hedge.

## Where to eat

Restaurants are fairly scarce, the best being the two-storey ***bar*** and ***restaurant*** attached to Hotel Yunost, one beside the Dom Kniga and one in the banya. There are also ***canteens*** in the market above the Pioneer building. The main markets, both covered and open-air (year-round), are behind the Pioneer building. They are organised by wares – meat, fruit and vegetables, housewares, car parts, clothes, sweets and so on – and are more like bazaars. There are a surprising number of traders from China and the Central Asian republics at the markets and Turkish music is common. (You will also meet North Koreans in the street.)

Tynda is blessed with well-stocked shops with the best being on ul. Krasnaya Presnya. The state department store complex also has a range of railway hats and badges on sale. However, as you need a railway purchasing permit to buy railway clothing, you may have to convince the salespeople with tales of being a collector in order to get them.

## Getting assistance

Nadezhda Ltd, owned by the energetic Nadezhda Konstantinovna Nizova, is licensed to organise travel for residents and tourism for visitors. It can set up local excursions and long-distance travel on the BAM. Nadezhda Ltd, Nadezhda Konstantinovna Nizova, General Director, 676080, Russia, g. Tynda, Amurskaya Oblast, ul. Festivalnaya 1, ☎ +7 41656 2-05-93, 📄 +7 41656 2-13-58, telex: 288126 DWC SU, 🖳 td_nadejda@amur.ru (676080, Россия, Амурская область, г. Тында, ул. Фестивальная, 1, Торговый дом «Надежда», Низова Надежда Константиновна, Генеральный директор).

The Tynda School-Youth Centre for Tourism and Excursions (Detsko-yunoshcheski tsentr turizma i ekskursi) organises outdoor events for local

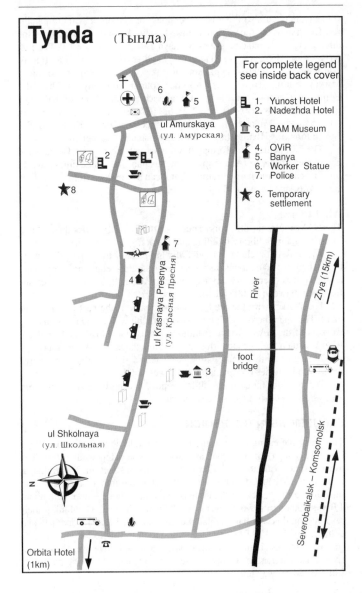

# Tynda (Тында)

For complete legend see inside back cover

1. Yunost Hotel
2. Nadezhda Hotel
3. BAM Museum
4. OViR
5. Banya
6. Worker Statue
7. Police
8. Temporary settlement

ul Amurskaya
(ул. Амурская)

ul Krasnaya Presnya
(ул. Красная Пресня)

River

Zrya (15km)

foot bridge

Severobaikalsk – Komsomolsk

ul Shkolnaya
(ул. Школьная)

N

Orbita Hotel
(1km)

students and can also organise excursions for visitors. For more details, see Excursions in the region below. Leonid Mikhailovich Yadrov, the director, can be contacted at Festivalnaya 7, ☎ 2-72-33 (676080, Россия, Амурская область, г. Тында, ул. Фестивальная, 7, Децко-юнощеский центр туризма и экскурсий, Ядров Леонид Михаилович, Директор). Another tourist company is The BID Company (General Director Igor Davidovich Brusilovski) at ul. Krasnaya Presnya 70A, ☎ 2-09-91, 📄 2-28-62 (676080, Россия, Амурская область, г. Тында, ул. Красная Пресня, 70A, ООО «БИД», Брусиловский Игорь Давидович, Генеральный директор).

The best source of information on what is happening in Tynda is the newspaper *Avangard* (Авангард), which is published three times a week. It is difficult to find it on the streets but it can be obtained from their office at ul. Krasnaya Presnya 70 (☎ 213-97).

## What to see

The BAM museum, ul. Profsyuznaya 3, ☎ 32-483 (ул. Профсоюзная, 3), is in the city's library building and is good.

The museum includes a model of what parts of the railway line were built when. It also contains displays of early settlers' equipment and gulag artefacts. It is open every day except Friday from 10.00-18.00 but closes for lunch between 13.00 and 14.00.

The Worker with the Sledge Hammer statue is the best BAM monument. This giant heroic sculpture was built with welded stainless steel by workers of the BAM Bridge Building organisation Moststroi-10 outside what was then their headquarters on ul. Amurskaya (ул. Амурская).

Next door to this statue is the city's banya. This is a genuine banya with birch branches on sale, a pool and wet and dry saunas.

Tynda is not much of a cultural centre, but the local Russian choir, Zernyshki (Зёрнышки), is worth hearing.

## EXCURSIONS IN THE REGION

The most interesting place in the region is the indigenous Evenk village of Zarya (Заря) also known as Pervomaiskoe (Первомайское). The town is small with about 200 families. The main street, ul. Tsentralnaya, is the only tarred road and it eventually peters out into a dairy farm. The most interesting aspect of the town is that it has a large school with about 1,000 students in it from several local Evenki villages. Combining their resources in this way has enabled the survival of the Evenki language and culture. Bus No 105 from Tynda's bus station travels to the village. The trip, which takes about 30 minutes, passes a stone bridge over the Getkan river. This functioning railway bridge is the only part of the original 1930s Little BAM railway left.

An excellent film on the Evenki was made by BAM Film Studios and they will supply a video copy of the film for a few dollars. They have also produced a number of films on the BAM. Viktor Nikolaevich Pozharov, BAM Kino Studios, ul. Krasnaya Presnya 34, ☎ 747-69, 🗎 22-004 (Кино корреспондентский пункт МПС на БАМе, ул. Красная Пресня, 34, Пожаров Виктор Николаевич).

As all along the BAM, there are excellent rafting expeditions through the wilderness. You can put in rubber rafts at Tynda and float down the Gilyui river (p. Гилюй) for seven days to the Zeya Reservoir (Зейское водохранилище), paddle across the reservoir to Verkhnezeisk (Верхнезейск) and bring the rafts back by train on the BAM. Along the way there are two huts but otherwise accommodation is in tents. Alternatively you can take the AYaM railway to Zolotinka (Золотинка) and raft down the Iengra river (p. Иенгра) to the Timpton river (p. Тимптон), taking out at Chulman (Чульман), also on the AYaM railway. If you miss this take-out point you can raft a further 250km to the Aldan river (p. Алдан) or a further 900km down the Aldan to Khandyga (Хандыга). Or you can take the BAM eastward to Larba (Ларба) and raft to Ust-Nyukzha (Усть-Нюкжа), then bring the rafts back from the BAM station at Yuktali (Юктали).

## 🚉 SHAKHTAUM (Шахтаум) 2,380km

The BAM and the AYaM railway head off together up the Gilyui river (p. Гилюй). Shakhtaum is the site of a wood-processing plant that makes fibreboard. The Evenk village Zarya is across the Gilyui and up the hill.

## 🚉 BESTUZHEVO (Бестужево) 2,391km

The station is named after a famous Decembrist family that saw all three sons participate in the anti-Tsar uprising on 14 December 1825. The St Petersburg uprising demanded a constitutional monarch rather than an omnipotent Tsar. All three brothers were sentenced to death, which was later commuted to exile in Siberia.

The first to be sentenced was Mikhail Aleksandrovich, a captain in the Moscow Imperial Guards Regiment, who led his regiment into Senate Square in St Petersburg and lined the soldiers up in front of the pro-government troops. He gave the command to open fire at the opposing forces and after his troops were routed by cannon fire, he tried unsuccessfully to rally them to storm Peter and Paul Fortress. His commuted sentence was 20 years in the Siberian city of Chita. The second brother was Nikolai Aleksandrovich, a lieutenant commander in the Naval Guards, who like his brother also led his troops into Senate Square in St Petersburg. He was sentenced to 20 years in the Siberian Nerchinsk mines. The last one was

Aleksandr Aleksandrovich, a writer, who was exiled to Yakutsk for his anti-Tsar writings and public meetings.

Accommodation can be organised at the **Recreation Base**, ☎ 38-83 (Бестужева База отдыха).

Just after you depart Bestuzhevo, the line divides into the AYaM railway for Berkakit, Aldan and Yakutsk in the north, and the BAM for Komsomolsk-na-Amure in the east. For details about the AYaM railway, see pp262-278). The BAM continues up the Gilyui through often clouded summits.

### 🚉 MAREVAYA (Маревая) 2,452km

This moderate-sized settlement was built by the Moscow Region BAM Construction company. It has a North Korean logging camp nearby. Accommodation can be organised at the **Railway Hostel** (☎ 2-71). The line crosses a pass and descends into a wide depression in the mountains, crossing many small creeks that empty into the Zeya Reservoir (Зейское водохранилище).

### 🚉 UNAKHA (Унаха) 2,511km

There is another North Korean logging camp near this settlement.

### 🚉 DIPKUN (Дипкун) 2,527km

This moderate-sized settlement was built by the Moscow Region BAM Construction company. Accommodation can be organised at the **Railway Hostel**. The line makes a wide loop to lose height.

### 🚉 DESS (Дёсс) 2,541km

This town derives its name from the Dess river, which eventually flows into the Zeya Reservoir.

### 🚉 MOSKOVSKI KOMSOMOLETS (Московский Комсомолец)

The station gets its name from Moscow's young communists who supposedly built it.

### 🚉 TUTAUL (Тутаул) 2,582km

This moderate-sized settlement was built by the Moscow Region BAM Construction company. It has a North Korean logging camp nearby. Accommodation can be organised at the **Locomotive Brigade Hostel** (☎ 2-22, Дом отдыха Локомотивной бригады).

## 🚉 ULAK (Улак) 2,700km

This station is on the west bank of the Zeya Reservoir (Зейское водохранилище). Six kilometres away is Gorni village, which has a population of 1,500, and the airport that services Verkhnezeisk.

### Zeya bridge 2,704km

The Zeya bridge over the Zeya Reservoir is the second longest bridge on the BAM. It is 1,100m long, stands 50m above the water and took the Leningrad Bridge Building Company (Ленинградмостстрой) nine years to build. Because of its significance, it is guarded by a platoon of soldiers.

## 🚉 VERKHNEZEISK (Верхнезейск) 2,707km

Verkhnezeisk/Zeisk is a small BAM town but its averageness is what makes it worth spending time here. It is large enough to have the aspects typical of BAM towns including a temporary settlement, shattered plans and isolation, yet small enough to be able to see everything and meet a range of people, which provides an insight into life in a rural town.

The mayor, Vladimir Ivanovich Natresenyuk, is happy to introduce you to all aspects of life there.

### Orientation

Verkhnezeisk is the name of the station, while the town is called Zeisk. The names come from the Zeya river whose name in Evenki means 'blade of a knife' due to its narrow, fast flow as it cuts through the taiga. Verkhnezeisk ('Upper Zeisk') was hacked out of virgin taiga on the flat, marshy Verkhnezeisk Plain (Верхнезейская Равнина) at the upper end of the 130km long Zeya Reservoir (Зейское водохранилище). The town Zeya, with the dam, is at the lower end. The Zeya river continues south to form the major stream of the Amur.

The plain, two-storey Verkhnezeisk station and the Locomotive Brigade Hostel are next to the railroad. A 500m road leads to the Zeisk town. A hollow square of five-storey buildings, a small commercial centre with an open-air market, another street of apartments and the blocks of the hospital, the school and the half-built House of Culture complete the urban core. Beyond are the ruins of the temporary settlements of works brigades and railway army troops, interspersed with stubborn settlers who prefer to live surrounded by their own gardens and greenhouses.

### History

In the early 1970s when the BAM was being planned, it was stated that the town would be a major railway headquarters looking after a large section of the BAM. A town of 15,000 was planned with schools for 6,000 children, cinema, pool, maternity hospital and a large civic centre. However, only the schools were built before the plans were changed and

❏ **VERKHNEZEISK**
**(Верхнезейск)**
Amurskaya Oblast,
  Verkhnezeisk, 676239
(676239, Амурская область,
  п. Верхнезейск)

Zeisk was downgraded to become just another BAM railway settlement. When the wind blows in summer, dust swirls create a impression of a ghost town with the small number of people dwarfed by the scattered housing blocks. This feeling is compounded by the lack of street names as the administration has held off naming them for over 15 years because they were waiting for decisions about the town's future. The inhabitants are also aware that they are under siege from the taiga and will tell you with great relish the story of a 17-year-old who was eaten by a bear just 15km away in 1993.

The downsizing of the town was an enormous disappointment to the inhabitants who had given up everything to move here. In addition, the number of trains has been reduced to two passenger trains and a few freight trains a day which has compounded the feeling of isolation. The town also lacks the typical Russian network of grandparents and relatives essential to compensate for the lack of childminding and other social services. The vast majority of inhabitants are young couples and there is only one Great Patriotic War veteran in town.

The town was sponsored by Ufa, which is in central Russia near the Kazakhstan border. The town's Central Asian inhabitants are not the original builders but people who have recently fled the ethnic problems in Central Asia and southern Russia. These people are welcomed by Zeisk's inhabitants as they increase the population and, as everyone is an immigrant, there are no ethnic tensions as found in many established Russian towns.

## Getting there and away

There is one long-distance train per day in each direction, which happen to coincide at Verkhnezeisk between 00.30 and 01.30 and stop for more than 30 minutes. There is also a daily local train running to the west to Dipkun (four hours) and another running to the east to Dugda (five hours).

Flights arrive from Zeya and Blagoveshchensk at the Gorni airport on the other side of the Zeya Reservoir. To get there, walk across the Zeya Reservoir bridge or catch the local train to Ulak (Улак) and then walk 6km to Gorni village and airport.

From January to early April, it is possible to drive over the frozen Zeya Reservoir. It takes three hours to drive to Zeya. In summer, driving to Zeya requires a long detour. You must drive 89km to Ogoron on the BAM then south to Zeya. The eight-hour trip is all on dirt roads.

## Where to stay and eat

The only accommodation in town is the ***Locomotive Brigade Hostel*** (☎ 2-14, Дом отдыха Локомотивной бригады) just in front of the station. Singles are $10, with shared toilet and showers. It is pleasant and friendly, with flowers and benches out front in summer. It also has a *24-hour cafeteria*.

## Getting assistance

The Mayor of Zeisk, Vladimir Ivanovich Natresenyuk, will make you welcome and gladly show you the whole town. Contact Vladimir Ivanovich Natresenyuk, Mayor, at 676239, Amurskaya Oblast, Zeisk Raion, Verkhnezeisk, House 34, Apartment 9, ☎ 4-50, ☎ 4-36 (rail) or telephone Zeya town at ☎ 841658 and ask for 75-2-30 (676239, Амурская область, Зейский район, п. Верхнезейск, дом 34, кв. 9, Натрасенюк Владимир Иванович, Администратор посёлка).

Vladimir Ivanovich is unusual. He is not an old party official only interested in power but just an ordinary man who really takes an interest in his town. The job is one with few privileges and perks and he even admits that he has a 'position of power with no power'. Power in a BAM town is divided between the railway and the civic authorities. However, as the railway invariably owns all facilities including schools, hospitals, shops, houses and hotels, there is little left for the civic authorities to manage. Therefore the mayor's main responsibilities are social services such as pensions, unemployment benefits and housing.

Although 30 people are officially unemployed, he believes that there will be more jobless in the future. 'I am trying to help but there are no jobs'.

Vladimir Ivanovich's main job is simply talking to everyone, finding out what problems everyone has, helping with solutions and keeping everyone informed. In many ways a thankless task but one that he believes will develop a community spirit. As you drive around with Vladimir Ivanovich pointing to the vacant spaces where the pool, sporting complex and more apartment blocks should be, he speaks of everyone's resentment with Gorbachev's *perestroika* and Yeltsin's economic reform. 'This has resulted in a lower standard of living for all. We are sick of talk and what we need is government help now!'

## What to see

The following description of the town's features is included not because they are unusual but because they are common to almost every BAM town. Their detailed description allows you to see and understand the reality of life in the BAM zone as you wander around the town.

**Schools** There is one school and two kindergartens in town. These were built in anticipation of 6,000 students but today there are only 580. For a tour of the schools, contact Annya Gorevnya Peshkova, Middle School No 47, ☎ 2-81 (средная школа, Пешкова Ання Горьевня).

**Temporary settlement** All BAM towns consist of a permanent and a temporary settlement. The temporary settlement is for the constructors of the permanent town and railway and is normally a collection of ramshackle wooden buildings that are torn down when the work is completed. However, in many BAM towns, the shortage of accommodation in the permanent settlement means that many people live in the temporary settlement. Zeisk is unusual in that demand for housing was less than expected and only 12 families out of the original 2,000 temporary settlement inhabitants remain in the temporary settlement, in a few wood houses with gardens and greenhouses, surrounded by collapsed and destroyed buildings.

**Bakery**  Bakeries are absolutely essential in every town, as bread is the central element in a Russian meal. The Zeisk bakery is run by one woman who makes 300 loaves a day. The ovens are wood fired and while wood is delivered, she must chop it up. Occasionally there are bread shortages due to lack of ingredients but these are rare. The bakery's smell and bread-making process make visiting here a must.

**Greenhouse**  The short 94-day growing season means that greenhouses are essential for all but the quickest-growing plants. Zeisk has a typical commercial greenhouse that was built to supply workers' needs. The 40m-long greenhouse is heated to 28°C by a line from the city's central hot water circulation pipes and lit by electricity. However, even with these, it

Vladimir Ivanovich Natresenyuk, Mayor of Zeisk, looks at his own picture in the first edition of this guide. Photo by Nicholas Zvegintzov.

---

❏ **Private enterprise still struggling in Siberia**

In post-communist rural Russia, the introduction of self-employment, free markets and capitalism still have a long way to go. While goods trading and money market speculation may be accepted by the government, there is still a great deal of official resistance to private ventures in agriculture, manufacturing and professional services.

Victor P Sulitski is typical of the unconnected Russian who is struggling to run a business. Victor was a naval dentist for years and would like to set up a private practice in Zeisk. However, the government maintains a monopoly on dentistry and it is a criminal offence for dentists to work outside the government. So Victor established the first commercial fishing company on the Zeya Reservoir. He purchased licences for 50 nets along a 40km stretch and, with his four employees, catches a tonne of fish a week. Despite the long hours and good catches, he is not earning much as the only purchaser is the state which pays him considerably below the market price. Life is very rough for Victor and his workers as during the fishing season they live under a canvas sheet on the fly-invested shores of the lake. During winter, Victor lives by himself in an airless, underground shelter with a built-in stove providing the only heat. From here he hunts bears and deer. Despite the long hours of arduous work and the little time he can spend with his wife in Zeisk, he is proud of his independence and would not return to a stifling state job. (Viktor P Sulitski, Verkhnezeisk, ul. Taezhnaya 1). (Виктор П Сулицкий, Верхнезейск, ул. таежная 1).

---

is only practical to grown plants until mid-October. The greenhouse is now run by one person who is having difficulty making it profitable with the recent substantial price rises for hot water and electricity.

**Central heating plant**  All hot water in the town is provided by the central heating plant powered by coal. The water is distributed by aboveground pipes that should be covered with insulation and a protective metal skin. However, insulation often falls off the pipes and is not replaced, resulting in a horrendous loss of energy in winter. The plant is worth visiting to appreciate the decrepit system.

**Hospital**  The town's medical complex consists of a polyclinic and a 100-bed hospital. These facilities lack a maternity ward which is surprising considering that most of the town's families are of child-bearing age. Mothers normally deliver in the Tynda maternity hospital. A tour of the hospital provides a disturbing insight into the failing Russian medical services.

**Commercial complex**  This is quite small with a bank, post office and food and clothing shops. They are all located in one area to minimise shoppers' exposure to the winter temperatures.

**Railway troops camp**  Most of the railway line between Tynda and Komsomolsk-na-Amure was built by military railway troops. Four thousand of these soldiers were based around Zeisk providing timber and construction earthworks until they left in 1990. A number of their camps can still be found. One camp is on the outskirts of Zeisk, halfway between the temporary settlement and the bakery. Guard towers, barbed wire fences, demolished buildings and a statue to the construction achievements of soldiers can still be seen.

## Excursions in the region

**Bomnak**  Near the shore of the reservoir on the west side of the Zeya river is the old Evenki village of Bomnak (Бомнак). About 120 families live here. When the reservoir was flooded, the village only lost one street. Buried here is G Fedoseev, the author of children's socialist heroic books including *By the path of experience* and *Pashka: From the Bear Ravine*. While there is a dirt road from Gorni to Bomnak, it is quicker to reach the village by boat from Zeisk.

Forty-seven kilometres to the east of Bomnak on the Tok river is an old landing strip for American Lend-Lease aircraft. Planes landed here from the USA and were refuelled before heading onwards to the warfront.

**Zeya Dam**  The Zeya Dam was built in 1972 130km south at Zeya, with 115m high walls, to become the largest hydro-electric station in eastern Siberia. The station provides power for both the Trans-Siberian, which is 120km away, and Tynda, which is 300km away on the BAM. The other advantage of the dam is to regulate the downstream flow of the Zeya before it runs into the Amur. This stopped flooding, increased the area available for agriculture and enabled ships to travel up to Zeya more regularly. The Zeya Reservoir is peculiar as it fills up during summer, not spring.

The filling of the dam did not have the human consequences of the Bratsk damming as the area was sparsely populated. The dam only drowned a children's camp and the gold-mining village of Khvoiny (Хвойный). Khvoiny has since been rebuilt on a new site. The flooding was done without clearing the trees in the area, which means that all the timber was wasted and boating is dangerous today as the trees are often just below the surface.

The other towns on the reservoir are Snezhnogorski (Снежногорский) and Beregovoi (Береговой), both of which are logging communities.

**Fishing**  Fishing is one of the highlights of the region. A large variety of fish can be caught including shuka, som, taimen, shevak, kharius, lenok and the rare kasatka (касатка).

Fishermen from as far away as Tynda come to the lake and spend a weekend fishing and camping before returning home with the month's fish. The most popular stop is the unmarked siding of Apetenok (Апетенок), 30 minutes from Zeisk.

## ☒ APETENOK (Апетенок) 2,723km

From Verkhnezeisk you pass through the flat Verkhnezeisk Plain (Верхнезейская равнина) which contains numerous creeks and rivers flowing into the Zeya Reservoir.

The unmarked siding of Apetenok is the most popular stop for fishermen and is about 30 minutes from Zeisk. The stop is about 300m from the water's edge and fishermen then walk around the lake to their favourite spots.

Along this stretch of the line you will see numerous kerosene tubes.The vertical tubes are designed to keep the ground frozen year-round which prevents it from subsiding. The tubes are filled with kerosene and penetrate several metres into the earth. As the kerosene absorbs heat from the ground, it vaporises and rises to the above ground part of the tube. The tube gives off heat which condenses the kerosene and the fluid then drips to the bottom of the tube where the process is repeated. While these tubes are effective, they are also very polluting as, after a few years, they start leaking kerosene into the ground.

## OGORON (Огорон) 2,796km

The town was sponsored by Ulyanovsk on the Volga river. There are considerable gas reserves between Ogoron and Verkhnezeisk but they are uneconomical to extract. After leaving the town, the train starts its long ascent over the Soktakhan and Dzhagdy ranges (хребты Соктахан и Джагды).

## MOLDAVSKI (Молдавский) 2,820km

The station is named after Moldova from where its constructors came.

## MIROSHNICHENKO (Мирошниченко) 2,850km

Miroshnichenko was a hero of the civil war who single-handedly defended a bridge. There is a bust of Miroshnichenko at Fevralsk station. On 29 April 1984 the eastern section of the BAM was joined at this station (memorial west of the station on the south side).

## TUNGALA (Тунгала) 2,863km

This ambitious two-storey station was built on slender piers to insulate it from permafrost, but even so the west section cracked in 1996 and is shored up on timbers. The town was sponsored by Novosibirsk.

## DUGDA (Дугда) 2,912km

This moderate-sized settlement was built by the Moldovan BAM Construction company (МолдоваБАМстрой). This is the terminus of local trains that run to the east and west. Accommodation can be organised at the *Railway Hostel* (Общежитие).

## 🏚 NORA (Нора) 2,932km

This station is named after the Nora river, a 305km tributary of the Selemdzha river.

## 🏚 FEVRALSK (Февральск) 3,033km

The line crosses the gold-bearing Selemdzha river (р. Селемджа) and stops at Fevralsk (Февральск).

Fevralsk is not the most attractive town but it offers several interesting side-trips to unusual parts of the BAM zone. The town of 12,000 people had a difficult birth, as its site was badly chosen. It is located in a swamp on permafrost while solid ground is located just a few kilometres away. Consequently, in its early years the sewerage system collapsed, masonry became dangerously cracked and foundations sank. Today the town looks much older than its 20-odd years.

The town was mainly built by railway troops although the Moldovans sponsored it. In the early 1990s there were about 3,000 soldiers based around the town and the last left in July 1994. Despite their lasting legacy, including the 350 bed hospital, a hotel on the banks of the Selemdzha river and the partly built railway line to Ogodzha, there are no monuments in town to their work. The monument on the station's platform is to the Russian Civil War hero, Miroshnichenko.

### Getting there and away

There is one long-distance train per day in each direction. There is also a daily local train running west to Dugda (Дугда) (four hours) and one running east to Etyrken (Этыркен) (four hours).

Along the Selemdzha river, buses run upstream to Ekimchan (Экимчан), 212km, on Wednesday, Friday and Sunday and downstream to Norsk (Норск), 129km, on Tuesday, Thursday and Saturday. To the south, long-distance buses run via Svobodny (Свободный) on the Trans-Siberian and then to Blagoveshchensk (Благовещенск) on Monday, Wednesday and Friday, or to Belogorsk (Белогорск) on Tuesday, Thursday and Saturday. The 304km highway linking Fevralsk with Svobodny is one of only two paved roads in the BAM Zone. The buses leave from the train station.

### Where to stay and eat

A *hotel* (☎ 22-90) is located in the station building. Its entrance is at the western end of the station. It has 10 standard rooms, $8, and one luxury room, all of which are quite noisy. There is no canteen or restaurant in town. You can buy food in the *market* and may persuade the hotel to let you use the kitchen.

## What to see

The highlight of the town is the city baths, which indicates Fevralsk's limited sightseeing possibilities! The banya consists of a municipal one on the ground floor and a private one upstairs. The contrast between the two in terms of facilities reveals that the town's powerbrokers live a good life. Asterid, the company that owns it, also has considerable commercial interests in the town and region. It is owned by the young entrepreneur Igor Yurevich Solomanov (Соломанов Игорь Юрьевич) ☎ 23-36.

Six kilometres away from Fevralsk is the 200-year-old settlement of Fevralskoe. This community of only about 40 houses contains traditional Russian houses surrounded by the river and trees and is a refreshing contrast to Fevralsk's concrete apartment blocks surrounded by a wasteland.

If you are interested in the area's history, talk with the local historian, Galina Yakova, ul. Ayanskaya 2a, kv 25, ☎ 33-71 (rail) (ул. Аянская 2a, кв 25, Якова Галина).

## EXCURSIONS: EXPLORATION OF THE SELEMDZHA VALLEY

The Selemdzha river flows south-west to join the Zeya and thus the Amur. The river valley is a beautiful and old area with several indigenous and ancient Russian villages. The roads are better than most in rural Siberia as the gold mines pay for regular grading which reduces the repair costs for their large fleet of vehicles. If you are travelling between June and August, make sure you take mosquito repellent, as the mosquitoes are big enough to carry you off.

### A loop to Novy Urgal

The most interesting route is a 600km loop starting in Fevralsk, up the Selemdzha through Ekimchan, over the mountains to the gold-mining town of Sofisk (Софийск) and finishing in the BAM town of Novy Urgal (Новый Ургал). Although Russian maps show that there is a road connecting Ekimchan and Sofisk, in reality this is little more than a dirt track. Scheduled buses run along the entire route except for this section; if you wish to travel it, you should hire a 4WD or try your luck at grabbing a rare lift.

### Rafting

Rafting down the Selemdzha river (р. Селемджа) is a popular summer sport. The 647km-long Selemdzha starts in the mountains to the north, flows past Ekimchan and Fevralsk, joining the Zeya a little above Svobodny. The river is navigable up to the village of Norsk (Норск) which is 129km from Fevralsk and occasionally as far as Ekimchan during high water. Before the BAM was built, the Selemdzha was identified as a river of enormous recreational value. However, the mining of railway ballast on its banks and upstream gold dredging of its tributaries has severely damaged the quality of the river. With a reduction in industrial activity and the settling of disturbed sediments, the river is slowly returning to normal. Rafting from Fevralsk to Svobodny takes a leisurely three days.

## Byssa hot springs

Sixty kilometres south of Fevralsk on the road to Svobodny is a famous sanatorium in the village of Byssa (Бысса). The sanatorium, whose condition is described as 'rough', is based around a 42°C radon hot water spring and claims to be able to relieve arthritis and rheumatism. It can accommodate 50 people and was built by the Fevralsk gas-production plant.

## Future railway to Ogodzha

A railway line is being built to the coal-rich region around Ogodzha (Огоджа). The region contains a massive 131 million tonnes of coal.

Ogodzha is 144km north of Fevralsk and when the line is finished, it will include five stations. The word Ogodzha means a 'sunny and warm valley' in Evenki.

## A drive to Ekimchan (Экимчан)

If you have limited time, the best and easiest trip is to Ekimchan. This 212km route takes six hours by car and you should stay overnight before returning the next day. The trip starts by taking you over the new railway line to Ogodzha, through the village of Fevralskoe to the Selemdzha river. A 24-hour car ferry takes your vehicle across the river for $2.

The first village you pass through is Selemdzhinsk (Селемджинск) and the next is the ancient gold-mining town of Stoiba (Стойба). This is about halfway to Ekimchan and it is a nice place for a picnic lunch on the banks of Selemdzha. The descendants of Volga Germans can be found here and in other nearby towns; they settled here during the 1800s colonisation of Siberia and in the 1930s when Stalin exiled them to Siberia.

A further two hours will bring you to the area currently being dredged. The giant 1940s-era dredgers crawl along the rivers scooping up all the rock pebbles and water and mechanically shifting it. Any alluvial gold falls into a tray and the water and waste rock is flung out the back of the machine. The area laid waste by the machines remains scarred for decades, as there is no rehabilitation process after dredging. The area has three dredges that work for six months of the year before the rivers freeze. Coming across them at night is surrealistic, as the machines appear to be giant monoliths devouring all with spotlight-like eyes looking for food. This region produces 26 per cent of the gold in Amurskaya Oblast.

The next major town is **Ekimchan** (Экимчан) which is the regional headquarters of the Selemdzhinski Raion (Селемджинский район). This is a small town that feels as if the 20th century passed it by. Most of the buildings are wood, the streets are dirt broken up with patches of asphalt and the pavements are covered with wood. The town was founded in 1887 as a gold-mining community and gets its name from the Evenki word for older sibling. It has a 16-person *hotel*. Contact the regional administrator, Sergei Nikolaevich Levanov, ☎ 21-311 (п. Экимчан, Леванов Сергей Николаевич, Главный Администратор).

## Tokur (Токур)

Tokur is 12km from Ekimchan up a side creek and is more interesting to stay in. It is the commercial hub of the region even though it is a smaller town and was only founded in 1939. It is the headquarters of the company Olimp and the Selemdzhinski gold mine. Three thousand people live in the town or work for these companies.

There are two hotels in town. One is the small, *all-suite hotel* in the administration block of Olimp and the other is the 21-room *local hotel* at 676561, Tokur, ul. Sovetskaya 2, ☎ 22-524 (Амурская область, 676561, п. Токур, ул. Советская 2). The best place to eat is at the excellent five-table *restaurant and bar* owned by Olimp.

Two interesting half-day trips from here are to visit the Selemdzhinski gold mine and the air navigation locator station.

## Selemdzhinski gold mine (Прииск Селемджинский)

The Selemdzhinski gold mine was established in 1939 and since then has extracted 30 tonnes of gold from its 200km of tunnels. In its best year it produced 1.5 tonnes, but today its 200 workers produce substantially less. The mine was a state company until it was privatised in December 1993. It is now 51 per cent owned by shareholders. Current production is being held back by a lack of investment and technology. The mine needs a refinery to extract gold from the crushed rock. Otherwise, the ore has to be trucked to the BAM and then shipped to a refinery. This is how production has always been done, but with the increase in the cost of freight and low extraction rates typical in Russian refineries, it is now not economical. Older refineries using mercury only extract about 60 per cent of the gold, while the newer process using zinc and chlorine still only extracts 80 per cent. So until a refinery is built incorporating foreign technology, which can extract up to 99 per cent of gold, the mined ore is piling up waiting to be processed.

A tour of the mine and its numerous tunnels is interesting, and make sure you visit the communist lecture theatre in the administration block. Contact Valentin Dovgaenko or Sergei Abramovich, Selemdzhinski Gold Mine, Amurskaya Oblast, 676561, Tokur (676561, Амурская область, п. Токур, Прииск селемджинский, Довгаенко Валентин, Абрамович Сергей).

## Air navigation locator station

On a nearby hill is an air navigation locator station. The station monitors and controls airspace within a 350km radius, which covers the major

Japan to Moscow flight path. Life here is extremely hard for the 20 technicians and air traffic controllers not only due to the isolated and harsh conditions on top of a mountain, but also because their pay is always several months late. With the arrival of the BAM, they were told that the station would move to Fevralsk in 1985. A decade later, they are still being told that there is no money for the move, despite the fact that their government organisation, AERO, receives about $150 million a year in fees for foreign airlines to fly over Russia. The staff of the station are pleased to show anyone around and it takes about 30 minutes to reach from Tokur.

### Zlatoustovsk (Златоустовск)
This town is 55km from Ekimchan. Just before you reach it you come across the Evenk village of Ivanovskoe (Ивановское).

### ZVONKOE (Звонкое) 3,040km
The line heads south across the marshy Selemdzha valley.

This station is named after Vasili Vasilevich Zvonkov (1891-1965), a transport scientist. Vasili Vasilevich graduated from the Moscow Institute of Railroad Communication Engineers in 1917. During his career he taught at the Leningrad Institute of Waterway Transportation and the Military Transport Academy. From 1955 to 1965, he was deputy director of the Institute for Problems of Integrated Transport Systems of the Academy of Sciences. He was awarded the Order of Lenin, four other orders and numerous medals. He is unusual in that he only became a member of the Communist Party late in his life in 1951.

### DEMCHENKO (Демченко) 3,065km
This station was named after the Soviet hero, Maria Sofronovna Demchenko, who became famous for her exploits in the 1930s in harvesting a massive 24 tonnes of sugar beet per hectare. Such devotion to duty earned her an Order of Lenin.

The line begins to ascend the Turana ridge (Турана хребет), with peaks up to 1,500m.

### ULMA (Ульма) 3,149km
The line makes loops around shoulders of the hill and crosses a small river on a high bridge at 3,141km. Look for the watch-tower on the right followed by the barracks beyond. Ulma gets its name from the Ulma river which flows into the Selemdzha river.

The line continues up the Isikan river over smaller bridges and through broken uplands over a pass and down the Tuyun river (р. Туюн). At 3,154km you pass the border of Amurskaya Oblast and Khabarovski Krai. Marking the border is a large monument on the left to the military

## ❏ Feudal capitalism

Tokur is a microcosm of the power shift occurring throughout Russian cities and towns. In the past, Moscow-controlled massive industrial enterprises dominated the economic life of an area through their factories, farms, bakeries, hospitals, schools, telephone systems etc. The state, through the Communist Party, dominated local government and it often provided similar infrastructure for those not working for the enterprises.

Nowadays, with the disappearance of control from Moscow and the Communist Party, local private organisations have tried to fill the void. Unlike the old system, the new power blocks are locally controlled and much more reactive to the market. Rather than competing against each other, the power blocks respect each other's spheres of influence and often work cooperatively by dividing up the market.

Frequently, there are only one or two organisations in small towns along the BAM and each is like a feudal empire with staff personally loyal to their lord. Despite popular media coverage, these leaders are not always lazy ex-communist party hacks. Old boy political connections will only get you so far and building up a dynamic organisation requires business acumen and hard work. Nikolai Malik, the head of Tokur's dominant company, Olimp, is typical of the true entrepreneurs that Russia should be proud of.

Olimp's primary activity is distribution of goods. The company is blessed with many gold miners with high disposable income and very little to spend it on. Olimp buys in bulk imported confectionery, clothes and white goods, as well as supplying staples. Nikolai has expanded his work to such activities as importing fresh fish. In the past, the only fish available in the region's shops were frozen fish from the Pacific Ocean supplied by the state several months after it was caught. Seeing the demand for fresh fish, Nikolai hired planes to fly to the fishing villages and buy it as soon as it is brought on shore. With a fleet of trucks, he supplies fish and other goods to his shops and others in the region.

What makes Nikolai different from the vast majority of Russian businessmen who are simply traders is that he is investing in local production. In 1994 he purchased Tokur's bakery and has expanded it to produce a range of breads and cakes which the previously state-owned bakery could never do.

Expanding into brewing beer was Nikolai's biggest investment. Establishing the brewery in 1995 cost $250,000 which included bringing Moscow technicians to Tokur to assemble the 40 tonnes of equipment. The plant now produces 63,000 litres per month for the region.

As well as distribution, Olimp has expanded into restaurants in Tokur, Ekimchan and Fevralsk.

Nikolai sees enormous opportunities in converting the region's timber wealth into furniture and semi-processed building materials. 'Most companies simply try to export the timber which does not lead to many jobs nor help the Russian economy', he said. 'If we can find a western company who could supply the technology, we would produce the wood products and benefit everyone.' With so many successes already, Nikolai's ideas are destined to become reality sooner or later. Nikolai Malik, General Director, Olimp, Amurskaya Oblast, 676561, Tokur (Николай Малик, Генеральный Директор, Фирма Олимп, Амурская Область, 676561, Токур).

constructors who built most of the eastern section of the BAM. It looks like a giant 'X'. The border also marks a time-zone border. To the west in western Amurskaya Oblast the time is six hours later than in Moscow, while in Khabarovski Krai it is seven.

### 🚉 ETYRKEN (Этыркэн) 3,179km

Accommodation can be organised at the *Railway Hostel* (Общежитие).

### 🚉 ALONKA (Алонка) 3,264km

This medium-sized town was built by the Moldovans. There are plans to dam the Bureya river (р. Бурея) in a narrow canyon near its junction with the Niman (р. Ниман). If this proceeds, Alonka will grow into a town of about 25,000.

### 🚉 BUREINSKI (Буреинский) 3,305km

This village is on the Bureya river (р. Бурея) near the ancient village of Ust-Urgal (Усть-Ургал). The line crosses the Bureya river.

The bridges over the Bureya river are an impressive sight. In BAM construction history, the bridges hold a special place due to the sacrifices and dedication of the railway troop builders. The wooden bridge for road traffic was built in 1954, which was adequate for the small amount of traffic from the only town in the area, Chegdomyn. However, when it was decided to restart the BAM and build Novy Urgal, construction of a new metal bridge for rail traffic started. To get the bridge built in a hurry was a monumental task and it required working throughout the winter regardless of the temperature. Technically, soldiers and other workers are not obliged to work outdoors when the temperature falls below -45°C on windless days and -35°C when the wind is blowing. This regulation is due partly to human compassion and partly to preserving equipment as axes shatter and bulldozers rapidly fail at these temperatures.

The metal bridge was opened in record time on 22 April 1975, but on 20 July 1975 the largest flood in 300 years looked certain to wash the wooden bridge away. All along the Bureya river, villages were evacuated as the torrent washed trees and houses away. While the bridge could withstand the water, if trees got caught under it, the water pressure behind any obstacle would simply push the bridge over. As it was impossible to get within 2km of the bridge due to flooding, troops were lowered by helicopter to string a safety line across the top of it. Soldiers then stood on the bridge working to free any trees or other obstacles that got caught underneath it. The troops stood for hours in the freezing water, constantly afraid that the bridge would give way under them. It didn't and many won bravery medals that day.

The wooden bridge can be seen from the train and you will notice the enormous wooden shields around its piers, which deflect trees and icebergs.

# Novy Urgal–Komsomolsk-na-Amure
## Новый Ургал–Комсомольск-На-Амуре

## THE ROUTE (see Route Map 4, p369)

The line heads east toward Komsomolsk-na-Amure, 300km as the crow flies but 522km on the railway. The straight route is blocked by two south-west to north-east ranges – the Bureinski range (Буреинский хребет) and the Badzhalski range (Баджальский хребет). It crosses the first by the Dusse-Alin (Дуссе-Алинь) tunnel, then heads 180km north-east down the Amgun river (р. Амгунь) and circles back south across lowland meadows to Komsomolsk-na-Amure. The time is Moscow time +7 hours.

## NOVY URGAL (Новый Ургал) 3,315km

Novy Urgal is one of several new BAM towns that splendidly dominate their hilltop sites. Coal-mining and logging are the local industries.

### Orientation

Novy Urgal is at the intersection of the west-east BAM mainline, built in the 1970s and the north-south line from the Chegdomyn coal-mines south to the Trans-Siberian, built immediately before and after the Great Patriotic War. It was founded in December 1974 when the first Ukrainian BAM builders arrived and is the headquarters of the eastern third of the BAM. Novy Urgal was sponsored by Ukraine and many of its streets honour the builders with names such as Donbas, Kharkov, Carpathia, Dnieper and Kiev. From the station, 300m below, the town is defined by a rampart of buildings, with circular windows and a tower.

A monumental stairway ascends from the station to the town; the road from the station winds around the hilltop on the east side. Both come out at a grand plaza with the shopping centre (торговый дом) and the house of culture (Дом култура) at the hilltop. The shopping centre has the form

---

❏ **NOVY URGAL (Новый Ургал)**
682071, Khabarovski Krai, Verkhnebureinski Raion, Novy Urgal
(682071, Хабаровский Край, Верхнебуреинский район, п. Новый Ургал)

badly sited; nobody wants to carry their purchases halfway up the hill. To the north of the station are the railway yards. On the road to the yards are old steam-train engine boilers that are used to supply hot water to the local villages. There is even one of these recycled locomotives providing steam in the railway yards.

The north-south railway and stretches of the west-east railway were built by gulag prisoners and Japanese POWs, and many older buildings in the area were built by the Japanese. Japanese groups tour the BAM region from here east to the Pacific to visit the graves of their relatives.

Chegdomyn (Чегдомын), the centre of the Verkhnebureinski (Upper Bureya) Raion, is 17km away. For information about sights in Chegdomyn, including the regional museum and the North Korean compound, see Chegdomyn–Novy Urgal–Izvestkovaya (pp210-15).

## 🏛 URGAL-1 (Ургал-1) 3,330km

The small village surrounding Urgal-1 was founded in the 1940s as the line to the Chegdomyn coal mines was being built. The abandoned barracks up the hill from the station building were built by Japanese POWs. Trains for Chegdomyn turn off the BAM near Urgal-1.

## 🏛 SOLONI (Солони) 3,383km

This small town was built by the Tadzhikistan Komsomol. The line twists and turns toward the pass and tunnel across the Bureinski range (Буреинский хребет).

## ⊠ DUSSE-ALIN (Дуссе-Алинь) 3,403km

This station is at the eastern end of the 2km Dusse-Alin Tunnel (Дуссе-Алинский Тоннель) – see the boxed text. Near the portal on the left side there is a small memorial cross, followed by the barracks and the station.

## 🏛 SULUK (Сулук) 3,421km

This small town, on the Suluk river, was sponsored by Khabarovsk Komsomol. After leaving Suluk, the train turns from the south-east to the north-east and travels 180km down the Amgun river (р. Амгунь), flanked to the north by the Bureinski range (Буреинский хребет) and to the south by the Badzhalski range (Баджальский хребет).

## 🏛 GERBI (Герби) 3,475km

This railway settlement is the terminus for local BAM trains running to Novy Urgal in the west and Postyshevo in the east. Accommodation is available at the *Locomotive Brigade Hostel* (Дом отдыха Локомотивной бригады).

## ⊠ URKALTU (Уркальту) 3,500km

Painted silver spikes were hammered into the track at this siding, signifying the completion of the 504km eastern section of the BAM in June 1978.

## 🏛 AMGUN (Амгунь) 3,581km

This town is named after the 723km Amgun river that runs beside the train line. Permafrost is widespread in this region making construction of the railway line difficult.

In 1989, between here and Duki (Дуки), 50km away, hikers found the wreckage of a American-built DC-3 that had disappeared on 4 October 1938 while searching for the Rodina aircraft which had just crashed in the region.

## ❏ Dusse-Alin Tunnel (Дуссе-Алинский Тоннель)

Of all the tunnels on the BAM, this one has had the longest and most tragic history. Work started in 1939 when prisoners from the BAM gulag complex, BAMLag, arrived on foot with only hand tools, one horse and a single motorised cart and orders to dig a 2km tunnel as quickly as possible.

Conditions were extremely harsh and starvation, coupled with overwork, was the most common cause of prisoners' death. The life of free workers was slightly better, but death was still common. For example, in 1940 the chief engineer, Vasili Konserov, was shot in the back by the military guard commander after a dispute. The death was officially called an accident and Konserov was buried with full honours, as he had previously received the Order of Lenin for constructing the famous Belomorski-Baltiski canal.

A suitable replacement, the well-known Moscow Metro engineer Ratsboum, was forcibly volunteered to finish the tunnel. He was shocked at the condition of the prisoners and demanded immediate improvements, including giving them their meagre back pay. After some dispute, his superiors acquiesced to his demands, more afraid of not completing the tunnel on time.

Returning to work, Ratsboum was faced with a far greater problem. There was no survey equipment so the tunnel was being dug from both sides of the mountain using just line-of-sight. This meant that there was an excellent chance that the tunnels would not meet. The inevitable consequences would be a charge of deliberate sabotage, followed by a firing squad.

Luckily, when the tunnels joined they were out by only 20cm and Ratsboum's life was spared. Work continued on enlarging it until work halted in December 1942 due to the Great Patriotic War. In 1947, work recommenced and Ratsboum resumed his post. The tunnel was officially opened on Stalin's birthday in 1950. As part of the tunnel's decoration, busts of Marx, Engels, Stalin and Lenin behind one another were chiselled into the rock face beside the entrance, with the inscription '1947-1950' above it.

Despite its completion, the tunnel was never put into regular service as work on the line between the tunnel and Komsomolsk-na-Amure was stopped following Stalin's death. A small maintenance detachment remained until 1959 and then when it became obvious that the BAM's construction would not be resumed, the tunnel was abandoned. Subterranean water slowly trickled into the tunnel, the freezing of the water resulted in rock falls and eventually it iced up.

Following the decision to restart construction of the BAM, railway troops arrived at the tunnel in December 1974. Despite being abandoned for 20 years, the barracks were still in good condition and the soldiers moved into them. The camp's wire enclosures, guard towers and signs left no doubt as to the original builders and as excavation work commenced, more reminders, including frozen corpses, were unearthed. Letters about the gruesome finds started to be received by the soldiers' families and even a candlestick holder made from a skull was sent home as a souvenir.

The outcry from the soldiers' families quickly snowballed into a military commission sent from Moscow. In a great hurry, the camp underwent a 'Potemkin village' renovation. (Potemkin was a one-eyed general and lover of Catherine the Great, who would precede the Tsarina on her tours around Russia, ensuring that each village was freshly painted and festooned with banners, and unsightly places and people hidden.) As part of the camp's renovation, a cloth was tactfully draped over Stalin's bust.

---

❏ **Dusse-Alin Tunnel (Дуссе-Алинский Тоннель) cont'd**
The verdict of the commission was that the political education of the soldiers was poor and it was ideologically inappropriate for them to live in prisoners' barracks. So, in just 10 days, the entire camp was levelled, including the cemetery, and all signs of the previous workers, including the busts and 1947-1950 inscription, were destroyed. The demolition work led to more grisly finds, among them numerous letters secreted away in the walls of the barracks. An example is: 'To the beloved leader and Comrade Stalin: My wife went on a business trip and never came back. I myself was arrested at night and the term was 10 years. And when I asked why, I was told 'you'll serve your term and then know'. Pray find out the truth and restore justice.'

To reopen the tunnel, the soldiers used the backblast from aircraft jet engines to melt the 32,000 cubic metres of ice that blocked the tunnel. Workers from both sides met on 11 April 1976 and the tunnel was officially opened in 1982 when the first train travelled from Novy Urgal through the tunnel to Komsomolsk-na-Amure. Sadly, the tunnel now just carries the letters '1982' on its portal with no mention of the previous tunnel builders.

---

All 18 Russians on the DC-3 were killed. The tail section of the DC-3 was recovered and now stands as a monument in Komsomolsk-na-Amure.

## 🏠 POSTYSHEVO (Постышево) 3,633km

Work resumed on the BAM after the Great Patriotic War, until again stopped in 1949. During this time, the eastern segment of the line reached Postyshevo and this section of track remained in operation ever since.

The handsome station, built after BAM work was resumed, was named after Pavel Petrovich Postyshevo (1887–1940) who was a prominent Ukrainian Bolshevik and ally of Stalin. In 1930, Stalin named him secretary of the Ukrainian Central Committee and he ran the Party apparatus there until he disappeared on Stalin's orders in 1938.

The town, Berezovy (Березовый), has a different name from the station and was sponsored by the Novosibirsk Komsomol. A 10-minute walk brings you to the Amgun river (р. Амгунь) which is famous as one of the best fishing rivers in eastern Siberia.

In late summer and autumn, you can flyfish for dog salmon and hunchback salmon, while in winter you can icefish for Brachymystax salmon, taimen and grayling. You need a licence but this is easily obtained once you arrive. The best fishermen in town are the father and son team of Viktor Ivanovich and Genadi Viktorovich Shchus. They can organise a fishing trip if you write to them well in advance. Contact them at 682638, Khabarovski Krai, Solnechny Raion, Berezovy, ul. Parkovaya 18 (682638, Хабаровский Край, Солнечный район, п. Березовый, ул. Парковая, 18, Щусь Виктор Иванович и Геннадий Викторович). Another useful contact is the adventure club Azimut (Азимут) run by Adolf Vaselovich Bovogov (☎ 292) and Sergei Chekashin (☎ 423).

Contact Azimut at 682638, Khabarovski Krai, Solnechny Raion, Berezovy, ul. Novomotornaya 4a, kv 10 (682638, Хабаровский Край, Солнечный район, п. Березовый, ул. Новомоторная, 4a, кв 10, Бовогов Адольф Васелович и Чекашин Сергей).

About 8km down the Amgun river is the Old Believers village of Tavlinka (Тавлинка, Деревня староверов). Old Believers are devout followers of the Russian Orthodox Church as it was prior to the second half of the seventeenth century. It was at this time that the church underwent reforms that included a revision of the prayer book and new statutes. Those that did not accept the reforms were labelled Old Believers and persecuted. Over the next 100 years they migrated eastward and, at the height of persecution, hid their villages in remote taiga. Today descendants of these Old Believers exist just as they did then, shunning smoking and drinking. You can distinguish Old Believer men by their long beards.

The line runs south-east again and skirts low-lying marshes at 150m above sea-level.

## 🐂 EVORON (Эворон) 3,697km

The station's name comes from nearby Lake Evoron (озеро Эворон) which means 'ghosts of the lake' in the Nanai language. The lake covers an area of 194 sq km, runs 30km north-south and is about 12km wide. This area is a major resting place for migratory birds and the Wildlife Institute in Khabarovsk, which provides survey information for the government's nature resource management, has recommended that this area become a national park. Over 200 types of birds have been identified here. In the late 1980s, it was planned to build a nuclear reactor at the lake. A combination of anti-nuclear protests in Komsomolsk-na-Amure and a cash shortage resulted in the 2.5 billion rouble project being dumped. However, the lake suffered considerably in May 1993 when a massive oil spill in one of its feeder rivers flowed into the lake.

## ⊠ KONDON (Кондон)

Five kilometres from this station is the Nanai village of Kondon, which is the location of one of Siberia's most important archaeological finds.

Archaeological digs first started here in the 1930s with major finds near the old post office in the centre of the town and at another site 2km away known as Kukelev (Кукелев) on the banks of the Paltsem river (р. Пальцем). These sites were about 5,000 to 6,000 years old and revealed a highly organised society that had disappeared overnight. It appears that the village was attacked, everything was burnt down and the inhabitants fled, never to return.

Among the finds were wooden objects, combs made from animal bones and shards of pottery with a well-known pattern of broad spirals.

Then, in 1965, workers discovered a statuette that for the first time revealed the physical shape of the original inhabitants. Called 'the Nanai Venus', it confirmed the link between the past and present indigenous people. The statue was of a woman with a soft oval face, broad cheekbones, a slender chin and small pouting lips. The woman's nose is long and thin, like those of the North American Indians. The eyes are long and narrow, like arched slits, while the forehead and upper part of the head is

---

### ❏ Rodina – when even a disaster breaks a record

The 1930s were the golden age of Soviet aviation with records being broken virtually every second month. New planes were developed, aero clubs sprang up throughout the country and record-breaking flights were common. Even though one such attempt resulted in the plane crashing, it only fuelled national pride.

In October 1938, an ANT-37 aircraft, nicknamed *Rodina* or homeland, left Moscow for the Russian Far East, crewed by three women in an attempt to break the non-stop distance record for women. The crew consisted of the navigator Marina Raskova, Captain Valentina Grizodubova and co-pilot Polina Osipenko. As soon as they passed the Urals, the weather turned ugly with a strong headwind and low visibility. Visual navigation became difficult and then the radio navigation signals stopped. They had no choice but to go on. When it became apparent that they were about to run out of fuel, Raskova was ordered to bail out as her position in the nose of the aircraft was deadly in a crash. She took her survival kit which consisted of a gun, matches and two bars of chocolate.

The plane struggled on for a few more kilometres before crashing. For the next 10 days Raskova struggled through the taiga until she reached the crashed Rodina and all the crew waited together until they were rescued. Despite the crash of the Rodina the flight captured the women's non-stop flying record with 26 hours, 29 minutes and more than 6,000km travelled.

This struggle captured the imagination of the Soviet people and when Raskova returned to Moscow, Stalin awarded her the Gold Star of the Soviet Union.

Raskova played a pivotal role in convincing Stalin to create women's air-combat regiments following the Soviet Union's entry into the Second World War. Due to Raskova's personal fame, thousands of women applied to join her new regiment called the 587th Dive Bomber Regiment which later was designated the 125th Guards Bomber regiment. Eventually 1,000 were selected and training started in October 1941. Raskova trained herself and other pilots to fly the notoriously hard to handle Pe-2 divebomber. Unfortunately as the regiment was flying from their training base to the front, Raskova's plane crashed killing all aboard.

While her death was a tragic blow to all women pilots, she advanced the cause of women in her country. According to Anne Noggle in her excellent book, *A Dance with Death: Soviet Airwomen in World War 2*, 'Without Marina Raskova it is doubtful that there would have been any women air regiments in the Soviet Union during World War 2'. Her importance was also recognised by the US government when it launched a supply ship called *Marina Raskova* in California on 22 June 1943.

broad and slanted back. Along the Amur and Lena rivers you still see people with these characteristics.

There are no hotels, but very basic **accommodation** can be organised in the town's Possovet. There is a local museum, but most of the important finds are now at Novosibirsk's Museum of History and Culture.

### 🏚 GORIN (Горин) 3,733km

This town is located on the Goryun river (р. Горюн). The BAM reached this town in 1942 but the rails were ripped up late that year to be used for the Stalingrad to Saratov line. The line was re-laid in the 1950s and upgraded in the 1970s. The line heads south toward Komsomolsk-na-Amure.

### 🏚 KHURMULI (Хурмули) 3,769km

This is a small indigenous village and is relatively famous for producing the first Nanai businessman of note, Inokenti Dyonovski.

### 🏚 KHALGASO (Хальгасо) 3,808km

For the really keen rail enthusiasts, this place is a must. When the line from Komsomolsk-na-Amure to Postyshevo was re-laid in the late 1940s, Lend-Lease rails were used and you can still see the words 'USA 1944' and 'Colorado 1943' stamped on the rails. These rails are not used on the current BAM but on a siding running parallel to the BAM.

Beside the rails are the remains of a camp that started as a hospital camp for forced labourers who laid the lines in the 1940s. The camp had two sections, Special Hospital Branch 3762 for Russian gulag prisoners and Camp No 5 for Japanese POWs. After the Soviet Union's gulags were closed in the 1950s, the camp was converted into a children's Pioneer camp. The camp was finally closed in 1984 when the BAM was completed and the number of trains rushing by presented a danger to young children. All that remains of the camp is the front gate and some rubble.

In the early 1990s, the Japanese built a memorial nearby honouring the Japanese POWs who died in the area. The Russian government has also indicated that it would like to build a similar memorial for the victims of Stalin's repression but does not have the funds to do so.

The site of the rails, camp and Japanese memorial is about 5km from Khalgaso station and is relatively easy to find. Simply follow the road in front of the station to the village of Start (Старт). The town earned its name as a launching base for explorations to the north of Komsomolsk-na-Amure including Solnechny. Two kilometres past Start, you pass a military settlement which houses a tank regiment. A further 1km on, the road does a left dog leg. Just before you cross over a railway line, take the left turn that runs parallel to the line through a rail lumber yard. About 400m further on, the road crosses the railway line and it is at this point that you will find the rails, camp remains and Japanese memorial.

## SILINKA (Силинка) 3,818km

Tin concentrate from the nearby Solnechny and Gorni mines is loaded here for smelting in China.

## KOMSOMOLSK-NA-AMURE 2 (Комсомолск-на-Амуре 2) 3,831km

A railyard and suburban station 6km from the main Komsomolsk-na-Amure station.

On the left, as you enter Komsomolsk-na-Amure proper, you will see the steelworks of Amurstal (Амурсталь), first the new rolling mill and melt shop, then the decommissioned open hearth blast furnaces and soaking pit.

# Komsomolsk-na-Amure and region
## Комсомольск-на-Амуре и окрестности

## KOMSOMOLSK-NA-AMURE (Комсомольск-на-Амуре) 3,837km

Komsomolsk-na-Amure is a major industrial city built in the wilderness since 1932 and closed until the end of the Soviet era. Situated on the Amur river 500km above its mouth, it is the end-point of the BAM route, which connects north Baikal with the Amur. Growing and prosperous since its foundation, the city reflects the majestic and expansive urban architecture of the 1930s, the 1950s and the 1970s. It is an attractive town on the beautiful Amur river and the gateway to the rarely-visited northern areas of the Russian Far East, to Nikolaevsk-na-Amure, ancient capital of the region, to the local towns of Solnechny, Amursk and Pivan, to the wild forested coasts of the far east, haunt of the Amur tiger and of course to the BAM.

> ❏ **KOMSOMOLSK-NA-AMURE**
> **(Комсомольск-на-Амуре)**
> Area code ☎ 42172
> 681021, Khabarovski Krai,
>   Komsomolsk-na-Amure
> (Хабаровский Край,
>   г. Комсомольск-на-Амуре)
> Moscow time +7 hours

## Orientation

Komsomolsk-na-Amure and its smaller neighbour Amursk were built in the wilderness on the Amur river between the old river cities of Khabarovsk, south and Nikolaevsk-na-Amure, north at the mouth of the river. On the west the BAM heads toward Tynda, Lena and Baikal. To the east the railway crosses the Amur over the last bridge on the river and then twists through coastal mountains to reach the Pacific. To the south Komsomolsk-na-Amure is linked with Khabarovsk by the railway, by a paved road and by the river itself.

The first urban core, the central district (Центральный район), is built in brick and stucco with turrets and cupolas on tree-lined avenues – Peace Avenue, formerly Stalin Avenue (проспект Мира, проспект Сталина) from the river to Metallurgists Square (площадь Металлургов) and Lenin Avenue (проспект Ленина) from Metallurgists Square to Railway Park (парк ЖД). North of this section is the first industrial site, the steel mill Amurstal (Амурсталь). Eastward, across a park in the meadows of the Silinka river (р. Силинка), is the Lenin district (Ленинский район) with the aircraft factories and shipyards, the Gagarin park and sports complexes and heavy avenues of 1960s apartments. On the western side of the city is the stupendous Pervostroitelei ('First Builders') Avenue (пр. Первостроителей), 80m wide and lined with 1970s and 1980s blocks with Soviet store fronts and signage intact, and with parks and playgrounds hidden behind.

Four tram routes cross at Metallurgists Square and link all quarters of the city.

The industrial city of Amursk is 63km south, the mining town of Solnechny is 43km north-west and the dacha town of Pivan is across the river.

## History

Komsomolsk-na-Amure was built in the unpopulated Russian Far East by fervent young communists as part of the 1930s nationwide industrialisation campaign designed to propel the Soviet Union into the modern world. It was from these workers, who were members of the Young Communist League, or Komsomol, that the city got its name. The full name, Komsomolsk-na-Amure, means 'Komsomolsk on the Amur river', which distinguishes the city from the other Komsomolsks dotted throughout Russia.

It was built in a remote area of the Russian Far East with the closest settlements being a small Nanai indigenous village and the small Russian village of Permskoe, founded in 1858. According to the 1890s Geographical and Statistical Dictionary of the Amur and Primorski Regions, in 1888 Permskoe consisted of just 26 farms, with 78 adult males and 82 adult females. 'The village provided supplies for the traders' and military's river boats and maintained a regional postal office.'

The isolated site chosen for Komsomolsk-na-Amure may seem strange, but its remoteness was ideal for building a military industrial complex of aircraft, ship building and steel plants. The Chinese border was over 400km away, the Pacific Ocean was 450km down the Amur river and travellers on the Trans-Siberian would never get closer than 350km.

Komsomolsk-na-Amure was founded on 10 May 1932 when the advance party arrived from Khabarovsk on the river steamers *Columbus* and *Comintern*. Thousands of builders followed and within seven years the town became the fourth largest in the Russian Far East. By the late 1930s growth had slowed due to workers' inexperience, harsh winters and a lack of management and supplies.

As Stalin's purges were sweeping the Soviet Union at this time, Komsomolsk-na-Amure's failure to meet targets became the justification for a local purge that started on the fifth anniversary of the city. The director of the steelworks, Amurstal, summed up the purging process in *Komsomolskaya Pravda* on 12 June 1937 with, 'We are mercilessly rooting out this scum of wreckers'. It was alleged that the 'wreckers' were active and ingenious: they mixed sugar with concrete to lower its strength, they put glass into ball-bearings to cause accidents and destroyed vital blue-prints. The town's leadership was quickly eliminated amid claims of poor security which had led to 'agents of foreign intelligence services, bandits and diversionists' penetrating the ranks of workers and technicians.

The victims of Stalin's purges throughout the Soviet Union created a vast pool of labour and as Komsomolsk-na-Amure was in need of labour, it became the gulag capital of the Russian Far East. An estimated 900,000 prisoners tramped through Komsomolsk-na-Amure's camps. Thousands died and unmarked mass graves litter the city. The Sewing Machine Factory, Railway Park, Maternity Hospital No 1 and Dalstalkonstruktsiya Enterprise all sit on prisoner cemeteries.

As the Great Patriotic War progressed, Komsomolsk-na-Amure's gulag population of Soviet citizens decreased from 67,742 in 1942 to 28,073 in 1944. However, this decline was more than offset by the flood of Japanese and to a much smaller extent German, POWs. At its peak, the prison complex had 49,500 Japanese POWs, which included 16,000 in 18 city camps and the rest working on the BAM and other projects in the region. In Komsomolsk-na-Amure, the Japanese worked in the steel plant, aircraft factory, brick plant and repair plant. They also constructed most of the city's stone buildings including the Amur Hotel, Polyclinic No 7, High School No 145 and 30th Anniversary of October Cinema.

In 1990 Komsomolsk-na-Amure became the first Russian town to allow Japanese ex-POWs to return to honour their dead. Over the next few years, the Japanese built 16 memorials around Komsomolsk-na-Amure. Rumour has it that even then the Russians were exploiting the Japanese as they charged them enormous amounts to build the memorials. Today, Komsomolsk-na-Amure has a sister-city relationship with the Japanese city of Kamo.

Today, Komsomolsk-na-Amure is suffering from high levels of unemployment and the population peaked at 312,400 in 1993 and is now declining as families leave for Khabarovsk and Vladivostok looking for work. Despite this, Komsomolsk-na-Amure is the Russian Far East's fourth biggest city and has a lot to offer travellers.

## Getting there and away

Komsomolsk-na-Amure is at the junction of railways west along the BAM, east to the Pacific and south to Khabarovsk. West, there is one train a day to and from Tynda (37 hours). East, there is one train each night to and from Vanino (12 hours) and Sovetskaya Gavan. South, the night train from Sovetskaya Gavan continues by day to Khabarovsk (10 hours), stopping at every station and railway halt and on to Vladivostok. There is also one night train to Khabarovsk. For information about this line, see Komsomolsk-na-Amure–Khabarovsk by train (pp215-24). Locally, trains go to the dacha villages to the south.

There are essentially no good roads west or east. South, there is a new

**The Emblem of Komsomolsk which is also called the City of the Dawn.**

500km highway to Khabarovsk (five hours); shared vans load outside the Komsomolsk-na-Amure and Khabarovsk railway stations and leave when they make up a full load. North, there is a wretched road to Lazarev (Лазарев) and Nikolaevsk-na-Amure (Николаевск-на-Амуре). These roads split at Selikhin (Селихин) after crossing the Amur rail-road bridge.

Local buses load at the bus station one block north of the River Station. They go to the local mining towns, to Amursk and across the river to Pivan and other villages. The bus station (☎ 38-62-91) is at ul. Naberezhnaya (ул. Набережная, Автовокзал).

The Amur river is navigable usually from 20 June to 31 August. There is one daily hydrofoil to Khabarovsk (south) and two daily hydrofoils to

## ❏ Balancing gender in Komsomolsk

The construction of Komsomolsk appealed to many communists who wanted adventure while building a brave new socialist world. They were invariably young and male, and the dearth of women made the population of Komsomolsk-na-Amure restless and transient.

This shortage created the Khetagurova Movement, which in conjunction with forced exile, became one of the major strategies for increasing the population of the Russian Far East in the 1930s. The movement was named after Valentina Khetagurova-Zarubina, the 22-year-old wife of a major serving in the Special Far Eastern Army. She felt so much compassion for the single males in Komsomolsk-na-Amure who had little chance of finding a wife that she wrote an open letter to the women of the Soviet Union encouraging them to migrate to the Russian Far East. The letter was published on 5 February 1937 and appeared in numerous forms over the following years. The needs of the Far East are great, she wrote. 'We need fitters and turners, teachers and draftswomen, typists and accountants – all to the same degree. We want only bold, determined people, not afraid of difficulties'. She described the Far East as an exotic dreamland, 'where still a short time ago there were only deer, tigers and lions' and where 'wonderful work, wonderful people and a wonderful future' would meet the girls. More importantly she implied that every girl would find a husband in the Far East and possibly even one who held a military rank or commanded a good salary. This appeal was picked up by others in the media such as Pavel Pavlenko who integrated it into one of his novels: 'From the polar tundra down to Korea, everybody dreams of women. Nowhere else do people get married as quickly as there. Widows do not exist in the Far East. Only the oldest women overcome by senility remain single.'

The Khetagurova movement was a brilliant success on paper and by the end of 1937, over 70,000 Soviet girls had registered as volunteers for the Far East, with 5,000 being selected in 1937 alone. How many actually married and stayed was never recorded.

Nikolaevsk-na-Amure (north). For information about this line, see Khabarovsk–Komsomolsk-na-Amure–Nikolaevsk-na-Amure by river (pp224-8). There are local ferries to the dacha villages. There are also occasional cruise ships that travel from China, through Blagoveshchensk, Khabarovsk and Komsomolsk-na-Amure to Nikolaevsk-na-Amure.

There are regular flights from Moscow, Krasnoyarsk, Khabarovsk, Nikolaevsk-na-Amure, Vanino, Bogorodskoe and several rural towns. The airport is 27km out of town and there are 12 buses a day that make the 45-minute trip. The city's Aeroflot office is at pr. Pervostroitelei 18, ☎ 303-93 (пр. Первостроителей, 18, Агенство Аэрофлота).

## Getting around

Four tram lines (and many buses) go to all parts of the city. The useful tram No 2 starts at the railway station and passes near all three hotels, the market and the Tsum shopping centre, the post and telephone office, the city government offices, the Polytechnic Institute and the art and regional museums and ends at the River Station (речной вокзал). The Nata-Tour company (see Getting assistance, pp174-176) will supply an excellent city map with transport lines and stops marked.

## Where to stay

*Hotel Voskhod* has the best facilities and is the closest to the station. It is the tourist and business hotel, set back in a small plaza used by the homeless on Pervostroitelei ('First Builders') Avenue at the intersection of Lenin Avenue. On the corner is a 'Beryoza' storefront, the former hard currency store. The Voskhod Hotel is cheerless, deserted, disobliging and expensive – $50 for a room for two. There is a small café on the 8th floor, a ground-floor restaurant and a hairdresser. The rooms are small but adequate, with a toilet and shower. Hotel Voskhod is at pr. Pervostroitelei 31, ☎ 303-36 (пр. Первостроителей, 31, Гостиница «Восход»).

The down-market *Hotel Amur* is on the second and third floors of a corner building on prospekt Mira, two stops from the River Station. The rooms start from $17 for a single. Most rooms have no facilities and the shower is on the ground floor. Hotel Amur serves ordinary Russians, Chinese traders working the market, and shady businessmen and their girlfriends. It has a cafeteria. Hotel Amur is at pr. Mira 15, ☎ 430-74 (пр. Мира, 15, Гостиница «Амур»).

The most interesting hotel is the *TsVEKS Hotel* – the Centre for Higher Economic and Cultural Relations (Центр внешн еэкономических и культурных связей). It is hard to find and easy to miss. Start at Metallurgists Square (площадь Металлургов); face away from the river; a tramline heads up a ramp over the railway; stay to the left of the tramline, on the flat, and follow a footpath past a row of tiny villas in their own gardens; take the paved street, ul. Khabarovskaya (ул. Хабаровская), to the left; on the left look for a large two-storey villa behind a fence, standing in a formal garden; go through the gate and buzz on the front door. The history of this hotel was revealed when one of the editors said to the Director 'Nobody in the city knows this hotel'. He replied, 'They would if you asked for Khrushchev's dacha'. A one-storey villa was built for Khrushchev's visit, and a second storey was added for later leaders. There are six guest rooms. Prices are $150 a night for the luxe suite, $120 for the half-luxe, a single at $90, and a double at $80. You can sleep in the bed that Brezhnev, Yeltsin and Gorbachev slept in and, like them, hold the shower nozzle with one hand while you wash with the other. Contact Hotel TsVEKS (Tsentr Vneshneekonomicheskikh i Kulturnykh Svyazei) at Khabarovskaya, 47, 681013, g. Komsomolsk-na-Amure, ☎/▤ 447-05 (ул. Хабаровская, 47, Гостиница ЦВЭКС).

## Where to eat

*Hotel Voskhod* has a restaurant and a café, the *Amur restaurant* has a cafeteria, *Hotel TsVEKS* has a kitchen, the *railway station* has a busy cafeteria and the *river station* has a small café. Komsomolsk-na-Amure has a good number of other restaurants and canteens. Several locations are shown on the map.

Of special mention is the *Pelmennaya* at 21 Lenin Avenue (пр. Ленина, 21) – a café that makes and serves pelmeni (plus other cooked delicacies). These meat-filled potato pastry dumplings are made on site with a small machine that is worth watching in action and the Pelmennaya itself is a Soviet-era original. Make sure you get the vinegar sauce and while these pelmeni are not as good as home-made they are quite tasty. (And admire the whole block with its excellent stucco, turret, balconies, star and the classic Stalin-era slogan that was posted over the gates of gulags: «ТРУД В СССР ЕСТЬ ДЕЛО ЧЕСТИ ДОБЛЕСТИ И ГЕРОЙСТВА» – 'LABOUR FOR THE USSR IS A MATTER OF HONOUR, VALOUR, AND HEROISM'.)

For an intimate, upmarket lunch or dinner in peace and quiet (a rarity in Russia) try *Café Assorti* (☎ 4-72-83), in the Avangard Stadium at ul. Komsomolskaya and pr. Mira, at ul. Komsomolskaya 26, (стадион Авангард, ул. Комсомольская, 26, кафе «Ассорти»).

The following upmarket restaurants are close together on Pervostroitelei Avenue.

*Rodnik bar-restaurant* offers traditional Russian cuisine and seafood. The restaurant produces its own beer called 'Flora' and there is a dance hall. Rodnik is at pr. Pervostroitelei 19, ☎ +7 42172 3-70-20, (пр. Первостроителей, 19, ресторан «Родник»).

*Heilungjian* is the only Chinese restaurant in Komsomolsk-na-Amure. It has Chinese cooks in the kitchen, a band out front, and is at pr. Pervostroitelei 21, ☎ +7 42172 3-22-72 (пр. Первостроителей, 21, ресторан «Хейлундзян»). Heilungjian is the Chinese name of the Amur river.

*Vstrecha bar-restaurant* offers traditional Russian cuisine, plus a wide selection of salads with tartaletki, plus seafood. Vstrecha is at pr. Pervostroitelei 20, ☎ +7 42172 3-71-35 (пр. Первостроителей, 20, ресторан «Встреча»).

## Getting assistance

Nata-Tour Co Ltd, run by Mikhail Radokhleb, organises adventure tours including white-water rafting and river floating, expeditions into the taiga on foot and by vehicle, train tours, and gulag and POW camp tours. Radokhleb was educated as a railway engineer; his hobby was outside sports, especially rafting. His fully-equipped office, with phone/fax, copi-

er, maps, photos, brochures and Internet access, is on the ground floor of
Voskhod Hotel; pr. Pervostroitelei 31, Hotel Voskhod, Room 104,
Komsomolsk-na-Amure, 681010 Russia, ☎/🖂 +7 42172 3-03-32, 🖳
natatour@kmscom.ru, www.amur.rosnet.ru/natatour (681010, Россия, г.
Комсомольск-на-Амуре, пр. Первостроителей, 31, Гостиница
«Восход», 104, «Ната-Тур», Радохлеб Михаил).

Dersu Uzala Tourist Centre, run by Alexander F Shelopugin, organises specialised tours (business, archaeological, geological) and adventure
tours (hunting, fishing, climbing, rafting, skiing), plus trips for young people and for foreigners. Contact Dersu Uzala at ul. Sevastopolskaya, House
12, Office 16, Komsomolsk-na-Amure, Russia 681000, (☎/🖂 +7 42172
47088, 🖳 shel@kmscom.ru (681000, Россия, г. Комсомольск-на-
Амуре, ул.Севастопольская, дом 12, оф. 16, Туристический центр
'Дерсу Узала', Шелопугин Александр Ф).

Marina Aleksandrovna Kuzmina is one of the Russian Far East's
experts on gulags, Japanese POWs and the history of the BAM. She has
written three books on these subjects. She is currently the Secretary of
the Japanese-Russian Friendship Society's Komsomolsk-na-Amure
branch and has organised a number of tours by ex-POWs from Japan. She
was the chairperson of Memorial and is also active in local politics. Her
address is 681013, Russia, Komsomolsk-na-Amure, ul. Vokzalnaya 37/4,
floor 10, ☎ +7 42172 3-47-63, 📄 (care of Nata-Tour) +7 42172 3-03-32
(ул. Вокзальная, 37/4, 10 этаж, Кузьмина Марина
Александровна).

A good source of information on what is happening is the local paper,
the *Dalnevostochny Komsomolsk*, based at ul. Kirova 31, ☎ 429-22 (ул.
Кирова, 31, Редакция газеты «Дальневосточный Комсомольск»).

---

### For complete legend see inside back cover

1. Voskhod Hotel
2. Amur Hotel
3. TsVEKS Hotel

4. Daker restaurant
5. Pelmennaya cafe
6. Voskhod restaurant
7. Good canteen
8. Uyut cafe
9. Novinka cafe
10. Rita cafe

11. Regional museum
12. Art museum
13. Outdoor tank museum

14. Japanese POW memorial
15. Great Patriotic War memorial

16. City administration
17. Drama theatre
18. Komsomol hall
19. Government departments,
    Russia-USA, Russia-Japan
    & Memorial

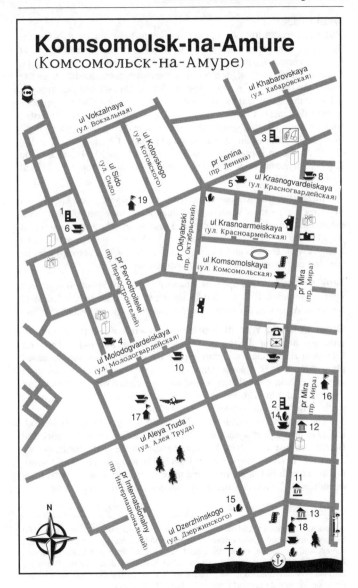

# Komsomolsk-na-Amure
(Комсомольск-на-Амуре)

ul Khabarovskaya
(ул. Хабаровская)

ul Vokzalnaya
(ул. Вокзальная)

ul Kotovskogo
(ул. Котовского)

ul Sido
(ул. Сидо)

pr Lenina
(пр. Ленина)

3

8

ul Krasnogvardeiskaya
(ул. Красногвардейская)

5

19

1
6

ul Krasnoarmeiskaya
(ул. Красноармейская)

pr Oktyabrski
(пр. Октябрьский)

pr Pervostroitelei
(пр. Первостроителей)

ul Komsomolskaya
(ул. Комсомольская)

7

pr Mira
(пр. Мира)

4

ul Molodogvardeiskaya
(ул. Молодогвардейская)

10

17

pr Mira
(пр. Мира)

16

2
14

12

ul Aleya Truda
(ул. Алея Труда)

11

pr Internatsionalny
(пр. Интернациональный)

15

13
18

N

ul Dzerzhinskogo
(ул. Дзержинского)

## What to see

**Regional museum**  A good introduction to Komsomolsk-na-Amure is the Regional museum, which is one of the best museums in the Russian Far East. It is unusually modern in its use of dioramas, models and displays. There are displays of the local Nanai indigenous people, rural life in the late 1800s, the building of Komsomolsk-na-Amure, the wartime factories, the gulags in the region, and the natural history of the Amur. Of interest are photos and documents of two Americans, Ann Stanley and Lloyd Patterson, who ran the English language propaganda radio during the Great Patriotic War which broadcast into Japan, China and much of Asia.

The museum is open daily except Mondays from 10.00 to 17.00. The Regional museum is at pr. Mira 8, ☎ 422-60 (пр. Мира, 8, Музей краеведческий).

**Art museum**  The Art museum consists of two floors of art. The ground floor has one room of Western art with another room housing short term exhibitions. Upstairs is indigenous and peasant art. The Art museum is at pr. Mira 16, ☎ 422-60 (пр. Мира, 16, Музей изобразительного исскусства). There is also a commercial art shop at pr. Pervostroitelei 20 (пр. Первостроителей, 20, Художественная лавка).

**Tank museum**  This open-air museum consists of about 30 armoured fighting vehicles. It is located in the park next door to the Regional Museum. As it does not have a fence around it, it can be visited anytime.

**Great Patriotic War memorial (Мемориал в честь земляков, павших в годы Великой Отечественной войны)**  The War Memorial is the finest sculpture on the BAM. On a wide marble-paved plaza three narrow obelisks stand above an eternal flame; seven giant granite heads face the flame; behind them are carved over 5000 names of the war dead, plus 126 Heroes of the war, an astonishing toll for a city founded from nothing only nine years before the war.

The memorial was sculpted by N S Ivleva who got the idea from reading a German officer's war diary: 'We have marched through France and Belgium in just three days. We have conquered the Netherlands, but we are unable to take a single step in Russia. The Russians are firmly standing in our path like stone rocks and there is no way to pass around them or turn aside.' Although the diary did not mention seven 'stone rock'

---

**(Opposite)  Top:** An Old Believer working on a fire-train at Postyshevo. Old Believers are Orthodox who refused to accept church reforms in the mid-seventeenth century and hid in the remote taiga, undisturbed until the coming of the railway. **Bottom:** The Great Patriotic War memorial at Komsomolsk-na-Amure. When the German invasion smashed its western armies, Russia reached deep into the Far East for resources to fight back. (Photos © Nicholas Zvegintzov).

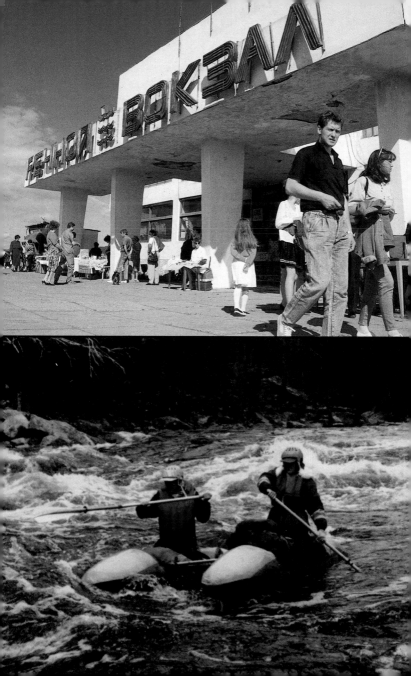

Russians, the number was chosen because it is a lucky one in Russia, according to Ivleva.

Komsomolsk-na-Amure takes the Memorial seriously. The flame often burns and sometimes high school boys and girls mount an honour guard.

**River Station and memorials to the First Builders** The River Station (Речной вокзал) was built to look like a ship when seen from the Amur river; hydrofoils and river-boats travel up and down the Amur from here. At one end are the ticket office, waiting rooms and a small café. From the station, you can see Pivan on the opposite side of the river, the Amur bridge and, if you have binoculars, the never completed Pivan BAM tunnel.

On the south side is the First Builders Monument (Монумент первостроителям города) at the foot of the 3km First Builders Avenue, pr. Pervostroitelei (пр. Первостроителей). It portrays a party of young people heading inland with equipment, including gun, guitar and surveyors' transit. The leader is digging with one foot and beckoning with one hand, giving rise to the local name for this statue – 'Let's go and dig fishing worms'.

On the north side of the station is a memorial stone at the landing site of the first builders who arrived on 10 May 1932 (Памятный камень высадки первостроитей города).

Yet further north near the central bus station is a half-built monument. It was intended to be the Soldier-Builders monument (Памятник войнам-строителям), depicting the 'heroic' arrival in 1934 of the construction troops who marched from Khabarovsk on the frozen Amur river. However, the reality was that while the soldiers did march over the ice, in front of them tramped prisoners who tested the ice and found the best route. Many prisoners died during this arduous trip. In addition, archives have revealed that these troops were the second military group to arrive but the exact date of the first is not known. So today all that exists to commemorate communist propaganda is a 3m-high concrete base with steel reinforcing sticking out of it. A monument is still planned for the soldier-builders as they did contribute significantly to the city, but a more appropriate monument and site may be selected.

**The Lenin district: aircraft factory, museum and Gagarin Memorial** The **Yuri Gagarin Aircraft Factory** is located in the Lenin district (Ленинскии район) (tram Nos 4 and 5 east from the city centre). The aircraft factory was renamed Gagarin Aircraft Factory to hon-

**(Opposite) Top:** The Amur and Lena rivers are vital for the transportation of freight and passengers. Every riverside community has a mooring barge or a river station. This one is at Komsomolsk-na-Amure. (Photo © Nicholas Zvegintzov). **Bottom:** The BAM and Lena regions encompass thousands of kilometres of wilderness-rafting rivers. This is on the Akishma river near Novy Urgal with five groups of rapids and a twelve-day float. (Photo © Irina Shcheglova).

our his three visits to the complex, although he never worked there. It is now run by KnAAPO, the Komsomolsk-na-Amure Aircraft Production Association (КнААПО, Комсомольское-на-Амуре Авиационное Производственное Объединение). On 25 February 1932, Moscow announced that an aircraft factory would be built in Komsomolsk-na-Amure, even though the first builders were yet to arrive. In 1936 the first plane, a Tupolev R6, rolled off the production lines. With the help of gulag inmates, the factory expanded and in 1941 started producing the famous IL-2 Shturmovik two-seater ground attack/light bomber. A total of 6784 were built in several factories across the Soviet Union, making it the most produced Soviet plane in the Second World War. These planes were used to bomb Berlin as early as December 1941, and it was at this time that Stalin made an appeal to the factories producing the IL-2 that they were 'as necessary for the Red Army as air, as bread'. Komsomolsk-na-Amure's factory produced a total of 2732 Il-2s. The factory started producing jets in 1949 with the Mig-15. In 1976, it produced its first Mig-17 fighter and one of these sits on a plinth at the front of the plant. In 1981, the SU-27 fighter rolled off the production line and is still being produced today, along with the SU-33, the Be-103 amphibian, and the S-80. Like most military complexes, the factory also produces consumer goods that use the same materials or equipment that its principal products do.

The **Factory Museum** at Pr. Kapylova 46/V, ☎ 6-85-54 or 6-81-018 or 2-89-46 (Экспоцентр КнААПО, пр. Капылова, 46/В) has numerous displays of the factory's aircraft, including the Il-2, Mig-17, SU-27, and BE-103, material on 'conversions' to civilian products, and a 'red corner' of flags and biblically-bound books of Soviet awards. It is open by appointment. Make arrangements with one of the tour organisers listed in Getting assistance (see pp173-174).

The **Yuri Gagarin Memorial** (Памятник Ю. А. Гагарину) sits in front of the Gagarin Aircraft Factory. The pink granite memorial depicts Gagarin holding a stylised book containing the Laws of the Cosmos (whatever they might be) with a cosmic train trailing behind him. From a distance, it looks like he is holding a brick with a towel draped over his arm, hence the locals' disrespectful name 'Brick and Towel Memorial'.

The tram ride (No 4 or 5) to the Lenin district is an excursion in itself, passing city streets, park, wasteland, railway lines, a narrow bridge with a chicane and an intact Komsomolsk-na-Amure city marker complete with its Order of Lenin.

**Japanese POW memorials** (**Мемориал знак военнопленным, умершим в Комсомольске**) There are 16 memorial stones in and around Komsomolsk-na-Amure, marking cemeteries or camps of

Japanese POWs. The central memorial is a large stone beside the Amur Hotel that was unveiled on 5 October 1991. This site was chosen because the POWs built the hotel.

Another important site is a graveyard where 1,513 Japanese were buried. This site is worth visiting though it is hard to find without a guide. To get to it, you travel down the Severnoe Shosse highway (Северное Шоссе) towards Solnechny for 20 minutes. When you come to an asphalt road to the left with a flag-shaped sign on the corner stating Autobaz 8 (Автобаз 8), you take the small dirt road on the opposite side of the road. (If you reach two large power stations on your left, you have gone about 1km too far and need to go back and find the Autobaz 8 sign.) The dirt road peters out after about 100m and you need to walk a further 50m on a track that goes under a raised section of the insulated hot-water tubes. The simple monument consists of a central pillar with Japanese writing on it.

Returning to Komsomolsk-na-Amure on the Severno-Shasse highway, you will pass a row of small red-brick houses on the right. These are distinctively not Russian looking and were built by the Japanese.

**Stalin's repression memorial stone (Памятник знак жертвам политических репрессий)** This stone is a memorial to those that suffered and died during Stalin's repression. The local government was pressured into creating this monument by an organisation called Memorial whose membership consists of relatives of repression victims. One of the important functions of Memorial was to search for information on the death of relatives and, equally important, on whether they were posthumously rehabilitated. After Stalin's death many Russians who died in camps were secretly retried and many found not guilty. Although it was cold comfort for the victim, posthumous rehabilitation was important for relatives as it removed the taint of being a relative of an 'enemy of the state'. This taint was sufficient to deny education, promotion, Communist Party membership and an internal passport that allowed them to leave their area. As the trials were secret, getting hold of documents relating to them was extremely difficult.

By 1990, these documents were no longer important due to the freeing up of society, but even now many relatives still do not know what happened to their loved ones. Memorial ceased to exist in the early 1990s as the city administration took over its role of finding out information about former prisoners. However, several ex-members claim that things have become worse as, while the government's policy is one of assistance, the reality is that the bureaucratic morass ensures that little happens.

The location of the stone, beside the City Court, is a poignant reminder of the failure of the Soviet justice system. The stone was taken from the Mount Novaya quarry on the outskirts of Komsomolsk-na-Amure, which was worked by prisoners.

**Industry and its importance**   There are three main industrial complexes in town: the Yuri Gagarin Aircraft Factory, the Amur Shipbuilding Factory and Amurstal steel works. It is possible to organise tours of these through the tour companies listed in Getting assistance (see pp174-176).

## Excursions in the region

Excursions around Komsomolsk-na-Amure include the Pivan BAM tunnel, rafting and floating, the Komsomolsk Nature Reserve and indigenous villages, cruising to the Shantar islands, skiing, the nearby mining towns and Amursk.

**Pivan BAM tunnel**   In 1939 work started on an 800m railway tunnel through a mountain that is opposite Komsomolsk-na-Amure and to the north of Pivan. The tunnel was to link a planned 2.5km bridge across the Amur river and the railway line from Pivan to Sovetskaya Gavan. The start of the Great Patriotic War stopped the bridge although the tunnel was finished. Consequently the tunnel, which was built at the cost of hundreds of gulag prisoners' lives, was never used. The tunnel's entrance, which starts 100m above the river's water level, can be seen from Komsomolsk-na-Amure's River Station with binoculars. This side is difficult and dangerous to get to, as the mountain face is sheer.

The other side is much easier to get to and makes an interesting half-day trip. To get to it, take the bus to Pivan, then walk through Pivan past the disused brick works to the dacha village. In the village there are numerous confusing roads; ask the way, but don't be surprised if many locals do not know where the tunnel is.

Once you reach the tunnel, you can walk in about 100m before you hit a fence that has been breached by vandals. It is possible to walk the length of the tunnel but it is dangerous and not recommended, as the walls and roof are unstable. Walking through this monument to worthless labour is an eerie experience. Remember to take a torch.

**Rafting and floating**   Close to Komsomolsk-na-Amure there are wilderness river stretches that offer river rafting and floating in pristine wilderness in moderate class 1 water.

The Gur river (p. Гур) takes three to four days, 90km. Take the railway west toward Vysokogorny, then float down the Gur, coming out on the Amur above Amursk.

The trip from Lake Evoron (озеро Эворон) along the Gorin river (p. Горин), three to four days, 130km, offers unique access to nature and to the indigenous lifestyle and culture. Take the BAM west to Evoron, put in at the lake and float down the Gorin through the Komsomolsk Nature Reserve (see below), coming out on the Amur below Komsomolsk-na-Amure.

For much more challenging white-water expeditions, see Rafting near Novy Urgal, pp160-161.

**Komsomolsk Nature Reserve (Комсомольский заповедник) and indigenous villages** An old forestry railway line runs 20km north-east of Komsomolsk-na-Amure, terminating at the logging town of Galichny (Галичный). Galichny is on the southern border of the Komsomolsk Nature Reserve (Комсомольский заповедник) which is centred on the Gorin river with its eastern boundary the Amur river. Where the Gorin flows into the Amur is the Nanai village of Bichi (Бичи) which can only be reached by boat. Nearby are other Nanai settlements of Dzemgi (Дземги) and Negigaltsy (Негигальцы). Komsomolsk Nature Reserve is an excellent place for birdwatching and over 240 species have been seen here. A regional bird expert is V A Kolbin (В. А. Колбин) who can be contacted through one of the tour organisers listed in Getting assistance (see p174-176).

On the far side of the reserve is the Nanai village of Nizhnie Khalby (Нижние Халбы). This settlement is famous for its dance ensemble. There is a boarding school in the town for Nanai and Russian primary school children with classes taught in both languages. Nearby are spectacular cliffs that have spiritual significance for the Nanai. The village hosts a Nanai festival early in August, with performances, recitations, crafts, costume, beauty contest, boat-races and Nanai cooking. The village welcomes travellers and homestay can be organised there through one of the tour organisers listed in Getting assistance (see p174-176).

**Cruising to the Shantar islands** The Shantar islands (Шантарские острова) are a group of uninhabited islands in a bay of the Sea of Okhotsk (Охотское море). They are a fascinating destination for watching birds, seals and whales. It is possible to arrange a small cabin cruiser for four people plus crew, sailing downstream from Komsomolsk-na-Amure or Khabarovsk to the mouth of the Amur, and north to the islands. The best time for this is mid-July to mid-September.

**Skiing** The skiing season is from November to mid-May. There are several downhill ski runs near Komsomolsk-na-Amure and cross-country skiing can be done anywhere. There are ski bases at Solnechny (Солнечный) and Gorny (Горный). The best runs with T-bars are three near Gorny in the Myao Chan mountains (хребет Мяо Чан). ('Myao Chan' means 'black head' in Evenk after the colour of the rocks, which you can't see in winter.) There are national and international ski meets at Solnechny throughout the winter, including extreme skiing down Myao Chan, 1,470m and Chalba (Чалба), 1,566m, cross-country skiing races, ski orienteering and ski tourism. There are several other runs in the region but their condition varies enormously. Rather than ski tows, some people hire a Buran Motor Sled to take them to the top of the run, then ski down. The cost of an all-inclusive day trip is about $50 from Komsomolsk-na-Amure and can be booked by one of the companies listed under Getting assistance (see p174-176).

**The tin towns of Solnechny and Gorny**  The three towns of Solnechny, Gorny and Festivalny could be known as the tin triangle, as they surround Russia's largest known deposit of tin. At one stage they were the industrial show pieces of the Far East but nowadays they are a shadow of their former selves. However, they are worth a day visit and can be easily reached by local buses.

Solnechny is the regional capital, the largest of the three towns and at the junction of the roads to the other two. Solnechny is 43km north-west of Komsomolsk-na-Amure while Gorny is 61km and Festivalny is 58km.

The Nanai called the region the Valley of Death and no people ever lived here. The reason for this is that the water is acidic and contains sulphur which explains the absence of wildlife in the area.

The trip to Solnechny was once on the communist tour circuit as the mountainous route is beautiful and you passed the 'major' socialist achievement of the bridge over the Tsurkul river (р. Цуркуль), where everyone was forced to marvel at the first rail bridge on the eastern sector of the BAM. While the road has deteriorated since then and no-one is very interested in the bridge, the trip is still pleasant. After leaving Komsomolsk-na-Amure, which is about 100m above sea level, you start to climb to 250m at Solnechny and 350m at Gorny. The change in height crosses a flora boundary and the dominant tree species changes from birches to pines.

### ⌖ SOLNECHNY (Солнечный)

Solnechny (area code ☎ 421-48) is a small modern city with about 20,000 inhabitants. The largest building is the headquarters of the mining enterprise that controls the mines. It dwarfs the city government building, which symbolises where the real power lies. The Solnechny mines are on the other side of the Solnechny valley but can be seen from the town.

The best explanation of the Solnechny mine and its history can be found in the local museum (☎ 91-2-11). Half of the museum is devoted to the history of the mine and of particular interest is the model of a smelter that was never built. Currently the tin concentrate is shipped to China for smelting but the Russians would like to build a smelter locally. While the predicted 70-year life of the mines initially attracted considerable foreign interest in the early 1990s, nothing came of it as Russia's instability and the legal conditions of joint ventures scared off all investors. The other half of the museum is devoted to the region's geology. Of particular interest is the locally found semi-precious gemstone, amethyst. This violet quartz is used in jewellery and is believed to be a cure for drunkenness if you carry it around with you.

A church is being built opposite the regional council building.

The only accommodation in town is at the ***Zarya Hotel***, at pr. Lenina 21a (пр. Ленина, 21-а, гостиница «Заря»). There is also the ski base, with accommodation (see Skiing pp181-182).

## 🏛 GORNY (Горный)

Gorny is a small, attractive township of 5,000 people. It is located in a pleasant, steep-walled valley with the Silinka river snaking through it.

At the northern end of the town is the concentrator that extracts tin from ore. Although tin is the major product, copper, tungsten, lead and zinc are also concentrated here. The concentrator consists of a crusher that grinds the ore into small particles. The particles are washed over massive banks of vibrating tables and each type of metal is separated on the basis of weight. At the end, the concentrated particles of metals are dried and loaded into giant bins and sent by truck to the BAM for smelting in China.

This process produces large amounts of tailings, which are dumped on a massive heap 400m downstream of the concentrator. Behind the heap is the used water dam where any remaining metals hopefully sink to the bottom before the water flows back into the Silinka river.

As there are no chemicals used in the concentrating process and no smoky chimneys in town, air pollution is zero. This helped Gorny win a Tidy Town Award in the mid-1980s. However, the Gorny and Solnechny concentrators are very polluting as a great deal of heavy metals leech from the tailings into the Silinka river. The river often has a bluish hue due to the copper wastes. The Silinka is one of the dirtiest rivers in the country and regularly features in the monthly ecological section of the regional newspapers.

A tour of the plant is quite scary with bank upon bank of tables vibrating away in dim light and no-one in sight. To organise a tour, go to the office and ask. They will either find someone to take you or simply say, 'just wander around'.

If you follow the single road through Gorny for another 11km you reach the famous lake of Amutinka (озеро Амутинка) which translates as 'black'. The lake is cold as it is filled by the mountainous Amut river (р. Амут) and exits to become the Silinka river. The lake's water is pure and it is a picturesque picnic spot. You need a 4WD to get there or good hiking boots.

Gorny also has a ski base, with accommodation (see Skiing pp181-182).

The settlement of Festivalny (Фестивальный) is now virtually a ghost town with only about 100 people living there.

## 🏛 AMURSK (Амурск)

Virtually everything ever written about Amursk (area code ☎ 421-47) states that the city was founded in 1958 in order to build a giant industrial complex producing cellulose, which is the basic ingredient of paper. This was a lie. The real reason for building Amursk in a strangely remote, uninhabited area was the giant military industrial Amurmash complex

(Амурмаш). Amurmash, which is short for Amur Machinery Enterprise, is officially described as producing non-standard equipment. In reality it produces tank shells and other ammunition. The enterprise consists of one building that is nearly 1km long. It can be seen on the left about 20 minutes out of town heading towards Komsomolsk-na-Amure. With the decrease in the defence budget, this factory is now producing buses and looking for overseas buyers for its munitions.

Amursk was designed soon after the 1955 decree that renounced Stalinesque decorative, classically inspired buildings in favour of plainer, more easily constructed buildings. The architects of Amursk applied this decree to the letter and produced a fine example of post-Stalinist construction. Consequently Amursk has some of the country's ugliest concrete box apartment buildings totally devoid of decoration.

## Getting there and away

Amursk is 63km south of Komsomolsk-na-Amure and 18km from the closest railway station of Mylki (Мылки). The easiest way to get there is on bus No 220 from Komsomolsk-na-Amure, which travels 18 times a day.

The most scenic route is via the Amur river on a hydrofoil from Komsomolsk-na-Amure. The Amursk River Station is just a floating barge with a few cabins and seats on it moored at the bottom of a cliff. Every winter the barge is moved to a place safe from the crushing effects of pack ice. For schedules and bookings, see Khabarovsk–Komsomolsk-na-Amure–Nikolaevsk-na-Amure by river, p224-8.

## Where to stay

The best place to stay is the *Sanatorium Rodnik* at pr. Mira 226, ☎ 236-21 or 264-53 (пр. Мира, 226, санаторий «Родник»). Rooms cost $7. The only other option is a *hostel* at pr. Mira 48 (пр. Мира, 48, Общежитие).

## What to see

The museum used to be devoted to the cellulose complex but since 1992 all reference to it has been removed. According to the museum's curator, Tatyana Ivanovna, 'no one was interested'. There is still one room dedicated to the early days of Amursk including a tent with wooden floors, stove and samovar. There is also one room devoted to the early settlers and more interestingly to the original indigenous people. On display are a number of archaeological finds that are over 5,000 years old, most of them recovered from the ancient settlement of Voznesenskoe (Вознесенское) across the river from Amursk. The museum is located at pr. Komsomolsk-na-Amure (☎ 245-533, пр. Комсомольский, Краеведческий музей).

Amursk contains the third biggest greenhouse botanical garden in the Russian Far East, after Khabarovsk and Vladivostok. It has its roots in the Amursk Society of Young Fans of Cactuses formed in 1982. With support

# Amursk (Амурск)

For complete legend
see inside back cover

1. Sanatorium Rodnik
2. Hostel

3. Molochnoe cafe
4. Utes restaurant
5. Ekssomak cafe
6. Cafe

7. regional museum

8. Police (formerly Hotel Amursk)
9. Palace of Sport

10. Port where hydrofoil stops,
   known as Port Galbon

11. Botanical Garden

Mulki railway station (18km) &
Komsomolsk (63km)

pr Stroitelei
(пр. Строителей)

pr Pobedy
(пр. Победы)

TsKK Paper Mill
(1km) & Amurmash
Military Complex
(10km)

N

pr Mira
(пр. Мира)

pr Komsomolsky
(пр. Комсомольский)

ul Pionerskaya
(ул. Пионерская)

pr Mira
(пр. Мира)

ul Amurskaya
(ул. Амурская)

Amur River

from members and the city council, the Botanical Gardens were created in 1988 and today have over 1,000 varieties of cactuses with the oldest being 25 years old and the heaviest being one tonne. It contains 13,000 species of plants.

Before the collapse of the Soviet Union, 30,000 visitors used to marvel at the Gardens with their summer temperature of 30-35°C and winter temperature of 18°C. However, with the collapse of the economy, few tourists visit the Gardens and the council now only pays wages and not capital repairs. In addition, the Gardens have been forced to save money be reducing the heating bill and in 1994 the winter temperature was just 8°C. Many plants unfortunately died. To raise money, the Garden is now breeding plants and raising birds and tropical fish for sale as well as contracting for revegetation work.

The industrial face of Amursk is TsKK or the Tsellyulozno-Kartonny Kombinat (Цкк–Целлюлозно-картонный комбинат). This giant complex was the second cellulose and cardboard plant in the Russian Far East after the Japanese built a plant on south Sakhalin Island (which was occupied by the Soviets at the end of the war).

TsKK consists of three plants, producing amongst other things worked wood products, paper, cardboard, fodder yeast, ethylene spirit and fibreboard. The biggest problem at the plant is air and water pollution. Despite claims that the 800,000 cubic metres of waste water a day discharged from the works remain in aerated ponds for several months before being pumped into the Amur river, untreated waste water often gets into the river. This often happens when the river floods, bringing its water level above the height of the pond walls. The other problem is the stench. As you can imagine, millions of tonnes of rotting water lets off a horrendous odour. According to locals, the only relief comes when the wind blows away from the city or when it rains. The plant's management claims that the cost of cleaning up existing industrial pollution and installing new filtration equipment was 500 million roubles in 1992 and they do not have this money.

The main TsKK plant is about 1km from the city on the road to Komsomolsk-na-Amure. The end of the blue main building closest to the city is the area normally visited by foreigners, as it is the end of the production process.

# Komsomolsk-na-Amure–Sovetskaya Gavan
Комсомольск-на-Амуре–Советская Гавань

## THE ROUTE (see Route Map 4, p369)

The line leaves Komsomolsk-na-Amure to the south past dacha halts, then splits off from the line to Khabarovsk and crosses the Amur on the impressive railway-road bridge. This is the lowest point of the BAM, less than 100m, until the ocean – but the railway has one more barrier to cross.

The line snakes through river-bank towns, then ascends the Sikhote Alin coastal range (хребет Сихотэ Алинь) to over 900m in a sequence of tight loops and steep gradients unique on the BAM that tortures squeals and sparks from the bogies. The mid-point of the 487km line is at the evocatively named Vysokogornaya (Высокогорная – 'High Mountain'). Here the eastward and westward trains cross beside a haunting station built by Japanese POWs. Then the line grinds down to Vanino (Ванино) and Sovetskaya Gavan (Советская Гавань) to reach the ocean on the almost land-locked Tatar Strait (Татарский пролив).

This stretch of railway is not technically the BAM, since it lies beyond the Amur, but effectively it completes the link from the Trans-Siberian at Taishet to the Pacific at Vanino. In this guide the distances are marked in kilometres from Pivan to agree with the markers on the railway.

The trip through the coastal mountains is both scenic and historic, but unfortunately both the eastward and westward trains run by night, co-ordinating with the ferry to Sakhalin Island (остров Сахалин).

The time is Moscow time +7 hours.

## History

This section of the BAM was the only one completed during the Great Patriotic War and it played an important part in the Soviet seizure of Sakhalin (Сахалин) and the Kuril Islands (Курильские острова) from the Japanese after Russia declared war on Japan on 8 August 1945. Ironically, after the capitulation of Japan on 2 September 1945 Japanese POWs captured in Sakhalin and Manchuria completed the line.

The line was built in two stages – a 468km section from the right bank of the Amur at Pivan to Sovetskaya Gavan completed in 1945 and the 19km branch line from Komsomolsk-na-Amure to Pivan including the 1,437m Amur river bridge completed in 1975.

The 468km section was mostly built by gulag prisoners and POWs under the control of the Ministry of Internal Affairs' Construction Unit No

500. There were six major camps along the line with headquarters at Gurskoe (Гурское) and the main Japanese POW Camp No 1 at Vysokogornaya. In October 1945, Construction Unit No 500 consisted of a total of 124,000 workers, which included 9,000 free workers, 2,600 escort guards, 1,600 railway troops, 34,000 Russian gulag prisoners, 12,800 exiled Russian ethnic minorities, 1,000 Germans POWs and 49,500 Japanese POWs.

The line was completed on 20 July 1945 and immediately started carrying soldiers to Vanino for the invasion of south Sakhalin Island, which was held by the Japanese. The first scheduled service started on 5 October 1946 but work continued for several more years building stations and improving the track.

Until the early 1990s, the area was considered a border zone and both foreigners and Russians needed special permission to travel to it. The area was also restricted as it contained strategic reserves stockpiled in preparation for war with Japan. Today the military bases are either closed or have been significantly scaled down.

## KOMSOMOLSK-NA-AMURE (Комсомольск-на-Амуре)

For information on Komsomolsk-na-Amure, see pp168-181.

## ⊠ AMURSKI (Амурский)

This station, on the left bank of the Amur river, is the closest one to the Amur bridge.

### AMUR BRIDGE (16km from Komsomolsk-na-Amure)

The 1,437m bridge spans the Amur river. Although it also carries road traffic, the bridge was primarily built to connect Komsomolsk-na-Amure on the left bank with the railway line to Sovetskaya Gavan on the right bank. The first train crossed on 26 September 1975 but it took another seven years before it was opened to cars on 9 June 1982!

Before the bridge was built, transporting freight across the river was difficult. In summer, spring and autumn train ferries would take three hours to transport rolling stock and many hours to load and unload. During winter, rails were laid over the frozen ice and the trains would go straight across it. There was normally a month's interruption to train services from when ferries could not break through the ice to when the ice was thick enough to support the rails and vice versa. This twice-yearly interruption would result in huge pile-ups of up to 3,000 freight cars on both sides of the river. Ice breaking ferries were tried in the early 1960s to overcome this problem but they were unsuccessful.

The Amur bridge is the longest of the BAM's 3,000 bridges and is considered one of the most innovative bridges in Russia. It was designed by Leningraders KS Shably and GL Katranov of the National Research Institute of Transport Engineering and consists of eight 159m spans and five 33m spans. It used four techniques which were novel at the time. Firstly, it used 304 hollow ferroconcrete supports instead of the traditional solid footings to support the bridge. Secondly, it was fastened with thousands of high-tension bolts that could each support 30 tonnes rather than the traditional tens of thousands of rivets. Thirdly, rails were directly bolted onto ferroconcrete slabs without the need for ballast, rather than onto sleepers supported by ballast. Finally, constructors used jet-rock drilling for the first time in bridge construction.

Using these innovations plus overcoming the natural obstacles of great water depth, sharp fluctuations in the water level and fierce winter winds, it was hardly unexpected that the construction time doubled to over 10 years.

It is forbidden to stop on the bridge or even walk over it. The soldiers who guard the bridge at both ends enforce this law and will even stop you from taking photos.

### 🏠 PIVAN (Пивань) 0km

This attractive settlement was built at the same time as Komsomolsk-na-Amure to supply construction materials to the city. Nowadays, the brick factory, quarries and industrial railway lines lie abandoned around the mostly wooden town. Nearby is a dacha village where the exit to the Pivan tunnel lies. See p180 for more information on the Pivan tunnel.

### 🏠 GAITER (Гайтер) 29km

To the south of the railway, you will see the large Khummi Lake (оз. Хумми) which is really a bay on the Amur river.

### 🏠 KARTEL (Картель) 41km

Near the station is the town of Bolshaya Kartel (Большая Картель) which was the site of a massive failed military project that publicly revealed the huge waste and gross mismanagement of the Soviet military.

The Bolshaya Kartel saga started with an article entitled *Mysteries of a Dead Object* in the regional newspaper, *Priamurskie Vedomosti* (Приамурские Ведомости) on 27 November 1991. It was then given national exposure when the article was reprinted in the national newspaper *Izvestiya* (Известия). The article described a massive experimental radio locator station as part of an anti-missile defence system. It consisted of a 2km diameter circle with 300 steel antennas outside and 270 inside, and a monitoring complex. The complex was built by the Scientific Research Institute of Remote Radio Communication under the Ministry of Radio Industry with funds supplied by the Ministry of Defence. When it was finished in 1981, it was of limited success, because in its first year of operation it didn't work for 173 days and in just the first quarter of 1982 it stopped working on 106 occasions. It worked intermittently until 1983 when it was permanently shut down, but it took until 1985 before it was decided to dismantle the complex. By then all the technical staff had left and there was no money or interest in actually carrying out the order. There was insufficient manpower to provide proper guarding and by the late 1980s most of the valuable equipment and materials had been looted and the monitoring complex had been burned down.

The article decried the incredible waste and mismanagement and Gorbachev personally organised an investigation commission. Its conclusions were that between six and 20 million roubles ($600,000 to $2,000,000) worth of precious metals and equipment had been stolen, but, strangely and probably for political reasons, the commission could not determine how much the project cost. In addition, the commission could not find anyone to blame so no charges were ever laid.

Until Gorbachev's policy of glasnost was introduced, this type of story was considered secret and never published. However, glasnost opened a floodgate of exposés which contributed significantly to the rapid loss of confidence in the Communist Party, military and bureaucracy. Today, the site remains unchanged and you can see part of the antenna complex north of the railway and road.

### SELIKHIN (Селихин) 51km

At this large town is the southward turn-off for the paved road to Khabarovsk (300km) and the northward turn-off for the vestigial road to Lazarev (Лазарев), 500km, which is 9km from Sakhalin Island. Selikhin is also the junction of a railway branch line to the north. It goes through the villages of Machtovy (Мачтовый), Oktyabrski (Октябрьский), Chuchi (Чучи), Nizhnetambovskoe (Нижнетамбовское), Shelekhovo (Шелехово) and Yagodny (Ягодный), before terminating at Cherny Mys (Черный Мыс).

This railway was approved on 5 May 1950 by the Council of Ministers of the USSR and it was intended to reach Cape Lazarev where it would enter a 9km tunnel under the Tatar Strait to Sakhalin Island. By 1953, 122km of rails had been laid as far as Cherny Mys and this length was opened for traffic. In March 1953 Stalin died and on 26 May 1953 the Council of Ministers stopped this and a number of Stalin's other pet projects. The line was transferred from the BAM Railway to the Far East Forestry Company (Гладальлеспром) and it became a forestry line. A few times, local and regional governments have proposed recommencing construction of the line to Nikolaevsk-na-Amure (Николаевск-на-Амуре), but this is usually used as a vote winner for the isolated people to the north. However, interest has been rekindled by Japanese interest in a ground route to Europe, involving a bridge from Hokkaido to Sakhalin and the tunnel to the mainland. The line does not carry passengers and consequently is not shown on most railway maps of Russia.

### 🚉 KUN (Кун) 95km

The town near the station is called Snezhny (Снежный). After leaving Kun, the train starts a long ascent through the Sikhote Alin Range (хребет Сихотэ Алинь).

### 🚉 GURSKAYA (Гурская) 112km

The medium-sized town Gurskoe (Гурское) derives its name from the Gur river, which travels parallel with the railway for about 50km. Gurskoe was the location of the headquarters of the prisoner camps that built the railway and most of the buildings in town were constructed by prisoners.

### 🚉 OUNE (Оунэ) 182km

At about 190km look up and right to see the line ahead heading beyond the tunnel into the final pass. At 196km the line makes a screaming horse-shoe bend to the right in a mountain cove, clings to the slope edging up and to the left, and crosses a shoulder in a 300m tunnel (the only tunnel on this section) which took prisoners 13 months to dig (199km). At 200-201km the line heads through a narrow cutting across the pass.

### 🚉 KUZNETSOVSKI (Кузнецовский) 203km

Contrary to what many Russians believe, the town is not named after the famous Russian admiral Kuznetsov but rather the little-known survey engineer, Arseni Petrovich Kuznetsov (Кузнецов Арсений Петрович), 1901–1943. Between 1935 and 1938 Arseni Petrovich surveyed much of the BAM and was then transferred to surveying the route for the Komsomolsk-na-Amure–Sovetskaya Gavan railway. When the war broke out, he was forced to resurvey the entire route, as there was no metal for the planned bridges and little labour for the envisaged tunnels. The route finally chosen was significantly longer and more twisting than the original route but it could be constructed with fewer resources. Kuznetsov died in his office of a heart attack induced by overwork on 15 November 1943.

A monument (planted with flowers in summer) was unveiled in Kuznetsovski on 1 July 1993 to commemorate Kuznetsov and the 50th anniversary of the joining of the east and west sections of the railway which occurred here.

### VYSOKOGORNAYA (Высокогорная) 220km

The eastward and westward trains often meet here and stop for 30 minutes, which is enough time to go to the popular water bore beside the station to have a wash. The major occupations of the inhabitants are gold mining and logging. The only accommodation is at the *Locomotive Brigade Hostel* (Дом отдыха Локомотивной бригады).

Vysokogornaya ('High Mountain') was the centre of the Japanese POW complex known as Camp Department No 1. Most of the town was built by the Japanese.

The station building has a triple-peaked portico, each peak supported on each side by a pair of narrow square-sectioned pillars; at the top they meet the gable in a complex joint of projecting beams. Inside the heavy wood doors there is a hall divided by a wood screen, with a high peaked ceiling with projecting beams with uptilted ends. It is painted a pea-soup green and looks hauntingly like a disused Japanese temple. At 2am in the dark and the mountain fog, with only a couple of provodnitsi gossiping and a wheel-tapper at work, and the immense train silent and sighing, it is a sobering but heartening memorial, a sign that the Japanese prisoners were not just slave labour. On the platform is an altar-shaped memorial carved with a route-map of the railway, commemorating its builders, though not specifying who they were.

The whole line is a regular place of pilgrimage of Japanese visiting the grave-sites of their comrades-in-arms and fathers and grandfathers.

### DATTA (Датта) 240km

Why this station is called Datta is a mystery as the village of Datta is 160km away on the Pacific Ocean coast near Vanino.

### KENADA (Кенада) 260km

A few kilometres beyond this stop is the village of Dzhigdasi (Джигдаси), about which the following story was told by N M Derevtsov, veteran of Labour and former engineer on the Komsomolsk-na-Amure–Sovetskaya Gavan railway. He now lives in Kislovodsk near the Black Sea.

'Although the Japanese POWs left a legacy of buildings and railways, there were only a few instances when they left something more precious – descendants. One such instance occurred in the town of Dzhigdasi, and

---

(**Opposite**) The Vysokogornaya station building was constructed by Japanese POWs in the style of a temple. The whole of the eastern section of the BAM is a place of pilgrimage for Japanese visiting the grave sites of their comrades-in-arms, fathers and grandfathers. (Photo © Nicholas Zvegintzov).

involved a Japanese engineer called Umoda and a Volga German telephonist named Marsha. Marsha was an internal exile as she and her parents had been deported to this region from their native Kazakhstan during the Great Patriotic War due to Stalin's suspicion about their nationality's loyalty.

Initially, when the Japanese came to Dzhigdasi in 1943, they were always under close guard and officers were separated from enlisted men. Political education was an integral part of camp life and prisoners were divided into democrats and non-democrats with the latter, which included monarchists, considered anti-Soviet and requiring a more fundamental education.

Political education included regular parades in support of communism, lessons on communist philosophy and the publication of a Japanese-language communist paper called Symbol. While most of the Japanese paid little attention to education, Umoda applied himself to learning Russian. Being an engineer, democrat and supervisor, he soon was trusted enough to walk around unescorted and because of his rare Russian ability, became a popular figure among the Russians. He developed a friendship with Marsha and they spent as much time as they could together, limited as she worked all day and Umoda had to be back in camp before evening curfew.

The Japanese character *Kotobuku*, meaning happiness.

Umoda told Marsha he loved her on her 18th birthday and gave her a beautiful red handkerchief, which had on one side in exotic calligraphy the Japanese character *Kotobuku* meaning happiness. Unfortunately, the Japanese repatriation started in spring 1947 and he was one of the first to be shipped home.

Unbeknown to him, Marsha was pregnant and returned to Kazakhstan to give birth to their child, Kolya. Despite all her efforts, Marsha died without finding Umoda and telling him that he was a father. Kolya now lives in Germany and is still trying to trace his father.'

## 🏚 TULUCHI (Тулучи) 303km

After leaving this town, the train passes over the Tumninski Range with the Primorski Range visible to the north.

---

(**Opposite**) **Top:** Spring sunrise over still-frozen Yakutsk. **Bottom:** Summer sunrise on the Olekma river as twin coal-burning Yea steam locomotives haul an excursion train. Yea locomotives were supplied by the USA as Lend-Lease and are kept running by the Russian railways for tourism or defence. (Photos © Nicholas Zvegintzov).

## 🚃 TUMNIN (Тумнин) 340km

There is a well-known hot-water spring about 10km out of this town along a dirt track. The town is named after the 364km Tumnin river, which starts in the Sikhote Alin mountains and flows into the Tatar Strait. The railway runs through the Tumnin Valley to the ocean. This river is a major salmon spawning river and in August and September fishermen sell jars of red caviar as the train stops along this section.

It is around this town and Vanino that most sightings have been made of the Taiga Yeti. About every six months the local newspapers report a new sighting of this monster, probably as a way of boosting circulation. The first real 'proof' was obtained in 1992 when footprints measuring 45cm were found. In the same year the Yeti claimed its first victim who was a fit and healthy geologist who died of a heart attack when he saw the monster.

If you see the Yeti, don't be too worried as it appears to be a vegetarian, having left the geologist's body untasted!

## 🚃 UST-OROCHI (Усть-Орочи) 380km

The Orochi is the Russian name for the local indigenous people who call themselves the Nanai. They mainly live in this area and around Komsomolsk-na-Amure. In 1979 there were just 1,200 left. They are commonly confused with the Oroki on Sakhalin Island, who are descended from Evenk, but the Orochi are a different ethnic group.

## 🚃 MONGOKHTO (Монгохто) 403km

Discretely hidden away from the station is the marine aviation base of Mongokhto. It was built as a staging post for Lend-Lease goods flown from the USA. There are claims that it is also the storage site of chemical weapons that pose a risk as their containers are physically deteriorating and the military has no money to destroy them. There is a road from here to the village of Datta on the Pacific coast.

The line turns south away from the Datta peninsula and the muddy shore on the east of the train is the Pacific Ocean (Тихий океан). This backwater is the Tatar Strait (Татарский пролив), almost walled off from the ocean by the 948km long Sakhalin island, which comes within 9km of the continent at Lazarev and within 48km of Japan at Omisaki.

The train passes coastal installations and refineries and squeals round a headland and down to the port city of Vanino.

## 🚃 VANINO-VOKZAL (Ванино-Вокзал) 441km

Vanino is infamous throughout Russia as the port of departure for gulag prisoners to the labour camps to the north. Nowadays, Vanino is a minor

Russian port on the Pacific Ocean and the
main gateway to Sakhalin Island.

Despite there being little to see in
Vanino, travellers often prefer to stay here
than the larger and more interesting
Sovetskaya Gavan. The reason for this is
that Vanino is easier to reach and is cen-

❏ **VANINO-VOKZAL**
**(Ванино-Вокзал)**
Area code ☎ 421-76
Khabarovski Krai
(Хабаровский Край)

trally placed for exploration of the region. Vanino is one place that it is
wise to have listed on your itinerary. (One of the editors had a long and
bizarre struggle with the railway station police to get permission to *leave*;
since all transport is booked in the railway station this can be a real problem. See Getting assistance, pp198-199.)

## Orientation
Vanino is built on the foothills with a pleasant view of the small harbour
inlet. Below the town is the road to Sovetskaya Gavan, the railway and the
port. The main gate of the port is 30m from the station. The main street of
Vanino runs up the hill between two channel-marker towers – the 'light-
houses' (Маяк). The main bus stop is at the lower lighthouse. The street
starting at the bus stop and following the contour, lined with trees and
kiosks, is 1st Line (1ая линия).

## History
Vanino was founded in 1944 as a transhipment point for gulag prisoners.
Before the Great Patriotic War, the main transit camp to the northern goldfields of Kolyma, Magadan, Sakhalin, Kamchatka and to the uranium
mines of Primorski Territory was Nakhodka, near Vladivostok. However,
with the opening of the BAM, part of the transit camp moved to Vanino.
These camps were like giant slave markets, with representatives from various camps coming to select the fittest workers. For instance, one large
mine in the region had a contract with the NKVD (the KGB forerunner) to
supply 12,000 prisoners a year. (For travel to the Kolyma region in modern
times, see pp279-83.)

Most prisoners only stayed in Vanino for a few days, which was just
as well as they mostly slept in tents or out in the open. However, some
were unlucky enough to be caught there at the end of the navigational season or when something unusual happened, such as when the harbour was
blocked when a load of explosives for the Kolyma mines blew up on board
the ship Dalstroi in 1946.

The following description of the Vanino transit camp was written by
Michael Solomon, in *Magadan*, 1971: 'When we came out on to the
immense field outside the camp I witnessed a spectacle that would have
done justice to a Cecil B DeMille production. As far as the eye could see
there were columns of prisoners marching in one direction or another like
armies on a battlefield. A huge detachment of security officers, soldiers

and signal corpsmen with field telephones and motorcycles kept in touch with headquarters, arranging the smooth flow of these human rivers. I asked what this giant operation was meant to be? The reply was that each time a transport was sent off the administration reshuffled the occupants of every cage in camp so that everyone had to be removed with his bundle of rags on his shoulder to the big field and from there directed to his new destination. Only 5,000 were supposed to leave, but 100,000 were part of the scene before us. One could see endless columns of women, of cripples, of old men and even teenagers, all in military formation, five in a row, going through the huge field and directed by whistles or flags. It was more than three hours before the operation was completed and the batch I belonged to was allowed to leave for the embarkation point.'

The numbers described by Solomon may be somewhat exaggerated as archives have revealed that there were only ever a maximum of 10 permanent and transit camps in Vanino with a total population of 15,000. Another description of the horrors of Vanino's transit camps can be found in *Kolyma: The Arctic Death Camps* by Robert Conquest, 1978.

In modern times, Vanino has become a commercial port, handling 5,000,000 tonnes per year, including timber to Japan, oil products and freight to Sakhalin and the Kuril islands. Vanino has a population of 22,000.

## Getting there and away
There is one long-distance train a day to Komsomolsk-na-Amure and Khabarovsk that leaves in the evening. There is a local train to Khabarovsk that also leaves in the evening. There is also a work train to Vysokogornaya every four days, which leaves in the morning. This might be an excellent option for sight-seeing, if you pick the right day.

To travel to Sovetskaya Gavan do not take the train. Take the 101 Express bus (автобус 101 экспресс) which meets the long-distance train in the station yard. At other times of the day (about six per day) it leaves from the bus stop at the lighthouse. The express bus 'does not go through the kolkhoz or take hunters'. There are also local buses to Sovetskaya Gavan from the bus stop. For reasons why not to take the train to Sovetskaya Gavan, see To Sovetskaya Gavan by train p200.

There are no roads out of the Mongokhto–Vanino–Sovetskaya Gavan area. There is an airport halfway between Vanino and Sovetskaya Gavan with flights to Khabarovsk and to Shakhtyorsk (Шахтёрск) and Yuzhno-Sakhalinsk (Южно-Сахалинск) on Sakhalin Island. Book plane tickets at the railway station.

In principle a ferry runs every day to the port city of Kholmsk (Холмск) on Sakhalin Island, but in practice the schedule is erratic because of bad weather and maintenance. There are also sporadically ferries to Japan and to Pusan, Korea. The first ferry, called *Sakhalin 1*, was

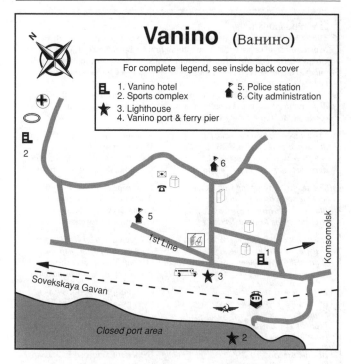

commissioned in June 1973, and carries passengers, railway wagons, cars and trucks. The 144km trip takes nine hours. Buy tickets at the railway station. You may have to show your itinerary with 'Sakhalin' typed on it to get a ticket. Get ferry information at the railway station, or from the ferry company. Sakhalin Shipping Company is at ul Pobedy, dom 16, Sakhalinskaya Oblast, Kholmsk, 694620 Russia, ☎ +7-42433-66-150 or 📄 +7-42433-66-123 or +7-42433-66-020 (694620 Россия, Сахалинская область, г. Холмск, ул. Победы, дом 16, Сахалинское Морское Пароходство).

From Kholmsk, buses and trains go all over Sakhalin island. From the southern port of Korsakov (Корсаков), ferries run for $40 to Yuzhno-Kurilsk (Южно-Курильск), Kurilsk (Курильск), and Malo-Kurilsk (Мало-Курильск) on the islands Kunashir, Iturup and Shikotan disputed with Japan since WWII. Also from Korsakov, a Japanese ferry runs to Wakkanai on Hokkaido approximately every three days for $275 (AO Higashi Nihonkai Ferry, ✉ info@kaiferry.co.jp, www.kaiferry.co.jp).

## ❏ Vanino Lament

The following song, by Aleksandr Galich (Александр Галич), is about the departure of gulag prisoners from Vanino to their probable death in the gulag camps of the north. As being sent from Vanino invariably meant that the prisoner would never return, most spouses never mentioned their disappeared partner and got remarried. This song describes this reality.

Following Stalin's death and the opening of prisons, many of the 'living dead' returned home to be ordered away by their former spouses afraid of the danger to their new family if another purge followed.

| | |
|---|---|
| *I remember that Vanino port,* | Я помню тот ванинский порт, |
| *at the side of the steam ships so sullen,* | И вид пароходов угрюмый, |
| *While we were going on board* | Как шли мы по трапу на борт |
| *deep into those cold and dull holds.* | В холодные мрачные трюмы. |
| | |
| *The sea fog was getting worse and worse,* | Над морем сгущался туман, |
| *and the sea was beginning to roar ...* | Ревела стихия морская. |
| *Magadan appeared before us -* | Стоял впереди Магадан – |
| *'Capital of the Kolyma Territory'.* | «Столица колымского края». |
| | |
| *It was not a song but a moaning cry* | Не песня, а жалобный крик |
| *that came out of every heart:* | Из каждой груди вырывался |
| *'Farewell the continent, farewell for good!'* | «Прощай навсегда, материк» |
| *that was the roaring cry of the steamship.* | Ревел пароход, надрывался ... |
| | |
| *Everyone was seasick* | От качки тошнило, зэка |
| *the prisoners embraced each other like brothers...* | Обнялись, как родные братья ... |
| *From time to time some curses* | И только порой с языка |
| *came out of their mouths.* | Срывались глухие проклятья |
| | |
| *Be damned, Kolyma,* | Будь проклята ты, Колыма, |
| *that is like an alien planet,* | Что названа чудной планетой, |
| | |
| *One can easily be driven mad* | Сойдешь поневоле с ума – |
| *There is no way back from here ...* | Отсюда возврата уж нету ... |
| | |
| *I know you are not waiting for me,* | Я знаю, меня ты не ждешь, |
| *and you don't read my letters.* | И писем моих не читаешь, |
| *I know you are not going to meet me,* | Я знаю – встречать не придешь, |
| | |
| *and even if you do, you'll not recognise me* | А если придешь – не узнаешь |

## Where to stay

The only hotel is *Hotel Vanino,* above the station, at ul. Chekhova 1, ☎ 51-228 (ул. Чехова, 1, Гостиница «Ванино»). A single with full facilities (and a view of the ocean) is $40.

## Where to eat

There are two *restaurants* next to the hotel, a *café* inside the foodstore at

the lighthouse, a bar with snacks in the station, and *food stalls* along 1st
Line (1ая линия).

## Getting assistance

The Passport Bureau (Паспортный бюро), (☎ 5-09-55), on the second
floor of the police station, may be able to extricate you from visa problems
(possibly after a small fine).

To find the police station, follow 1st Line (1ая линия) from the lighthouse past the town heating plant to a two-storey building behind a car park.
Go in the side door past the bust of Feliks Dzerzhinski (Дзержинский
Феликс Эдмундович), founder of the Cheka or Political Police, up to the
second floor to the second office on the left.

## What to see

The only place of interest in town is the port and unless you have a ticket
for the ferry, you won't see even this. Foreign ships are a common sight in
Vanino, particularly from Japan and the Chinese port of Taijin. A museum
that included material on the gulag transit camp was closed by the city.

## TO SOVETSKAYA GAVAN BY BUS
(Highway kilometre markers from Mongokhto (Монгохто))

### Vanino (Ванино) 29km

Take the 101 Express bus (автобус 101 экспресс) in the station yard
when it meets the long-distance train, or at the bus stop at the lighthouse.
Pass the port and go up the creek to cross the bridge and drive up the hill.

### Oktyabrski (Октябрьский) 35km

The town is quite large, as it is the region's main railway depot. There is
a *railway hostel* here.

### ☒ Zavety Ilicha (Заветы Ильича) 39km

Stops at the gate of the navy base, whose name translates as 'Precepts of
Ilich' (Lenin).

### Gavan (Гавань) 42km

Road sign at the boundary of the city, with the date '1853'. Pass the village of
Maiski (Майский). The road turns inland to cross the Khadya river (р. Хадя).

### Turn-off to Gatka (Гатка) 53km

Cross the Khadya river (р. Хадя). Head down the other side of the river and
come out above the bay with the southern headland visible. Cross the railway.

### Prison camp 64km

A high-security prison with a patrol perimeter between barbed wire fences
with guard-towers at the corners, and more wire around the huts. Violent
criminals are sent here (we were told), but not murderers. 'Murderers are
sent to Siberia.'

**⛴ Sovetskaya Gavan (Советская Гавань) 68km**

The main bus-stop is on ul. Pionerskaya (ул. Пионкрская) near the war memorial and the *hotel*. The bus turns right on ul. Lenina (ул. Ленина) and takes the third left to turn around at the stadium. This is a good place to catch the bus on the return trip to secure a seat.

For more on Sovetskaya Gavan, see below.

## TO SOVETSKAYA GAVAN BY TRAIN

**🚉 Sovetskaya Gavan-Sortirovka (Советская Гавань-Сортировка) 449km**

Getting to Sovetskaya Gavan by train is not straightforward. Although there is a Sovetskaya Gavan station and the long-distance trains have 'Sovgavan' (Совгаван) written on their destination plates, these trains do not actually reach Sovetskaya Gavan town but Sovetskaya Gavan marshalling yards, called Sovetskaya Gavan-Sortirovka (Советская Гавань-Сортировка), in Oktyabrski (Октябрьский). Sovetskaya Gavan-Sortirovka is 8km from Vanino and 26km from Sovetskaya Gavan. At Sovetskaya Gavan-Sortirovka, passengers change for a two-carriage local train for Sovetskaya Gavan City station. The station's ticket office hours are 11.30 to 14.30 and 17.00 to 20.00.

The frilly fretwork turreted station building was built as the backdrop for the 1945 opening of the railway.

**⛴ SOVETSKAYA GAVAN-GOROD (Советская Гавань-Город) 467km**

This station is stuck in the middle of nowhere about 8km from the town. To get to the city, walk through the forest for 200m up a hill until you reach a bus shelter on the road and take bus No 1 to the city. To get to the station from the city, get off at the second stop. The 8km railway extension to the city has been planned for decades but work has yet to start.

Beware the timetable at Sovetskaya Gavan City station, which states the time of departure for the train at Sovetskaya Gavan-Sortirovka even though it just says Sovetskaya Gavan. The connecting train from Sovetskaya Gavan to Sovetskaya Gavan-Sortirovka leaves Sovetskaya Gavan about 90 minutes before the long-distance train departs Sovetskaya Gavan-Sortirovka.

From the day the gulf of Sovetskaya Gavan was discovered in 1853 by Admiral Boshnyak, the area has been militarily significant both as a naval base and as a forward defence against Japan. The city was originally known as Imperatorskaya Gavan or Emperor's Harbour and in 1926 became Sovetskaya Gavan ('Gavan' means 'harbour' or 'haven'). The city administration has so far resisted pressure to return to its original name.

## Orientation

The city is built on the south side of an deep water inlet, 11km long, with three bays. The gulf provides one of the few good deep harbours in the Far East and, although the bay ices over from November to April, ships can move in and out with the assistance of ice-breaking tugs. Fogs are common during May, June and July.

> ❏ **SOVETSKAYA GAVAN-GOROD** (Советская Гавань-Город) Area code ☎ 421-71 682880, Khabarovski Krai (Хабаровский Край)

The city's older main street, ul. Lenina (ул. Ленина), is lined with solid two-storey buildings with shops below and apartments above, and has the House of Culture and the library. The newer ul. Pionerskaya (ул. Пионерская) has 1970s office buildings. At the intersection is Victory Square with the war memorial, the main bus stop, the shopping area and the hotel.

## History

The gulf was discovered and fortified for the Russians in 1853 by Admiral Boshnyak (though known earlier to the Japanese and Chinese). In a distant skirmish of the Crimean War, the British captured the admiral's flagship Pallada and in the peace settlement of 1856 the Russians agreed to scuttle it in the harbour.

From 1905, the Japanese ruled the lower half of Sakhalin Island, which is about 120km away. The gulf was an ideal invasion place for the Japanese who occupied parts of the Far East after the 1917 Revolution until 1922. For this reason, there are numerous old trenches, bunkers and observation points built before the Great Patriotic War dotted around Sovetskaya Gavan's coastline.

Sovetskaya Gavan was one of the three most important naval bases of the Pacific Fleet. At its height in the 1950s and 1960s, it normally had seven to 10 major surface combatants such as cruisers, destroyers, frigates, coastal patrol ships and submarines and their small support vessels harboured there. The base also housed a submarine school. The navy started using the base for fitting out half-built ships and submarines from the Komsomolsk-na-Amure shipyards when the first floating dock of 5,000 tonnes arrived in 1939.

After the Soviet occupation of Sakhalin Island, which removed the direct Japanese threat, the region's priority shifted from forward defence to the support of Soviet forces on Sakhalin. The post-war Soviet strategy was to prepare for an invasion of Japan by dispatching forces through Sakhalin across the narrow straits to secure Japan's Hokkaido Island. The Japanese response was a strategy called Look North, which involved placing their most powerful defence units on Hokkaido. The Fleet Air Arm airbase at Sovetskaya Gavan provided, and still does, long-distance reconnaissance bombers including Tu-16 Badgers and Tu-142 Bears.

To support the Soviet strategy, about 20 per cent of the Russian Far East's 11 million tonnes of war material was stored in the region's coastal area.

With the collapse of the Soviet Union, the military forces in the area have been disbanded or significantly reduced. Vessels are now rare in the Zavety Ilicha naval base and ship-building work is no longer carried out. Few planes fly out from the military airport and troops aren't seen that often around Sovetskaya Gavan.

Commercial activity has now replaced the military focus in the region. The Sovetskaya Gavan port is now owned by the Terminal company which is made up of numerous Far East, Altai and Sakhan enterprises. From the number of imported Japanese cars running on the 100km of local roads, the babies, and the status-symbol big dogs in town, it appears that many locals have prospered because of this arrangement.

The city has actively sought international connections and already has sister-city agreements with Everett in the USA, Rymo in Japan and the Port of Sligo in Ireland. Of particular interest to foreign companies are forestry concessions.

Sovetskaya Gavan has a population of about 40,000. This is lower than the peak of 50,000 in 1959, which coincided with the height of the Cold War, but significantly higher than the low of 26,000 in 1967.

## Getting there and away
See Getting there and away under Vanino-Vokzal on p196. See To Sovetskaya Gavan by bus (see pp199-200) for details about travelling to Vanino and beyond. Plane tickets are sold at the Aeroflot office on ul. Goncharova (ул. Гончарова).

## Where to stay
The only hotel is a friendly modern hotel, the *Sovetskaya Gavan Hotel*, at ul. Pionerskaya 14, ☎ 7-2783 (ул. Пионерская, 14, Гостиница «Советская Гавань»). A single with full facilities costs $40.

## Where to eat
There are limited choices in this city; the only restaurant is at *Sovetskaya Gavan Hotel*. As Sovetskaya Gavan is the base for much of the northern Pacific Ocean fishing fleet, the shops are stocked with excellent fish. Kamchatka crabs are quite common as the crab beds to the north produce about 80 per cent of the world's canned crab. In addition, the city's cannery produces tins of red caviar, which fill the local shops. In summer you can discern the region's relatively mild coastal climate, with raspberries and gooseberries in the market.

## What to see
The regional museum, ul. Sovetskaya 29, (ул. Советская, 29, музей), contains a small collection on the revolutionary and Civil War-era history

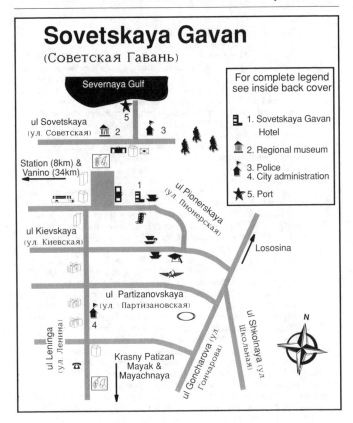

# Sovetskaya Gavan

(Советская Гавань)

Severnaya Gulf

ul Sovetskaya
(ул. Советская)

Station (8km) &
Vanino (34km)

ul Pionerskaya
(ул. Пионерская)

ul Kievskaya
(ул. Киевская)

Lososina

ul Partizanovskaya
(ул. Партизановская)

ul Leninga
(ул. Ленина)

ul Goncharova (ул. Гончарова)

ul Shkolnaya (ул. Школьная)

Krasny Patizan
Mayak &
Mayachnaya

N

For complete legend
see inside back cover

1. Sovetskaya Gavan
   Hotel

2. Regional museum

3. Police
4. City administration

5. Port

of the region plus excellent material on the indigenous people, but nothing on gulags. It has wood banisters, a few beams, some decorative trim, a door-handle and an oven brick from the scuttled Pallada, which was excavated in the 1980s.

It also has a room of stuffed animals and birds including a huge Siberian tiger, shot in 1983 and said to have weighed 380kg. The curator will apologise for the taxidermist's choice of staring fiery eyes, which makes the handsome animal resemble a Japanese print. (In January 1998 a tigress with two cubs was seen in the suburbs of Sovetskaya Gavan and had to be chased away). The museum is open every day except Saturday and Monday from 10.00 to 18.00 with a lunch break from 13.00 to 14.00.

### ❏ The Siberian tiger (Амурский тигр)

The largest cats in the world still roam the coastal mountain ranges of Khabarovski krai and Primorski krai south of Vanino and north of Vladivostok. The Siberian tiger, *Panthera tigris altaica*, called the Amur tiger in Russian, is the second rarest of the five species of tigers worldwide. Adult males are up to 3m long and weigh up to 375kg; adult females weigh up to 225kg. They prey on wild boar and elk. According to wildlife biologists, fewer than 400 Siberian tigers survive in the wild, with almost all in the Primorye region and approximately 40 of them on the 390,000 hectares of the Sikhote-Alin Reserve.

At one time the tiger roamed the whole of the Russian Far East, but by the 1930s it had mostly been exterminated. In the 1930s a determined effort to preserve the tiger resulted in the creation of the Sikhote-Alin *zapovednik* in 1935, a five-year ban (1936-40) on hunting red deer, a massive restriction in the number of hunting licences issued after 1941 and a ban on the capture of tiger cubs.

The tiger population slowly rose until the mid-1980s. Since then the numbers have dwindled, principally because of logging of the tigers' habitat and expanding agricultural land which has brought tigers closer to humans, with the animals invariably coming off the worse. There have been a number of incidents of tigers taking domestic animals, including dogs, and in March 1986, a sighting of a tiger in a main city street in Vladivostok and in 1998 in the suburbs of Sovetskaya Gavan.

Officially, only 35 tigers have been legally or illegally shot each year from 1985 to 1990. However, the actual number of killings far exceeded this because of a combination of the collapse of the Soviet Union, the destruction of the scientific and law enforcement agencies, and the opening of the border with China which resulted in a surge of poaching. Tiger bone is particularly valuable in the folk medicine of China, Taiwan, North and South Korea, and other Asian countries.

Tigers are territorial and radio-tracking data shows that an adult female requires a home range of 450 sq km. There are approximately 150,000 sq km of tiger habitat remaining in the region, which would provide for 333 breeding females if it were all prime habitat. The situation requires that no further habitat loss can be allowed. A Siberian tiger protection plan, co-ordinated by Russian authorities and international conservation organisations, calls for the creation of a new protected territory for the conservation of tiger habitat in Khabarovski and Primorski krais, co-ordinated development of conservation measures, viable economic alternatives for local people, and an anti-poaching campaign.

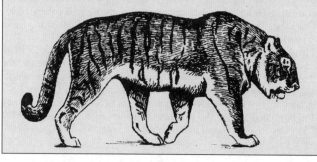

The only part of the port that is easily accessible is near the museum. Until 1992, a ferry used to leave this pier for Vanino. If demand increases, it may be resumed.

An interesting day trip is to the Pacific Ocean to see the remains of anti-Japanese paranoia. To get there, you catch a bus for 30 minutes to the village of Lososina (Лососина). As you walk through the town you pass a monument to Admiral Boshnyak. Three hundred metres from the bus is a junction with the good quality road veering to the right. Take the dirt track to the left and after three to four kilometres (40 minutes) you come to the sea with a road leading to a lighthouse which is called mayak (маяк) in Russian. From here you can see Vanino and Sakhalin with binoculars. Three hundred metres to the right of the lighthouse is a two-storey building with a radar dish on its roof. Five hundred metres to the left are concrete artillery bunkers, which are 2m high, 2.5m wide and 3m long and have 50cm thick walls. All the guns have been removed. These fortifications and the trenches were built prior to the Great Patriotic War as a defence against the Japanese.

In front is a small island and although it is possible to climb down to the sea, it is dangerous. In October and November locals collect edible seaweed which is called sea cabbage (морская капуста) from the base of these cliffs. As can be seen by the surrounding 50cm-high stunted pines and mountain ashes, the wind is extremely strong, so harvesting the sea-weed is both dangerous and freezing work. The return walking trip from Lososina takes four hours.

Another day trip to the coast is to visit the Krasny Partizan Lighthouse (Маяк Красный партизан) and memorials on Cape Nikolaya (мыс Николая). Beside the lighthouse is a memorial with a beautifully deco-rated bell which was the original lighthouse bell and dates from 1895. Also beside the lighthouse is a monument dedicated to the lighthouse keepers who were tortured to death by the White Army in 1919.

The lighthouse is in a naval area that was once closed, but now no-one seems to mind you wandering in. To get there, take the bus from Sovetskaya Gavan to Mayachnaya (Маячная) and then it is a short walk to the lighthouse.

# PART 4: BAM BRANCH LINES
## Описание путей по веткам

## Khrebtovaya–Ust-Ilimsk
### Хребтовая–Усть-Илимск

### THE ROUTE (see Route Map 1, p366)

The 214km railway between Khrebtovaya and Ust-Ilimsk was primarily built for the construction and maintenance of the Ust-Ilimsk hydro-electric station and links the BAM to the station. The railway line, opened in 1970, passes through scenic countryside and is a pleasant four-hour trip. It winds among wooded 1,000m ridges east of the Ust-Ilimsk reservoir (Усть-Ильимское водохранилище). There is only a rough road parallel with the railway; the road connecting Bratsk with Ust-Ilimsk is on the other side of the reservoir. The time is Moscow time +5 hours.

### Getting there and away

There are two passenger trains a day along the line. They start in Ust-Ilimsk, turn west on the BAM, go through Bratsk, join the Trans-Siberian at Taishet and turn east to Irkutsk, the oblast capital.

### 🚉 KHREBTOVAYA (Хребтовая) 0km

Khrebtovaya is located at 575km on the BAM. See Khrebtovaya, p76.

### 🚉 IGIRMA (Игирма) 70km

This station serves the town of Novaya Igirma (Новая Игирма) which means 'New Igirma'. The town is on the south bank of a flooded valley, with the original Igirma village 30km to the south-east. A reasonable road from Khrebtovaya ends at Novaya Igirma.

### 🚉 TUBINSKAYA (Тубинская) 160km

Tubinskaya is located on the north side of the flooded valley which used to be known as the Tuba river and is now known as Tuba Straits (залив Туба).

### 🚉🏚🚉 UST-ILIMSK (Усть-Илимск) 214km

The town is located below the junction of the Angara and Ilimsk rivers and owes its existence to the Ust-Ilimsk hydro-electric dam. The power station is one of three giant hydro-electric stations on the Angara river, with the others being in Bratsk and Irkutsk. Work started on the dam in 1963 with the building materials being floated down the Angara or trucked from Bratsk. Much of the 3840 MW 16-turbine capacity of the Ust-Ilimsk hydro-electric station is used to power the BAM. The dam and town are built on permafrost and consequently all the buildings, most notably the station, are built on insulated piles. Besides the dam, the main industry here is the wood-processing factory, reached by a 10km tramway.

The main part of Ust-Ilimsk and its station are on the east shore of the Ust-Ilimsk reservoir, with the port on the western shore. The station is 12km from the town and there are regular buses between the two.

Ust-Ilimsk Brewery (Уст-Илимский Пивоваренный завод) was founded by experts from the Czech Republic. A beer festival is held annually.

Ust-Ilimsk can be reached by two daily trains from Khrebtovaya (four hours), Bratsk (8½ hours), Taishet (15 hours) and Irkutsk (26½ hours). It can also be reached by daily buses from Bratsk and flights from Bratsk, Irkutsk, Krasnoyarsk, Magadan and St Petersburg. The area code is ☎ 39-535.

# Bamovskaya–Tynda (The Little BAM)
## Бамовская–Тында (Маленький БАМ)

### THE ROUTE (see Route Map 3, p368)

This 180km stretch connecting the Trans-Siberian Railway to the BAM mainline was the first section of the BAM to be built. It offers a striking contrast to the busy Trans-Siberian. The unelectrified Little BAM has only one track which winds through the taiga, compared to the two- or three-track electrified Trans-Siberian with its broad curves cut through farming land. Three long-distance trains crawl along the Little BAM daily at 46km/h compared to the 50 trains screaming along the Trans-Siberian at 100km/h.

The Little BAM leaves the Trans-Siberian at Bamovskaya, winds up to cross the Yankan range (хребет Янкан) at 750m, then follows the Tynda river down, north to Tynda. The highway also runs north from the Trans-Siberian to Tynda. It starts at the Trans-Siberian station at Bolshoi Never (Большой Невер), about 40km from Bamovskaya, then takes a more hilly route via Solovevsk (Соловьевск).

The time is Moscow time +6 hours.

Both the Little BAM and the highway are the southernmost portions of the 'mainlines' that link the Trans-Siberian railway over land to the great northern city of Yakutsk. For more on the AYaM railway, see pp262-78.

### History
The Little BAM was first proposed in the early 1930s as part of the initial BAM concept. Originally it was envisaged that the line would run north

from the Trans-Siberian station of Urusha (Уруша), but in 1933 the planners opted for a new location 64km to the east. A new station was built here called BAM, which was renamed Bamovskaya to prevent confusion with the railway line. Work started in early 1933 with many of the original workers being prisoners in Stalin's gulags. The Little BAM officially reached Tynda on 7 November 1937. Until the invasion of Russia by Germany in June 1941, when all work on the BAM stopped, Tynda was simply a supply base for the railway lines being pushed north, east and west.

In 1942 the rails were pulled up and shipped to the warfront and it was only on 5 April 1972 that work started on rebuilding the Little BAM. Virtually nothing of the old line remained as the taiga, permafrost and swamps had reclaimed the old embankments and even the buildings. It is interesting that it was two years later that the first trainload of the Komsomol arrived on 3 May 1974 and it is this date that most Soviet-era books name as the start of the Little BAM.

As this was the first section of the BAM to be laid, it attracted enormous media attention within the Soviet Union. Daily building achievements and statistics were splashed over the front pages of newspapers such as 'On 10 May 1972, work started on the first bridge' and 'On 14 September, No 1272 Diesel Locomotive pulled the first passenger train to the first completed station of Shturm'.

On 9 May 1975, to coincide with the anniversary of the defeat of Germany in the Great Patriotic War, the Little BAM was officially opened. Over its 180km length, 104 large and medium bridges and 140 other structures were built and 10.7 million cubic metres of earth and road metal were used.

## Getting there and away
On the Little BAM, and there is a train every other day from Neryungri and Tynda to Novosibirsk, west on the Trans-Siberian. There is a train every day from Neryungri and Tynda to Khabarovsk and every other day to Blagoveshchensk, east on the Trans-Siberian.

If you want to change to a Little BAM train from a Trans-Siberian through train, make sure that you change at a station where both trains stop. The closest major stations where all Trans-Siberian trains stop are at Yerofei Pavlovich (Ерофей Павлович) on the west or Skovorodino (Сковородино) on the east.

## BAMOVSKAYA (Бамовская) 0km

There is not much to Bamovskaya. It is a small town, with a sprinkling of stores, no hotel and only a few trains a day. The best thing in Bamovskaya is the big word 'BAM' in white blocks lying on the sloping ground in front of the station. It is not advisable to get off an express train here without knowing when your connecting train up the Little BAM will arrive.

## 🚉 MURTYGIT (Муртыгит) 49km

This medium-sized town was sponsored by the Voronezh Komsomol from western Russia. You will see the word *Voronezh* (Воронеж) with the year 1977 written in white brick on the red water tower next to the station. This is the terminus for local trains that run on the Little BAM from Tynda. A crashed American Lend-Lease bomber was found about 12km from Murtygit in 1993 but it has yet to be recovered, as there is no money to restore it.

The town has two *railway hostels* (Общежитие): a larger mixed sex one (☎ 2-84) and a male only one (☎ 4-20).

## 🚉 ANOSOVSKAYA (Аносовская) 82km

You will notice that the station looks as if it's about to fall down. This is because its foundations have sunk into the earth due to engineers ignoring the lessons of permafrost construction. By the time the evidence of inadequate construction had become indisputable, other Little BAM towns had been built and were similarly suffering, including Murtygit where both the school and sewage treatment plant collapsed.

The town has a *Railway Hostel* (Общежитие ) ☎ 2-75, 2-89, or 2-07.

After leaving Anosovskaya, you pass through the Yankan range (хребет Янкан), the windiest part of the route.

## ☒ ZABOLOTNOE (Заболотное) 113km

This station deserves its name, which is derived from the word meaning swamp.

## 🚉 BELENKAYA (Беленькая) 133km

This town was sponsored by the city of Orenburg (Оренбург) in the South Urals. The township is about 500m north of the station. There were Stalin-era gulag camps around the town. Accommodation can be organised at the *Locomotive Brigade Hostel*, ☎ 2-23 (Общежитие).

## 🚉 SETI (Сети) 160km

This is the headquarters and the largest of North Korea's logging camps in the Tynda area. There used to be about 5,000 North Korean workers in the region but this has been dramatically reduced over the last few years. You can see their camp from the railway on your right as you approach the station from the south. You can wander to the camp but don't attempt to take photos. An explanation about the North Korean camps is included under Chegdomyn in the Chegdomyn–Novy Urgal–Izvestkovaya section (see pp213-15).

The other notable aspect of Seti is that it has a UFO society of five people which has 'sighted' a 3m-high Yeti in the area.

### ⟨image⟩ TYNDA (Тында) 180km

Tynda is at 2,364km on the BAM mainline. See Tynda, p135.

# Izvestkovaya–Novy Urgal–Chegdomyn
## Известковая–Новый Ургал–Чегдомын

This 360km railway connects the Trans-Siberian station of Izvestkovaya with the BAM town of Novy Urgal, before terminating 32km later at Chegdomyn. The line was built to ship coal out from the massive Chegdomyn coal deposits. Much of it was built by Japanese POWs and Japanese graves litter the area.

There is a daily train between Khabarovsk and Chegdomyn (18 hours) leaving the Trans-Siberian at Izvestkovaya (Известковая) (12 hours).

There are daily local trains from both ends of the line, Chegdomyn and Izvestkovaya, which travel as far as Tyrma, halfway along the line.

There is no road between Chegdomyn and Izvestkovaya.

The time is Moscow time +7 hours.

### THE ROUTE (see Route Map 4, p369)

The line leaves Izvestkovaya up the Kuldur river to the spa town of Kuldur. Then it crosses the Little Khingan range (хребет Малый Хинган) over a winding pass, follows the Yaurin river (р. Яурин) down, then skirts the uplands of the Bureya river (р. Бурея), meeting the Bureya at Elga (Эльга). It joins the BAM through Novy Urgal (Новый Ургал) and Urgal 1 (Ургал 1) and then branches off up the Urgal river to Chegdomyn.

### ⟨image⟩ IZVESTKOVAYA (Известковая) 0km

This town is in the Jewish Autonomous Oblast (Еврейская Автономная область) on the Trans-Siberian. Despite being the junction of the Chegdomyn–Trans-Siberian line, most of the Trans-Siberian express trains do not stop here. It is a typical small town of about 2,000 people with a canteen, post office, dairy farm and market but little else. The old part of town, with its rustic wooden buildings and household garden plots, is hidden in the trees to the west of the town. Stopping here, unless you have to change trains, is not recommended.

## 🏛 KULDUR (Кульдур) 30km

This is the location of the Kuldur Health Resort, which is famous throughout Russia. The balneological resort is located in the scenic Kuldur river valley where the summer is moderately warm, with a mean July temperature of 18°C, but the winter is very cold with a mean January temperature of -27°C.

The attraction of the resort is the therapeutic 72°C hot mineral water. Bathing in the cooled water is allegedly good for patients with skeletal-muscular, gynaecological, dermatological, nervous, or digestive disorders. The health resort actually consists of two sanatoria, Kuldur (Кульдур) and Zhemchuzhina Khingana (жемчужина Хингана) – 'pearl of the Khingan'. *Kuldur* is located 2km from the station and is the main health resort. *Zhemchuzhina Khingana* is located in town and designed for parents with children aged from 7 to 14. Its accommodation is mostly twin rooms.

It is necessary to book to stay in either of these sanatoria. The address is 682032, Jewish Autonomous Oblast, kurort Kuldur, sanatoriums Kuldur and Zhemchuzhina Khingana (682032, Еврейская Автономная область, курорт Кульдур, санаторий «Кульдур» или «Жемчужина Хингана»).

## 🏛 PEREVALNY (Перевальный) 51km

'Perevalny' means 'at the pass'. This station is at the crossing of the Little Khingan range (хребет Малый Хинган) and just over the border into Khabarovski krai (Хабаровский край).

## 🏛 YAURIN (Яурин) 57km

The railway crosses the Yaurin river (р. Яурин) and snakes along beside it to near Tyrma.

## 🏛 TYRMA (Тырма) 169km

This is a railway town and there is accommodation at the *Locomotive Brigade Hostel* (Дом отдыха Локомотивной бригады). A local train runs from here to Chegdomyn in the north and another to Izvestkovaya in the south. The town is on the banks of the 334km Tyrma river, which flows into the Bureya river. The railway does not follow the river, but continues northward across the Bureya watershed.

Tyrma is the burial site of many Japanese POWs and is a popular pilgrimage site for Japanese.

## 🏛 ELGA (Эльга) 285km

Elga is near the small port village of Chekunda (Чекунда) on the Bureya river. There are no regular passenger vessels from here down the Bureya.

### NOVY URGAL (Новый Ургал) 328km

Novy Urgal is located at 3,315km on the BAM. For more information, see Novy Urgal (pp157-60).

### URGAL 1 (Ургал 1) 343km

Urgal 1 is located at 3,330km on the BAM. See Urgal 1 (p161).

### CHEGDOMYN (Чегдомын) 360km

Chegdomyn exists because of its coal deposits, which the indigenous Evenki knew about as the town's name means 'black stone' in their language. The town is one of the oldest on the BAM as it was connected to the Trans-Siberian in the late 1940s. The line and town were built by Stalin's gulag prisoners and Japanese prisoners of war. A legacy of this is the name of the regions around the town. In a conventional Russian settlement, the satellite regions are called mikroraions. In Chegdomyn they are called zone (зона) which is the typical nomenclature for the area of a gulag settlement. Many other cities, such as Komsomolsk-na-Amure, were once also surrounded by zones but it is a mystery why only Chegdomyn still retains this name. Chegdomyn is the administrative centre of the Verkhnebureinski (Upper Bureya) raion and is situated on the left bank of the Chegdomyn river.

#### Getting there and away
Trains running along the BAM do not pass through Chegdomyn, as it is 17km north of the closest BAM town, which is Novy Urgal. There is a daily train between Chegdomyn and Khabarovsk (18 hours) connecting with Izvestkovaya (Известковая) (12 hours) on the Trans-Siberian. There are three daily local trains between Novy Urgal and Chegdomyn, two of which meet the mainline trains.

#### Where to stay and eat
The only hotel in town is the grim *Bureya Hotel*, ul. Pionerskaya 1, 2nd floor ☎ 519-63 (ул. Пионерская, 1, этаж 2, гостиница «Бурея»), starting at $16 a dormitory bed, or $52 for a single. There is a *market* next to the hotel and a *cafeteria* on the main street.

> ❏ CHEGDOMYN (Чегдомын)
> Area code ☎ 42170
> 682080, Khabarovski Krai,
> Verkhnebureinski raion,
> Chegdomyn
> (682080, Хабаровский край,
> Верхнебуреинский район, п.
> Чегдомын)

#### What to see
The regional museum, ul. Parkovaya, 8, ☎ 5-29-15 (ул. Парковая, 8, Музей), is in a communal building used for weddings and basketball. The most interesting place to visit is the coal

mines. Coal has been mined here for over 50 years and currently two million tonnes a year are extracted. There is one main open-cut mine with
three more planned.

One of the more popular places for locals is a sulphur water spring on
the outskirts of town. The water continuously flows out of a pipe that is
housed under a small pavilion. Everyone believes in the health benefits of
the water, even the hospital which sends ambulances loaded with old milk
churns to fill up with the water for patients. The spring is 30 minutes from
town.

## The North Koreans in Chegdomyn

Of all the BAM towns, this is the one where you will see the most North
Koreans, wearing Chairman Mao-style suits and Kim Il Sung badges on
their lapels. This is because there is a North Korean consulate here. The
consulate consists of barracks and administration buildings surrounded by
a typical Russian 2m high concrete fence. At the left entrance is a small
gift-shop selling Asian trinkets (but no Kim Il Sung badges). Flanking the
entrance is a large display window with colour photos revealing 'great
socialist achievements', happy Korean life and the guiding hand of the
now dead 'Great Leader' Kim Il Sung and the current leader, his son, the
'Dear Leader' Kim Jong Il. In many ways, the staged photos of waving
Korean tractor drivers, smiling miners and sunbaking holidaymakers are
identical to the posters extolling the virtue of hard work, communism and
a spartan lifestyle during the Brezhnev era.

Although the gate only consists of a boom bar, the guards at the front
will quickly stop you from entering unless you have an official reason. If
you try to speak to one of the guards, invariably his partner will sprint off
and return with a translator. While the translator understands Russian, he
will invariably only say 'Nyet'.

Taking photos of a North Korean or of the consulate is risky. Your
Russian guide will gleefully tell you the story of a German photographer
who tried this and had his camera destroyed as a result. With each
retelling, the story gets progressively more gruesome with the most outrageous version being that the photographer was set upon by a pack of
chainsaw-wielding Korean lumberjacks. If you are determined to take a
photo, do it unobtrusively or from your car.

A number of North Koreans defect each year but helping them can be
a death sentence, as the Vladivostok-based South Korean Consul Choi
Duk-keun found out in 1996. Although the case is still unsolved, it is
believed that he was murdered by the North Koreans because he was
involving in helping loggers escape from Siberian logging camps.

In 1997 TASS reported that there were 20,000 North Korean workers
employed in logging operations, in agriculture, and on construction projects in the Amur region, Khabarovsk and Maritime territories, and in the

### ❏ North Korean gulags

Chegdomyn offers a rare and fascinating insight into one of the world's most secretive countries, North Korea. Officially known as the Democratic Peoples' Republic of Korea (DPRK), North Korea is the world's last communist cult-of-personality state.

During the Soviet era, North Korea and the USSR were fraternal brothers bonded together against the capitalist threat from the 'puppet regime' of South Korea and the imperialist USA. As one reward for being communism's Asian bastion, North Korea was allowed to run logging camps in eastern Siberia. Camps opened in 1967 in the Khabarovsk region and in 1975 along the BAM. The deal involved the Russians supplying logging equipment and fuel, in return for about 70 per cent of the timber the Koreans felled.

The Soviet government did not meddle in the operations of these camps and even allowed the Koreans to administer their own harsh laws. For example, if a Korean ran away from a camp, hoping to flee to China or South Korea, and was captured by the Soviet police, he was handed over to the North Korean camp authorities. These prisoners were chained and returned to North Korea to face probable execution. Today, the situation has changed slightly with the Russian police now less likely to try to capture defectors.

It is claimed by some, such as Sergei Kovalyov, Russia's former human rights ombudsman, that some of the camps are prison labour camps. He alleges that there is a secret protocol between the Russian and North Korean governments that gives North Korean intelligence services permission to have prisons on Russian territory. This has not been confirmed or denied by the Russian government, but none of the numerous camps that can be seen along the BAM appears to be encircled with barbed wire or patrolled by guard dogs. Most have a simple gate with the standard 2m wood or concrete Russian fence.

Propaganda pictures like the one above adorn the North Korean consulate in Chegdomyn. This statue symbolises the unity of a worker, peasant and intellectual towards building a society based on *Juche* (self-reliance). The imagery is Soviet socialist realist with the interesting twist of the intellectual being symbolised by the man in a Western suit holding a calligraphy pen.

---

---

fishing industry of Primorye. According to the South Koreans, loggers are also used as couriers for a state-sponsored drug smuggling ring. The allegation is that the North Korean Workers' Party formed large-scale opium farms in 1993 and the opium is then processed into heroin and morphine at the Nanam Pharmaceutical Plant. The loggers pick up their consignments, carry them onto the Pyongyang to Moscow train, and drop them off to buyers along the route. Proof of this drug ring included two arrests in 1997 of North Korean loggers for supplying opium, the suicide of a liaison official of the North Korean Forestry Ministry in 1996 while in a Russian jail, after being caught attempting to smuggle raw opium worth $800,000, and the arrest of a North Korean Public Security Ministry official for attempting to smuggle 8kg of heroin into Russia along the same route in 1994.

# Khabarovsk–Komsomolsk-na-Amure by train
Хабаровск–Комсомольск-на-Амуре поездом

This is probably the least interesting railway section in the Far East. There are only five reasonable-sized towns en route with the rest of the stops being either forestry camps or railway sidings. The route is mostly flat as it runs across the Amur river flood plain between the river front and the foothills. There is no road along the length of the railway as the Khabarovsk to Komsomolsk-na-Amure highway is 100km to the east on the other side of the Amur river, see route map 4, p369.

  The settlements are accessible only by the railway, not by road or by river. Along the line you may encounter the Miloserdie ('Charity') train (Милосердие), bringing medical and dental care, education, entertainment and food to the settlements, a successor to the propaganda trains of early Soviet times (although now it includes a church car sent by the Archiepiscopate of Irkutsk, complete with priest and baptismal font).

There is one day train from Vladivostok and Khabarovsk (10 hours), stopping at every station and railway halt, and one night train from Khabarovsk. There are a number of local trains along parts of the line. The best advice for travelling on this route is to catch one of the overnight trains and sleep through the journey, or travel on the river (see Khabarovsk–Komsomolsk-na-Amure–Nikolaevsk-na-Amure by river, pp224-8).

The time is Moscow time +7 hours.

## KHABAROVSK (Хабаровск) 0km

Khabarovsk was founded as a military outpost in 1858 and today it is the second largest city in the Russian Far East with over 600,000 inhabitants. It is located on the right bank of the Amur river, just below its confluence with the Ussuri (р. Уссури).

### Orientation
Khabarovsk is an important gateway to the north-east, since it is on the Trans-Siberian railway and has the largest airport in the Russian Far East, with international flights from USA, China, Japan and other countries.

It is also a fascinating city, with theatres, museums, restaurants, a university and fine pre-Revolutionary buildings. You can spend several days exploring it. In this guide we cover only the essentials. For more on the city, see *Russia by Rail with Belarus and Ukraine*, by Athol Yates, *Trans-Siberian Handbook*, by Bryn Thomas and other guidebooks (see p356).

In Khabarovsk do not drink water from the tap. Drink only bottled or boiled water.

### Getting there and away
Khabarovsk is on the Trans-Siberian railway and on the BAM branch line to Komsomolsk-na-Amure. On the Trans-Siberian there are frequent trains west to Moscow or east to Vladivostok and good connections to China and North Korea. On the BAM branch line there is one day train (very slow) and one night train to Komsomolsk-na-Amure. All trains leave from the station on ul. Leningradskaya (ул. Ленинградская).

> ❏ **KHABAROVSK (Хабаровск)**
> Area code ☎ 4210
> 680000, Khabarovski Krai,
> Khabarovsk
> (Хабаровский Край, г.
> Хабаровск)
> Moscow time +7 hours

Shared taxis for Komsomolsk-na-Amure (along one of the few paved roads in the far east) load outside the railway station.

The bus station for other long-distance services is at shosse Voronezhskoe 19, ☎ 343 309 (шоссе Воронежское, 19).

Khabarovsk is also on the Amur river (p. Амур). In the summer there is daily hydrofoil service to Komsomolsk-na-Amure and Nikolaevsk-na-Amure. The hydrofoil loads at the River Station (Речной вокзал) at the foot of ul. Shevchenko, ☎ 398 832 or 398 690 (ул. Шевченко, 1). For more on this route, see Khabarovsk–Komsomolsk-na-Amure–Nikolaevsk-na-Amure by river, pp224-8.

Khabarovsk has the largest and most modern airport in the Russian Far East. It has international flights from China, Japan, Kazakhstan, Thailand and Vietnam. It also has flights to Russia, including far east destinations such as Kholmsk (on Sakhalin island) and Kamchatka and BAM towns of Neryungri and Aldan. The airport is at the end of ul. Karla Marxa (ул. Карла Маркса) and the Aeroflot office is at bul. Amurski 18, ☎ 335 346 (бул. Амурский, 18).

## Getting around

Ul. Karla Marxa (ул. Карла Маркса) forms the spine of Khabarovsk, running from Komsomolskaya Square (Комсомолская пл.), above the Amur river, to the airport. The excellent trolley-bus No 1 runs the length of ul. Karla Marxa, passing close to most of the hotels – Intourist (end of the line and two blocks walk), Lyudmila, Tsentralnaya, Amur, Dalny Vostok, Turist, Amethyst and Zarya – and useful buildings. The railway station is on bus No 2 which leaves the railway station down the wide ul. Serysheva (ул. Серышева) to Komsomolskaya Square, then back along ul. Karla Marxa as far as ul. Leningradskaya, then along it to the railway station, passing the Advance Purchase Railway Ticket Office (Предварительная железнодорожная касса). The River Station is two blocks down the hill toward the river from Komsomolskaya Square.

## Where to stay

The basic *Hotel Mayak* (☎ 330 935), ul Kooperativnaya 11 is in a normal apartment block behind some shops and justifiably charges only US$3 per person but is reluctant to take foreigners. The old *Hotel Turist* (☎ 370 417), ul Karla Marxa 67, is popular with Chinese tour groups. It costs US$8/16 for single/double rooms.

The following hotel rooms all have attached bathrooms. The most centrally located and best value is the good *Hotel Tsentralnaya* (☎ 336 731), ul Pushkina 52. Comfortable single or double rooms with attached bath cost US$10/20, but you may have to persevere with the receptionist before a room becomes available. *Hotel Amur* (☎ 335 043, 🗏 221 223), ul Lenina 29, is newly renovated and charges US$10/19 for a single/double. *Hotel Lyudmila* (☎ 388 665) ul Muravieva-Amurskovo 33, charges US$10 but they may tell you to stay at the Intourist Hotel instead!

*Hotel Amethyst* (☎ 334 699, 🗏 (509) 01-600131), ul Tolstovo 5a, is very good value and has singles/doubles for US$55/80.

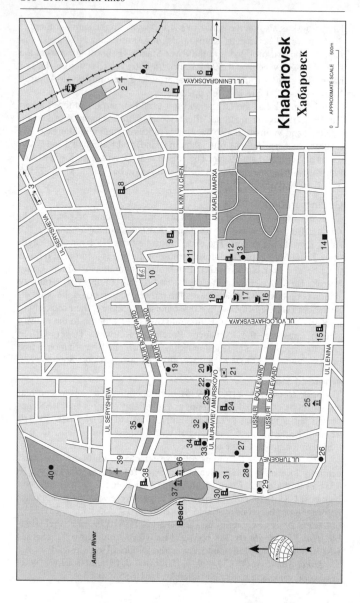

Khabarovsk
Хабаровск

0   APPROXIMATE SCALE   500m

## HOTELS AND RESTAURANTS

5  Hotel Zarya  Гостиница Заря
6  Hotel Turist  Гостиница Турист
8  Hotel Mayak  Гостиница Маяк
9  Hotel Amethyst  Гостиница Аметист
12 Hotel Tsentralnaya  Гостиница Центральная
14 Restaurant Okean  Ресторан Океан
15 Hotel Amur  Гостиница Амур
16 Pizzeria  Пицца
17 Café Kasam  Кафе Касам
18 Hotel Lyudmila  Гостиница Людмила
20 Café Dauria & Cinema  Кафе Даурия и Кино
23 Bistro Erofe  Бистро Ерофе
24 Hotel Dalny Vostok  Гостиница Далний Восток
30 Hotel Parus & Restaurant  Гостиница Парус + ресторан
31 Syangan Restaurant  Ресторан Сянган
32 Restaurant Rus  Ресторан Русь
34 Hotel Sapporo  Гостиница Саппоро
38 Hotel Intourist  Гостиница Интурист

## OTHER

1  Railway Station  Железнодорожний Вокзал
2  Church  Церковь
3  To Bus Station  Автовокзал
4  Advance Purchase Rail Ticket Office
   Предварительная Железнодорожная Касса
7  To War Cemetery

## OTHER (cont'd)

10 Market  Рынок
11 Japanese Consulate  Кулсульство Японии
13 Internet  Интернет
19 International Airlines Office  Касса Аэрофлота
21 Central Post Office  Почтамт
22 Tainy Remesla Art Store
   Художественный Магазин Тайны Ремесла
25 Geological Museum  Геолоúий Музей
26 Victory Monument  Слава Памятник
27 Eurasia Trans Inc
   Предприятие Eurasia
28 United States Foreign Office
   Американский Центр
29 River Station  Речной Вокзал
33 ATM
35 Domestic Airlines Office  Касса Аэрофлота
36 Military Museum  Музей Истории Краснознаменного
   Дальневосточного Военного Округа
37 Museum of Local Studies  Краевелческий Музей
39 Church of St Innocent  Иннокентьевская Церковь
40 Sports centre & Open-air Pool
   Спорт центр + Открытный Бассейн

*Mar Kuel Apartment Hotel*, at per Derzhinski 3, (note that this is not ul Derzhinski, but a small road between ul Derzhinski and ul Zaparina toward the Amur River from ul Lenina), has studio apartments with kitchen for US$80.

The main tourist hotel, *Hotel Intourist* (☎ 399 317), per Arseneva 7, is expensive (US$88/92 for 1/2 persons) but is, however, surprisingly well organised and pleasant. There are a number of good shops on the ground floor, an excellent restaurant on the eleventh, and the unhelpful service bureau on the second offers a wide range of excursions. Aeroflot and Asiana also have offices here. In its brochure, the hotel is described as 'a twelve storey modern-style building with a clear-cut architectural silhouette' – basically just another modernist block, painted white.

*MNTK* (☎ 399 401, ▤ 352 121) is situated a fair way from the centre of town, at ul Tikhookeanskaya 211. The rooms, however, are clean and comfortable; they cost from US$115.

There is an ever increasing number of excellent hotels and these are popular with business travellers. You're advised to book in advance, but you might be lucky if you just turn up. *Hotel Parus* (☎ 33 72 70, ▤ (7-509) 31 436 123 via Sprint) at ul Shchevchenko 5, and has single rooms for US$90 and doubles for US$120. There is a business centre in the hotel and the restaurant serves European food which is reputed to be the best in town. *Hotel Sapporo* (☎ 236 745, ▤ 234 418) at ul Komsomolskaya 79 is the best of them and caters to Japanese business people and tour groups, charging US$110/140 for a single/double room.

The *Hotel Dalny Vostok* (☎ 335 093), ul Muravieva-Amurskovo 18 is being refurbished but is in a great location; and the *Hotel Vassily Payarkov* (☎ 398 201) is on a boat tied up at the City Pier.

## Where to eat

The Japanese restaurant, *Unikhab* (☎ 399 315) on the top storey of the Hotel Intourist, is reliable but expensive.

*Sapporo Restaurant* (☎ 330 8082) on ul Muraveva-Amurskovo 3 is the next best place to eat but it's expensive. It has three floors of food with Russian cuisine on the first two and Japanese on the third. There is an ATM in the wall outside which gives you an idea of the prices inside.

On Komsomolskaya Square, you could join the tour groups downstairs in the new *Syangan* Chinese restaurant.

If you're staying at MNTK, the closest restaurant is the *Chinese Samovar* (Kitayski Samovar). Some dubious dealings go on behind the scenes but the food's not bad. Despite being only 50m from the main road, it's difficult to find. Take tram No 5 to Avtodorozhny Technikum.

A great find is the small *Pizzeria* at ul Dzerzhinskovo 36. There is a sign for the place but it's inside an unassuming entrance. Service is quick and the pizzas are good for US$1/2. Khabarovsk's bright young things hang out at *Café Dauria*, ul Muraveva-Amurskovo 25. *Café Kasam* sells good coffee and cakes and is at the top of ul Muraveva-Amurskovo. Further down the same street is the *Bistro Erofe* which sells decent pizza and coffee for US$0.50. There are various cafés along the river side which are pleasant for a drink and a snack.

### 🚊 AMUR (Амур) 9km

The railway takes the main line of the Trans-Siberian north through residential and then industrial areas of the city.

The settlement of Amur sits on the right bank of the Amur. The railway crosses the 2.6km combined rail-road bridge across the Amur river, completed in 2000. On the left bank of the Amur the railway crosses 3km of swamp and levees.

### 🚊 PRIAMURSKAYA (Приамурская) 17km

This town is just inside the border of the Jewish Autonomous Oblast (Еврейская Автономная область). The only thing of interest in the town is the silica brick factory, which produces insulation bricks for furnaces.

### 🚊 DEZHNEVKA (Дежневка) 38km

This is the actual junction of the Trans-Siberian and the line to Komsomolsk-na-Amure.

### 🚊🚊 VOLOCHAEVKA 2 (Волочаевка 2) 44km

This is a large railway complex 9km from the junction of the line to Komsomolsk-na-Amure and the Trans-Siberian. Trains from Komsomolsk-na-Amure for the west (Irkutsk) go through Volochaevka 2 and join the Trans-Siberian at Volochaevka 1. Trains from Komsomolsk-na-Amure for the east (Khabarovsk) go through Volochaevka 2 and join the Trans-Siberian at Dezhnevka. There is a hotel in Volochaevka 2.

Volochaevka 2 is in the Jewish Autonomous Oblast (Еврейская Автономная область) and some of the station signs are written in Hebrew. This region was established in 1935 to create a homeland for Russian Jews. The area was virtually uninhabited, as it is unsuitable for agriculture. Settlement has progressed slowly and today about 100,000 people live in the region, which has its capital at Birobidzhan (Биробиджан). Just five per cent of the population is of Jewish descent.

Volochaevka is famous as the scene of a major battle during the Russian Civil War. The Battle of Volochaevka ran from 5 to 14 February 1922 in the vicinity of the railway station and was one of the last battles of the Russian Civil War in the Russian Far East. In late 1921, General

Molchanov's White Guard forces launched an offensive from the Maritime Region to the north and on 22 December 1921 they seized Khabarovsk and advanced westward to Volochaevka. After a defeat near the railway station, the White Guard forces (4,500 men, 63 machine guns, 12 artillery pieces and three armoured trains) were forced onto the defensive. The Red Forces were under the command of V Blyukher (7,600 men, 300 machine guns, 30 artillery pieces, three armoured trains and two tanks) and attacked on 5 February. Although the temperature was as low as -35°C, the Red troops attacked the enemy without pause. The Whites' defences were finally broken on 12 February and by 14 February the communists had retaken Khabarovsk.

The train soon crosses over the Tunguska river (р. Тунгуска) which is the northern boundary of the Jewish Autonomous Oblast.

### ⊠ UTINY (Утиный) 55km

This railway siding is named after the poet, Iosif Pavlovich Utkin (1903-44) who was born in a village in the Khabarovsk region. His works were first published in 1922 and he won fame with the narrative poem, *The Tale of Motele the Redhead* (1925) which deals with the changes introduced by the October Revolution in a small Jewish town. He was the author of the narrative poem, *My Beloved Childhood* (1933) and of the collections *A First Book of Poems* (1927) and *Lyrics* (1939). The combination of revolutionary fervour and tender lyricism made Iosif Pavlovich's poetry popular, especially among the youth of the 1920s and 1930s. His published poetry includes *Verses from the Front* (1942) and *On the Motherland, Friendship and Love* (1944). He died in an aeroplane crash while returning from the German-Soviet war front in 1944.

### 🚉 PARTIZANSKIE SOPKI (Партизанские Сопки) 83km

Less than 1km east from here is the ancient Russian village of Golubichnoe (Голубичное) on the Darga river (р. Дарга) close to an inlet of the Amur.

### 🚉 DALNEVOSTOCHNY (Дальневосточный) 143km

The small forestry settlement around the station is known as Lesnoi (Лесной).

### 🚉 LITOVKO (Литовко) 154km

This is the major railway town between Komsomolsk-na-Amure and the Trans-Siberian. There is a ***railway hostel*** here. Three kilometres from the station is the village of Ukrainka (Украинка).

## 🏚 SANBOLI (Санболи) 172km

A dirt road from Sanboli skirts to the north and west of the Vandan Mountain Range (хребет Вандан). Nearby are about 17 caves with the longest being 300m. The region is hilly as the station on the Amur river flood plain is at 150m above sea level while the 848m Mount Elovaya (г. Еловая), the highest peak of the Vandan Mountain Range, is just 6km away from Sanboli.

## 🏚 BOLON (Болонь) 275km

This 5,000 inhabitant railway and logging town takes its name from the nearby Lake Bolon, a deep bay of the Amur. The town is wedged between the Alyur and Syumnyur rivers (р. Алюр и Сюмнюр) which flow into the lake. The lake is also know as Bolen, Nuri-Odzhal, or Boulen-Odzhal, and is the largest lake in the flood plain of the lower Amur, being 338 square kilometres, 70km long, 20km wide and having an average depth of 3m. In the centre of the lake is the volcanic island of Yadasen (о. Ядасен). The lake flows into the Amur river along a 9km channel and on its shores is the village of Achan (Ачан). This indigenous village is believed to be one of the first settlements on the Amur river.

The Lake Bolon area is a major stopping place for migratory birds so the Wildlife Institute in Khabarovsk, which provides survey information for the government's nature resource management, has recommended that this area becomes a national park. Over 200 types of birds have been identified here.

From Bolon town, you can reach the lake by a 10km road. On the lake's shore is the village of Dzhuen (Джуен).

## 🏚 KHARKOVSK (Харьковск)

This station is named after the west Russian city of Kharkov.

## 🅇 TEISIN (Тейсин) 301km

Besides the station, there is nothing at this stop. However, 5km east of here is the old village of Teisin which is on the edge of Lake Bolon. A good road runs 78km from the lakeside village to Komsomolsk-na-Amure.

## 🏚 ELBAN (Эльбан) 311km

This town has a machine-building plant, dairy farms and a large number of vegetable farms.

### 🚃 RAZ. 303km (Раз. 303км) 338km

Surrounding the station is the small town of Izvestkovy (Известковый).

### 🚃 MYLKI (Мылки) 352km

This is the closest station to the industrial city of Amursk. Although there is a railway line to the city, it only carries freight trains. There are regular buses between Mylki and Amursk and between Amursk and Komsomolsk-na-Amure. For information on Amursk, see pp183-6.

### 🚃 KHURBA (Хурба) 367km

This small town is wedged between the Big Khurba and Little Khurba rivers (р. Хурба).

### 🚃 KOMSOMOLSK-NA-AMURE (Комсомольск-на-Амуре) 374km

Komsomolsk-na-Amure is located at 3,837km on the BAM. For more information, see Komsomolsk-na-Amure and region (pp167-82).

# Khabarovsk–Komsomolsk-na-Amure–Nikolaevsk-na-Amure by river
## Хабаровск–Комсомольск-на-Амуре–Николаевск-на-Амуре
### по реке

The massive 4,440km Amur river forms in Mongolia and travels along the Chinese–Russian border before discharging into the Pacific Ocean just to the east of Nikolaevsk-na-Amure.

Few foreigners have travelled along the Amur river in the past due to Soviet-era travel restrictions and a lack of information. However, the river in summer is by far the most exciting and comfortable way to travel from Khabarovsk to Komsomolsk-na-Amure, and on to the river mouth at Nikolaevsk-na-Amure. The route has a daily service; the biggest of the hydrofoils, the *Meteor*, eats up the river at an awesome 60kph.

The *Meteor* has a front cabin with a panoramic view ahead (at least if you pull back the dainty curtains), a centre cabin with the purser's office and a tiny snack-bar and, between the centre and rear cabins, a raised open walkway where passengers gather to drink, smoke, flirt, or let the slip-stream blow in their faces. Skim along the roiling red river where the only sign of mankind is the channel markers hacked out of the encroaching forest, stopping at the floating jetties of tiny villages. This is the far eastern

**Hydrofoil timetable – Khabarovsk to/from Nikolaevsk-na-Amure**

| Downstream from Khabarovsk | | Upstream from Nikolaevsk | |
|---|---|---|---|
| Arrive (local time) | Place | Arrive (local time) | Distance (km) |
| 06.30 (depart) | Khabarovsk (Хабаровск) | 20.05 | 0 |
| 09.40 | Troitskoe (Троицкое) | 17.25 | 102 |
| 10.45 | Malmyzh (Малмыж) | 16.10 | 271 |
| 11.30 | Amursk (Амурск) | 15.02 | 312 |
| 12.30 | Komsomolsk-na-Amure (Комсомольск-на-Амуре) | 14.30 | 354 |
| 20.30 (arrive) | Bogorodskoe (Богородское) | 06.00 (depart) | 741 |
| 06.30 (depart) | | 19.10 (arrive) | |
| 10.30 (arrive) | Nikolaevsk-na-Amure (Николаевск-на-Амуре) | 15.00 (depart) | 933 |

route used by generations of conquerors, traders, exiles and even Anton Chekhov on his way to inspect the penal colonies of Sakhalin.

The hydrofoils and ferries officially run between 20 June to 31 August when the Amur is guaranteed to be completely clear of ice. Local ferries may start and end earlier depending of the river ice in their area of operation.

Tickets for the hydrofoils are bought at the river stations, or, if the town is small, on the vessel. As tickets are expensive for locals, there are invariably spare seats. Remember to keep hold of your ticket as you may be asked to show it during the trip and when you get off the boat.

In winter the Amur river freezes and becomes a road. The driving trip to Nikolaevsk-na-Amure takes 24 hours.

The time is Moscow time +7 hours.

## KHABAROVSK (Хабаровск) 0km

See pp216-221.

The River Station (Речной вокзал) is at the foot of ul. Shevchenko, ☎ 398 832 or 398 690 (ул. Шевченко, 1). The ticket office is in a low building in the square. Embarkation is from the green and cream barge built like a small country mansion.

### Getting there and away

The hydrofoil leaves Khabarovsk daily in the early morning and reaches Komsomolsk-na-Amure about midday, then continues to Bogorodskoe. Here passengers stay overnight, since the hydrofoils only run during daylight. The journey continues to Nikolaevsk-na-Amure, arriving at midday and returning to Bogorodskoe by evening. The upstream hydrofoil leaves Bogorodskoe in the early morning and arrives at Khabarovsk by evening.

The one-way fare from Khabarovsk to Komsomolsk-na-Amure is approximately $15. There are many smaller landings between these places, at which the hydrofoil will also stop. Discuss this with the ticket office or the purser.

### TROITSKOE (Троицкое) 102km

Small logging town on the right bank, linked to the Khabarovsk–Komsomolsk-na-Amure highway.

### MALMYZH (Малмыж) 271km

Evenk village is on the right bank under a headland. Confusingly, there is another Malmyzh close to Amursk on the left bank.

### AMURSK (Амурск) 312km

For information on Amursk, see p183. The River Station (Речной вокзал) is in a small cove below the centre of the town.

### KOMSOMOLSK-NA-AMURE (Комсомольск-на-Амуре) 354km

For information on Komsomolsk-na-Amure, see pp167-82. The River Station (Речной вокзал) is in a splendid ship-shaped building at the foot of pr. Mira (пр. Мира) at the tram turnaround. The ticket office is at the downstream end.

The river station at Komsomolsk-na-Amure (photo © Nicholas Zvegintzov).

## Getting there and away

Beside the daily hydrofoil described on p225 that heads both north and south in the middle of the day, a daily hydrofoil leaves early in the morning and reaches Nikolaevsk-na-Amure by the end of the day (see below). The one-way fare to Nikolaevsk-na-Amure is approximately $47.

There is a similar daily schedule for the return from Nikolaevsk-na-Amure, starting at 06.30.

## BOGORODSKOE (Богородское) 741km

The hydrofoil overnights at Bogorodskoe. A reasonably good 90km road leads from Bogorodskoe to Lazarev (Лазарев), which is 9km from Sakhalin Island. Eight km from Lazarev is the abandoned shaft of the proposed rail tunnel to Sakhalin island, decommissioned after the death of Stalin in 1953.

Bogorodskoe has a simple *hotel* (toilets in the corridor).

## NIKOLAEVSK-NA-AMURE (Николаевск-на-Амуре) 933km

Nikolaevsk-na-Amure (area code ☎ 42135) lies at the mouth of the Amur river where it empties into the Pacific Ocean in a shallow estuary sheltered by the north end of Sakhalin Island.

The settlement was founded in 1850 by Gennadi Ivanovich Nevelskoi (Невельской Геннадий Иванович), 1813-76, Russian explorer of the Far East, and became a town in 1856. Nevelskoi explored Sakhalin in 1848-49 and found out that it was an island (the Chinese and Japanese already knew this). It has 36,000 inhabitants, with ship-building and ship-repairing facilities. There is a museum of local history.

| Hydrofoil timetable: Komsomolsk-na-Amure–Nikolaevsk-na-Amure | |
|---|---|
| **Arrive (local time)** | **Place** |
| 08.00 (departs) | Komsomolsk-na-Amure (Комсомольск-на-Амуре) |
| 12.00 | Kiselevka (Киселевка) |
| 12.25 | Tsimmermanovka (Циммермановка) |
| 12.50 | Bystrinsk (Быстринск) |
| 13.35 | Sofisk (Софийск) |
| 14.20 | Mariinsk (Мариинск) |
| 15.05 | Bulava (Булава) |
| 15.50 | Savinskoe (Савинское) |
| 16.20 | Bogorodskoe (Богородское) |
| 17.25 | Susanino (Сусанино) |
| 18.00 | Tyr (Тыр) |
| 18.35 | Takhta (Тахта) |
| 19.35 | Innokentevka (Иннокентьевка) |
| 20.45 | Nikolaevsk-na-Amure (Николаевск-на-Амуре) |

Anton Chekhov, in his book *The Island* about his 1890 investigation of the penal settlements of Sakhalin, describes his traveller's distress on being disembarked from the Amur river steamer onto the jetty with all his luggage and no place to stay. Fortunately, he was rescued by the coastal steamer to Sakhalin.

The modern traveller need not be stranded, but can stay at the **Sever Hotel**, ul. Sibirskaya 3, ☎ +7 42135 6-31-34 (ул. Сибирская, 3, гостиница «Север»).

Passengers can travel with oil company supply ships from Nikolaevsk-na-Amure to Moskalvo (Москальво) on Sakhalin island, and from there by bus to Okha (Оха) and the rail-head at Nogliki (Ноглики).

# PART 5: REPUBLIC OF SAKHA
## Республика Саха

# Sakha and Yakutsk
# via the Lena River and AYaM
### Саха и Якутск по реке Лена и по АЯМ

This chapter describes routes into the Republic of Sakha (Yakutiya) (Республика Саха (Якутия)).

Covering 3,103,200 sq km, Sakha is one of the most prosperous and one of the wildest states in the Russian Federation. It lies in the north-eastern part of Asia, stretching 2,000km north-south, from the Arctic Ocean to the Stanovoi mountains, and 2,500km east-west, forming more than one-sixth of the total area of the Russian Federation. But it has fewer than 1,100,000 people, less than one person per three square kilometres – far less in most areas since two-thirds of the population live in cities and settlements.

Most of Sakha is taiga woods, mountain rivers with hundreds of kilometres between settlements and coastal delta tundra. Sakha includes the northern hemisphere's 'pole of cold' (Полюс холода) – the coldest place in the northern hemisphere – -71°C at the meteorological station between the villages of Oimyakon (Оймякон) and Tomtor (Томтор). It is home to the native long-haired Yakut horses, which live outdoors through the winter (according to agronomists, 'a good meat producer, with a high milk yield').

At the same time, Sakha is a rich region, producing diamonds, coal, gold, strategic metals, furs and energy. (The gold deposits of Sakha are alluvial and regularly yield nuggets – the largest found being 9.6kg.) Sakha's capital, the old and sophisticated city of Yakutsk, has a rich culture mingling indigenous Sakhan and Russian themes, a famous university and excellent internet connections.

There are three routes to this fascinating and paradoxical area. The mighty Lena river, 4,400km from its source near Lake Baikal to its giant delta at Tiksi (Тикси) on the Arctic Ocean, sweeps through Sakha in an immense S-bend between the mountains, with Yakutsk in the elbow of the upper crook; it forms a busy summer thoroughfare. The AYaAD highway, an engineering feat from Soviet times and later, makes a south-north land link to Yakutsk. The Kolyma Highway ('the road of bones') runs eastward into Magadanskaya oblast. To the west there is no road.

The Republic of Sakha is a state within the Russian Federation. It was previously known as the Yakut Autonomous Soviet Socialist Republic. 'Sakha' is the indigenous Sakhans' name for themselves – 'Yakut' was a mispronunciation by 17th-century Russians.

Sakha is far more autonomous than other regions in the Russian Far East as it has an elected president and parliament, greater economic self-determination and its own visa requirements (see below).

The population of Sakha is 976,000, with 228,000 in Yakutsk and 106,000 in Neryungri. The largest ethnic group is Russians (50 per cent), with Sakhans (33 per cent), Ukrainians, Evenki, Tatars, Evens, and Yukaghirs, with Russians predominating in the south and Sakhans predominating in the north, including Yakutsk. The Yakutian language, which is Turkic, is written in Cyrillic plus extra characters for Yakutian sounds. (In Yakutsk signs are often, disconcertingly, in Yakutian and English.)

Republic holidays are the major festival of Ysyakh (Ыһыах) at the summer solstice, and the last Sunday in March, Day of Reindeer Herders (День Оленевода).

The time zone in most of the Republic of Sakha (Yakutiya) is six hours later than Moscow.

## VISAS

Sakha has its own visa and residence regulations in addition to those of Russia. You need the names of the towns you wish to visit on your Russian invitation. In addition, Sakha requires an AIDS and hepatitis certificate for a stay of over 13 days, differing from the three month requirement for the rest of Russia. This rule is enforced by airlines, airports and hotels. There is no checking of visas on the AYaM railway trains from Russia.

The visa requirement was introduced in 1994 as a way of reducing the number of visitors to the region, which in turn reduces the consumption of limited food and goods. In addition, the visa system allows the government to control the visits of foreign businessmen, which ensures that they are informed of all commercial activity. The fine for not having a visa is $2.50 but there may be additional arbitrary punishments.

If you want to go to Sakha it is best to get one or more Sakhan towns listed on your invitation before you leave home. If you arrive in Russia without them, it is virtually impossible to find anywhere outside Sakha to add them. If you do not have a contact to get an invitation from, try one of the organisations listed under Getting assistance in Yakutsk or Neryungri, p237/p270.

# Yakutsk
## Якутск

Yakutsk (Якутск, Туймаада in Yakutian) is the capital of the Republic of Sakha. Founded in 1632 by Cossacks on the east bank of the Lena, it was later moved to the west bank. Yakutsk is now a vigorous modern city of

200,000 people, with theatres and music, cafés and a famous university and research organisations.

The mostly cream-coloured low-rise buildings are set on harmoniously proportioned streets and plazas. A few buildings, mostly joint ventures with Swiss, Austrian, or Canadian firms, and some glass-

❑ **Yakutsk (Якутск)**
Area code ☎ 4112
677000, Russia, Republic of Sakha (Yakutiya), Yakutsk
(677000, Россия, Республика Саха (Якутия), г. Якутск)
Moscow time +6 hours

clad, are springing up. Little is left of pre-Soviet Yakutsk and you may have a hard time recognising locations on the photographs in the museum, but behind the main streets you can catch glimpses of the sumptuous log mansions of old Yakutsk. Unfortunately the older buildings subside because their poorly insulated foundations melt the permafrost.

Yakutsk has an extreme continental climate, with winter temperatures of less than -50°C and summer ones in the high 20°Cs. The town is built on permafrost; the newer buildings are all built on piles.

In 1999, Yakutsk and Magadan were the most expensive cities in the country for a basket of basic food items.

## HISTORY

Yakutsk was founded in 1632 as a stockade on the east bank of the Lena river. During the 1640s it was moved to the opposite bank due to flooding. In the 1680s the town's stockade was rebuilt as a wooden fortress and the main guard tower still stands today. The town quickly became the administrative and trading hub for the region and served as a springboard for the Russian colonisation of the Far East. From the mid-1700s Yakutsk became one of the main destinations for convicts and exiles to Siberia (11 Decembrists were exiled here). The harsh treatment of these prisoners led to a number of bloody protests, notably in 1889 and 1904, and a number of monuments around the town commemorate these.

Soviet power was proclaimed in July 1918 but Yakutsk was recaptured by the White Guard from August 1918 to December 1919.

In 1991 an agreement was signed between the presidents of Russia and Sakha, giving the latter a certain degree of autonomy within the Russian Federation. The idea was to have more local control over the proceeds of gold and diamond mining and use these to improve local living conditions.

## GETTING THERE AND AWAY

### By river

In the summer there is transportation in many directions on the Lena river and its tributaries. The following is a summary; for more details see pp241-61.

All river traffic goes from the River Station, which is north of the centre of the city on pereulok Energetikov at the terminus of the No 8 bus (переулок Энергетиков, речной вокзал). River transport is run by a variety of shipping groups. You may find information and schedules on bulletin boards or hand-lettered flyers in the River Station (though the cashiers do not open up unless a boat is leaving), or from the agents listed in Getting assistance (p237), or from the individual shipping groups.

From the River Station frequent car ferries and passenger hydrofoils cross the river to Nizhni Bestyakh (Нижний Бестях).

From Ust-Kut (Усть-Кут) upstream, junction with the BAM railway, river steamers make nine round-trips with passengers and seven round-trips with passengers and automobiles between May and September. These are operated by AOOT 'KREB' (Kirenskaya Remontno-

**YAKUTSK MAP KEY**

1  Stadium (Стадион)
2  Farmers' Market
   (крестьянский рынок)
3  Catholic Church
   (Католическая церковь)
4  Russian Orthodox Church of St
   Nicholas (Никольская церковь)
5  Bus station (Автовокзал)
6  Hotel Yakutsk, Intourist-Yakutsk
   (Якутск, Интурист-Якутск)
7  TV tower
   (телетрансляционная мачта)
8  Literary Museum
   (Литературный музей)
9  Sakha Theatre
   (Саха театр)
10  Yakutsk Musical Theatre
    (Якутский музыкальный театр)
11  Former Trinity Cathedral
    (бывший Троицкий собор)
12  Geological Museum
    (Геологический музей)
13  TourService Center Ltd
    (ТурСервис Центр)
14  Pushkin Library
    (здание Публичной библиотеки)
15  Shergin's Shaft
    (Шергинская шахта)
16  Museum of Music and Folklore
    (Музей музыки и фольклора)
17  Hotel Tygyn Darkhan
    (Тыгын Дархан)
18  Lenin statue
    (памятник В.И. Ленину)
19  Russian Drama Theatre
    (Русский драматический театр)
20  Town Hall
    (Администрация города)
21  Globus map shop (Глобус)
22  Hotel Kolos (Колос)
23  Aeroflot (Аэрофлот)
24  Telephone (Телефон)
25  Hotel Lena (Лена)
26  Hotel Sterkh (Стерх)
27  Hotel Parus (Парус)
28  Post office (Главпочтамт)
29  LenaRechFlot (Ленаречфлот)
30  State Museum
    (Государственный музей)

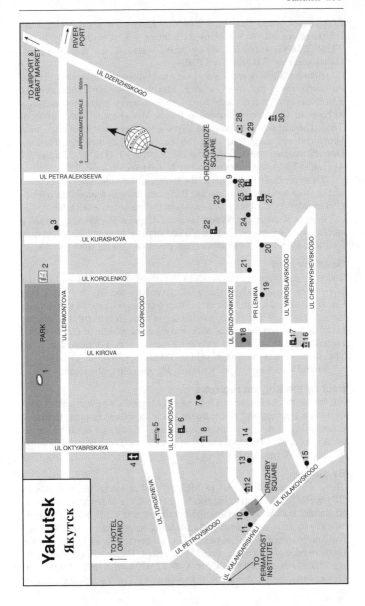

# Yakutsk
## Якутск

TO AIRPORT & ARBAT MARKET

RIVER PORT

UL DZERZHISKOGO

APPROXIMATE SCALE

ORDZHONIKIDZE SQUARE

UL PETRA ALEKSEEVA

UL KURASHOVA

UL KOROLENKO

UL LERMONTOVA

PARK

UL GORKOGO

UL KIROVA

UL ORDZHONIKIDZE

PR LENINA

UL YAROSLAVSKOGO

UL CHERNYSHEVSKOGO

UL LOMONOSOVA

UL OKTYABRSKAYA

UL TURGENEVA

DRUZHBY SQUARE

UL KULAKOVSKOGO

UL PETROVSKOGO

UL KALANDARISHVILI

TO HOTEL ONTARIO

TO PERMAFROST INSTITUTE

Ekspluatatsionnaya Baza Flota), 666710 Kirensk, Irkutskaya oblast, ul. Partizanskaya 30, ☎ +7-39568-3-23-06 or +7-39568-3-24-10, 🖹 +7-39568-2-16-09 (666710, Иркутская область, г. Киренск, ул. Партизанская, 30, АООТ «КРЭБ»).

Between Yakutsk and Tiksi (Тикси), downstream beyond the delta of the Lena river, the river steamer Mekhanik Kulibin («Механикик Кулибин») makes five round-trips with passengers, plus two round-trips to Kyusyur (Кюсюр) and three to Bykov Mys (Быков Мыс), short of Tiksi. The trip downstream from Yakutsk to Tiksi takes three days, nine hours and upstream four days, 16 hours. Contact LenaRechFlot, ul. Dzerzhinskogo 2, next to the post office, ☎/🖹 +7 4112 42-27-62 or +7 4112 42-57-61 (ул. Дзержинского, 2, «Ленаречфлот»).

There are daily hydrofoils to the mouth of the Aldan river (р. Алдан) and up to Khandyga (Хандыга). There are daily hydrofoils up river to Olekminsk (Олёкминск). Inquire about these also at LenaRechFlot.

A river steamer, the *Stepan Vasilev* («Степан Васильев»), makes a weekly round trip to Nyurba (Нюрба) down to the mouth of the Vilyui river (р. Вилюй) and up it, with other boats travelling onward from Nyurba.

## South by land

Twice a week there is a bus south to Neryungri, $95 for 730km, from the bus station, at ul. Oktyabrskaya 24, served by the city bus No 8 (ул. Октябрьская, 24, Автовокзал). From Neryungri trains go to Tynda on the BAM railway. The bus crosses the Lena river, therefore it does not run between April and the end of May and from the middle of October until December between the ferry and the ice road seasons. For more details see The AYaM: Tynda–Neryungri–Aldan–Yakutsk, pp262-78.

From December to April ice roads are open along the rivers.

## East by the Kolyma Highway

For the adventurous there is a road east to Magadan, which at least in winter (when marshes and rivers freeze over) sees some through traffic. A patchwork of rides, possibly including an air hop and hitch-hiking, is needed to reach Magadan. For more details see The Kolyma Highway: Yakutsk to Magadan, p279-90.

## By air

There are near daily flights to Moscow and at least weekly flights to Blagoveshchensk, Bratsk, Irkutsk, Khabarovsk via Aldan and Ust-Maya, Krasnodar via Omsk, Neryungri, Novosibirsk and Vladivostok, and periodically to most settlements with a landing strip within Sakha. The airport, at Novoportovskoi Kvartal (Новопортовской квартал) on the northern edge of the city, is served by bus No 4. The Aeroflot airline booking office is at ul. Ordzhonikidze 8, ☎ 42 0204, 42 5139, 42 0265 (ул. Орджоникидзе, 8, Агентство Аэрофлота). The Yakutavia Computer

Centre (ВЦ Якутавия) offers an on-line search of flight schedules and prices at 🖥 www.yakutia.ru, ☎ +7-4112 242554 or +7 4112 424656, 📄 +7 4112 242554, (г. Якутск, ул. Орджоникидзе, 10, каб 614, ВЦ Якутавия).

## GETTING AROUND

Yakutsk is on the west bank of the Lena river, on the inside of a giant bend. It is built (barely) back from the marshes and old ox-bows of the river can be seen in the town as lagoons.

The plan of the centre of the city is simple. The main street is Prospekt Lenina (пр. Ленина), some seven blocks long. At the street's southern end is the Friendship of Nations Square (пл. Дружбы народов), in the centre is Lenin Square (пл. Ленина), the statue of Lenin, and government buildings, and at the northern end is Ordzhonikidze Square (пл. Орджоникидзе). There are two blocks east of Pr. Lenina and six blocks west. The river station is on an inlet of the river north of the city centre. The airport is at the edge of the city on the north. The University and the Permafrost Institute are at the southern end of the city.

There is a dual bus system in operation: public buses are cheaper, but run infrequently and are packed like sardine cans; smaller private buses run the same routes with the same route numbers and will almost always have free seats, but they cost a little more. There may be subtle differences between the itineraries of public and private buses with the same number (ask the driver or conductor about your destination). Bus No 8 goes to the river station, along most of pr. Lenina, and past the bus station. Bus No 4 goes to the airport and along pr. Lenina. Both pass most of the hotels.

The Federal Service of Geodesy and Cartography of Russia operates an excellent and friendly map-shop, Globus, at Pr. Lenina, 16, ☎ 42-30-72 (677892, г. Якутск, пр. Ленина, 16, «Глобус»). Among many other maps, it sells:

● a city map with the bus routes and a huge variety of public, cultural, governmental, religious and commercial sites marked
● topographic maps
● a Sakha travellers' map (Пути сообщения – 'paths of communication'), which shows petrol stations, avtobazy, and the important distinction between all-weather and winter roads.

For getting around in cyberspace, visit the telephone company Sakhatelecom's *Internet Café*, at ul. Kurashova, 22, (corner of pr. Lenina), Yakutsk 677000, ☎ 42-05-72, 🖥 http://telecom.sakha.ru, (677000, Россия, г. Якутск, ул. Курашова, 22, «Сахателеком» Интернет Кафе), with networked terminals and fast internet connections (but no coffee) at the intercity telephone office.

## WHERE TO STAY

The best hotel in Yakutsk is ***Hotel Tygyn Darkhan*** (гостиница «Тыгын Дархан»), named after the legendary Sakhan warrior who led the Yakuts before the Russians colonised the region (formerly the President Hotel). The Tygyn Darkhan is the government hotel, in the heart of the city just off Lenin Square. It was recently luxuriously renovated by a Swiss company, with a swimming pool, sauna and weight-room (you may nevertheless wonder what is in that sausage, pale pink with dark specks, served with a smear of ketchup at breakfast). A single starts at $100. Contact the hotel at 677018, Yakutsk, ul. Ammosova 9, ☎ +7 (4112) 43-51-09, 43-53-09, 43-52-13, 43-55-09, 📠 43-53-54 (677018, г. Якутск, ул. Аммосова, 9, гостиница «Тыгын Дархан»).

The Canadian-built ***Hotel Ontario*** is in a quiet location in a park zone about 20-minutes' drive out of the city centre. It has a restaurant, and a sports-sanatorium complex is in a neighbouring building. A single starts at $34. Contact the hotel at Sergelyakhskoe shosse, 13km, building 7, ☎ +7 (4112) 265058, 7 (4112) 422066 (Сергеляхское шоссе, 13 км, строение 7, гостиница «Онтарио»).

***Hotel Sterkh*** was renovated in 1992 and has its own bar and restaurant. A single starts at $60. Contact the hotel at 677000 Yakutsk, pr. Lenina 8, ☎ +7 4112 242701, 📠 242955 (677000, Якутск, пр. Ленина, 8, гостиницу «Стерх»).

The more basic ***Hotel Lena***, next door to and once part of Hotel Sterkh, has singles from $26. The hotel is at 677000, Yakutsk, Prospekt Lenina 8, ☎ +7 4112 42-48-10, 42-48-92, 42-47-94, 📠 +7 4112 42-42-14 (677000, Якутск, пр. Ленина, 8, гостиница «Лена»).

***Hotel Parus*** belongs to the Lena River Shipping Company. A single starts at $60. The hotel is at 677000, Yakutsk, Prospekt Lenina 7, ☎ +7 4112 423727, 📠 +7 4112 422762 (677000, Якутск, пр. Ленина, 7, гостиница «Парус»).

***Hotel Yakutsk*** is the former Intourist hotel. It charges $35 a single and is near the bus station at ul. Oktyabrskaya, 20/1, ☎ 250 700 (ул. Октябрьская, 20/1, гостиница «Якутск»).

A 'Russian' hotel is ***Hotel Kolos*** ('ear of grain'). A single with full facilities is $15. The Kolos has a small cafeteria and is at ul. Khurashova 28 (ул. Хурашова, 28, гостиница «Колос»).

All of the hotels except for Hotel Ontario are located in the centre of the city.

TourService Center Ltd (see Getting assistance p237) can also organise ***homestay***s.

For more information on Yakutsk hotels, see 💻 www.yakutiatravel.com/hotels.htm.

## WHERE TO EAT

Do not drink water from the tap. Drink bottled water or boiled water.

Yakutsk has many places to eat. There are buffets in many office and shopping buildings. There are *Magic Burger* stands, where the special sauce is heavy on the dill. *Hotel Tygyn Darkhan* has an excellent and fashionable restaurant with Yakutian, Russian and international food at surprisingly reasonable prices. Another good choice is the restaurant at *Hotel Ontario*. There is a fast-growing number of expensive private restaurants such as *Fregat* at the LORP building on pl. Ordzhonikidze, *Traktir Yamschika* on ul. Ordzhonikidze, *Antalia* and *Margarita* on pr. Lenina, and *Café Delfin* at ul. Kirova 21. *Kafe Manhattan Avenue* (Кафе Манхэттен Авеню, ☎ +7 4112 251-051) on ul. Lenina, 45a, next to the Lena cinema and near Yakutsk State University, has both American and Russian fast foods in a lively recreation of a national chain (one only to date).

## GETTING ASSISTANCE

TourService Center Ltd, under General Director Vyacheslav Ipatiev, offers tours including trekking, cultural/indigenous, sport-fishing, bird-watching and river cruises along the Lena river. It also organises business visits for Russians and foreigners and holidays for Russians. TourService Center Ltd also maintains the useful 🖥 www.yakutiatravel.com and is at 5, ul. Oktyabrskaya, Yakutsk, Russia 677000, ☎ +7 4112 25 11 44, 🖹 +7 4112 25 08 97, 🖥 tours@online.ru (677000 Якутск, ул. Октябрьская, 5, Компания «ТурСервис Центр»).

Intourist-Yakutsk is at Hotel Yakutsk, ul. Oktyabrskaya, 20/1, ☎ +7 4112 25-40-90, 25-38-20 (ул. Октябрьская, 20/1, ГП «Интурист-Якутск»). For hunting and fishing expeditions to remote areas Ilin Tour at Vilyuiski pereulok, 8, Yakutsk 677008, ☎ +7 4112 25-13-32 or 25-40-606, 🖥 ilintour@sakha.ru (677008 Россия, г. Якутск, Вилюйский переулок, 8, Илин Тур) has a fleet of An-2 biplanes and a helicopter.

## WHAT TO SEE

The **State Museum of the History and Culture of the Peoples of the North**, housed in what was formerly the Bishop's Palace, is one of the oldest museums in Siberia. An extension is currently being built, maintaining the same style of architecture. On the ground floor are exhibits about the history and customs of Yakutiya and an impressive exhibition of animal life, culminating in the complete skeleton of a mammoth. On the upper floor a whole section is dedicated to Yakut religion. Outside, under a shelter, is the sadly deteriorated skeleton of a giant fish (a whale?). Two more buildings form part of the museum complex: the original Eastern Tower (built between 1682 and 1687) of the former Yakutsk wooden stockaded town and a small wooden house, where the history of Yakutsk

238  Republic of Sakha

is presented. The museum is at Prospekt Lenina 5/2 (in the middle of the block, behind the pr. Lenina buildings), ☎ 234 734 (пр. Ленина, 5/2, Государственный объединный музей истории и културы народов Севера им. Е.М. Ярославского).

Behind the museum, on the other side of ul. Yaroslavskogo, is the **Political Exile annexe** of the museum in a two-storey log-house where political prisoners staged an armed revolt from 18 February to 7 March 1904. Here the curator can show material on the 11 Decembrists exiled to Yakutsk. The annexe is at ul Yaroslavskogo, 5/1 (ул. Ярославского 5/1, Музей «Политическая ссылка в Якутске»).

The **Permafrost Institute** is not actually a museum, but the Institute welcomes tourists as a way to top up its meagre finances. You are taken 12 metres underground to see part of the old river bed, where the temperature never varies from -5°C. The walls of the cavern, of sand and flecks of wood, are as sturdy as concrete as long as they do not thaw. Permafrost is said to affect 25 per cent of the planet and 50 per cent of Russia. This institute claims to be the only one in the world engaged in fundamental study of permafrost (as opposed to specific applications) and it was here that the guidelines were developed on how to build on permafrost. To get in, you will probably have to book through a tour agent. Outside the Institute is a model of a baby mammoth that was found preserved in permafrost. You can see the actual preserved mammoth in the St Petersburg Natural History Museum. The Institute is at the end of bus line 17 at ul. Merzlotnaya (ул. Мерзлотная, Институт мерзлотоведения).

Shergin's Shaft (Шергинская шахта) is a 116.6m deep shaft dug between 1827 and 1837, and was the first serious attempt to study permafrost. The shaft started when a merchant named Shergin discovered that no matter how deep he dug a well outside his house, he never hit water. He contacted the Russian Academy of Sciences in Moscow with this curiosity and it dispatched a team of experts that came to the conclusion that the water in the soil was permanently frozen. The shaft was still in use for measurements as late as 1942. It is near the intersection of ul. Kulakovskogo and ul. Yaroslavskogo, but all there is to see is the little wooden cabin built over it, without a sign to indicate its existence.

The **Literary Museum**, ul. Oktyabrskaya 12, (Литературный музей, ул. Октябрьская, 12) is built in the form of a Yakut yurt. The **Geological Museum**, ul. Petrovskogo 2, (Геологический музей, Петровского, 2) is part of the Science Centre. The **Museum of Music and Folklore**, ul. Kirova 8, (ул. Кирова, 8, Музей музыки и фольклора) has an interesting display about Yakut shamanism.

The **Sakha Theatre** (for performances in Yakutian) is on Ordzhonikidze Square (пл. Орджоникидзе, Саха академический театр им. П. А. Ойунского). The **Yakutsk Musical Theatre** (opera and ballet) is at pr. Lenina 46 (пр. Ленина, 46, Якутский музыкальний театр). The **Russian Drama Theatre** is at pr. Lenina 21 (пр. Ленина, 21, Русский драматический театр).

**Yakutsk State University** faces the lagoon on ul. Kulakovskogo (ул. Кулаковского, Якутский государственный университет).

Several churches are now open. The **Russian Orthodox Church of St. Nicholas**, ul. Oktyabrskaya 31, was built in 1852 and until recently served as the Communist Party archive (ул. Октябрьская, 31, Никольская церковь). A modern **Catholic Church** is at ul. Lermontova 36 (ул. Лермонтова, 36, Католическая церковь). Outside the centre are a **Russian Orthodox Church**, ul. Ushakova 20 (ул. Ушакова, 20) and a **Baptist Church**, ul. Pilotov 14 (ул. Пилотов, 14).

A number of **19th-century buildings** can be seen at the foot of ul. Ammosova beyond Hotel Tygyn Darkhan. These are listed as historic buildings but have not been restored. A number of mansions in old Yakutsk, some stuccoed, some of squared logs with tracery balconies and veneered pilasters, can be found on back streets west and south of pr. Lenina. The last buildings built of the traditional materials, squared logs, are rows of two-storey apartment buildings built along ul. Dzerzhinskogo (ул. Дзержинского) after the Great Patriotic War and before the establishment in the region of precast concrete building technology. The **former Trinity Cathedral**, built of brick in 1708, converted to a variety theatre (театр Эстрады), is at ul. Kalandarishvili 2 (ул. Каландаришвили, 2, бывший Троицкий собор); ask in the lobby to be let in. The auditorium is built into the west end of the church but you can still see the brick inside of the (truncated) tower where the sanctuary was. The **Pushkin Library** at the corner of pr. Lenina and ul. Oktyabrskaya, built of brick in 1911, is slowly being restored (пр. Ленина, 40, здание Публичной библиотеки). A number of historic wooden buildings have been collected at the **Druzhba Historical Park** (see below).

One of the most popular markets is the **Arbat Market**, though it is a fair way out of town to the north, beyond the airport. It specialises in clothes and if you want to buy a *shapka* (winter hat) guaranteed to keep your brain warm at -50°C, this is the place to go. To get there, take one of the private buses that have 'Arbat' (Арбат) written on their windscreen. The **Chinese Market** is a short distance from the Arbat.

For beautiful (and useful) fur clothes and reindeer boots, visit Sakhabult store, pr. Lenina, 25, ☎ 45-61-86 or 45-61-74 or 46-06-95 (Магазин Сахабулт, Национальный концерн охотничьего хозяйства, пр. Ленина, 25), the local hunting products company. (Unfortunately, only a tiny selection will be on display in the summer).

The **Farmers' Market** (крестянский рынок) is at Komsomol Square next to the Park (пл. Комсомольская). Do not be misled by the dense array of stalls selling all kinds of junk – the food you are looking for is sold inside the market hall.

## EXCURSIONS IN THE REGION

### Druzhba Historical Park (Ленский историко-архитектурный музей-заповедник «Дружба»)

Druzhba Historical Park (Ленский историко-архитектурный музей-заповедник «Дружба») is near Ogorodtakh (Огородтах), on the right bank of the Lena, near the site of the original pre-Yakutsk fort. It comprises historical wooden buildings, both Sakhan and Russian, from all over the north. They include dwellings, forts, churches and stores, plus funeral structures, ritual pillars and crosses, a wind-mill and a replica of the first Cossack settler boat. You can spend the night on site in simple bungalows. To get there take the raketa hydrofoil from Yakutsk (twice daily, $13 one way) and walk for about 3km. You would have about three hours on site if you want to catch the afternoon raketa back to Yakutsk. One of the agents listed under Getting assistance (see p237) can arrange visits for individuals and groups.

### Excursions on the Lena river

Besides passenger services (see Getting there and away pp231-4), LenaRechFlot operates a river cruise ship *Demyan Bedny* (Демян Бедный), named after a proletarian poet of the early Soviet period. Built in Austria in 1985, the ship is comfortable by anyone's standards, with all cabins having private facilities. The food in the restaurant is of the kind you find in a good Russian restaurant and the service is charming and friendly; there is also a bar, lounge, movie theatre and sauna.

At the height of summer the *Demyan Bedny* makes one or two cruises down the Lena to the ocean with Western tourist groups aboard. There are barbecues, sing-songs, fish feasts, visits to native villages and wildlife-watching in the park preserves. The ship also makes shorter cruises around Yakutsk, such as the Lenskie Stolby excursions described (see below).LenaRechFlot is at ul. Dzerzhinskogo 2, next to the post office, ☎/▤ +7 4112 42-27-62 or +7 4112 42-57-61 (ул. Дзержинского, 2, «Ленаречфлот»).

### Lenskie Stolby (Ленские Столбы) excursions

The only Lena river excursion still being organised on a regular basis is to the Lenskie Stolby ('Lena Pillars'). (See Travelling the Lena river, p258.)

The excursions generally leave on Friday evening and take two days. These excursions are mainly organised for the benefit of the locals. The Stolby are not so much the aim as a pretext to forget the sorrows of everyday life.

---

**(Opposite)** *Khomus* (Jew's harp) instruction at a master class in Yakutian music at Yakutsk Music College. Instructors and senior students are wearing traditional dress for the occasion (Photo © Nicholas Zvegintzov).  **Bottom left:** Statue of an extinct baby mammoth outside the Permafrost Institute in Yakutsk.  **Bottom right:** Ice caverns under the Permafrost Institute in Yakutsk. The foundations are in sand, mud and driftwood, solidly frozen. (Photos © Bryn Thomas).

Everything is done to make your trip as pleasant as possible. A bar is open for most of the trip and, weather permitting, a discotheque is organised on the upper deck in the evenings. The ship leaves at 19.00, stops for several hours during the night, so as to arrive at the Pillars after lunch on the next day. You have about five hours to do whatever you like. It is a strenuous but rewarding one-hour climb to the top of the pillars for a magnificent view of the river and cliffs. Many locals, however, stay close to the ship to take a dip in the river, have a picnic, or organise a barbecue.

At 19.00 (dinner time) you start your return journey and again during the night the ship stops for several hours. In the morning it ties up at a flat island with meadows and trees, where you can go walking, play football, or just sit back and relax. Here you stay for most of the day, before the two-hour return to Yakutsk, arriving at 19.00.

Prices according to class (one, two, or four persons per cabin) vary from $240 to $120 per person and tickets can be bought through travel agents or directly from LenaRechFlot. Prices do not include food. Bring your own (hot water is provided) or eat in the restaurant, in which case the normal procedure is to buy a voucher on board at the reception ($80) for the six meals. Alternatively, you can pay for individual meals (you would need a good appetite to stow away all six meals anyway), but you will probably only be accepted after the people with vouchers have had their meal.

# Travelling the Lena river
## Путешествие по реке Лена

The mighty Lena river (река Лена), called Grandmother Lena ('Лена эбэ') by the Yakuts, carries the second largest volume of water in Russia (after the Yenisei), yet it is virtually unknown outside of Russia. The 4,400km river starts in the mountains to the west of Lake Baikal and snakes through north-eastern Siberia until it flows into the Laptevykh Sea (море Лаптевых) in the Arctic Ocean. Since the mid-1600s, the river has been the lifeline to Yakutsk, the capital of north-eastern Siberia, supplying it with grain, salt, guns and adventurers. It was from here that the exploration, conquest and eventual colonisation of eastern Siberia and the Russian Far East were launched.

Like the vast majority of Russian rivers, the Lena flows north. (This contrasts with the USA, where the major rivers flow south.) The river is navigable from about 150km below its source to the Arctic Ocean; in the summer months regular services ply the river from Zhigalovo to the Arctic

---

(**Opposite**)  The Lena Pillars form colonnades, arches, and minarets of honey-coloured eroded limestone over gentle green meadows, a favourite Lena river excursion from Yakutsk.(Photo © Bryn Thomas).

❏ **Lena river facts**
● The 4,400km Lena river is the ninth longest river in the world.
● High water is in June, when its water level is 10-18m above the winter level.
● Each year the Lena carries out to sea 12 million tonnes of sediment, 540 cubic kilometres of water and 41 million tonnes of dissolved substances.
● The Lena is ice-free for five to six months in the south and four to five months in the north.
● The Lena freezes on average 10 days after its tributaries.
● The revolutionary Vladimir Ilyich Ulyanov chose the Lena river as the basis for his revolutionary name – V I Lenin.
●In the Yakutian language, the Lena's name translates as 'very big river'.

Ocean. It is usually ice-free from May to September and its frozen surface provides ice-roads from December to March. Its June temperature ranges from 14°C to 19°C.

The Lena is a godsend for travellers as it is one of the most interesting ways of exploring hidden corners of Russia. As few foreigners travel these routes, you are guaranteed an extraordinary insight into the lives of river villages, both Russian and indigenous. The river's other major attraction is its excellent fishing. Common fish include muksun, omul and white salmon.

## THE ROUTE (see Route Map 5, p370)

The Lena river rises in a small mountain pond less than 10km from the western shore of Lake Baikal about 200km from the northern end of the lake. The Lena and its tributary streams are separated from the lake by the narrow band of the Baikal Range (Байкальский хребет) with peaks up to 2,200m and they run west and a little south down from the range. The Lena avoids Baikal's drainage via the Angara and the Yenisei; instead it flows north and east, to meet the Arctic ocean far east of the Yenisei. Some 150km below its source, the Lena becomes navigable at Kachug (Качуг), 4,222km from the mouth, and there are passenger services on the river 114km further down at Zhigalovo (Жигалово), 4,108km from the mouth. The river flows north, protected by a band of mountains, 410km to the major trading port of Ust-Kut (Усть-Кут), 3,698km from the mouth. It then flows east, bounded by eastern mountains, and forms a giant S-bend with Yakutsk in the lower crook (1,710km from the mouth). Finally the Lena flows north, still bounded by mountains, to empty into the Arctic Ocean at a giant delta.

The time on the lower Lena river is Moscow time +5 hours. Beyond the border of the Republic of Sakha (Yakutiya) it is Moscow time +6 hours.

## SERVICES ON THE LENA RIVER

Hydrofoils and river steamers ply the Lena river in the summer season and provide passenger service from Zhigalovo down to the ocean. For details about the various hydrofoils and river steamers, see pp42-5. It is quite difficult to plan a trip in advance, as timetables change and departures can be cancelled with hardly any notice. The river steamers (Ust-Kut to Yakutsk and Yakutsk to Tiksi) are the most reliable, and photocopied timetables can be found in river stations along the route. Hydrofoils, being more expensive to run, operate only when there is sufficient demand; the decision about the departure or destination of a hydrofoil may only be announced after passengers have bought tickets. Timetables are hard to find and sometimes it is even hard to discover who is running the hydrofoils. So if you want to be sure about having a successful trip, allow a lot of leeway in your travel schedule and be prepared to ask questions at the river station.

Nevertheless it is possible to travel from Zhigalovo down to Ust-Kut by hydrofoil, from Ust-Kut to Yakutsk and Tiksi by river steamer, or from Ust-Kut to Yakutsk and below by leapfrogging between hydrofoils and by being ready to hole up in a river town until the next sailing.

## Getting boat tickets

Ust-Kut and Yakutsk have large river stations; book tickets there. In smaller towns, check if there is a shipping office in town that sells tickets. Otherwise, buy tickets on board the hydrofoil or steamer. There are no separate fares for foreigners. Because of Sakha visa regulations (see p230), it is advisable to have some Sakhan cities listed on your Russian visa. It is best to be safe and list Yakutsk on your visa regardless of which way you travel. To take the river steamer upstream from Yakutsk, you should buy your ticket as early as possible. The steamer, while relatively expensive, is still the cheapest means of getting out of Yakutsk and as frequency is low, demand is high.

Most people seem to travel within Sakha, and more particularly between Lensk and Yakutsk. Between Lensk and Ust-Kut it is much quieter and you should not have a problem buying a ticket in Ust-Kut. You will always get passage on the steamer, but you could be consigned to the 3rd class cells, or even sleep in the corridor.

Hydrofoils are generally lightly loaded. One major exception is the Yakutsk–Olekminsk daily service, which

Veteran of the Great Patriotic War on the Lena river steamer. Photo © Nicholas Zvegintzov sells out regularly, especially the day after a service cancellation. Make sure you buy your ticket the day before sailing. Remember to keep hold of your ticket as you may be asked to show it during the trip and when you get off the boat. This is especially true for the hydrofoils where tickets are sold on board – don't think you'll get away with sitting quietly in a corner and not buying a ticket.

## The river steamer
## Ust-Kut–Yakutsk

Without a doubt the river steamer is the easiest, cheapest, most comfortable and most romantic way to travel between Ust-Kut and Yakutsk. The stately progress along the immense quiet river, the still bays, the majestic mountains and the off-shore stops at tiny stockaded villages give an unforgettable experience of Siberia. In 2000 the sister ships *Krasnoyarsk* («Красноярск») and *Blagoveshchensk* («Благовещенск») made 14 round trips. The passenger trip downstream takes four days, nine hours, while the upstream trip takes seven days, one hour. If you want to see some of the towns on the way, you will probably have to supplement your

| ❏ Passenger steamer schedule | | | |
|---|---|---|---|
| Km from Ust-Kut | Schedule* downstream | Place (Место) | Schedule upstream |
| 0 | 09.00 depart | Ust-Kut, Osetrovo river station (Усть-Кут Осетрово) | 15.00 |
| 301 | 05.00 | Kirensk (Киренск) | 10.00 |
| 622 | 21.30 | Vizirny (Визирный) | 06.30 |
| 743 | 03.30 | Vitim (Витим) | 20.20 |
| 767 | 05.00 | Peledui (Пеледуй) | 17.00 |
| 954 | 14.10 | Lensk (Ленск) | 02.00 |
| 1,008 | 16.45 | Saldykel (Салдыкель) | 21.25 |
| 1,037 | 18.20 | Nyuya (Нюя) | 18.45 |
| 1,083 | 20.40 | Tinnaya (Тинная) | 14.40 |
| 1,111 | 22.10 | Chapaevo (Чапаево) | 12.00 |
| 1,151 | 24.00 | Macha (Мача) | 08.20 |
| 1,232 | 03.35 | Delgeiskaya (Дельгейская) | 01.20 |
| 1,361 | 10.30 | Olekminsk (Олёкминск) | 15.10 |
| 1,426 | 15.10 | Khorinskaya (Хоринская) | 09.10 |
| 1,485 | 18.00 | Uritskoe (Урицкое) | 04.40 |
| 1,581 | 22.20 | Sanyyakhtakh (Саныяхтах) | 21.05 |
| 1,622 | 00.35 | Malykan (Малыкан) | 17.40 |
| 1,661 | 02.40 | Isitskaya (Иситская) | 14.20 |
| 1,893 | 12.40 | Pokrovsk (Покровск) | 21.00 |
| 1,988 | 18.00 arrive | Yakutsk (Якутск) | 13.00 depart |

* **Important note**: All these times are Ust-Kut and Irkutsk times. Yakutsk time is one hour later.

trip with hydrofoils, as you may not want to spend up to two weeks in any of these places, which are mostly just small villages.

The *Krasnoyarsk* and *Blagoveshchensk* have paddle-wheels amidships, powered by twin horizontal single-cylinder steam-driven oil-powered engines. Built in Hungary in 1959, with length 71.4m, breadth 15.2m, height 10.5m, and draught 1.6m, they carry 148 passengers with bunks and an unbounded number of passengers without bunks.

The cost for a one-way fare from Yakutsk to Ust-Kut is $160 first class, $100 second-class soft, $70 second-class hard and $50 third class.

For information and bookings, contact AOOT 'KREB' (Kirenskaya Remontno-Ekspluatatsionnaya Baza Flota) at 666710 Kirensk, Irkutskaya oblast, ul. Partizanskaya 30, ☎ +7-39568-3-23-06 or +7-39568-3-24-10, ▤ +7-39568-2-16-09 (666710, Иркутская область, г. Киренск, ул. Партизанская, 30, АООТ «КРЭБ»).

## Hydrofoil services

There is a string of hydrofoils from Zhigalovo above Ust-Kut to the Aldan river below Yakutsk and you should be able to travel the whole stretch by hydrofoil, though with some awkward waits in the unpopulated stretch below Olekminsk. They include:

● Twice a week from Ust-Kut to Zhigalovo upstream (Усмь-Кут – Хигалово), and back the next day, about $25.

● Every other day from Ust-Kut to Peledui downstream (Усть-Кут–Пеледуй) and back the next day, about $35.

● Daily except Sunday from Peledui to Lensk (Пеледуй–Ленск) and back the same day, with a hop to Vitim (Витим) and back at the beginning and end of the day.

● Once a week from Lensk to Olekminsk (Ленск–Олёкминск). This is the most problematic stretch of the river for transportation, below the gold and diamond areas and above the Yakutsk-Olekminsk stretch. Population densities in this area are below five per 100 square kilometres.

● Daily from Olekminsk to Yakutsk (Олёкминск–Якутск). It takes 12 hours and costs about $110.

● Daily from Yakutsk down to the mouth of the Aldan river (р. Алдан) and up to Khandyga (Хандыга).

Apart from these services, there are local services from some places (eg around Ust-Kut, Kirensk and Yakutsk).

## SOURCES OF THE LENA 4,400km

The Lena rises in the Baikal Range (Байкальский хребет) on the west shore of Lake Baikal, among peaks up to 2,200m. The area of the upper Lena is within the Baikal-Lena Reserve (Байкало-Ленскии заповедник) where access is closely controlled. Before entering this area, you should check with local travel organisers about fees and registration.

The Lena river rises in this lake near Lake Baikal. (Photo © Elliot Mainzer).

The easiest way to get to the source is via Cape Pokoiniki (мыс Покойники) or Cape Sharshlai (мыс Шаршлай), nearly level with Ushkanaya Island (остров Ушканая).To get there, either hire a boat from Severobaikalsk or arrange for a local with a dinghy to meet the Severo-baikalsk–Irkutsk hydrofoil. At Pokoiniki there is a Reserve ranger station and a weather station. The walk up the east escarpment of the Baikal Range is steep but no special equipment is needed. The distance is 10km as the crow flies but may be 40km by foot.

The Lena rises at a small natural lake at about 1,800m. A treeless escarpment rising to 2,100m forms the barrier with Lake Baikal.

## Rafting down the mountains

The Lena flows roughly north for 19km, losing 600m. Here the Lena has gathered enough water to make floating feasible. The river turns roughly west and then south, and drops another 600m in 120km to Chanchur (Чанчур), where there is a ranger station. This float trip takes about six days and includes at least two waterfalls that require portages, and involves Class 3 or 4 water, depending on flow. From here it is a gentle 40km float to Biryulka (Бирюлька) where the road starts.

The area is rugged and remote, and the ascent to the Lena sources, either from the downstream side or from Lake Baikal, is a rugged expedition, and should not be attempted without knowledgeable guides; try Tourist Club Kedr (Туристический клуб «Кедр»), see pp75-6, based in Zheleznogorsk.

## KACHUG (Качуг) 4,222km

The Lena cascades down the Baikal Range and slides along a marshy valley, where it is joined by several broad tributaries before reaching Kachug. From Kachug there is a good road to Irkutsk, with two daily buses taking six to seven hours.

## VERKHOLENSK (Верхоленск) 4,197km

Verkholensk is opposite the mouth of the Kulenga river (р. Куленга). Until the revolution Verkholensk was a place of Tsarist exile with the most famous being Feliks Dzerzhinski, who went on to create the Soviet secret police, the Cheka. The river snakes north-west through narrow cuts in the mountains.

## 🏛 ZHIGALOVO (Жигалово) 4,108km

Zhigalovo is where regular services on the river start. A Zarya hydrofoil travels between Zhigalovo and Ust-Kut every other day, leaving in the morning and arriving late in the afternoon; the trip costs about $30. This high section of the river is particularly sensitive to water level; for example, in 1997 the service was cancelled during the whole of August because of lack of water. There is also a daily bus between Zhigalovo and Irkutsk, taking nine to 10 hours.

A little upstream from Zhigalovo at the junction of the Tutura and Lena rivers is the village of Tutura (Тутура). There is a house-museum dedicated to the communist revolutionary V V Kuybyshev (В. В. Куйбышев), 1888-1935, who was exiled here by the Tsarist government

---

### ❏ Petroglyphs and rock drawings

Between Kachug and Verkholensk, and upstream of Verkholensk on the Talma tributary (р. Тальма), are some of Russia's best prehistoric petroglyphs and rock drawings. The cliff drawings, dating from the Neolithic period to the Bronze Age, provide a fascinating insight into indigenous people's lives and beliefs over thousands of years. The drawings include elk, deer and humans.

The most famous drawings are on a 2.5km stretch of cliffs near the village of Shishkino. Of particular importance is one drawing of a red horse on a high cliff about 40-60m above the river and near an old mill.

This picture predates the other drawings in the region as it is from the Palaeolithic period. It is similar in style to the famous Palaeolithic cave paintings of Western Europe. When it was found in 1941, it destroyed the accepted theory that stone-age culture evolved in Western Europe and spread outwards, by proving that a similar culture evolved simultaneously in Siberia and therefore probably in several other places.

It is difficult to organise a trip to these areas as few people other than archaeologists have visited them. A group that can help is the Tourist Club Kedr (Туристический клуб «Кедр») see pp75-76.

between 1915 and 1916. During his career, Kuybyshev was arrested eight times and banished on four occasions to Siberia. He was a member of the first USSR Politburo and is buried in the Kremlin wall in Moscow.

The route up the Lena is fascinating with its small villages and varied scenery including dense taiga, river flats and canyons. One of the deepest canyons, with walls rising 150m, is just downstream from Zhigalovo.

## UST-KUT (Усть-Кут)
### 3,705km on the Lena, 715km on the BAM

Ust-Kut is 40km long and lies at the junction of the Lena river and the 408km Kuta river. The town sits astride the BAM, which runs parallel with the Lena river. It is a major rail and river terminal for the Lena river and the Republic of Sakha (Yakutiya) and ships 80 per cent of all cargo for the Sakha region.

Present-day Ust-Kut was created in 1954 by amalgamating several settlements. From west to east they are Kirzavod (Кирзавод), Ust-Kut,

> ❑ **UST-KUT (Усть-Кут)**
> Area code ☎ 395-65
> 665780, Irkutskaya Oblast,
> Ust-Kut
> (665780 Иркутская
> область, г. Усть-Кут)

Lena (Лена), Rechniki (Речники), Rechniki-2 (Речники-2), Geologists (Геологи), Neftebaza ('Oil Terminal') (Нефтебаза) and Yakurim (Якурим). The freight port is located near Ust-Kut station. The Lena River Passenger Station, known as Osetrovo, is 7km downstream at Lena. The main passenger station of Ust-Kut, Lena, is a short walk from Osetrovo. For more on Ust-Kut see pp77-81.

## LENA (Лена) 3,698km on the Lena, 722km on the BAM

The Osetrovo River Passenger Station, for river steamers and hydrofoils up and down the river, is a short two-block walk from the main passenger railway station of Lena. The station is at ul. Kalinina 8, ☎ 2-63-97 (dispatcher), 2-65-06 (chief), 🖹 2-07-28 and 2-15-00 (attention: Osetrovo River Port), ☎ 2-32-53 general (ул. Калинина, 8, Речной вокзал Осетрово). For more on Lena see pp78-81.

The river ducks under the BAM bridge and heads north-west across a rolling plateau.

## KIRENSK (Киренск) 3,397km

Originally built on an island at the confluence of the Lena and Kirenga rivers (р. Киренга), Kirensk was turned into a promontory in the 1970s. A wide dam was constructed to prevent the water from the Kirenga from taking the short cut to the Lena upstream from the town, thus creating havoc in the bottleneck at the down-stream end of the island. (The museum has some interesting photographs with houses completely torn apart by the blocks of ice being forced through in spring.)

> ❏ **KIRENSK (Киренск)**
> Area code ☎ 395-68
> 666710, Irkutskaya Oblast,
> Kirensk
> (666710 Иркутская
> область, г. Киренск)
> Population 12,000

## History

Kirensk was founded in 1630 by a Cossack detachment under the command of Vasili Bugor. One of the first large settlers was the brutal Yerofei Khabarov in the early 1640s. Khabarov did not take kindly to more settlers arriving and an undeclared war started, with many new settlers being killed. It was only when Khabarov departed in 1649 to rape and pillage the Amur region that the town developed quickly. The outpost finally gained respectability when in 1775 it was granted the title of a town.

During its three centuries of existence, it witnessed the departure of a number of successful and not-so successful expeditions to Yakutiya, the Far North and north-east Siberia. The former include the 1864-66 Olekma-Vitim expedition led by P A Kropotkin, geographer, geologist and revolutionary, the 1890-1901 expedition led by V A Obruchev, geologist and geographer and the 1881-82 Nizhnyaya Tunguska expedition led by I D Cherski, geologist, geographer and palaeontologist.

Kirensk has always had an important transit function and not only for expeditions. It was a staging post for some of the Decembrists on their way to exile; commemorative plaques at some houses indicate where they have lived. The number of politically-conscious people in town (exiles of the Tsarist regime), meant that the communists took power almost as soon as they did in St Petersburg, but they lost it again in the summer of 1918, only to take it back for good (well, for 70 years) in 1920.

During the 1930s, the town housed three gulag camps including one that contained a large number of Baptist, Pentecostal and other Christians. It was also supposed to be a transit camp under Soviet rule, but a find of over 80 bodies under the former offices of the NKVD (forerunner of the KGB) as recently as 1991 has proved that for many it also was the final destination.

In the Great Patriotic War, Kirensk's airfield became a staging post for American bombers given to the Soviets as part of the Lend-Lease programme. In the museum you can see a map of their itinerary through north-east Russia to the Western Front. The transit route started in Fairbanks and finished in Krasnoyarsk, with the last staging post being Kirensk. The supply line operated from 1942 to 1945 and in all 8,110 US planes were delivered. A considerable number of planes were lost en route. For example in 1942, 131 planes left Fairbanks and only 41 arrived in Krasnoyarsk, while in 1943, 2,464 left Fairbanks and 1,917 arrived. In 1986 one of those planes was found in the region and a monument has been erected in memory of the pilots at ul. Lenina. (If you are interested in this history, there is also a small display on it in Irkutsk's Regional Museum.)

During the first year of BAM railway construction, equipment and materials were brought down the Lena to Kirensk and then up the Kirenga river to the future BAM station of Magistralny. This allowed work to be carried out simultaneously on two sections of the western end of the BAM and contributed to its quick construction time.

In more recent years, the port was important for transferring goods on their way between Ust-Kut and Yakutsk, as the bigger ships could not go upstream from Kirensk due to the shallowness of the water. However, the general downturn in the economy has significantly reduced the amount of freight coming through and the smaller boats now go all the way to Yakutsk.

## Getting there and away
**By river** Upstream, you can get to Ust-Kut daily by *Polesye*, and every other day by *Zarya*. Downstream, *Zarya* goes weekly to Vizirny. Every other day a *Raketa* passes through on its way to Peledui.

The river steamer to Ust-Kut or Yakutsk picks up passengers directly from the beach opposite the hydrofoil terminal, next to the ferry. Kirensk is also the headquarters of the river steamers: AOOT 'KREB' (Kirenskaya Remontno-Ekspluatatsionnaya Baza Flota), at 666710 Kirensk, Irkutskaya oblast, ul. Partizanskaya 30, ☎ +7-39568-3-23-06 or +7-39568-3-24-10, 🖹 +7-39568-2-16-09 (666710, Иркутская область, г. Киренск, ул. Партизанская, 30, АООТ «КРЭБ»). The shipyard is in a dead-end arm off the Lena river to the north. At the end of it you may find more mothballed river steamers.

**By air** There are daily flights to Irkutsk, and weekly ones to Olekminsk and Bodaibo, all by AN-24 (44 seats). There is a weekly flight to Bratsk, several times a week to Vizirny and Ust-Kut, all by AN-2 for that unforgettable 1940s experience. There are also at least weekly flights to remote settlements north of Kirensk on the Tunguska river, a tributary of the Yenisei. The airport is about 3km out of town across the dam.

## Getting around
Central Kirensk is easily covered on foot. There is an hourly bus from the market to the airport. Ferries across the Lena and Kirenga rivers go to the outlying quarters of town every half-hour. There is a daily *Zarya* hydrofoil down the Lena to Petropavlovskoe, which may be an interesting day-trip, allowing you to spend a couple of hours in some real out-of-the-way villages.

## Where to stay and eat
There is only one hotel, the rather simple *Hotel Sever*. It is a short walk from the hydrofoil terminal, to the west (upstream) along ul. Lenrabochikh. There are no restaurants or canteens left in Kirensk, but a *café* between the hydrofoil and the hotel offers hot snacks.

**Kirensk**

Ferry Ports

FERRY

SHIPYARD

N

Hotel Sever

Market

Church

Museum

UL KOMMUNISTICHESKAYA

LENA RIVER

PATH TO LOOKOUT

TO AIRPORT

WW2 Monument

Pilots Monument

FERRY

DAM

UL KALANDARISHVILI

UL SOVETSKAYA

UL LENINA

Old Vodka Factory

KIRENGA RIVER

FERRY

## What to see

The main enemies of the town are water and fire, and the latter means that little has been preserved from early history. The town centre on the island has escaped the horrors of Soviet housing blocks and still consists mainly of one and two-storey wooden houses. It is a pleasant place to stroll around, even if there are no major tourist attractions as such, just enjoy the quiet labyrinthine streets, or sit on the river bank and watch the boats go by. The most interesting part of town is the higher half (east side) of the island, bordered by ul. Kalandarishvili, and is about 1-2km across.

The regional museum, at the intersection of ul. Sovetskaya and ul. Kommunisticheskaya, has the usual exhibits of local village life and nature, plus an interesting collection of pictures of old Kirensk and a section on the transfer of Lend-Lease American planes.

The island's south-east quarter was once taken up by a monastery, containing three churches, but not much is left of this now. One church, sitting astride the entrance gate, was destroyed in the first half of the 20th century. Another wooden one was burned down in 1996 as the result of youngsters building a campfire. A brick one (minus the bell tower) now houses a TV transmitter. The only working church is now at ul. Kalandarishvili. A picture inside the 'lobby' shows how it once looked, before the Soviets removed the towers and turned it into a cinema. A small bell-tower now replaces the two original big ones.

The ruins of red-brick buildings at the south end of ul. Sovetskaya were originally a vodka factory (Vinzavod, Винзавод). The office building was used by the NKVD (forerunner of KGB, now also extinct) as a prison. Officially no executions took place here, but in 1991 over 80 bodies were found in a pit in the basement. All had been hit on the head, apparently so as to avoid any noise and so hide the executions. The top bodies had not rotted and were mummified, making identification relatively easy. They had all been killed on one day in 1938. In 1997 the museum was preparing an exhibit with pictures of the find and the reburial ceremony.

Across the Lena river to the east, a path leads up the steep bank behind a group of houses. From up here you have an excellent view of the area. The river heads north-east and then east hemmed in by a giant massif with peaks over 2,000m, pierced by river canyons.

## ⊠ CHERTOVA DOROZHKA (Чёртова Дорожка) 3,101km

'Chertova Dorozhka' means 'Devil's Path'. This one-kilometre section is treacherous in flood when it becomes difficult to see the main channel. Consequently, numerous ships have run aground in these shallows.

## ⊠ SHCHEKI (Щёки) 3,096km

Shcheki means 'cheeks' and this aptly describes this dangerous stretch of the Lena river, where it is forced in between giant cheeks, copper-red coloured vertical rock faces towering 200m above the river. As this section is narrow compared to the rest (at most 200m), the passage between the cheeks is impressive. Make sure you are on deck at the right moment, as the passage is fairly short, half an hour at most. If you pass at night, the Captain will turn on the steamer's searchlight.

Going downstream the first cheek is on the right bank and you seem to run right into it, but the river is deflected to the left upon hitting this rock. Just a bit further on a similar rock on the left bank ricochets the water onto the third and largest on the opposite bank again. This one is called Pyany Byk (Пьяный Бык) meaning 'drunken bull'. Legend has it that in the days before the installation of the beacons, when a pilot joined the ship to ensure safe passage, one ship smashed against its solid rock after the whole crew had had too much of the local vodka.

## ⛴ VITIM (Витим) 2,955km

The Vitim logging settlement is located just over the border in the Republic of Sakha (Yakutiya). It is at the confluence of the Vitim and Lena rivers. There is an air connection by AN-2 to Lensk.

The border also designates a time-zone change. In Irkutskaya Oblast the time difference is five hours later than Moscow while in the Republic of Sakha (Yakutiya) it is six hours.

### Vitim river (река Витим)

This 1,837km tributary of the Lena starts in the Vitim Plateau (Витимское плоскогорье) west of Lake Baikal, heads south, passing just 144km from the Trans-Siberian town of Chita. Then it heads north in deep cuts through ranges, including the rugged Stanovoe plateau (Становое нагорье). It crosses under the BAM railway east of Taksimo, then loops northward through further ranges with peaks up 2,300m, racing over the fearsome Parama Rapids (Парама пороги) and Uronski Rapids (Уронский пороги), before passing the famous gold town of Bodaibo and the city of Mama. (For more on running the Vitim river and its tributaries, see Parama Rapids and Long-distance rafting on the Vitim river system, pp113-114.)

While the Vitim is navigable by river steamers as far as Bodaibo, nowadays they rarely go to it. Tugs used to pull barges past Bodaibo as far as the BAM railway but today this also rarely happens. The river peaks in June and freezes from November to May.

The history of trade on the Vitim river gives a fascinating insight into the enormous difficulties in establishing and maintaining settlements such as Ust-Muya, Mama and later Bodaibo on the Vitim river. Due to the Vitim's speed as it entered the Lena, it was difficult to bring goods up the river. So from the early 1700s, goods were first hauled 144km from the Trans-Siberian town of Chita to the Vitim river town of Romanovka, and from here the goods were floated down river nearly 1,600km in boats. At Romanovka, single-use wooden boats were constructed. Each of the broad-bottomed, high-bowed boats took 45 cubic metres of pine and was assembled using wooden larch pegs instead of nails. To enable the boats to be steered easily even during the high water following the spring thaw, the boats were fitted with a special board called an *opleukha* that could be raised and lowered in the water.

Every summer, hundreds of these boats floated down the river, reaching their destination in six or seven days. There they were either abandoned or broken up for fences or wooden pavements. Within a decade, Romanovka's surrounding forests were depleted of timber and planks also had to be carted in. These boats, which each cost 1,500 roubles which was equal to six months average wage, were used until just after the Great Patriotic War. After the war, reusable metal boats were used but while this reduced the cost, supplying the towns was still a problem. For example, in 1965 there was little rain and the Vitim became so shallow that the loaded boats were laid up all summer until late autumn, resulting in a hard winter for the towns. Despite the nearby new BAM railway, and regular air flights and barges from Ust-Kut, life is still more difficult in isolated Bodaibo than in most Siberian towns.

When the Vitim river joins the Lena, the Lena river widens. As the river carries many dead trees, navigation is difficult for small passenger vessels like hydrofoils. Often departures are delayed or cancelled because of damage to the hull or propellers.

### 🖼 Vitim river town: Mama (Мама)

Mama owes its existence to the rare muscovite mica, a prized mineral that is found in thin translucent sheets. From 1705 until the invention of sheet glass, mica was mined in Mama for use in glass manufacturing.

The settlement was abandoned until the early 1920s when mica's other property of being an excellent insulator resulted in mining being resumed. Mining was again abandoned in the late 1930s when a manufactured insulator was discovered. Mama is now a small river community.

### 🖼 Vitim river town: Mamakan (Мамакан)

This small workers' settlement revolves around the Mamakan hydro-electric dam. This 86 MW station was completed in 1961 and was one of the country's first hydro-electric dams to be built on permafrost (frozen ground). This was a major achievement considering permafrost melts and subsides under pressure, such as that generated by the dam wall's weight, which in turn could lead to cracks in the walls of the dam which would spell a major disaster.

In the kitchens of the river steamer *Krasnoyarsk*, (Photo © Nicholas Zvegintzov).

## Vitim river town: Bodaibo (Бодайбо)

The town was founded in 1864 when gold was discovered. Gold still justifies its existence which is well symbolised by the giant scoop of a gold dredge mounted on a memorial block on ul. Uritskogo (ул. Урицкого).

### History

Gold mining in the region was infamous as most of it was done by convicts during the Tsarist times and then by gulag prisoners during Stalin's lifetime. In addition, Bodaibo had a large gulag transit camp for prisoners who worked in the Marble Canyon uranium mines near the BAM railway town of Novaya Chara and in the surrounding forestry camps of the region.

Just upstream of Bodaibo is the settlement of Luzhki (Лужки). This old port was the start of the road to the Lena goldfields, which were famous in communist history as the site of the 1911 Lena Workers' Massacre. In early 1911, the region's 6,000-strong mining workforce went on strike over the appalling conditions in the goldfields, demanding an eight-hour day instead of their 15-hour day, a decrease in accidents, which in 1910 ran at seven injuries per 10 workers and a 30 per cent increase in wages. Tsarist troops arrived from Kirensk and Bodaibo and in the early hours of 4 April arrested the strike committee. Later that day hundreds of miners went to Nadezhdinski field to demand their release. The soldiers responded with gunfire killing 270 and wounding 250. The massacre resulted in a government commission arriving and conditions improving. For the communists, this was the year when northern Siberian workers developed class consciousness.

**Getting there and away** The easiest way to get to Bodaibo is by plane from Bratsk, Kirensk, Taksimo, Chita and Yakutsk.

It is also possible to travel up the Vitim river and there are occasional vessels from Vitim and Peledui on the Lena river.

In some Soviet publications, it is claimed that there is a good road to the BAM station of Taksimo. This is not true. The dirt road is shocking and there are no scheduled buses to Taksimo.

**Where to stay** An *hotel* is located at ul. Stoyanovisha 42.

## PELEDUI (Пеледуй) 2,931km

Peledui was founded in 1933. Nearly all its buildings are made from wood. There is a small *hotel* in an unmarked wooden building in one of the more inland parts of the town. The price for a single is about $10. The town's most important employer is the Lorp ship-repair company in the Lenski Rayon which is along the 398km long Peledui river. Common salt is mined nearby at the mouth of the Peledui river. There is an air connection by an AN-2 to Lensk.

Below Peledui, high up on the left bank is a gigantic statue of a robed and hooded woman gazing eternally upstream. Disregard the many other romantic tales that you may be told; this represents Sakha holding in her cupped hands the riches of diamonds.

The area code is ☎ 411-37

## LENSK (Ленск) 2,744km

This town is a major port and the hub for the north Siberian diamond fields. Construction of the town started in 1963 on the site of the ancient rural settlement of Mukhtuya (Мухтуя). Mukhtuya was founded in the 1800s as a stopping point for postal couriers on the Prelenski Trakt (Преленский Тракт) to Yakutsk. Lensk is a major regional town with a regional museum. It has a good road to the inland diamond town of Mirny. Lensk is the only port of any significance between Kirensk and Yakutsk.

*Lena Hotel*, which has a restaurant, is situated near the river about 500m downstream from the river landing. Prices for the very basic single room range from $2 to $2.50. There are air connections with Yakutsk, Irkutsk, Ust-Kut, Peledui, Vitim, Olekminsk and Mirny. There is a bus to the airport. Four-wheel drive taxis wait at the river-landing for passengers wanting to travel to the more important city of Mirny.

In May and June 1998 a late thaw caused devastating floods on the Lena and Aldan rivers. The Lena crested at 6.26m above flood-stage at Lensk and 90 per cent of the town (plus 20 other towns) was under water. There was a huge struggle to evacuate and re-house people, and a race to break up the ice-jams to avert flooding at Yakutsk downstream. On the right bank, where the ground is steep, you will see the scour of the flood.

## MIRNY (Мирный)

Mirny is located 230km north of Lensk. Massive diamond deposits were found in the region in 1955 and, with the attraction of excellent pay, the town rapidly mushroomed. By 1959 the settlement was granted the title of a town. The town is now the industrial and administrative centre of western Sakha and even boasts a museum dedicated to its industrial past. The town's main sight is the giant man-made crater where diamonds are mined and which may be seen in virtually any picture book about Sakha.

A regular bus service (at least once daily) operates between Lensk and Mirny. There is a one-lane track from here to Ust-Kut which is mostly used by heavy trucks hauling supplies.

(Opposite) Reindeer racers from all over Sakha compete on the Yakutsk Harbour Inlet to celebrate the Day of Reindeer Herders in late March (Photo © Nicholas Zvegintzov).

## ⚓ CHAPAEVO (Чапаево) 2,587km

This village was the site of a Decembrist prison. The village was renamed early in the 20th century in honour of Vasili Ivanovich Chapaev, a revolutionary commander in the Russian Civil War.

Chapaev was made famous following a novel about his life written by Dmitri Andreevich Furmanov (1891–1926). At one time during the war, Furmanov was Chapaev's political commissar. According to the *Great Soviet Encyclopaedia*, the Chapaev novel was 'one of the best works of Soviet prose in the 1920s, realistically depicted the semi-partisan peasant masses and conveyed the romantic spirit of the revolutionary struggle. The figure of Chapaev, portrayed in all its complexity, was an embodiment of the contradictory but innately heroic traits of the people.'

This novel was made into a classic Stalinist propaganda film in 1934, which elevated Chapaev to the status of folk hero. Because of his fame and the obviously biased film, Chapaev was the butt of innumerable jokes.

One of them relates to a scene in the film in which Chapaev explains the plan of attack on Odessa to his peasant soldiers. Rather than using a map, he uses potatoes to represent each component of his unit and their role in the upcoming battle, which involved swimming across a river and storming the fortifications. According to the joke, Chapaev's adjutant packs the potatoes into a sack and ties them around his waist to be eaten later and the troops move out. Everyone swims across the river under a withering hail of fire and as Chapaev gets across he turns around to see his adjutant disappearing under the water weighed down by the potatoes and his troops fleeing. 'Why are you running?' Chapaev screams. An escaping soldier yells out in reply as he passes, 'It's hopeless – the attack plan has been lost!'

## ⚓ MACHA (Мача) 2,547km

This village was the site of a Decembrist prison.

## ⚓ OLEKMINSK (Олёкминск) 2,337km

Founded in 1635 as a small fort, Olekminsk quickly grew into an agricultural centre with its excellent climate for vegetables and grain. It was a place of political exile before the 1917 revolution.

Olekminsk has a museum devoted to the history of agriculture in Sakha and several wooden houses are preserved as architectural monuments to the 18th and 19th centuries.

---

**(Opposite) Top**: Drinking water for the winter – blocks of ice cut on the Lena river – stored outside a cottage in the Yakutia countryside. **Bottom**: The M-56 main highway from Yakutsk heads across the Lena river as an officially posted dual carriageway *zimnik* (winter road). (Photos © Nicholas Zvegintzov).

Originally the town was virtually opposite the mouth of the Olekma river (р. Олёкма), but regular flooding caused it to be moved 12km upstream. Just above its mouth, the Olekma river is joined by the Chara river (р. Чара). Both rivers flow from the south, cutting through the mountains. The BAM meets the Olekma below Khani (Хани) and climbs it for nearly 100km to Yuktali (Юктали). The Chara river crosses the BAM at Chara and then cuts through the Kodar range (see pp124-32.) After the Olekma joins the Lena, the Lena widens to 2km and is flanked by extensive floodplains.

### 🏛 URITSKOE (Урицкое) 2,213km

This town was originally named Chekurskaya (Чекурская) but was renamed Uritskoe after the Bolshevik, Moisei Solomonovich Uritski (M С Урицкий), who was exiled here from 1902 to 1905. Uritski (1873-1918) was a dedicated communist who became the Chairman of the Petrograd Cheka (precursor of the KGB) before he was assassinated. He was buried in St Petersburg's Field of Mars, which is where many heroes of the revolution and the communist era are buried.

### LENSKIE STOLBY (Ленские Столбы) 2,030-1,850km

Lenskie Stolby ('Lena Pillars') is a stunning rock formation that stretches for 180km on the right bank. Cliffs of honey-coloured limestone form towers, colonnades, arches and minarets, some of which reach 100m above the water. Wind and water have carved these shapes by eroding softer rock around them. Gentle meadows nestle in clefts between them and fold over their inland slopes to make pathways to the heights. The Lenskie Stolby are grouped in three sections but the most impressive part is the downstream section. They are Yakutsk's biggest tourist destination. For details of excursions from Yakutsk, see Lenskie Stolby excursions under Yakutsk, pp240-1.

### 🏛 SINSK (Синск) 1,937km

As well as being the location of the Ordzhonikidzevski collective farm, the confluence of the Sinsk and Lena rivers also contains petroglyphs and rock paintings from the Neolithic Period.

On a cliff on the left bank of the Lena, close to the village of Elanka (Еланка) and Cape Toion-Ary (Тойон-Ары), are petroglyphs from the Neolithic Period. They depict hunters, riders and scenes from daily life.

### 🏛 MOKHSOGOLLOKH (Мохсоголлох) 1,820km

Mokhsogollokh is a company town supported by the cement maker, Yakutcement. There is a paved road between Mokhsogollokh and Yakutsk and a daily bus service. There is a car ferry across the Lena river. As the ferry trip is shorter here than the one at Yakutsk, many travellers to Aldan drive to Mokhsogollokh. For details about travel on this road see The AYaM: Tynda–Neryungri–Aldan–Yakutsk (pp277-8).

## 🏠 POKROVSK (Покровск) 1,805km

Built on the site of an old Russian village, Pokrovsk grew from virtually nothing in 1941 to a moderately-sized working town supplying construction material to Yakutsk and new industrial enterprises and mines in the area. Pokrovsk has a museum to the revolutionary G K Ordzhonikidze (Г. К. Орджоникидзе), 1886-1937, who was exiled here for three years. He put his time in Sakha to good use as he organised Soviet councils in the region that played an important role in defeating the White forces. Ordzhonikidze eventually became Commissar for Heavy Industry and a Politburo member. However, he became disillusioned by Stalin's purges, notably after his deputy, Pyatakov, was arrested and executed and his eldest brother was shot after torture. The day after one particularly argumentative phone call with Stalin, Ordzhonikidze was found dead, allegedly a suicide.

Below Pokrovsk, at Diring Yuriakh (Диринг Юриах), archaeologist Yuri A Mochanov (Юри А. Мочанов) has excavated thousands of chipped and flaked rocks similar to tools found in the Olduvai Gorge of Africa, dated to 2,000,000 years ago. The Siberian site has yielded no human or animal remains, and the identification and dating are disputed.

## THE APPROACHES TO YAKUTSK

After Pokrovsk, the river turns to the north. Thirty kilometres below Yakutsk (1,740km) you pass a narrows, only 2.5km wide, formed by the Tabaga cliffs (Табагинскаий утёс) on the left bank and you cross under the high-tension electricity lines. From Nizhni Bestyakh (Нижний Бестях) on the right bank ferries run to Yakutsk. On the left, far across the flats, you can see the TV tower (телетранслязонная мачта) in the centre of Yakutsk. The steamer makes a loop around low wooded islands to enter the city harbour from the north.

## 🏙️ YAKUTSK (Якутск) 1,710km

Yakutsk is the capital of the Republic of Sakha. See Yakutsk (pp230-41) for more on this ancient and fascinating city. All river traffic goes from the River Station, which is north of the centre of the city on pereulok Energetikov at the terminus of bus No 8 (переулок Энергетиков, речной вокзал). See Getting there and away – By river under Yakutsk (pp231-4) for a summary of services by river hydrofoil, steamer and cruise-ship.

After passing Yakutsk, the Lena river flows north to join the Aldan from the east and then turns north-west to join the Vilyui from the east. Then it flows north, always bounded on the east by the Verkhoyanski range (Верхоянский хребет), crossing the Arctic Circle, some 1,000km to the Arctic Ocean, where it creates a delta 200km wide by 100km long.

## MOUTH OF THE ALDAN RIVER (р. Алдан) 1,560km

The 1,600km Aldan river joins the Lena from the east. It makes a loop parallel to the Lena 300km to the east and rises close to the southern border of Sakha in the Stanovoe range. The chief towns on the Aldan river are Khandyga (Хандыга), Ust-Maya (Усть-Мая) and Tommot (Томмот). For more on reaching the upper Aldan river, see The AYaM: Tynda–Neryungri–Aldan–Yakutsk (pp274-7).

## SANGAR (Сангар) 1,373km

Sangar is a coal-mining settlement that provides much of the energy for the Republic. Sangar is as far as the daily hydrofoil goes from Yakutsk, out in the morning, back in the afternoon.

## MOUTH OF THE VILYUI RIVER (река Вилюй) 1,313km

The 2,450km Vilyui river joins the Lena from the west. The towns of Vilyuisk (Вилюйск) and Nyurba (Нюрба) are on the Vilyui. The diamond town of Mirny (Мирный) is on a tributary. Higher up the Vilyui is dammed for the Vilyui Reservoir, and it rises west of the Sakhan border in the north-central Siberian uplands.

## ZHIGANSK (Жиганск) 939km

Zhigansk is the first settlement beyond the Arctic Circle, which crosses the river 20km above Zhigansk. Zhigansk's fortress was founded in 1632, making it the same age as the fortress in Yakutsk. The name of Zhigansk comes from the indigenous Evenk language, meaning an inhabitant of the lower part of the river.

## AGRAPHENA (Аграфена) 865km

Agraphena Island is home to a legendary Russian princess who dispatches diseases onto the Yakut people as punishment for any passing sailor who does not leave a gift.

## SIKTYAKH (Сиктях) 545km

Siktyakh is the oldest settlement beyond the Arctic Circle. 'Siktyakh' means 'wet place'. The settlement is a famous archaeological site as artefacts have been found here which prove that the locals knew how to melt metal over 3,000 years ago.

## KYUSYUR (Кюсюр) 385km

Kyusyur was founded when the indigenous Evenk and Yakut people were pressured by the Soviet government to renounce their nomadic lifestyle and settle down. Nowadays Kyusyur is a regional cultural centre boasting schools, libraries, shops, hospitals and kindergartens.

## THE LENA DELTA 222km

Below Tit-Ary (Тит-Ары) the river enters the Lena delta in the Laptevykh Sea (Море Лаптевых), a bay of the Arctic Ocean. The delta is 200km wide by 100km long. Much of the delta is a nature reserve. The delta, with its mix of fresh and salt water, is a key location for supporting the Arctic salmon species. It is also the main area for the nesting of migratory birds in the Arctic; 118 species have been observed. The intercontinental ties, direction and distance of the delta bird populations are unique in the Arctic.

The river breaks up into a number of channels as it passes around islands in its path. The largest of the channels is Trofimov, which accounts for 70 per cent of the Lena's discharge into the sea, followed by Bykov and Olenek. The 106km long Bykov channel (протока Быковская) connects the Lena with the region's principal sea port, Tiksi (Тикси).

## TIKSI (Тикси) 0km

Tiksi, on the mainland east of the delta, is the sea gate to the Republic of Sakha (Yakutiya). In the Yakut language, 'tiksi' means a moorage place. Tiksi appeared on the map in the mid-1930s when Soviet vessels travelled regularly to the region. Murmansk at the edge of the North Atlantic is 3,600km and Provideniya in the North Pacific near the Bering Strait is 2,800km. The navigation period for vessels sailing the Arctic Ocean is two and a half months. Tiksi also has an airport.

As Tiksi is 5° north of the Arctic Circle, the city is in complete darkness 24 hours a day over winter. You will see the first rays of the sun on 7 February and by 19 February you can see all of the sun for a few short minutes.

# The AYaM:
# Tynda–Neryungri–Aldan–Yakutsk
### АЯМ: Тында–Нерюнгри–Алдан–Якутск

## ABOUT THE AYAM

'AYaM' stands for 'Amuro-Yakutskaya Magistral' (АЯМ–Амуро-Якутская Магистраль), ie the Amur-Yakutsk Mainline. This 'mainline' is the land link between the Amur river (effectively, the Trans-Siberian railway) and the great northern city of Yakutsk. Until the building of the AYaM, old and prosperous Yakutsk was only accessible by the Lena river, either 2,000km eastward downstream, or 1,700km upstream from the Arctic Ocean.

## The AYaAD Highway

The AYaAD, the Amur Yakutsk Automobile Highway (Амуро-Якутская Автомобильная Дорога), was built in 1930-37. It is 1,157km long and links Bolshoi Never on the Trans-Siberian to Yakutsk and is designated M-56. One of the engineering feats of the early Soviet era, it anticipated the strategy of the BAM – to create a direct path of transportation that cuts across existing lines of communication, regardless of cost or engineering difficulty. The AYaAD highway heads almost due north from the Trans-Siberian, crossing two major chains of mountains and then edges north and a little east toward Yakutsk, ignoring and bypassing the chaotic pattern of the mountain rivers. It emerges on the east bank of the Lena and crosses to Yakutsk by ferry or over the ice.

The AYaAD highway is a three-lane gravel and dirt track with occasional patches of asphalt, an ordeal of dust in late summer and autumn and of packed snow in winter, and a nightmare of mud in spring and early summer. In winter it is notorious for its treacherous ice patches and steep descents, and the shoulders are lined with memorials to the drivers who have died. The route is especially demanding in winter because trucks can't stop moving in the -50°C temperature as their tyres and engine blocks freeze and shatter.

Though no superhighway, the AYaAD highway is well-travelled (perhaps 10 vehicles an hour in each direction), with regular services, including petrol stations and rest-stops, and continuously maintained. It is hard surfaced only through towns and on occasional random stretches. However, it is excellently signed, with kilometre markers and other highway signs, such as 'Извините за неудобство – Мы работаем на дороге' ('Forgive the inconvenience – We are working on the road').

## The AYaM railway

Roughly parallel to the AYaAD highway is the partially built AYaM railway. The logic of building the AYaM is that a railway is the only effective all-weather land route to the far north-east mountains.

The AYaM railway has four segments according to its construction status:

● The 180km section from the Trans-Siberian to Tynda, completed in 1937, is commonly known as the Little BAM. It is covered in Bamovskaya–Tynda (The Little BAM), pp207-10.

The remaining three segments are covered in this section:

● The 210km section from Bestuzhevo (Бестужево), 27km north of Tynda along the BAM, to Berkakit (Беркакит), with a short branch line to Neryungri (Нерюнгри), was completed in 1978.

● The 380km section from Berkakit to Aldan (Алдан) and Tommot (Томмот) was opened all the way to Tommot to freight traffic in 1997 but in 1999 it is still not open to passenger trains.

● Work has only recently started on the 456km section from Tommot to Yakutsk (Якутск) and it is unlikely that it will be finished for several years.

The building of the AYaM railway is a monumental construction project in terms of overcoming the natural barriers of permafrost, rivers and mountains. When it is completed, the railway will require some 200 bridges, 21 of which will be more than 1km long, 85 million cubic metres of moved earth and land fill, 540 structures other than bridges, seven major railway stations, six new settlements and 2,100 workers to staff the new line.

**When will the AYaM railway be complete?**  Given the need for a land route to Yakutsk, the logic of the railway is inescapable. It would provide a cost effective freight route to Yakutsk and give access to the region's enormous natural resources. It would also be usable in nearly all weathers, with a far greater capacity than the highway. The high cost of freight to Yakutsk has always limited development. As virtually everything has to be imported and up to 50 per cent of the cost of goods is the freight component, the cost of living in Yakutsk is one of the highest in Russia. Currently 50 per cent of freight travels along the Lena river downstream from the BAM town of Ust-Kut and 8 per cent upstream from the Arctic Ocean, but the river is only navigable for three months a year. Only 28 per cent of freight moves on the AYaAD highway, while another 13 per cent moves on another dirt road to the east known as the Magadan Highway, and just one per cent by air. The government optimistically predicts that when the AYaM railway is finished it will carry 65 per cent of the freight to Yakutsk and the line will pay for itself in just seven years.

Seven hundred and seventy kilometres have been built; 456km remain. Unlike the built section, which crosses several major mountain ranges, the remaining section will cross the gently rolling watershed of the

Lena, plus a 10km bridge over the Lena river. Construction estimates predict that it could be completed in six years. The fundamental factor that controls the construction of the AYaM railway is political will. In 1994 construction of the AYaM railway was transferred from Russia's Ministry of Transport Construction to the Republic of Sakha. With the introduction of multi-party elections in the Republic of Sakha, the AYaM railway is a major voting issue. Most city dwellers want the railway as it will lower the cost of living, but villagers and indigenous peoples are afraid that it will destroy their lifestyle and possibly their environment. Due to the disproportionate weighting given to rural votes, the current government is only lukewarm on the AYaM railway. However, as of 1999, construction is continuing on the AYaM railway. (There is also a regrading of steep slopes and rebridging on the AYaAD highway.)

## THE ROUTE (see Route Maps 3 and 5, p368 and p370)

The railway heads north from Tynda up the Mogot river valley (p. Могот), climbing to 600m, then snakes up a side canyon to cross the Stanovoi range (Становой хребет) and the border with the Republic of Sakha (Республика Саха) on a narrow ledge at 1,100m. The railway crosses another crest of the ridge in a short tunnel and drops to a mountain plateau around Neryungri (Нерюнгри). The AYaM railway heads further north through jagged ridges and across the Tommot ridge (Томмотская гряда) to Aldan (Алдан) and heads east to cross the Aldan river at Tommot (Томмот), where the completed section of the railway ends. The road continues north and a little east, crossing the Amga river (p. Амга) and the watershed of the Lena river (p. Лена), meeting the Lena near Bestyakh (Бестях). Here there is a ferry or an ice road to cross to the hard road to Yakutsk (Якутск) on the west bank, or you can continue on the east bank to Nizhni Bestyakh (Нижний Бестях) and take the ferry or ice road into Yakutsk. The time is Moscow time +6 hours.

### 🚂 TYNDA (Тында)

Tynda (see pp135-41) is at 2,364km on the BAM mainline.

### 🚂 BESTUZHEVO (Бестужево) 0km

Bestuzhevo (see pp141-142) is at 2,391km on the BAM mainline. Just after you depart Bestuzhevo, the line divides into the AYaM railway to the north and the BAM mainline to the east. The AYaM railway begins to climb the Mogot river (p. Могот).

### ⊠ GILYUI (Гилюй) 19km

Gilyui is a settlement confusingly located on the Mogot river, which flows into the Gilyui river.

## 🏨 MOGOT (Могот) 44km

Mogot is a small industrial town with two-storey buildings. There is a North Korean timber complex on the outskirts of the town and there was a Stalin-era gulag camp nearby.

This town is one of the best examples of poor construction on the BAM. The town rests on permafrost and therefore all buildings are on piles that insulate the buildings from the ground and prevent subsidence. Although the piles should have been driven many metres through the permafrost, many didn't even go down two metres. During the town's first summer when the top layer of the permafrost melted, the piles sank and dragged the buildings down. By spring 1981, the town's heating pipes, water mains and its sewerage system were out of order, the pavements had collapsed, and the administration and shopping block were boarded up due to the danger of further collapses. The town's administration appealed for help but the construction authority, the Ministry of Transport Construction, denied responsibility. Today, the patched-up town again has most of its facilities although it looks years older than it actually is.

Accommodation can be organised at the *Railway Hostel* ☎ 4-29 (Комната отдыха).

## ⊠ RIKHARD ZORGE (Рихард Зорге)

This settlement is named after the Russian spy Rikhard Zorge, born in Baku, who informed the Soviet Union that the Germans intended to attack on 21 June 1941, and later worked in Japan where he was executed as a spy. The AYaAD highway, which crosses the hills directly rather than climbing the Gilyui and Mogot rivers, joins the railway and both snake up a side canyon, criss-crossing each other several times. They climb to 1,200m to cross the Stanovoi range (Становой хребет) which runs for hundreds of kilometres on the northern boundary of the BAM zone.

## ⊠ YAKUTSKI (Якутский) 80km

This is the last stop before the pass. The railway breaks out of a cut onto a narrow ledge over the winding valley of the Timpton river (р. Тимптон) far below. Simultaneously you cross the border from Amurskaya oblast to the Republic of Sakha (Yakutiya), marked by a huge rough-cut stone head. The railway makes a mighty U-bend to the left to cross a tributary of the Timpton.

## 🏨 NAGORNAYA YAKUTSKAYA (Нагорная Якутская) 93km

This station services the medium-sized town of Nagorny (Нагорный) which means 'uplands'. The railway continues through the high ridges at an elevation of over 1,100m and passes through a 1.2km tunnel and then drops to an open plateau at 900m.

## 🏛 ZOLOTINKA (Золотинка) 135km

There's not much to this settlement except for the Olensky sovkhoz reindeer-breeding farm. Near the station is the start of a popular rafting route down the Iengra river (р. Иенгра) to the Timpton (р. Тимптон) which takes you to the town of Chulman. There were Stalin-era gulag camps around Zolotinka. Accommodation is available at *Railway Hostel No 1* (☎ 2-67) (Общежитие 1).

Several kilometres north of Zolotinka the train passes over the Iengra river. Guarding the bridge is a large military post. From the height of the bridge you can see the plan of the camp and, most notably, the zigzag trenches along both sides of the banks designed to repel a water-borne attack.

Two kilometres past the bridge on the left is the old town of Iengra (Иенгра).

## 🚆 BERKAKIT (Беркакит) 192km

The group of towns – Berkakit, Neryungri, Serebryany Bor and Chulman – lies in a plateau or basin of low open hills. The whole area is underlain by a deep seam of high quality coal.

'Berkakit' means 'place of death' in Yakut although why it is called this is not known. The AYaM railway arrived at Berkakit in 1977. The only accommodation in town is at the *Locomotive Brigade Hostel*, (☎ 20-43) (Дом отдыха Локомотивной бригады). The nearby city of Neryungri is a better place to stay.

Neryungri is presently the terminus of passenger service on the AYaM railway. However, in the design of the AYaM railway, Neryungri is on a spur, while Berkakit is on the main line. For transport on the AYaM railway, see Getting there and away under Neryungri below.

## 🚆 NERYUNGRI-PASSENGER (Нерюнгри-пасс.) 202km

Neryungri is the second largest city in the Republic of Sakha, with a population of about 70,000. It is a brand new city, built on a hilltop well away from the gigantic coal-mine that supports it, with plain but harmonious blocks on wide avenues around a central park.

### Orientation
Berkakit, Neryungri, Serebryany Bor and Chulman are a cluster of towns sharing a basin of low open hills drained by the Chulman river. Berkakit (see above) is the furthest south. Neryungri is 10km north. North-east from Neryungri across the Chulman river is the gigantic open-pit mine. Serebryany Bor (Серебряный бор) is 8km east of Neryungri, with a reservoir and hydro-electric station. Chulman (see p271) is 30km north, with airport.

Neryungri-Passenger station is the main passenger station for Neryungri and should not be confused with Neryungri-Gruz.

(Нерюнгри-Груз.), also known as Ugolnaya (Угольная), which is 8km further on at the mine and is the Neryungri freight station.

❏ **NERYUNGRI-PASSENGER**
**(Нерюнгри-пасс)**
Area code ☎ 841147
678922, Republic of Sakha
(Yakutiya), Neryungri
(678922, Республика Саха
(Якутия), г. Нерюнгри)

## History

Neryungri was a rural village with a population of 1,000 before 1970. Following the discovery of one of the world's largest coal deposits, a geological and working settlement was quickly built in 1972. In 1974 the settlement was granted the title of a city.

The new city was a Komsomol project, which is reflected in the large number of communist statues in the town. Today, Neryungri consists of five- and nine-storey apartment buildings accented in cream and sea-blue and set on wide streets. The buildings are built on piles due to permafrost and are designed to withstand powerful earthquakes.

## Getting there and away

All the passenger trains leave southward. There is one train a day via Tynda (five hours) and the AYaM railway to Blagoveshchensk (21 hours). There is a train every other day via Tynda and the BAM to Moscow.

The nearest airport is 30km away at Chulman with flights to Blagoveshchensk, Khabarovsk, Moscow, Novosibirsk, Omsk, Rostov-na-donu, Ufa and Yakutsk.

Southward, a bus to Tynda departs from the station every Sunday, Monday, Wednesday and Friday at 14.00. There is also a bus that travels the 648km along the AYaAD highway from Neryungri to Bolshoi Never on the Trans-Siberian.

North, along the AYaAD highway, a bus runs daily to Aldan and departs at 07.15 from Neryungri railway station, 07.30 at Neryungri, 08.05 at Chulman airport and 14.00 at Aldan. Twice a week there is a bus to Yakutsk. The bus trips are quite expensive – Aldan $35 and Yakutsk $95.

Bus No 102 runs about every hour between Berkakit and Neryungri.

## Travelling by freight train

Currently the AYaM from Berkakit north to Tommot carries only freight trains. For permission to travel on a freight train, contact Severny express (Северный експресс), ☎ 27062 in Neryungri, 24602 or 24704 in Aldan.

If you travel in a freight train, you will travel in the guards' van. The van is a converted passenger carriage with a stove, beds, wash basin and batteries to run the van's electric lights. The guards are called *vagon-shchik*i (вагонщики) and their main role is to load and unload the wagons. They sometime check the wagons en route but this is normally the job of rail wagon checkers who are based at stations. Vagonshchiki normally work 15 days on and 15 off but this depends on how long each trip lasts.

Be warned, travelling in a freight train can be very slow. On one trip, it took one author 14 hours to travel the 280km from Berkakit to Aldan.

## Where to stay

Closest to the centre of Neryungri and best value (used by graduate students and Chinese traders), is *PNILZ Hotel*, in a two-storey wooden dorm building next to a ball-field. PNILZ is the Scientific Research Earthquake Laboratory of Yakutsk State University (Проблемная научно-исследовательская лаборатория землетрясений Якутского госуниверситета). A single, sharing a toilet and washbasin with one other room, with showers downstairs, is $17. PNILZ Hotel is at 678922 Neryungri, ul. Yuzhno-Yakutskaya 18/5 (678922, г. Нерюнгри, ул. Южно-Якутская 18/5, Гостиница ПНИЛЗ).

*Hotel Sosnovaya* is the former Communist Party hotel, with the predictable overstuffed furniture and suspicious attitude. A single with full facilities is $56. Hotel Sosnovaya is at ul. Bolnichny Kompleks, ☎ 41-258 (ул. Больничный Комплекс, Гостиница Сосновая). For reservations, see Getting assistance, p270.

*Horizon Sanatorium*, up the hill from the Sosnovaya, has beautiful rooms with full facilities, a balcony and views over the town and the mountains, with options for exercise, massage, dental care and full catering. For reservations, see Getting assistance (p270). The sanatorium is at ul. Bolnichny Kompleks, ☎ 4-26-87 or 4-06-16 (ул. Больничный Комплекс, Профилакторий «Горизонт»).

*Shakhtyor ('Miner') Sports Complex* has some rooms on the second floor. Sports-complex 'Shakhtyor' is at ul. Churapchinskaya, ☎ 6-92-56 (ул. Чурапчинская, Спортскомплекс «Шахтёр»).

You can also stay at the *NGRES hydro-electric station hotel* at Serebryany Bor, which is about 30 minutes out of Neryungri. NGRES Hotel is at Serebryany Bor (Серебряный бор, Гостиница НГРЭС).

## Where to eat

Of the hotels, only the *Horizon Sanatorium* has full meals. However, Neryungri is well-supplied with cafeterias and snack-bars in the shopping areas, restaurants, night-clubs and ice cream and confectionery stores. Near the PNILZ Hotel is *Café Fenix* (Кафе Феникс) – look for its name in coloured lights – which is a cafeteria by day and a restaurant by night. On ul. Karla Marksa almost opposite the new churches is a confectionery and snack bar. The *pizza house* next to the post and telephone office is a fashionable hang-out for snacks, drinks and espresso.

You will see many purchasers in stores and cafés using a card. These are not credit cards but Zolotaya Korona smart debit cards. In an isolated one-industry town like Neryungri, these help to solve Russia's perennial cash problem, since most of the wages circulate within the town.

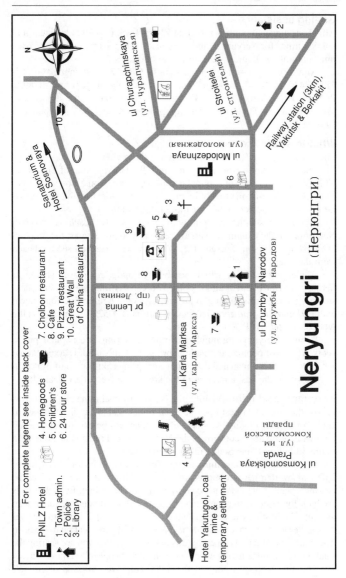

## Getting assistance

Alfa Tour, under its director, Galina Zhuravlova, organises business and holiday travel for Neryungri, and specialised activities for outsiders – river runs, hunting, geological, scientific, and trading.

Alfa Tour Agency is at pr. Lenina 6, 678922, Neryungri, ☎/🖹 +7-41147-43058, ☎ +7-41147-64210, 🖳 juravlev@yakutugol.ru (678922 Россия, Республика Саха (Якутия), г. Нерюнгри, Пр. Ленина, 6, «Дом книги», Туристическая фирма «Альфа-Тур», Журавлева Галина).

## What to see in the region

There are several interesting attractions in the region.

There is a reindeer-breeding farm near the BAM station of Zolotinka, which is also the start of a popular summer rafting route down the river Timpton (р. Тимптон) to Chulman. The river is ideal for inexperienced rafters. See Zolotinka (p266) for more information.

A popular swimming spot with a rare sandy beach is close to Neryungri on the Chulman river. To get to it, you go just past the junction of the Neryungri spur line and the AYaM railway. You can see the beach from the road.

A pleasant half-day trip is to the hydro-electric power station at Serebryany Bor (Серебряный бор). You can visit the station and occasionally there is hang gliding in the area around the reservoir. You can eat at the *Olongro restaurant* (Олонгро ресторан) ☎ 520-59 and stay at the *NGRES Hotel* (НГРЭС).

Around Neryungri, a number of mineral springs are popular picnic spots. The most popular are the hot springs called Nakhot (Нахот) about 30km north of Chulman and the cold water springs 5km south of Berkakit.

However, the best attraction in the area is the Neryungri Coal Mine.

**Neryungri coal mine**  Visiting the Neryungri coal mine is a must. It is one of the world's largest open cut coal mines with 12 million tonnes of coal a year being dug up. At this rate, the mine will be exhausted by 2007 but this is of no great concern as the Neryungri coal mine is just one field in the 40 billion-tonne South Yakutiya coal basin.

Everything about this mine is big. The coal seam is 25m thick; up to 250m of overburden is removed to reach it. The trucks are massive, the crushing plant is huge and the coal trains are never-ending. Even the roads are built for giants with 60cm thick reinforced slabs of concrete rather than asphalt. The best way to appreciate the sheer size of the mine is to fly over it. Another way is to drive around the mine from one open cut pit to the next. There are no restrictions on doing this but be aware that you are sharing the road with 200-tonne trucks which have an unchallengeable right of way.

The first stop on a tour of the 3,000-employee mine is the mine's headquarters. This nine-storey building is about 10km out of Neryungri on the road to the mine. This is the end of most bus routes to the mine. You can catch bus Nos 3 and 6 from the town to this stop. There is no museum in the building, but it has a good canteen and several well-stocked shops on the ground floor. One kilometre further on, to your right, is the headquarters of the mine's truck company, ATA Yakutugol (ATA Якутуголь), and its giant repair workshop is a further 500m onwards. You can wander around this workshop without a pass and crawl over the mammoth 2,300 horsepower trucks with their 5m diameter tyres.

This workshop maintains only 170 big dump trucks out of the mine's fleet of 2,500 vehicles. The majority of these giant tip trucks are 180-tonne Russian Belaz, 120-tonne Japanese Komatsu and 200-tonne US Dresser trucks, but there are also a few US Caterpillar trucks. The average cost of each truck is about $2 million. The trucks are crucial to the mine because every lump of overburden is moved by truck to valley fills beyond the mine and every lump of coal is moved to the coal-washer.

Maintaining the fleet is demanding as the trucks have to work 24 hours a day, 365 days a year, in temperatures as low as -50°C. In summer, the problems are just as bad with coal dust storms choking and even destroying the truck's engines. The drivers work 12-hour shifts with two months of holiday a year. They are only allowed to drive for five months each year as longer exposure to the continuous vibration and constant physical effort in controlling a 200-tonne truck can do them permanent damage. The workers spend the remaining five months a year working in the vehicle repair shops and on other less demanding jobs in the mine. In addition to the Russian maintenance staff, nine foreign specialists work at the mine, maintaining their respective company's vehicles.

Another interesting place to visit is the coal-washer at Ugolnaya, 8km north-west of Neryungri. This complex is the largest and most modern washer in Russia and annually reduces nine million tonnes of dug up coal to five million tonnes of coal concentrate ready for exporting. Trucks dump their loads of coal into the washer's crushers, which reduce lumps of coal to 0.3mm fragments. The coal is then concentrated by flotation and solid-magnetic suspension. The wet concentrate is then conveyed to one of four giant dryers that remove all moisture. The dry concentrate is then carried by conveyers the length of a football field to waiting coal trains; 870 workers run this computer-controlled plant.

## CHULMAN (Чульман) 232km

Chulman is the region's airport and is 30km north of Neryungri. The town sits on the right bank of the Chulman river opposite a spectacular white limestone cliff that rises on the left bank. It was from this that the town derived its name, which means 'white rock' in the Evenk language. Nowadays the cliff is grey with soot from an old 72 MW coal power station. Chulman has two industries, underground coal mining and limestone mining.

## FROM CHULMAN TO ALDAN ON THE AYAM RAILWAY

The railway and the highway run roughly parallel. The railway runs east of the highway to near Bolshoi-Nimnyr, then crosses the highway and runs west of the highway to Aldan.

### 🚊 Chulbass (Чульбасс) 246km

When the rail-builders named this small town, they were rather optimistically expecting that the region would boom. The name of this station derives from the words Chulman Basin (Чульманский Бассейн) which signifies a giant industrial area similar to the heavily industrialised Donbass or Donets Basin in European Russia.

### ⊠ Taezhnaya (Таежная) 351km

After this stop, the train passes over the highest ridge between Tynda and Aldan and the mountains here are permanently covered in snow. The turn-off from the AYaAD highway for Kankunski (Канкунский), 50km to the east, is near the station.

### 🚊🚂🚊 Bolshoi Nimnyr (Большой Нимныр) 416km

This medium-sized town is a major railway settlement on the AYaM.

### 🚊 Kosarevski (Косаревский) 470km

This station is also known as Orochen 1 (Орочен 1). About 2km from the station is the gold-mining village of Lebediny (Лебединый). Freight trains often terminate at Kosarevski and to get the last 16km to Aldan, you can catch one of the regular buses from Lebediny to Aldan, which take 40 minutes. You can also catch a bus to the larger village of Yakokit (Якокит) to the east, from where regular buses also travel to Aldan.

## FROM CHULMAN TO ALDAN ON THE AYAAD HIGHWAY

This section describes the route on the AYaAD highway, which has far steeper grades and tighter turns than the railway. Kilometre distances, corresponding to the road markers on the highway that count road kilometres from Bolshoi Never on the Trans-Siberian, are given within [ ]. To work out the distance from Yakutsk, which is listed on the north side of the road markers, subtract from 1157.

### 🚊🚂🚊 Chulman (Чульман) [404km]

The highway climbs out of the Chulman-Neryungri plateau. At [415km] look back for a fine view of the plateau.

### Chumakan pass (перевал Чумакань) [424km]

The first of three high passes and a giant U-bend. Beyond the pass the highway crosses the Chumakan river at [427km].

## Durai pass (перевал Дурай) [433km]

Another pass, followed by the small settlement of Bolshoi Durai (Большой Дурай).

## ☒ Khatymi (Хатыми) [475km]

A small village at a creek, with a petrol station and two pleasant truck-stop *cafés*.

## Tit-Ebe pass (перевал Тит-Эбэ) [500km]

A pass around the tundra slopes of the 1,600m peak of Evota mountain (Гора Эвота). A few kilometres further on is an elaborate commemorative marker of the AYaM and the AYaAD and an abandoned construction town.

## 🏚 Maly Nimnyr (Малый Нимныр) [523km]

Near this village is the turn-off to Kankunski (Канкунский), 50km to the east. Kankunski was a Stalin-era mica gulag complex and now a mining town. A trucker described it as 'a city that is like a settlement, surrounded by a lunar landscape – they care for nothing'. The AYaAD highway continues straight over rolling uplands.

## ☒ Vasilevka (Васильевка) [536km]

Two wooden crosses to the west behind the snow fences mark the burial grounds of the Stalin-era uranium-mining gulag of Vasilevka. Two kilometres further on there is a two-storey barracks of hewn stone on the east side and a cluster of low huts on the east, all abandoned.

## 🏚 Bolshoi Nimnyr (Большой Нимныр) 416km [569km]

At [550km] the railway crosses over the highway. The highway drops down to cross the Bolshoi Nimnyr river at Bolshoi Nimnyr.

This medium-sized town is a major railway settlement on the AYaM railway. It has a lumber mill and a petrol station and truck-stop. The road climbs into a region of small steep hills in a bend of the Aldan river (p. Алдан).

## 🏚 Lebediny (Лебединый) [628km]

A gold-mining village. The name is the adjective from 'swan'.

At about [633km] is one of the strangest headstones in Russia – a gravestone with a pair of bicycle handlebars sticking out of it. The highway, particularly south from here to Neryungri, is lined with memorials to dead drivers. It is common for drivers who get killed on the road to have steering wheels attached to their headstones but a bicycle is unique. Some memorials have faded flowers; a few have a two-litre soda bottle of petrol – enough to get the departed to the first truck-stop on the other side.

## ALDAN (Алдан) 486km [641km]

Aldan exists for its gold and mica. When gold was found in the 1920s, the indigenous village in the area was called Nezhametny, which became the Aldan settlement in 1924. It became the city of Aldan in 1939 and the city council always has a celebration on its anniversary on 15 July. The town now boasts a population of 30,000 with 60,000 in the region.

The satellite town of Leninski, 10km south of Aldan, was known as Nizhnestalinsk (Нижнесталинск) or Lower Stalin until 1962.

The power behind the town is Aldanzoloto (Aldan Gold Co) which has its headquarters 27km away in the smaller but wealthier town of Nizhne-Kuranakh.

Aldan was closed to foreigners from the 1930s to the early 1990s and then opened for a few years until the Sakhan government redeclared it a closed town in 1992. The government did this because it was concerned

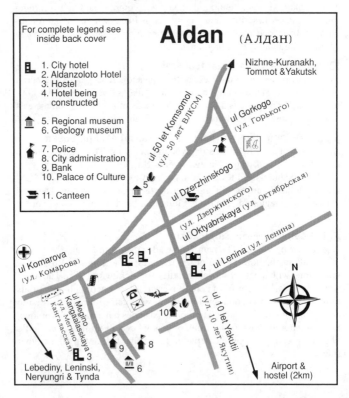

For complete legend see inside back cover

1. City hotel
2. Aldanzoloto Hotel
3. Hostel
4. Hotel being constructed

5. Regional museum
6. Geology museum

7. Police
8. City administration
9. Bank
10. Palace of Culture

11. Canteen

**Aldan** (Алдан)

Nizhne-Kuranakh, Tommot & Yakutsk

ul Gorkogo (ул. Горького)

ul 50 let Komsomol (ул. 50 лет ВЛКСМ)

ul Dzerzhinskogo (ул. Дзержинского)

ul Oktyabrskaya (ул. Октябрьская)

ul Komarova (ул. Комарова)

ul Meghno Kangaalasskaya (ул. Мегино Кангаласская)

ul Lenina (ул. Ленина)

ul 10 let Yakutii (ул. 10 лет Якутии)

Lebediny, Leninski, Neryungri & Tynda

Airport & hostel (2km)

N

about the possibility of gold theft in the guise of business. This means you should have Aldan on your visa to buy a ticket to the city. However, if you arrive by train or bus, no-one checks.

> ❏ **ALDAN** (Алдан)
> Area code ☎ 411-45
> 678900, Republic of
> Sakha (Yakutiya), Aldan
> (678900, Республика
> Саха (Якутия), г.
> Алдан)

### Getting there and away

Although freight trains reach Aldan, it will be a few years yet before passenger trains make it. For information on how to catch a freight train, see Travelling by freight train on p267.

A more reliable way of travelling between Neryungri and Aldan is on a bus. There are daily buses departing Aldan at 07.00 and arriving at 13.25 at Chulman airport, 14.00 at Neryungri and 14.15 at Neryungri railway station. The trip is $35. Buses run to Yakutsk on Wednesday and Saturday for $60.

Local buses run daily between towns such as Kanku (Канку), Nizhni-Kuranakh, Khatystyr and Tommot. There are flights from Yakutsk, Chulman and Khabarovsk.

### Where to stay and eat

The only public hotel is a two-storey, wooden *hostel* with a number of shared rooms. Toilets and showers (with a bare trickle of water) are downstairs. The price is an outrageous $22 for a single. The hostel is at ul. Oktyabrskaya, (22002 (ул. Октябрьская).

There is also a *hotel* owned by Aldanzoloto and a *workers' hostel* which may give you a room. A multi-storey hotel was started more than 10 years ago a block away but so far has not been completed. A better place to stay is in Nizhne-Kuranakh as there is a good hotel owned by Aldanzoloto.

The excellent *canteen* on ul. Dzerzhinskovo (ул. Дзержинского), a block down from the hotel, is bright, friendly and with tasty food.

### Getting assistance

This is one place where it is great to have someone who can organise accommodation and access to the museums. The best contact is Olga Yakovlevna Korneva. Olga Yakovlevna was formerly Director of the Aldan Bureau of Travel and Excursions, but is now in private business. Contact her at 678900, Aldan, PO Box 26, ☎ 2-29-63, home ☎ 2-94-03 (678900, Республика Саха (Якутия), г. Алдан, а/я 26, Корнева Ольга Яковлевна).

### What to see

There is a regional museum and a geological museum in Aldan. The first contains halls dedicated to the history of gold mining in the region, the creation of the town and work from local artists. The second displays the history of the geologists who worked for the Aldan Geology Co and the region's rocks.

There is the usual collection of monuments to revolutionary leaders, heroes of the Great Patriotic War and explorers dotted around the town.

However, the most interesting sights are not in the town but around it. A nice day-trip is to the Sakhan indigenous village of Khatystyr (Хатыстыр) which is 60km away on the Aldan river. The main occupations of the inhabitants are reindeer breeding and fishing. To get there you need to catch a bus that goes through Nizhne-Kuranakh.

On all the roads out of Aldan, you will notice that the river valleys have been stripped of all vegetation. These valleys have been dredged for alluvial gold and as there are no regeneration programmes they will stay barren for decades.

### GLUBOKI KURANAKH (Глубокий Куранах) [519km]

### Nizhne-Kuranakh (Нижне-Куранах) [674km]

The station Gluboki Kuranakh serves the medium-sized settlement of Nizhne-Kuranakh. This town houses the headquarters of the region's largest gold-mining company, Aldanzoloto. The town has excellent facilities including a hotel, brewery and salami factory. There is a road from here to the Sakhan indigenous village of Khatystyr (Хатыстыр) which is 30km away on the Aldan river.

Near here is the enormously rich Kuranakh gold field. The areas with high gold content are now close to exhaustion. The present yield is comparatively low, ranging between 1.6 and 1.7 grams of gold per tonne of

ore. Western companies have been eyeing the area as large-scale ore enrichment using modern technology could turn this into one of the world's largest gold-mining enterprises. A feasibility study has showed that for a $209 million investment, about 13.5 tonnes of gold could be produced from 20,000,000 tonnes of ore mined annually.

### ⌧ YAKOKIT (Якокит) 533km [688km]

This stop should not be confused with Yakokut (Якокут) village which is 42km south of here. Near the railway station is a pioneer camp.

Berry-sellers on the AYaAD Highway, August. Photo © Nicholas Zvegintzov

## TOMMOT (Томмот) 568km [715km]

This small city is on the Aldan river. In the past, boats sailed from Yakutsk, up the Aldan river via Khandyga (Хандыга) and Ust-Maya (Усть-Мая) to Tommot. Tommot is the furthest upstream point that can be reached on the Aldan river. The town is an iron and steel centre and coal is shipped in from Neryungri and iron ore from the nearby Aldan deposits.

The AYaM railway reached Tommot in August 1997. The railway bridge is in place although its approach embankments are not.

The highway crosses the river and climbs out of the river valley. From here north to its meeting with the Lena river (p. Лена) the highway crosses relatively rolling hills, ever gentler, angling toward the river across its watershed. The original surface of the highway was hard-rolled gravel, but wherever the road has heaved or sunk it has been patched with mixed gravel and dirt dug out of improvised quarries that can be seen all along the highway. This surface is loose and treacherous.

## VERKHNYAYA AMGA (Верхняя Амга) [826km]

The highway crosses the Amga river (p. Амга), which runs into the Aldan river at Khandyga. This settlement has a petrol station and truck-stops. Railway construction can be seen in the area.

## KUR KEN-KI (Курь Кен-Ки) [862km]

A spring by the side of the road.

## KYRBYKAN (Кырбыкан) [881km]

A small village at the crossing of the Kyrbykan river (two bridges), with a police post and a villainous truck-stop.

## ULUU (Улуу) [907km]

A small village at the crossing of the Uluu river, with petrol station and truck-stops.

## MUNDURUCHCHU (Мундуруччу) [991km]

A small village at the crossing of the Munduruchchu river.

## CROSSING THE LENA RIVER TO YAKUTSK

The AYaAD highway arrives at the east bank of the Lena river; Yakutsk is on the west bank; the river is 10km wide, including marshy verges. Crossing is by ferry in summer and by ice road in winter. Keep in mind that you cannot cross the river between April and the end of May and from the middle of October until December. A planned 10km road and rail bridge will be the biggest construction on the AYaM railway and is expected to take at least eight years to build.

There are two crossings with ferries – at Bestyakh (Бестях) and Nizhni Bestyakh (Нижний Бестях). Bestyakh has a shorter crossing and a private ferry.

To cross at Bestyakh, watch for the GIBDD (highway police) post at the intersection at [110km]. Turn left off the AYaAD highway and follow the road past the highway maintenance brigade town down to the bank of the river. Take the ferry or the ice road to Bestyakh. The city on the bluffs is Mokhsogollokh (Мохсоголлох), which fabricates pre-cast concrete building elements. Then drive up the bluff, through the town of Bestyakh and turn right on the easy hard road to Yakutsk.

To cross at Nizhni Bestyakh, continue on the AYaAD highway to Nizhni Bestyakh on the right bank on the Lena river opposite Yakutsk. From there take the city ferry or the ice road into the city.

For river travel see Travelling the Lena river on pp241-5.

## 🚌🚆🚕 YAKUTSK (Якутск) 1,046km [1,157km]

Yakutsk is the capital of the Republic of Sakha. See pp230-41 for more on this ancient and fascinating city.

The buses arrive at and leave from the bus station at ul. Oktyabrskaya, 24, served by city bus line No 8 (ул. Октябрьская, 24, Автовокзал).

Crossing the Lena at Mokhsogollokh. Photo © Nicholas Zvegintzov

# PART 6: KOLYMA HIGHWAY
## Колымская трасса

# The Kolyma Highway: Yakutsk–Magadan
### Колымская трасса: Якутск–Магадан

In Russia it is called the Kolymskaya trassa (Колымская трасса), which is usually translated as 'Kolyma Highway'. But trassa can also mean 'line' or 'sketch' and in some places this may be a more appropriate description, as the road is not much more than a line on a map. The Kolyma region is named after the Kolyma river (р. Колыма), which drains the huge mountainous mineral-rich region north of Magadan (Магадан). The Kolyma Highway, once called 'Road of Bones' because it was built by slave labour, links Yakutsk on the Lena river to Magadan on the coast of the Sea of Okhotsk (Охотское море).

## THE ROUTE (see Route Map 6, p372)

The Kolyma Highway does not take the easy route. The old highways of Russia sought paths that were already open, typically following rivers that had already found or made their way through mountain barriers. This highway, as befits the engineering of the Soviet era and of an era with abundant slave labour, makes its own path. From Khandyga (Хандыга), the easternmost point reachable on the Lena river system, it heads 800km east into successive ranges of formidable mountains, before turning south across 300 more kilometres of mountains to reach Magadan.

The time in Yakutsk is Moscow time +6 hours. Three hundred kilometres beyond Khandyga, near Kyubeme, the time changes to Moscow time +8 hours.

## HISTORY

Life has a long history in these parts. However, most of the human life you will see along the road has come here with the road. The main exception is the area around Tomtor and Oimyakon. Yakuts lived here long before the arrival of the Russians and even now they are the main inhabitants of this region. They did not escape the Soviet collectivisation and their villages now look much like any other *sovkhoz* or *kolkhoz* (collective farms), but they continue the work of their ancestors. They work in the fields and breed their native Yakut horses, which will be out grazing in the severe Sakhan winters, looking for grass under the snow while the air temperature is -50°C.

The Russian presence in the region is much more recent and can be explained in one word: gold. In pre-Revolutionary times there was a Russian presence consisting of a route (not a road), a settlement on the sea of Okhotsk and a few inland, and reputedly a remote prison-camp. Transit was on foot, with the help of reindeer and dog-sleds. Most of the travellers were geologists. Where they found the most promising lodes, a settlement was established to mine the precious metal.

For this a workforce was needed and as few people wanted to live in this remote and hostile environment, a workforce was invented by the state. In 1932 Dalstroi (Дальстрой) was created, a subdivision of the Gulag system, to exploit the mineral riches of the Soviet Far East. A couple of years later the first shiploads of prisoners started to arrive in Magadan to be sent up north to work in the mines of the Kolyma river basin. As this labour was virtually free and disposable, they worked in extremely harsh conditions using only the most primitive of equipment, some of which can be seen in regional museums along the way and especially in the one in Magadan, which has a whole section devoted to Dalstroi. For eyewitness accounts of life in the camps see the books by Varlam Shalamov and Michael Solomon in Appendix E (see p358).

Soon 80,000 prisoners were toiling for Dalstroi and, at its peak, over 100,000 prisoners were in the system. The whole region was shut off from the outside world – even Russians needed a special permit to come here.

After Stalin's death the Gulag system was abolished and 1956 saw the official end of Dalstroi. Even if the area was once littered with camps, it is difficult to find a trace of them today. In more than 40 years since their closure, towns have been built over some of them, while the access roads to the more remote ones have all but disappeared. In some cases, such as Nelkan, south of Ust-Nera, you can still see some remains if you know how to get there by truck or on foot.

With no more prisoners to work in the mines another way had to be found to get people to go to the Kolyma. Since the end of the Great Patriotic War many people had already arrived in the region, especially Ukrainians fleeing the desperate situation in their home country. People were lured to the north by financial incentives and other perks. Every other year they could take three to six months' holidays in the south and often they were able to keep their flats or houses in their home regions. Even if the financial advantage was partially offset by the higher cost of living in the north, it was possible to set enough

Колыма, Колыма
Чудная планета
Двенадцать месяцев зима
Остальное лето

*Kolyma, Kolyma*
*Strange planet*
*Twelve months winter*
*The rest summer*

Quoted in Michael Solomon,
*Magadan*, 1971

money aside for a comfortable retirement on the *materik*, 'the mainland' as they called Russia.

The Russian north-east suffered even more than the rest of the country from the implosion of the system when savage capitalism was let loose on the country after 1992. First of all the rouble went crashing through the floor and a lifetime's savings which yesterday still bought a decent house were now just enough to get a couple of bottles of vodka. Secondly, the centre withdrew the region's financial subsidies that were essential to maintaining a way of life that was similar to the one in western Russia. Thirdly, the rapid privatisation of industry, which often meant that the bureaucrats accepted gifts to sell companies cheaply, resulted in massive price rises for monopoly goods and services such as electricity and transport. This ruined many companies and collective farms that depended on cheap inputs.

Life, which had never been easy, became next to impossible. Salaries are not paid for several months, sometimes even years, and one arrives at the paradox that people are living in poverty on top of a gold mountain. Some have taken to gold panning as in the bad old days of Yukon fame. Others are leaving or trying to leave, which is not always easy, as not only do you need money for this, but also you need a place to go to.

All along the road there are ghost villages and even the surviving towns are more than half empty and in ruins. It is eerie walking around the overgrown towns with streets still called Sovetskaya and Lenina and surrounded by many windowless buildings emblazed with fading communist slogans.

It is easy to run around with a camera and take pictures of death and decrepitude, but please spare a thought for the people around you and do not hurt their sensibilities. Even if only few of them may have been real communists, all have been working all their lives in order to carve a human existence out of the frozen soil and to build a brighter future, only to be told one day that it was useless and to no avail.

## THE CHANGED ROUTE

The history of the Kolyma Highway follows closely the ups and downs of the region. The original road was largely built by prisoners. It served as a supply line to the camps and mines from both the sea port of Magadan and the river ports on the Lena river system. In the days of Dalstroi, the prisoners were also responsible for the upkeep of the road; at regular intervals (8km) was a little hut with a prisoner whose task it was every day to check his stretch of the road and repair it when necessary.

The original road went from Khandyga straight east through Kyubeme and Tomtor to Kadykchan and on to Susuman. When Ust-Nera was founded in 1937 a dead-end road was built there from Kadykchan. This meant that Ust-Nera, which is in Sakha, could only be reached from Yakutsk via a 500km detour through Magadanskaya Oblast. So a short cut was created, leaving the highway near Kyubeme to run north to Ust-Nera. This road was intended to become an all-year route, but it has not been finished yet. About 50km of roads through swamps and marshes and a couple of major bridges are still required, but in the meantime it is an adequate winter highway. At the same time maintenance was abandoned on the eastward all-year route, so that its cuts and bridges are virtually impassable.

As far as real traffic is concerned, the Kolyma Highway is two distinct systems. The eastern road network from Magadan is the supply line and industrial artery of the mining regions as far west as Ust-Nera and beyond. The western section, including the new winter road, links Sakha with its eastern communities. Since Ust-Nera and the surrounding towns are both mining regions serviced by Magadan and administrative regions of Sakha, the two highway systems are still linked. Probably the only traffic going between Sakha and Magadan are the limited number of adventurous foreigners passing through with their 4WDs, bicycles, motorbikes and thumbs.

## WHEN TO GO

Judging by the endless array of memorial stones along the entire road, travel here can be dangerous in any season. Danger not only comes from the road itself and the weather conditions, but also from drunk or exhausted drivers. Summer and winter are the best times to travel, with spring and autumn being times to avoid at all costs. From one year to the next the weather can be very different, so the beginning and ending of each season should be taken as approximations only.

● **Summer (June to August)**  The river connection between Yakutsk and Khandyga is open; the all-year roads from Khandyga to Tomtor and from Ust-Nera to Magadan are passable; the new link to Ust-Nera is probably not passable. To bridge this gap you can fly – there are several flights a week between Ust-Nera and Tomtor, a distance of 120km, about 20-minutes' flight. The main problems of the season, apart from the bad condition of the road in places, are water, fire and dust. Water can keep you stopped for several days because sections of road have been washed away or because the river in front of you is too deep to cross. The worst time for rain is June but massive downpours can occur at anytime. Fire can be a hazard in July when temperatures are high and the forest is dry. In 1996 the smoke from forest fires around Khandyga prevented planes from using the airport at Ust-Nera, over 500km away. Dust can cause accidents by hiding the road and oncoming cars in the huge clouds in the wake of trucks.

● **Autumn (September to November)**  The main danger comes from slippery roads due to fresh snowfalls on top of a layer of ice. The winter roads are truly impassable and travel is dangerous on all roads.

● **Winter (December to March)** This is the season when roads appear where there are none on the maps. At the onset of winter, usually in December, when the ice on the rivers is judged sufficiently strong, bull-dozers are used to clear a path, tractors are positioned along the road at regular intervals to help the stranded and the winter road, *avtozimnik* or just *zimnik* (автозимник, зимник), is declared open. There is also an official end to the zimnik, after which all travel is at one's own risk. The main problems in winter are slippery roads and extremely low tempera-tures (-50°C is common). Truck engines are kept running day and night and trucks travel in convoy. This is because even a simple mechanical problem can stop a vehicle, causing first the engine and then the driver to freeze. Many drivers prefer to drive at night (the days are pretty short any-way), so as to notice oncomers from a distance and get out of the way well in advance. One experienced traveller recommended March for a land trip. 'The winter roads are still frozen, but it's not so cold.'

● **Spring (April to May)** Possibly the most dangerous season as the ice on the rivers and swamps is often too thin to carry the weight of vehicles. The winter roads are truly impassable and travel is dangerous on all roads.

## TRAVEL OPTIONS

Most foreigners hitch a ride with trucks. Truck drivers are usually willing to take passengers so as to have someone to talk to. However, you may have problems getting a ride in winter (when you are an additional burden and responsibility they can well do without) or if the cab has no extra sleeping space, which may make the nights uncomfortable. For the same reason two or more people travelling together may have a hard time finding someone to take them. Whether or not it is legal for drivers to take passengers is not clear, though it does not seem to cause too many problems and it has been the traditional form of passenger travel since the Gulag era.

While you can hitch a ride by waiting at the roadside, for longer dis-tances it is probably a better idea to contact the local *avtobaza* or transport company (автобаза) and see if they have any trucks going your way. Most of the trucks on this highway are owned by an avtobaza.

You can hire a car and driver for about $50 per day plus petrol.

If you intend to drive yourself, have a look at the website 💻 www.turtleexpedition.com, which contains an account of Gary and Monika Wescott's trip from Magadan to Yakutsk on the winter road in 1996.

# Route descriptions

## YAKUTSK–KHANDYGA (Якутск–Хандыга), 380km by land, 530km by river

The Kolyma route starts from Khandyga, which is 300km west and a little north of Yakutsk on the Aldan river.

The road east from Yakutsk peters out in the marshes between the Lena and the Aldan rivers. There is only a winter road to Khandyga. In winter there is a bus service to Ytykh Kyuel (Ытых Кюёль) on this route; beyond there is truck traffic.

In summer a daily raketa hydrofoil leaves both Yakutsk and Khandyga at 05.00 and arrives about 10 hours later.

## KHANDYGA–KYUBEME (Хандыга–Кюбеме), 320km

From Khandyga buses only go as far as the airport at Tyoply Klyuch (Тёплыи Ключ), 70km east.

From Tyoply Klyuch the highway leaves the plain and heads into the Suntar Khayata range (хребет Сунтар Хаята) up the steep Vostochnaya river (р. Восточная – 'East River'), crossing a pass at 1,200m to the plateau around the small settlement of Kyubeme, which has a petrol station. Kyubeme is the junction with the unfinished short cut to Ust-Nera.

Near Kyubeme the time changes by two hours to Moscow time +8 hours.

## KYUBEME–KADYKCHAN (Кюбеме–Кадыкчан) on the original highway, 405km

A maintained highway continues east into the wide valley of the Indigirka river (р. Индигирка) to Tomtor (Томтор), 155km. Tomtor has a petrol station and an airport with weekly flights to Yakutsk and Ust-Nera.

Between Tomtor and the village of Oimyakon (Оймякон), 40km down the valley, is the meteorological station famous in weather circles for recording the northern hemisphere's lowest winter temperature – -71° C – the 'pole of cold' (Полюс холода). The valley floor is at 750m, the valley walls go up to 1,100m, cold air pools in the valley and the temperature rises with the height. The mean temperature in Oimyakon in January is -50°C (in July it is +15°).

From Tomtor to Kadykchan the original highway heads directly towards Kadykchan across a broken plateau among 2,300m peaks, crossing the border into Magadanskaya oblast. Maintenance is minimal or non-existent, most bridges are out of order and there is virtually no traffic all year-round.

## KYUBEME–UST-NERA (Кюбеме–Усть-Нера), on the new road, 240km

From Kyubeme a winter road, gradually being upgraded to an all-weather road, runs direct to Ust-Nera on the upper reaches of the Indigirka river (р. Индигирка) below Tomtor. The road runs north crossing the creeks and shoulders of the Indigirka, climbing two passes at 1,362m and 1,380m. The winter road meets the existing road, which is in good condition, near Elginski (Эльгинский). The road continues east toward Ust-Nera.

## UST-NERA (Усть-Нера)

Ust-Nera is a substantial gold-mining town, home of the Indigir Zoloto Gold Company, whose production of several tens of tonnes a year is safely whizzed away by plane. It has petrol, a hotel and an airport with flights to Tomtor and other places in Sakha.

Ust-Nera has a splendid location on the confluence of the Nera and Indigirka rivers, surrounded by mountains topped with natural standing stone formations. (According to the Russians, these are 'Yakuts queuing for beer'.) There are some small freight ships on the Indigirka to provision the outlying mining communities downstream. However, the river is not navigable all the way to the Arctic Ocean from here; some 100km downstream there are dangerous rapids – even the fish cannot make it through there – and different species are found north and south of this divide. Russian adventure groups have organised difficult (and dangerous) expeditions from here.

> ❏ **UST-NERA (Усть-Нера)**
> Area code ☎ 41154
> 678730 Republic of Sakha
> (Yakutiya), Oymyakonski
> Rayon, Poselok Ust-Nera
> (678730, Россия, Республика
> Саха (Якутия),
> Оймяконский район, пос.
> Усть Нера)

There is a small museum in Ust-Nera, showing the history and the hopeful beginnings of the place (the first geologists arrived in 1937) and including a reconstructed interior of a Yakut dwelling.

## UST-NERA–SUSUMAN (Усть-Нера–Сусуман), 378km

Most supplies for Ust-Nera and the surrounding mining towns are carried in from Magadan, so traffic is heavier between Ust-Nera and Magadan (1,011km).

From Ust-Nera there is a weekly bus to Susuman).

The road leaves Ust-Nera up the Nera river (p. Нера) heading east, passing several more mining towns and the spoil-piles of mining. North-west is Mount Pobeda (гора Победа – 'Mount Freedom'), Sakha's tallest mountain at 3,003m. The road turns south-west with the river, passes a Sakhan border post at Artyk (Артык), and crosses the border into Magadanskaya oblast at Delyanki (Делянки). The road follows the Nera almost to its source and then crosses a 1,452m pass to drop steeply into Kadykchan. Coming in from the west is the original highway from Khandyga.

### Kadykchan (Кадыкчан)
Kadykchan is the logistics centre for the coal mines at Tal-Yurakh, which supply coal to the Magadan region. Kadykchan is high up on the watershed of the Kolyma river.

The main road to Susuman heads off to the right. A more direct, but abandoned, way passes through Myaundzha (Мяунджа), site of a colossal Stalin-era uranium-processing project described in Michael Solomon's *Magadan*, 1971 – gigantic buildings, a model town for free workers and barracks for 10,000 prisoners.

### SUSUMAN (Сусуман)

Susuman is headquarters of several mining companies. This town of 17,000 people has petrol, two hotels (one above the bus station, the other two blocks away) and an airport. From here there is a daily bus to Magadan, taking about 16 hours and costing about $50, including a two-hour stop at Magadan airport. There are two to three buses a day to Kadykchan and a weekly bus to Ust-Nera. The local telephone code is ☎ 41345.

The road north, along the Berelekh river (р. Берелёх), heads into territory reputed to be populated by illegal gold-panners who shoot first, then ask questions.

The road south beyond Bolshevik (Болшевик) is the more direct, but secondary, road to Magadan via Matrosova (Матросова) and Ust-Omchug (Усть-Омчуг). It is less travelled and there is no public transport.

### SUSUMAN–MAGADAN (Сусуман–Магадан), 633km

The main road heads east over a rocky pass to Yagodnoe (Ягодное), 107km, a sizeable town named after *yagoda* (ягода), berries, rather than after Genrikh Yagoda (Генрих Ягода), head of the NKVD political police, 1934-36, shot in 1937.

The road heads down a creek to cross the main stream of the Kolyma river on a one-lane bridge controlled by manual traffic lights at Debin (Дебин), 74km. Debin, once called 'Left Bank', was the major administrative centre of the gold-mining region in Dalstroi days. Before the bridge is the junction with the road to Sinegore (Синегорье), site of the dam of the huge Kolyma Reservoir (Колымское водохранилище).

The road continues east up a small creek to Orotukan (Оротукан), 58km. ('A wood and canvas settlement, in other words, tents with holes in them but overlaid with rough boards. The newly arrived prisoner transport ... saw even before being led in through the door: every tent in the settlement was surrounded with piles of frozen corpses on three out of four sides, except where the door was. (And this was not to terrify. There was simply no way out of it: people died, and snow was six feet deep, and beneath it there was only permafrost.)' – Aleksandr Solzhenitsyn, *The Gulag Archipelago*, vol 3.)

The road then heads south across rugged uplands of tundra, almost totally unpopulated, for 300km, via Atka (Атка), 194km, leaving the headwaters of the Kolyma river and finally dropping down to the coastal lowlands at Palatka (Палатка), 109km. From here it is 32km to the Magadan airport at the town of Sokol (Сокол) and then 59km to Magadan itself.

There is an alternative road between Susuman and Palatka via Bolshevik and Ust-Omchug, shorter but less travelled. On this route there is at least one bus a week from Magadan to Matrosova north of Ust-Omchug, but no buses go beyond this point to the junction with the main road at Bolshevik.

## MAGADAN (Магадан)

Magadan is a port city on the Sea of Okhotsk (Охотское море), the arm of the Pacific closed off by the Kamchatka Peninsula, the Kuril Islands and Sakhalin Island. Its climate is cool oceanic, with mean temperature -25° in January (the coldest month) and mean temperature in August (the warmest month) +13°. The time zone in Magadanskaya oblast is eight hours later than Moscow.

Magadan was founded in the 1930s as the headquarters and transhipment point for the slave labourers of Dalstroi (Дальстрой), the subdivision of the Gulag system created to exploit the mineral riches of the Soviet Far East. Magadan became a city in 1939. When Dalstroi was disbanded after the death of Stalin, Magadan continued to be the administrative and commercial centre of the region.

Magadan is the capital of Magadanskaya oblast, which includes the Chukotski Autonomous Region (Чукотский автономный округ) in the far north-east. This is the region of

> ❏ **MAGADAN (Магадан)**
> Area code ☎ 41322
> Magadan, Magadanskaya
> Oblast, Russia 685000
> (685000, Магаданская
> область, г. Магадан)
> Population 152,000
> Moscow time +8 hours

Russia closest to the USA on the Bering Strait, where it is possible to drive, walk, or indeed swim (it's been done) between the two countries. Since the end of the USSR, commercial, social and religious contacts have opened up across the strait.

Mining accounts for most industrial output. The region is a leading producer of gold for Russia (about 40 tonnes in 1994), as well as silver, tin and tungsten, plus four million tonnes of coal and 100,000 tonnes of fish from the north Pacific. The port of Magadan is open all year (with ice-breakers). Agriculture is centred on mink farms and reindeer husbandry (enjoy tasty reindeer sausages).

Magadan has a standardised Soviet look, with wide avenues of featureless blocks and without the flamboyance of the architecture of the BAM zone. The people of Magadan, in spite of their grievous history and difficult environment, are cheerful and outgoing. They remember the past, both in museums and in person, but they look to the future.

## Getting there and away

The Kolyma Highway, described above, is Magadan's only land connection to the rest of Russia. The bus station is at the intersection of Prospekt Lenina and ul. Proletarskaya ☎ +7 41322 2-16-02, 2-18-87 (Проспект Ленина и ул. Пролетарская, Автовокзал).

The airport is in the town of Sokol (Сокол) 59km north (take a bus from the bus station). The Aeroflot office is opposite the Magadan Hotel, ☎ +7 41322 2-88-91. There are flights to Ekaterinburg, Irkutsk, Khabarovsk, Krasnodar, Moscow, Novosibirsk, St Petersburg, Ust-Ilimsk, and to the towns and settlements of Magadanskaya oblast.

If heading for Yakutsk or other places in Sakha see Visas, p230

For telephone, email and internet service, use the Telephone-Telegraph station of MagadanSvyazInform, at ul. Proletarskaya 10, ☎ +7 41322 97-211, 🖃 +7 41322 97-025 (ул. Пролетарская, 10, Филиал ОАО «МагаданСвязьИнформ», Телефонно-Телеграфная Станция).

## Where to stay

**Business Center Hotel**, the former Intourist Hotel, with reasonable prices, is at Proletarskaya 84v, ☎ +7-41322 589-44, 585-46 (ул. Пролетарская, 84в, Гостиница «Бизнес Центр»).

**Magadan Hotel**, a large, grim block with moderate prices, is at Proletarskaya 8, ☎ +7-41322 210-14, 212-46 (ул. Пролетарская, 8, Гостиница « Магадан »).

There is a **hotel** in Sokol, opposite the airport, ☎ +7-41322 9-33-84.

## What to see

The main geological museum is on ul. Portovaya. You may have to find someone to open it, or go when it is open for a school tour. It gives an

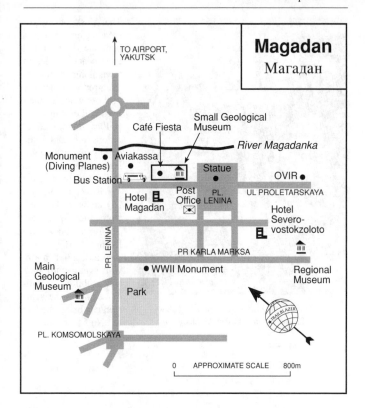

overview of the history of life on earth, has lots of meteorites and samples of the semi-precious stones from the region as well as a replica of the baby mammoth found in the north of the Oblast.

In the same building as the Fiesta café there is a small geological museum, but you may have to ask around to find someone to open it. In the rear room (locked with a special key) are all kinds of gold nuggets (the gold in Magadan area is alluvial) and stones with gold traces.

The Regional Museum (Музей краеведческий) is not big, but the quality of the displays (especially of the stuffed animals) is excellent, not the old stuffy ones that bore school children, but lifelike compositions in a modern, well-lit room. It also has a full floor of memorabilia of the gulags in a room completely covered in black, with letters of arrest, letters from prisoners, and wheelbarrows and other tools from the camps.

The Mask of Sorrow (Маска скорби), above Magadan. (Photo © Paul Geldhof).

The Mask of Sorrow (Маска скорби) is a huge head on a hill crest near the edge of town along the road to the airport, in memory of those who lost their lives in the camps.

Pleasant local expeditions are along the coast to the fishing village of Ola (Ола) in the east or west to the Yana river (р. Яна) – buy crabs ready to eat from the fishermen. The resort, Snezhnaya Dolina (Снежная долина), 23km north, with skiing until June and a children's holiday camp in the summer, can be reached by bus No 5.

# APPENDICES
Приложения

## Appendix A: History of the BAM
История БАМа

### WHY THE BAM WAS BUILT (Почему был построен БАМ)

There were two main reasons for building the BAM: military and economic. The military threat posed by Japan and China was the primary justification during the late 1930s, mid-1940s and again in the late 1960s, while the potential economic benefits of the region dominated justifications in the mid-1930s, 1970s and 1980s. There were a number of other reasons for building the railway such as Brezhnev's personal glory, but they were of secondary importance.

### THE MILITARY VALUE OF THE BAM

Since the Russian conquest of eastern Siberia and the Russian Far East, the areas have been vulnerable to invasion and there was little Moscow could do about it. The only route to Vladivostok until the late 1800s was the Great Siberian Post Road, which was little more than a mud track. In the event of conflict, the road was totally inadequate for quick communications or military support. After decades of procrastination, in 1891 Tsar Alexander III finally ordered the Trans-Siberian Railway to be built. While this single-track railway provided a lifeline to the Russian Far East, it was a fragile one. Many sections of the Trans-Siberian Railway ran virtually alongside the Chinese border, which meant that rail traffic could be interrupted with minimal effort.

The vulnerability of the Russian Far East was brought home to Moscow following the area's occupation by American, British and Japanese troops in 1918. It was only in 1922 that the Japanese finally left the Russian mainland.

The Japanese invasion threat resurfaced in 1931 when they occupied Manchuria and set up an independent state of Manchukuo. Inner Mongolia became a Japanese sphere of influence and the same fate appeared inevitable for Outer Mongolia. The Russian Far Eastern territories were outflanked and they could be cut off at a moment's notice by a Japanese military thrust anywhere to the east of Lake Baikal. In addition, in 1935 the Soviet leadership was forced by Japan into a humiliating sale of the valuable Soviet-owned East China Railway, which travelled through Manchuria to the sea port of Port Arthur (now called Lushun) in the Yellow Sea. The Japanese bought the railway for just 55 million gold roubles while Russia spent over 500 million on its construction.

The immediate response to the Japanese threat was to improve the Trans-Siberian by laying a second track. As an additional defensive measure, new bridges were built rather than widening existing ones as this doubled the number of targets for enemy bombers.

However, the only real insurance against interdiction was to build a northern rail line outside bombing range. But by the time construction work started on the northern line of the BAM, the Japanese threat had been neutralised with their defeat in the Japanese Mongolian war in 1939. In 1941, work on the BAM was stopped, with the exception of the Komsomolsk-na-Amure–Sovetskaya Gavan line, as all resources were thrown towards stopping the Nazis' advance in western Russia. The Komsomolsk-na-Amure–Sovetskaya Gavan line was completed just in time to be the only part of the BAM to play a significant role in the Great Patriotic War. In 1945 it was used to ferry troops and equipment to the Pacific coast in preparation for the invasion of the Japanese-held end of Sakhalin Island, the Kuril Islands and the northern Japanese island of Hokkaido.

The discontinuation of construction work on most of the BAM was unknown to Western observers. Perversely, the Soviet media's silence on the BAM was taken as evidence that the project had become a military secret and work on it was accelerating.

By the time Western intelligence services realised that the reason the BAM was not mentioned was because it was not being built, tension had risen between the former communist allies of the Soviet Union and China, and the debate was reopened on the military need for a second Trans-Siberian Railway. Debate within the Soviet Union peaked following the 1969 Sino-Soviet fighting, the rapid construction of underground nuclear shelters in northern China, and the proliferation of multi-warheaded nuclear missiles in China. However, a dispassionate analysis would have shown that the increased range of bombers, long lead time for construction of the BAM and the likelihood of nuclear conflict rather than railway sabotage had eliminated any significant military advantage likely to be gained by constructing the BAM.

## THE ECONOMIC BENEFIT OF THE BAM

The economic justification for the BAM was best expressed in the second Soviet Five Year Plan (1933-37). The plan stated that the BAM will 'traverse little investigated regions of eastern Siberia and bring to life an enormous new territory and its colossal riches – timber, gold, coal – and also make possible the cultivation of great tracts of land suitable for agriculture'.

Over the following 60 years, variations on this economic theme were propounded, including that the BAM would implement Lenin's theory of regional development, facilitate development in the Russian Far East, reduce traffic on the congested Trans-Siberian Railway and create a faster alternative container traffic route from the Pacific Ocean to Europe.

Siberia had long been seen as a frozen asset to be melted for future generations. Extracting this wealth started under the Tsar with furs, gold, diamonds and timber exploitation. However, its enormous mineral wealth was mainly left undisturbed until Stalin's massive industrialisation campaign. Throughout the Soviet Union, large-scale industries were built virtually overnight and raw material was needed to feed them. The shortage of hard currency, combined with the Soviet fear of being dependent on imported raw materials, resulted in a nationwide exploration programme.

Siberia became a priority area for raw material extraction and processing in Stalin's early Five Year Plans and his coercive apparatus provided the labour and money to achieve it. In the Russian Far East, Komsomolsk-na-Amure at the eastern end of the future BAM was selected to be the centre for heavy industry and in the 1930s rapidly grew into eastern Siberia's largest shipbuilding and steel-production centre.

Following the devastation of the Great Patriotic War, reconstruction of western Russia took precedence over building new industries in Siberia. Siberia lay forgotten until Khrushchev awoke to its economic importance in 1956. As a result, he doubled the capital investment under the sixth Five Year Plan. In the seventh Five Year Plan, 10 per cent of the Soviet Union's capital investment was in Siberia with the focus on energy production, raw material extraction and heavy industries.

Over the next 15 years, a quiet debate raged within Russia about the wisdom of investing such large sums in developing Siberia and in the BAM in particular. The anti-Siberians, as they were maliciously called, believed that investing in European Russia was more productive as it was possible to develop existing mineral reserves at less cost, as the existing

---

❏ **What they said**

'Let the crumbling green bosom of Siberia be clad in the cement armour of cities, armed with the stone muzzles of factory chimneys and fettered with the close-fitting hoops of railways. Let the taiga be burnt and chopped down, let the steppes be trampled underfoot. Let all this be, for it is inevitable. It is only on cement and iron that the fraternal union of all peoples, the iron fraternity of all mankind will be built.' – V Zazubrin at the first Siberian Congress of Writers in March 1926, declaring his support for industrialisation and the BAM.

'We are confident that the short but meaningful word 'BAM' will become a symbol of the enthusiastic work, mass heroism, and courage of the youth of the seventies.' – The first Secretary of the Komsomol Central Committee, Evgeny Tyazhelnikov, announcing that the BAM would become a Komsomol Shock Project at the 17th Congress of the Komsomol in April 1974.

infrastructure was already paid for. In addition, wages and infrastructure costs were lower in the relatively milder climate of European Russia than in eastern Siberia. The pro-Siberians believed that the economic advantage of European Russia was short-term, as the area was energy-deficient. In addition, as most extraction projects have a long life, there is a long-term benefit to building processing plants near the source of raw materials and power.

A more subtle argument against the BAM was that its construction would actually be detrimental to the region. The reasoning was that the BAM's massive construction costs would soak up nearly all the investment capital in Siberia and consequently other projects, particularly those outside the BAM Zone, would not be funded. In addition, there would be enormous pressure to start repaying the investment, which would create a mono-culture of cash crops in the region. This imperative would result in underfunded civic services, transient populations and environmental degradation.

One significant factor in convincing Brezhnev to proceed with the BAM was the opportunity it offered for economic blackmail of the West.

The 1973 Arab oil shock combined with the astronomical rise in the price of raw materials in the early 1970s created a worldwide belief that whoever controlled raw material supply could control the industrialised nations. As the Soviet Union contained the world's largest reserves of many raw materials, this belief promised enormous economic and strategic power to the Soviet Union. Two specific events instigated by the Soviet Union proved the correctness of this belief to Brezhnev. Firstly, the Soviets and their agents were engaged in raw material price-rigging schemes in the mid-1970s and some Americans claimed that this was the main cause of the 1974-5 US recession. Secondly, in 1978 and 1979, Soviet and Cuban activities in central and southern Africa contributed to a tenfold increase in the price of cobalt, a doubling of the price of platinum and a similar jump in the price of chromium. In all these cases, the Soviet Union reaped huge profits. Therefore, it was believed that unlock-

---

❏ **Why no-one spoke out against the BAM**

When Gorbachev came to power, he immediately criticised the BAM and this was quickly echoed throughout the government and media. Reports were quickly produced to demonstrate what a waste of money it was. So if everyone knew it was a white elephant, why didn't anyone protest earlier?

The answer is best illustrated by an anecdote told about Khrushchev's speech denouncing Stalin in 1956. During his criticism of Stalin, there were shouts from the audience demanding to know why he didn't raise his voice against Stalin when he was alive. Khrushchev stopped mid-sentence, glared at the audience and shouted, 'Who asked that?' A long silence followed. Quietly he continued, 'That's why'.

ing Siberia's enormous raw material reserves via the BAM would allow the Soviet Union to manipulate the world's markets. Other anticipated benefits of the BAM included opening up a new transport route to carry west Siberian oil and gas to the Pacific Ocean for the lucrative markets of Japan and the USA.

However, the disappointing results of Siberian oil fields and BAM Zone mines, combined with the early 1980's recession which saw the world awash with natural resources, finally destroyed Brezhnev's grand dream of economic power arising from the BAM. Gorbachev was left to pick up the pieces.

## THE BAM BECOMES A 'WHITE ELEPHANT'

Gorbachev inherited a state on the brink of collapse. Years of stagnation, nepotism and gross mismanagement had forced Gorbachev into a corner; either rebuild the Soviet Union or watch it die.

He attempted the former course with his economic policies of *perestroika* (which means restructuring), scrapping of large projects and introducing financial responsibility. Gorbachev championed a new philosophy called 'intensive growth policy' which was similar to the anti-Siberian development position. The new policy involved a more effective use of existing plants and equipment, increased reliance on scientific research and development, modernisation and reduction of waste in industry. The net outcome was a transfer of investment from developing greenfield sites in eastern Siberia to expanding and modernising existing plants in European Russia.

It was obvious that the BAM could not be justified in terms of opening up eastern Siberia, so the Ministry of Railways portrayed the line as a cost-competitive new transport bridge for container traffic from the Pacific Ocean to Europe, which would also reduce traffic on the congested Trans-Siberian line. However, a close analysis of these claims showed them to be false.

Theoretically the BAM route from Sovetskaya Gavan (Pacific Coast) to Taishet (junction of the BAM and the Trans-Siberian) would be attractive for high-value container traffic, as it is 450km shorter than the Trans-Siberian line from Vladivostok to Taishet. However, four problems prevent the BAM from being a viable alternative.

Firstly, the speed of container ships has increased considerably over the last two decades and the time taken for a ship to travel from Japan to Amsterdam is now the same as transport by rail across Russia.

Secondly, the route from Hong Kong, through Urumqi (north-west China), Kazakhstan and Moscow to Europe is shorter than the BAM.

Thirdly, the speed of the BAM is about one-third of the average speed of the Trans-Siberian line.

Fourthly, theft on Russian railways is a major disincentive, so that all Russian railways, including the BAM, are unattractive.

The claim that the BAM will relieve pressure on the Trans-Siberian is equally false. While the BAM will lead to some relief on the Trans-Siberian section from Vladivostok to Irkutsk, the major congestion is on the section from Novosibirsk to Ekaterinburg, which both lines feed into. In addition, double-tracking, electrification and better train control over the last decade on the Vladivostok to Irkutsk section of the Trans-Siberian has resulted in greater traffic flow.

In democratic post-Soviet Russia, the BAM has received even less attention than in Gorbachev's time. This can be attributed partly to the bankruptcy of the Russian government, which cannot further fund the railway's development, the general decline in all sectors of the Russian economy and the small number of voters in the BAM Zone.

## THE UNCERTAIN FUTURE

The BAM's outlook is bleak. The collapse of the Soviet Union buried all economic hopes for the BAM. At least 10 industrial complexes had been planned along the railway, but the financing never arrived. Only one industrial complex in the region, the Neryungri coal mine, is functioning. The Udokan copper deposit, the second biggest in the world, was never developed. Forestry turned out to be more expensive than anticipated. The railway has virtually no passenger traffic and some of the highest freight tariffs in the country. The region's population is declining, rail services have been slashed and government revival plans have amounted to little. In 1998, the BAM transported less than 15 per cent of its potential, which is 10 millions tonnes of cargo annually and lost 1.7 billion roubles.

To develop the region, business people with a long-term view of at least 10 years are needed rather than the current crop of mostly asset-strippers and short-term opportunists. If Russia was a stable, law-based market economy, then investment funds would come and the BAM Zone would become a boom region. However, it is unlikely that Russia will transform itself in the short or medium term so the future of the BAM remains poor. Whether anything will come of the 1999 Russian governments plans to develop the BAM Zone is yet to be seen but given the past failures, the chances do not look good.

## CONSTRUCTION HISTORY (История строительства)

From the mid-1800s, building a railway across Siberia was a popular topic among the powerful in St Petersburg, with the two main route options being either north or south of Lake Baikal. After extensive geological and engineering investigation, the northern route was discounted due to the region's difficult geography and limited agricultural potential. So, in

1886, work started on the now famous Trans-Siberian Railway and by 1916 the route from Moscow to Vladivostok was complete.

Despite the disappointing assessment of the northern route, Russians and foreigners still believed that such a railway line was viable and even inevitable. One of the most famous development proposals was from a French entrepreneur, Loik de Lobel, acting on behalf of US rail companies in 1904. He proposed a Siberian-Alaskan railway starting near north Baikal, through Yakutsk and then across the Bering Straits to Alaska. The construction would be privately funded on the condition that the bankers had a 90-year lease on all land within 25km of the railway. Not surprisingly, the Tsar rejected the proposal in 1904.

Following the 1917 revolution, the desire for massive industrial development in Siberia became a mass movement with railways becoming the symbol of progress and the tool for achieving it. The BAM was an idea whose time had come.

## BAM construction timeline

**1911** The western segment of the BAM from Taishet to Ust-Kut was planned but the First World War thwarted its construction.

**1921** In December, the Congress of Soviets announced the GOELRO plan that proposed a massive programme of nationwide electrification including a railway to the north of Lake Baikal. H G Wells summed up the world's opinion of this ambitious plan when he wrote, 'Can one imagine a more courageous project in a vast flat land of forests and illiterate peasants with no technical skill available, and with trade and industry at the last gasp?'

**1924** The Planning Commission of the Council of Labour and Defence elaborated a long-term plan for the development of the USSR's railways. The plan included a map on which the BAM appeared. A total of 1,000km of the projected route was identical to the present-day route.

**1926** Two engineers, Mazurov and Lvov, surveyed a railway line route between the Amur river and Sovetskaya Gavan.

**1932** On 13 April the Soviet government passed a secret decree to start survey work on the BAM to select the best route. The organisation was based at Svobodny on the Trans-Siberian, which was also the headquarters of the Amur railway. Taishet and Sovetskaya Gavan were selected as end points. An extensive survey began of the Taishet–Ust-Kut–Kirensk–Bodaibo–Tynda route under the direction of the engineer M A Petrov on behalf of the People's Commissariat for Railways.

**1933** Plans for the BAM were announced in the Second Soviet Five Year Plan (1933-1937).

The BAM 'will traverse little investigated regions of eastern Siberia and bring to life an enormous new territory and its colossal riches – amber, gold, coal – and also make possible the cultivation of great tracts of land suitable for agriculture. Two-thirds of the BAM will go through the Far Eastern region, the length of which is 1,800km. The line will be completed in the Third Soviet Five Year Plan'.

The first railway builders began laying track from Oldoi (near Bamovskaya) on the Trans-Siberian line towards Tynda.

**1937** On 17 August, a new organisation, BAMProek, was created which oversaw all the enterprises and government departments working on different aspects of the BAM. BAMProek reviewed all the route plans and discovered that the previous surveys were inadequate except for those between Tynda and Urgal. This prompted a massive purge of BAM geologists, administration staff and engineers. One of the victims was the famous explorer Arsenev whose geologist wife was executed. Many others ended up in the chain of railway construction gulag camps called BAMLag. These camps also had their headquarters at Svobodny.

A single track was completed connecting the Trans-Siberian with Tynda.

**1938** Construction of the Taishet–Bratsk–Ust-Kut line began. This line was a state priority, as it would link up with the massive Bratsk hydroelectric scheme.

**1939** The search for the BAM's optimum route accelerated. Expeditions of surveyors and explorers used 26 aircraft, 133 motor vehicles, 28 tractors and cross-country vehicles, 28 motor boats, 1,500 horses and hundreds of reindeer sleds in their survey work.

**1940** The first grand plan of the entire BAM route was completed. It estimated that 284,800,000 cubic metres of earth works and 618,000 tonnes of metal bridging would be needed.

Work on the Komsomolsk-na-Amure–Sovetskaya Gavan section began.

The first BAM tunnel at Pivan was completed but then abandoned as a new route was chosen.

**1941** Work started on two branch lines connecting the Trans-Siberian with the future BAM, Izvestkovaya–Chegdomyn and Volochaevka 2–Komsomolsk-na-Amure.

Construction stopped on the BAM with the exception of the Komsomolsk-na-Amure–Sovetskaya Gavan line following the Soviet Union's entry into the Second World War.

**1942** The railway lines between Bamovskaya and Tynda, Urgal and the Dusse-Alin tunnel, and Komsomolsk-na-Amure and Postyshevo were relaid between Saratov and Stalingrad during the battle of Stalingrad.

**1945** The final route for the BAM was selected and 200 numbered copies of the secret technical details were published.

The Pivan–Sovetskaya Gavan line was opened.

**1946** Construction of the western BAM sector resumed.

**1947** Track-laying between Taishet and Bratsk (315km) was completed. Japanese POWs completed relaying a freight line from Komsomolsk-na-Amure to Postyshevo.

**1949** The massive Udokan copper deposits were found halfway between Tynda and Severobaikalsk.

**1950** Work commenced on a new 500km line from near Komsomolsk-na-Amure to Sakhalin Island. This included a 9km undersea tunnel linking the Russian mainland to the island of Sakhalin.

The Taishet–Ust-Kut section of the line was opened. As the incomplete Bratsk dam wall would eventually be the bridge across the massive Angara river, rails were laid across the ice as a short-term measure.

**1953** Following Stalin's death, all work on the BAM was abandoned.

**1958** The construction of the Bamovskaya–Chulman railway (which would reach the massive Neryungri coal deposit) was proposed at a conference on industrial development of eastern Siberia, organised by the USSR Academy of Sciences.

**1960** Interest in the BAM was rekindled with the USSR Council of Ministers ordering specialists and researchers to draw up technical and economic plans for industrial exploration of the Udokan copper deposits. The reports indicated that the deposit was worth developing.

**1961** The Leningrad Institute of Transport supported restarting the construction of the BAM along the 1945 route from Ust-Kut to Tynda through Nizhneangarsk, Taksimo, Chara and Ust-Nyukzha, with a branch line to the Udokan copper deposit. The Institute of Industrial Construction threw its weight behind the proposal with the only change being an alteration to the route on a small section between Vitim and Larba, which took into account the district's developing economy and recent surveys.

**1967** A new construction plan for the BAM was released by the Moscow Transport Institute, which was then responsible, for the BAM's overall planning. The guidelines envisaged the building of a single-track railway carrying diesel locomotives with provision for subsequent building of a second track and electrification of the railway.

**1970** Plans for the difficult Kunerma–Nizhneangarsk section were completed. This included replacing three short tunnels with a single 6,698m tunnel in the Baikal mountains.

**1972** Re-laying of the Bamovskaya–Tynda route started a few kilometres west of the original 1937 line. The railway bed of the rebuilt line was 1m wider than old line and the grade was reduced to 14m per kilometre. The new line was 5km longer than the pre-war one. To build the 180km line, 200 bridges had to be constructed, seven million cubic metres of soil removed and 2,000 hectares of rail cuttings made.

**1974** On 4 January, work started on the western end of the BAM. On 9 January, the abandoned village of Polovinka, 20km east of Ust-Kut, was selected as the starting point for the winter road to the first BAM town of Zvezdnaya. Rail workers started building the BAM from here even though the line from Ust-Kut had yet to arrive. This started the pattern of leap-frog construction that was so important to building the line on schedule.

On 15 March, the General Secretary of the Communist Party, Leonid
Brezhnev, gave a speech in Alma-Ata stating that the BAM would become
a huge Komsomol construction project. The BAM's master plan was
released calling for its completion in 1982 with high-speed services operating in 1983.

In April, the 17th Congress of the Komsomol in Moscow rubber-
stamped Brezhnev's request and on 2 May the first detachment of
Komsomol workers arrived in Ust-Kut, direct from the 17th Congress of
the Komsomol, to an enormous reception.

On 25 July, the first big shipment of equipment was sent from Ust-Kut
to Magistralny by river barge in an effort to build a large bridge there
before the railway line arrived from Ust-Kut. The shipment included an
80-tonne power station and a large number of prefabricated houses, and it
had to navigate 600km of rivers while the distance was only 170km in a
straight line.

On 10 September, the first issue of the *Baikal-Amur Railway
Construction Worker* newspaper came off the press.

On 6 October, at 11.27 local time, the railway crane operator Ivan
Zhunin laid the first rail section on the new rail bed at Ust-Kut.

**1975** On 18 March, the three newspapers, *Eastern Siberia*, *Trans-Baikal*
and *Soviet Far Eastern* all printed a BAM commemorative issue as part of
a media strategy to raise interest in the BAM.

On 8 May, the Bamovskaya–Tynda line was completed.

**1977** The final design for the BAM was approved. It is interesting to note
that construction was already in full swing by then.

**1978** Brezhnev toured eastern Siberia and the Russian Far East with the
BAM being the focus of all his speeches.

The Soviet government now acknowledged that the 1974 construction
targets were too optimistic.

**1982** The government media organisation, TASS, released figures that
showed the BAM was between 70 and 80 per cent completed. However,
these figures included the Izvestkovaya–Urgal branch line which was finished decades before.

**1983** Achievements to date included constructing 126 large bridges across
rivers and gorges, 3,335 railway structures, and 200 stations and sidings.

**1984** On 29 April, the eastern section of the BAM was joined at the siding called Miroshnichenko.

On 24 September 1984, the golden spike connecting the eastern and western sections of the BAM was hammered into place at Balbukhta, near Kuanda.
No foreign media were invited to attend this historic event, as the Soviets did
not want questions asked about the line's operational status. In reality, only
one-third of the BAM's 3,115km of track was fully operational. Of the remaining, some 1,500km was suitable for partial service and 500km for work trains
only. Only one of the BAM's tunnels was fully operational.

**1985** The most difficult construction year. Following the completion of the relatively simply track-laying, workers were released for tunnelling, bridge laying and construction of railway infrastructure. However, this work required different skills so a mass retraining programme took place. Targets would not be met for two years.

**1986** Construction targets were still a major problem. Railway troops achieved their goals in the eastern section of the BAM, while members of the Komsomol accomplished only half to three-quarters of their plans on the western end.

In July, Gorbachev toured the Russian Far East and only mentioned the BAM twice in his Vladivostok speech. This signalled the end of official interest in the BAM.

In August, the director of the BAM, V Gorbunov, complained that money was so tight that only the most important construction projects would proceed. The BAM was only given 150 million roubles ($180 million) for the AYaM railway when it was estimated that it would need two billion roubles ($2.4 billion) to complete it.

**1988** In September, Gorbachev gave his famous Krasnoyarsk speech and didn't mention the BAM at all. The USSR Academy of Sciences' Scientific Council on BAM Problems was disbanded. Both events reflected the official view that the BAM was unimportant to Siberia's future.

Gorbachev described the BAM as the greatest monument to the period of stagnation (период застоя) and an example of Brezhnev's personal economic adventurism (авантюризм). Soviet journalists slavishly followed this with many stories about the line's pointlessness.

**1989** During the period from November 1989 to March 1990, the BAM became operational along its entire length.

**1990** Locals discussed creating a BAM Republic due to Moscow's lack of support for the region. The Ministry of Railway discussed cutting up the BAM and giving it to other regional railways. However, these railways rejected the offer, as they did not want to be lumbered with a loss-making operation.

**1991** On 18 April during his speech in Japan, Gorbachev highlighted the opportunities for Japanese firms to expand the ports of Vanino at the eastern end of the BAM and to modernise the Russian Far East's roads and railways, including the BAM.

**1993** The Berkakit–Aldan section opened for freight traffic.

**1994** The construction management of the AYaM railway was transferred from Moscow to the Republic of Sakha (Yakutiya).

The Ministry of Railways announced the need for massive reductions in the number of railway workers.

Several large price rises in freight and passenger tariffs decreased the operating losses on the BAM.

**1995**  The BAM got into dire financial straits. To stem mounting losses, the number of rail services was cut and the BAM's non-core assets, such as shops, clubs, schools, hospitals, apartments, boilers and water pumps, were hurriedly transferred to local authorities.

As a means of increasing interest in the region, the Ministry of Railways initiated an investment fund, BAMInvest. Organisations paid 100 million roubles ($20,000) to join which gave them access to information on developments in the region while membership fees for individuals were one million roubles ($200).

**1996**  The BAM gained the unenviable title of the least profitable of Russia's 19 railways, due to high operational costs and low freight volumes.

The BAM Railway Division (covering the line from Lena to Komsomolsk-na-Amure) was dissolved, with the western section of the railway transferred to the East-Siberian Railway and the eastern section to the Far East Railway Divisions.

**1997**  The Russian government announced a plan to encourage the economic development of areas adjacent to the BAM railway.

On August 15, the first train broke through the symbolic ribbon at Tommot, opening the Tommot–Berkakit section of the AYaM railway.

In December, the people digging the service tunnel from each end of the Severomuisk Tunnel met. Only 349m of the main tunnel remain to be dug.

**1998**  Work started on a 70-km railway line from Novaya Chara to the Chineyskiy ore deposit, which contains some of the world's richest vanadium ores, plus iron and titanium.

**1999**  As part of the reconstruction of the BAM Zone, state contractors have produced a list of their investment priorities in the region.

**2000**    Passenger service on the BAM up. Construction continues on the AYaM between the Aldan and Amga rivers.

**2001**    Severomuisk Tunnel bore-through completed.

## WHO REALLY BUILT THE BAM? (Кто действительно построил БАМ?)

The Soviet-era propaganda portrays the BAM builders as young communists devoted to building the country and socialism. However, the reality was that communists made up only a small proportion of the builders. The majority were Stalin-era slave labourers, German and Japanese prisoners of war, workers attracted by incentives, and railway troops.

### The original BAM builders: Gulag prisoners and POWs

During the 1930s and 1940s, the word BAM struck fear into the hearts of Russians. Rather than being the great heroic undertaking of Brezhnev's time, working on the BAM in Stalin's-era was synonymous with a Siberian death sentence.

The numerous labour camps along the BAM route were known collectively as BAM Corrective Labour Camps or BAMLag. Despite its

## ❑ Camp food

All prisoners received the same rations, which meant that physically large inmates invariably died first. There were normally five levels of camp rations, called *cauldrons*.

**First cauldron**: Thin soup twice a day and 300g of bread. This was for those who failed to achieve the daily work target and day labourers within the camp.

**Second cauldron**: Thin soup twice a day, 700g of bread and buckwheat in the evening. This was for those who had achieved the daily work target and office workers.

**Third cauldron**: Soup twice a day, 900g of bread, buckwheat and a small piece of meat or fish in the evenings. This was for those achieving 15 to 25 per cent above the norm.

**Fourth cauldron**: 750g of bread, and a meal twice a day containing some meat or fats. This was for privileged clerical workers.

**Fifth cauldron**: A meal three times a day which contained fats and 700g of bread. This was for hospitalised inmates.

The daily routine started with the first meal between 4 and 6am and ended with the evening meal between 5 and 7pm. The prisoners' brigade leaders had the prisoners' lives in their hands as they filled in the work certifications which determined the food rations. If the brigade produced above the norm, they were entitled to extra rations. However, the rations were inadequate to compensate for the extra energy expended so the brigade was unlikely to get extra rations for long. Conversely, if the brigade produced less than the norm, their rations were reduced. Falling below 30 per cent of the norm generally resulted in each brigade member being treated as refusing to work which meant *first cauldron* food rations and if the poor performance continued, they went to the isolator (solitary confinement). If a prisoner actually refused to work, he was referred to court and the usual sentence was a firing squad.

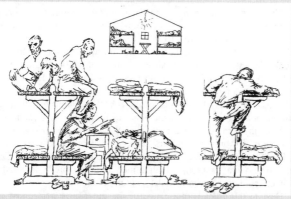

The interior of a prisoners' barracks. Picture reproduced with permission from *The Gulag Handbook* by Jacques Rossi, Overseas Publications Interchange Ltd, London, 1987.

inmate population of 400,000 prisoners between 1932 and 1941, BAMLag was just a small cog in Stalin's giant network of labour camps. Until the Russian archives were opened in 1992, it was believed that between five and 30 million Soviet citizens were imprisoned in Russian gulags between 1934 and 1953. While the truth is closer to five million, this does not diminish the enormous suffering and misery caused by the years of Stalin's brutal repression.

BAMLag was created in 1937 by amalgamating a number of eastern Siberian gulag complexes with the express aim of guaranteeing a continuous supply of labour for the BAM. Its headquarters were at Svobodny on the Trans-Siberian line, which was also the head of BAMProek, the BAM project-planning enterprise. BAMLag rapidly grew into dozens of camps. It was incorporated into the nationwide Railway Collective Labour Camps Administration or GULZhDS on 4 January 1940 following a purge of the BAMLag management due to perceived poor performance.

Prior to the Great Patriotic War, prisoners of the BAMLag built the western end of the BAM from Taishet to Bratsk, the eastern end of the BAM from Komsomolsk-na-Amure to Postyshevo, and the branch lines between Bamovskaya and Tynda and between Izvestkovaya and Urgal. The war stopped further track-laying except for the Komsomolsk-na-Amure–Sovetskaya Gavan line, which was built by Japanese and German POWs and Soviet prisoners. After the war, both Russian gulag prisoners and the POWs resumed work on several lines and started new ones such as the tunnel under the straits between the mainland and Sakhalin Island. In 1953 when Stalin died, work on the BAM again stopped and the gulags were disbanded with most of the prisoners being released.

The death toll of Japanese and German POWs before they were repatriated home in the late 1940s and mid-1950s was enormous. For example, only 10 per cent of the 100,000 German POWs who worked on the western end of the BAM in the Ozerlag camp complex, located to the west of Lake Baikal, survived to repatriation. In total, 46,082 Japanese POWs died in the Soviet Union, with most in the Russian Far East and many while working on the BAM.

Today, virtually all evidence of the BAMLag camps has disappeared with the notable exception of the chain of tunnel building camps on the shores of the remote Tatar Straits, near Sakhalin Island. However, there are several well-preserved non-railway gulag camps within easy reach of the BAM that are certainly worth visiting. The best is the Marble Canyon camp near Chara station, which mined uranium ore, and another is Akukan camp near Severobaikalsk, which mined mica.

Despite the crucial importance of the gulag prisoners, most of the region's museums unfortunately carry only fragmentary mention of them. This will change as the self-censoring of the past gives way to the truth.

## Young communists flock to the BAM

Following the 17th Congress of the Komsomol in 1974, which rubber-stamped Brezhnev's request that the BAM become a Komsomol Shock Project, the public face of the BAM became the self-sacrificing young communist. Being a Shock Project, the BAM was elevated to a national priority, which meant that it was given precedence over other projects in terms of equipment, materials and staff.

The Komsomol was given the responsibility of attracting workers and it did this by a nationwide appeal for volunteers through its thousands of offices, its newspapers and its TV programmes. In the early years, they had no trouble attracting workers; the Khabarovsk Region Komsomol was given the responsibility of surveying the Urgal to Komsomolsk-na-Amure route and over 200 surveyors applied for the 50 positions.

Most volunteers probably believed in the ideals of communism and considered it an honour to work on the BAM. A few may have been attracted to working in the 'romantic' great Siberian wilderness, but the vast majority would have been pragmatic enough to view working on the BAM as a wise career move. Rapid promotion was common on Shock Projects and it was possible to become a foreman at just 26. This experience gave the workers an enormous head start when they returned to normal life, particularly

The emblem of the Komosomol
(Communist Youth League)

if they sought a career in the Communist Party. Examples were Victor Lakomov and Tatyana Vasina, both of whom arrived in the first detachment direct from the 17th Congress of the Komsomol in 1974 and later became deputies in the Supreme Soviet of the Russian Federation.

An important source of labour was the two million students who graduated each year. In order to receive their degree and to repay the State for the cost of education, the students were given a three-year assignment by the Komsomol. Many served their indenture on the BAM even though the mostly manual work was a waste of their skills.

## Free workers attracted by incentives

The majority of workers didn't have the idealism of the Komsomol volunteers but were attracted by incentives. When the idea of incentives was proposed in the late 1970s it became a hotly debated subject in ideological circles as it contradicted basic socialist tenets. The crux of the matter was identified in *Soviet Sociology* in Spring, 1983. 'Obviously, the primary emphasis on offering people the privilege of receiving scarce goods as a way of attracting a work force to the BAM region cannot be considered an adequate method ... It stimulates consumerist attitudes among young people, paving the way for various kinds of speculation and intrigue, and damage is done to the patriotic spirit which should prevail on an urgent construction project.'

Despite these ideological arguments, pragmatism and the realisation that 'no incentives would result in no workers' won out.

The Logo of GlavBAMstroi, the main civilian organisation responsible for building the BAM

One of the first incentives offered was that when workers moved to the BAM, the flats they left behind were not reallocated to someone else.

This was comforting to know as being allocated a flat in the first place could take up to 10 years. If the worker did not have a flat to leave behind, by working on the BAM they would jump the accommodation queue when they returned to normal life.

Jumping the car queue was another major incentive, but problems caused by this scheme nearly resulted in the first BAM strike. In the late 1980s, workers on the BAM and other northern projects were offered a queue-jumping scheme in order to buy a new car. To be eligible, you had to work in the north or BAM for three years. This enabled you to open a car account and after putting money into it for three more years, you could buy a car voucher. You then took the voucher to a government vehicle-supply organisation and swapped it for a car. As well as retaining workers, the scheme built up massive bank reserves and reduced demand for goods already in short supply.

The scheme was a great idea until workers started to redeem their vouchers. The collapse of the Soviet Union's, and then Russia's, economy sharply reduced the supply of cars and increased their price. The government hoped that the price would stabilise and postponed the 1991 distribution of cars for vouchers until 1992. But in January 1992, the price increased again. When the automobile sellers suggested that the holders of vouchers pay the difference between the old and new prices, the northern workers responded with a hunger strike in the city administration building in Yakutsk and a campaign of bombarding government officials at all levels with telephone calls and telegrams. President Yeltsin attempted to redeem the vouchers by an emergency increase in the Yakutian government's sales of diamonds. But the price of cars went up again in April 1992, stopping all redemptions. This time the government did not do anything and the workers responded with plans for strikes, blocking the BAM and even seceding from the Russian Federation. However, this was at a time when the whole nation was undergoing massive turmoil – the protest plans were soon forgotten because everyone had more pressing things to worry about. Today, most of the long-term workers on the BAM still hold the vouchers hoping for redemption even though they know deep down that it will never happen.

The most attractive incentive for working on the BAM was the hardship bonuses, which boosted wages to over three times the Soviet average. These bonuses, which multiplied the standard Russian wage, included a regional wage allowance of 1.7 for working on the BAM, an additional 1.5 for working in the harsh northern region and another 1.4 to compensate for continual relocation.

BAM workers got the normal 24 days' holiday plus 12 more for working on the BAM and an additional 12 for working in the northern regions. People in hazardous occupations, such as tunnelling and demolitions, received a further six extra days. In addition, workers were given free return rail

The corps badge of the railway troops

tickets to their choice of destination in the Soviet Union every year and free plane tickets every third year. Furthermore, they were given considerable discounts at holiday resorts for themselves and at Pioneer camps for their children.

## Railroad troops

The role of the military in building the BAM has been virtually ignored in Soviet history. This is despite the fact that they were responsible for the whole eastern BAM section from Komsomolsk-na-Amure to Tynda where they laid over 1,459km of track and built over 32km of bridges.

The full name of the railway troops is Railway Forces for the Construction and Maintenance of Railways (Железнодорожные Войска по Строительству и Восстановлению).

They wear the standard Russian military uniform with the addition of their own corps badges and are headed by a General Colonel. Until the early 1990s, they were a part of the Ministry of Defence, but nowadays they are under the control of the Ministry of Transport Construction. This ministry is responsible for the construction of all new railways and roads in Russia.

In theory their mission is to manage, build and maintain the railway in the event of war. In reality, they are the Ministry of Transport Construction's main contractor, doing 25 per cent of its heavy work such as excavating and ballasting. From the ministry's viewpoint, railway troops have two attractions. Firstly, being a military unit, they can be ordered to work anywhere. Secondly, as railway troops' work is considered training, they are paid much less than equivalent civilian workers.

In many ways, they have replaced the forced labourers since Stalin's gulags were closed.

Railway troops have a long history in Russia, first being established in 1851 under the Tsar. They played an important part in ensuring troops and supplies reached the war fronts in both the Russian Civil War and the Great Patriotic War. Railway troops are classified as rear echelon forces and have their own academies and training schools. To become an officer, students must complete four years at St Petersburg's Higher Command School of Rail Troops and Military Communication.

After graduating and serving for two years as a Lieutenant, you are promoted to Senior Lieutenant. After three more years, you are eligible to become a Captain, then four more years to be a Major with another four to become a Colonel. After five further years of service, you are eligible to study at the Academy of Rear Services and Transport which is essential to climbing the promotional ladder.

As in other corps, soldiers and officers in the railway troops are not allowed to go abroad for five years after leaving military service. This is a Cold War security measure that is meaningless considering the work railway troops undertake.

## Who were the best BAM builders?

Both the railway troops and the civilian constructors regard their work as superior and, years after the completion of the BAM, argument still rages about who best completed the work on time, on budget and on specifications. This argument has become more heated in the mid-1990s as both groups compete for a dwindling amount of government construction work.

Ironically, from anecdotal evidence, it appears that the gulag prisoners and POWs in the 1930s to 1950s built the most durable sections.

## THE ENGINEERING CHALLENGE (Почему БАМ было трудно построить)

### Russia's largest-ever construction project

Constructing the BAM and the BAM Zone was the largest civil engineering project ever undertaken by the Soviet Union and probably by any country in the world. It devoured the same gigantic amount of resources as were used to conquer space in the 1950s and 1960s.

The Soviet Union is probably the only country in the world that could have undertaken such a massive project as only a single-party superpower coupled with a command economy could have marshalled the necessary political will, labour, finances and technical skill.

In the 1970s, probably 20,000 people lived in the BAM Zone with another 300,000 people at the east and west ends around Komsomolsk-na-Amure and Ust-Kut respectively. Today over one million live in the area in the Zone's three new cities and 100 settlements.

---

❏ **BAM and BAM Zone construction facts**
These figures apply to the railway from Ust-Kut to Komsomolsk-na-Amure.

| | |
|---|---|
| Length of the BAM | 3097.6km |
| Length of sidings, yards and passing loops | 445km |
| Number of urban settlements built in the BAM Zone | 100 |
| Number of cities built in the BAM Zone | 3 |
| Number of BAM workers excluding the military in 1981 | 40,000 |
| Number of BAM workers excluding the military in 1988 | 60,000 |
| Percentage of workers aged under 30 in 1984 | 75% |

**Embankments**

| | |
|---|---|
| Total length of embankments | 2,446.9km |
| Embankments higher than 12m | 59.9km |
| Embankments on swamps and marshes | 640 |

**Excavations**

| | |
|---|---|
| Excavations greater than 12m | 112.2km |
| Excavations in permafrost | 196km |
| Excavations at an angle greater than 1:3 | 122km |

**Bridges**

| | |
|---|---|
| Number of small bridges | 844 |
| Length of small bridges | 17.7km |
| Number of medium bridges | 638 |
| Length of medium bridges | 31.3km |
| Number of large bridges | 113 |
| Length of large bridges | 22.8km |

**Tunnels**

| | |
|---|---|
| Number of tunnels | 5 |
| Total length of tunnels | 31.7km |
| Number of railway structures (excluding bridges) built | 2,600 |
| Amount of earth moved | 570 million cubic metres |

---

The BAM was a national effort and every republic sent construction units to the BAM. Over 60 of the nation's hundred plus nationalities worked on the line. In addition, 14 of the 15 Republics and 30 Oblast governments sponsored individual BAM towns, and built and paid for 500,000 square metres of housing, 18 kindergartens, 12 medical facilities and four banyas between September 1974 and October 1984.

## How much did the BAM cost?

Don't believe any answers given to this question. While most books give the cost as $11 billion dollars, in reality this and any other answers are meaningless.

The fundamental problem is that in a command economy, the value of money does not represent what it represents in a market economy. In a command economy, Moscow tells its factories how much to produce of each good and how much money they will receive as a result. The money exchanged is simply a bookkeeping exercise and the prices do not reflect the true cost of production. In a market economy, prices and quantity produced are determined by the market.

This means that while the official cost of the BAM was about nine billion roubles (in 1984), it is meaningless to apply any exchange rate to determine its cost in US dollars. If this was not the case, then it would be reasonable to assume that the line could be built for $11 billion dollars (which equals nine billion roubles at the 1984 exchange rate). However, the author estimates the cost of building the BAM's infrastructure using Western construction companies was $30 billion in 1984 dollars.

A second problem is the veracity of the Soviet cost figures. In 1984, the cost was stated to be nine billion roubles, which is suspiciously close to the 1977 Soviet estimates of 8.4 to 9.5 billion roubles. By 1989, the total spent on the BAM and its related lines had officially increased to 10.7 billion roubles. However, it is unclear whether these figures include all the related lines, the work of the railway troops and the cost of the rolling stock.

## Numbers always win in Soviet construction

Inadequate planning, massive errors and poor workmanship are all charges levelled at virtually every large Soviet-era construction project, including the BAM. While many of the criticisms were justified, they must be balanced against the fact that invariably the problems only slowed but never stopped the ambitious projects.

Unlike the West, it was not money that guaranteed success in the Soviet Union but rather political will. If a problem occurred, then more labour and resources were simply channelled into overcoming it.

The BAM provides an unique insight into the problems of large-scale Soviet construction projects, as it was being completed just as the Soviet media started to take advantage of Gorbachev's policy of *glasnost* (openness) and to report on the previously unreportable.

## Planning problems

Poor planning was evident from the start. Following the announcement that the BAM would be built, an article in the *Izvestiya* newspaper of May 1974 highlighted that no-one knew what the project would involve, let along how much it would cost. 'At this point, it is difficult to say with precision how many stations, settlements, and cities will spring up on both sides of the BAM.' It was only in 1977 when construction was in full swing that the plan of the final route, rail infrastructure programme, and budgets were completed. The BAM planners were aware that problems would inevitably occur, so they set aside 10 per cent of the total budget for unforeseen work and another 15 per cent for rebuilding badly built and temporary structures.

While these amounts may seem high, they are understandable considering the sheer enormity and complexity of the BAM's construction.

The terrain's variety and inaccessibility were two of the major impediments facing the planners. As the route passed through 640km of marshes, 120km of landslide-susceptible terrain and along 1,330km of permafrost and semi-permafrost, re-routing was a common occurrence. The type of terrain affected the rate of track-laying. In 1975 and 1976, track-laying averaged 1.5km a day at the western end of the BAM but by 1979 it had decreased to between 0.2 and 0.3km a day as the difficulty of the terrain increased and lack of experience showed. As more experience was gained, this increased to 0.4-0.5km a day by the early 1980s.

The quantity and quality of the supplied equipment was also outside the control of the planners. Between 1975 and 1977, 13,000 heavy-duty trucks, 1,100 excavators, 2,000 bulldozers and 1,200 mobile cranes were supplied to the BAM. While this may sound an enormous number, most equipment lasted only one season before it became uneconomic to repair. Even the cost of maintaining a vehicle during its one year of operation was enormous. For example, the yearly maintenance cost of a bulldozer was about 12,000 roubles, which was almost twice its cost price. The principal reason for the high attrition rate was that the equipment was underpowered. In normal operation, 100hp bulldozers are required for earth moving and 250hp for work in permafrost. However, most of the BAM's bulldozers were converted Kirovets agricultural tractors of 55-75hp.

Similar supply problems occurred for track-laying materials. Sleeper supply was a common bottleneck, which reached a peak in 1981 when all the sleeper factories supplying the BAM failed to meet their production quotas. Consequently by the end of the year the constructors were 130,000 sleepers short. As 2,000 are needed for each kilometre of track, this meant that an extra 65km of track could have been laid but wasn't.

Another variable outside the planners' control was the weather and its effect on work rates and equipment. When the temperature dropped below -45°C without wind or -35°C with wind, workers legally downed tools. However, bulldozers seized up and axes shattered before these temperatures were reached, so workers would have to stop earlier than planned.

One problem that can be blamed on the planners was their inability to anticipate the skill shortage following the completion of the relatively simple track-laying in 1984. This released large numbers of workers for station and rail facilities construction but they didn't have the skills to do this work. Consequently a massive crash-training programme was instigated but it took two years before projects were back on target.

## Permafrost: The bane of constructors

The biggest geological difficulty faced by the constructors was building on the permanently frozen ground, permafrost. The BAM passes through about 330km of permafrost and about 1,000km of thawed ground dotted with islands of permafrost. The deepest permafrost on the BAM is 600m deep at Udokan near Chara.

The difficulty of constructing on permafrost is that if the insulating surface of moss and grasses is broken or if the ground is compressed, the ice in the soil melts. As frozen water occupies a greater volume than liquid water, the thawed soil subsides. The average depth of subsidence following construction is 90cm but up to 2m has been recorded. It normally takes two years for the ground to settle following construction on permafrost. Another option is not to disturb the permafrost by constructing buildings on insulated stilts which leave an air gap between the building and the ground as well as transferring the building's weight to the bedrock rather than the permafrost. This solution is expensive, as the cost of constructing permafrost tolerant infrastructure is 2½ times that of buildings built on solid ground.

Despite knowledge gained from years of experience building the permafrost cities of Norilsk, Yakutsk and Vorkuta in the 1940s, all the construction lessons were forgotten when the BAM was built in the 1970s. In one media report in the early 1980s, it was stated that at seven major BAM stations there were over 70 completed structures, such as buildings, sid-

Chuna station on the western BAM, was built in the 1940s. (Photo © Nicholas Zvegintzov).

ings and signal systems, which had sagged, collapsed, or were otherwise unusable because of design ill-suited to permafrost conditions.

The earliest towns suffered the most and particularly bad were the those of Belenkaya, Anosovskaya, Tynda and Khani. However, the worst example of poor permafrost engineering practice was Mogot on the AYaM railway. It was built in the late 1970s and by spring 1981 the town's heating and water mains had broken, its sewage system had failed and its sidewalks collapsed. Several buildings were condemned, including the midwife's station, the administration building and the railway terminal. The basic problem was that most of the buildings' insulated foundation piles were sunk only 2m rather than until they hit bedrock.

Laying rail lines on permafrost poses several problems. Firstly, while it takes two years for disturbed permafrost to settle, the track-layers do not have the luxury of waiting this long. Consequently, it is essential that engineers accurately estimate the subsidence and compensate by building an embankment this much higher. Secondly, as the BAM passes through many geologically-different regions of permafrost and semi-thawed ground, the most appropriate engineering approach must be used for each. The most common approaches were either to remove the permafrost or to build on it. The first method is only suitable in areas of scattered permafrost and involves refilling the excavated hole with rock and ballast. The second, more common method involves building an insulated embankment on the permafrost made of large rocks and boulders at the bottom with ballast at the top.

However, the shortage of building materials and time pressures often resulted in these principles being only partly complied with. The result was that track often had to be re-laid after the ground beneath it subsided. Typical of this problem was one report that stated that 10 million roubles a year was being spent in the early 1980s just relaying sagging rail foundations west of Tynda. The best-documented track problem case was the Little BAM connecting the Trans-Siberian with the BAM, which involved both permafrost and poor-quality materials problems. Originally the line was laid with low-quality rails on a mixed sand-gravel ballast. This resulted in the 187km trip taking eight hours and, during four months in 1987, line subsidence and ballast washouts caused three train wrecks. Since 1988, the line has been rebuilt with 1.5 million cubic metres of earthworks and the rails have been replaced with heavy-duty rails, but still the train crawls along at 46km/h.

## Tunnels on the BAM

Tunnels have been the bane of the BAM and even today, after 20 years of work and billions of roubles spent, not all the tunnels have been completed. The last tunnel, the Severomuisk tunnel, will not be finished until early in the 21st century.

The cost of the tunnels accounted for an astronomical one-third of the BAM's total construction budget. This was because the tunnels go through complex geological areas, including permafrost, multiple fault lines and underground waterways. A number of new tunnelling techniques had to be developed which further slowed construction.

Work on the tunnels started well before the rail line arrived as it was planned that the tunnels would be completed just as the rails arrived. However, due to faster than expected rail-laying and slower than expected tunnelling, temporary above-ground bypasses were built for most tunnels. The only tunnel that was finished before the rails arrived was the Dusse-Alin Tunnel, which was completed in 1950 but did not see its first train until 1982.

In retrospect, several of the tunnels should never have been built as a more cost effective route could have been found had more time been spent on survey work. However, this does not diminish the heroic achievements of the tunnellers. A number of tunnellers died during construction but the Russian authorities have never stated how many.

Although some Western experts claim that up to several hundred have died in mishaps, it seems that less than 20 lost their lives in the tunnels west of Tynda. While there are monuments to the tunnellers at each of the tunnels, there is only one memorial to those who died, which is at the Mysoviye tunnels.

There are six tunnels on the BAM, with four to the west and two to the east of Tynda. They are the:

● 15.7km Severomuisk Tunnel which is also known as the North Muya Tunnel (Северомуйский тоннель)
● 5km Mysoviye Tunnel which is made up of four tunnels. The tunnel is also known as the Cape Tunnel (Мысовые тоннели)
● 6.7km Baikal Mountain Tunnel (Байкальский тоннель)
● 1.94km Kodar Tunnel (Кодарский тоннель)
● 2km Dusse-Alin Tunnel (Дуссе-Алинский тоннель)
● 300m Kuznetsovski Tunnel (Кузнецовский тоннель).

Details of each tunnel are included in the route sections.

### THE COLD WAR AND THE BAM (Холодная война и БАМ)

#### Western intelligence agencies target the BAM

From the Soviet Union's earliest days, a veil of secrecy cloaked the country. Typical of the silence was the lack of Soviet press coverage of the BAM from the mid-1930s to the early 1970s. During this time, only one announcement was made and that was in 1938 when it was stated that the BAM would be built during the Soviet 1938 to 1942 Five Year Plan.

To justify such a massive undertaking, the West knew that there must be enormous resources in the region and that the BAM was militarily significant. Before the Second World War, both German and Japanese military intelligence sought information on this railway, but its remote location made gathering first-hand information difficult. Getting access to the region was made even harder as it was a closed region due to its gulag camps.

## Western intelligence efforts

Unlike the images portrayed in spy movies and novels, the vast majority of intelligence information is gathered from innocuous sources such as radio, newspapers and general conversations. Often the subject matter is unrelated but important information can be inferred. For example, in 1941 the Soviet newspaper, *Pravda*, reported that chickens were air-freighted from Irkutsk to Bodaibo. At the time, the BAM was thought to go through Bodaibo before joining Tynda so this revealed that the line to Bodaibo was a long way from being completed. Another clue was the report in *Pravda* on 2 November 1942 that the people of Yakutsk donated presents for the soldiers at the front and these were despatched by train from Irkutsk. This implied that they were flown from Yakutsk to Irkutsk, which meant that there was no close railway line, otherwise the presents would have been rail-freighted along the BAM.

## Soviet counter-intelligence efforts

The secret to destroying the intelligence value of everyday information is to plant misinformation which makes the intelligence assessor unsure of what is correct. The incorrect information on the BAM that prevailed for 40 years can partly be attributed to a clever Soviet misinformation campaign and partly due to Western intelligence services beating up the story to justify a bigger defence budget.

One of the first widely published inaccuracies was aired in the 1943 book by Emil Lengyel, *Siberia*. 'An American traveller in Siberia brought back the story in 1941 of the building of another railway line in the Soviet Far East. He did not see it himself, only heard about it from a young Communist. This line was to have its southern terminus at Komsomolsk-na-Amure and from there run along the Okhotsk Sea, eventually reaching Kamchatka peninsula and the Bering Sea. The building of the railway would be a formidable enterprise on what is probably one of the worst terrains on this globe. It is difficult to see how the Soviets could complete it on short notice, and it is even more difficult to see how they could overcome the obstacles placed in man's way by nature.'

An article in the *New York Times*, 'Soviet Completes Far East Rail Link', 11 August 1950, is indicative of the misinformation at the time. It quoted a Russian geologist liberated from a European displaced persons camp as reporting that the line was complete. In fact only about 30 per cent was completed and several sections were abandoned until the project was restarted in the 1970s. To put this article in perspective, it must be remembered that it was written leading up to the McCarthy-era of communist witch-hunts. On the same page of the paper were two other articles notable for communist paranoia.

One entitled 'Reds Say Cake-Bake Song Proves We Are Starving' claims that the American singer, Jack Smith, stated that the communists were using his song lyrics to prove that the masses were starving under capitalism. 'Mr. Smith said a former Berlin cabaret manager had told him that the words to 'If I knew you were coming, I'd have baked a cake' were being used to show that rationing existed in the United States.'

The other article concerns the arrest of Rose Lightcap, the wife of a reporter for the *Daily Worker*, a US communist paper. She was charged with being a member of an organisation which 'writes, circulates, distributes, prints and publishes and displays written and printed matter advising and teaching the overthrow by force and violence of the government of the United States, to wit, the International Workers Order'.

## Cold War paranoia lingers on

Despite the collapse of the repressive Soviet Union and the passing of Russian decrees allowing freedom of movement for foreigners, cold war paranoia still lingers.

The most obvious form of this paranoia is inaccurate maps that contain imaginary streets, don't show existing towns and move landmarks hundreds of metres.

The logic behind the misleading maps was that in a time of war, captured maps would be of little use to the invading army. However, this ignored the fact that space satellites could produce far more accurate maps than the Soviets ever printed. So the only confusion the maps created was for the Russians who used them.

Nowadays the larger cities have accurate maps, but in the smaller cities, such as those on the BAM, you still have to rely on inaccurate Soviet-era maps. For the traveller, it is important to be aware that any Russian map you buy may be inaccurate.

Another cold war legacy is the reaction of the military to taking photos of railway stations, bridges and tunnels. In the past this was strictly forbidden and even stated on visa applications. Although it has now been deleted on the forms, many officials are not aware that photographing railway infrastructure is no longer stealing a state secret. This problem is more pronounced off the beaten track, such as on the BAM, so the best policy is discretion when taking photos.

In the preparation of this book, the author was interviewed by the former KGB when he was spotted photographing the Vitim River bridge on the BAM and in another incident he was detained by an armed guard for taking photos around Khabarovsk's station. If this happens to you, simply explain in a friendly manner and hopefully everything will be laughed off.

# Appendix B: Life in the north-east
## Жизнь на северо-востоке

On the well-worn tourist routes of Moscow, St Petersburg and the Trans-Siberian, it is difficult to experience the real Russia. However, in the north-east you are guaranteed to see 'pristine' Russia, as few foreigners travel to the area. There is no tourist infrastructure so you will eat in Russian restaurants, stay in hotels for locals and experience Russian life first hand. The rareness of foreigners ensures that you will be greeted with enthusiasm by virtually everyone you meet. This makes the north-east one of the most interesting regions in Russia and this chapter will provide you with the background necessary to understand how everything works.

## PEOPLE (Люди)

The people of the north-east have a frontier character. The earliest surviving inhabitants belong to the central Asian nomads who lived by hunting, herding and horsemanship. On the Arctic coast are fishing nomads related to the native Alaskans. Europeans began to settle the region in the 17th century. Many were hunters, trappers, freebooters and settlers who preferred a region where the feudal relations of serfdom and personal service had never taken hold. 'God is high, the Tsar is far' («Бог высоки, Царь далеки»), says the Russian proverb – and here the Tsar was particularly far.

Nevertheless the Tsar, and later Stalin, perceived the advantage of the distant provinces as a prison. Under the Tsars, thousands of political prisoners were imprisoned or exiled in the far east, and in Stalin's time, millions. After Stalin's death in 1953, the forced labour system was cut back and the political prisoners (and common criminals) amnestied. Prisoners who had families or means went home, but many stayed behind.

In the 1960s, 1970s and 1980s young people were attracted to the adventure of building a new region. A revealing question that you can ask all across the region and one that always elicits an interesting answer, is 'How did your family come to be here?'

'We came with Khabarov [in the 1630s]' – Retired machinist, born in the village on the Ilim river that bears his surname.

'My ancestor was Polish and he was exiled after the Polish rebellion of 1830. They settled down and prospered and at the time of the revolution my grandfather owned 10 cows and 20 horses and three mills. During collectivisation he was dispossessed and moved to a *kolkhoz*.' – Electric power executive in Severobaikalsk.

'My grandfather was distributing *Iskra* [the Socialist newspaper founded by Lenin in exile] and was sentenced to hard labour in Sakhalin after the 1905 revolution. When he was released he settled there and married my grandmother, who was exiled there also. He took part in the Revolution and was a member of the Communist Party. In the 1930s he was arrested in the purges and shot.' – Shipping engineer in Sakhalin.

'My great-grandparents were peasants in the Ukraine. They were moved, with all their possessions and farm equipment, first to western Siberia and then again to the Far East.' – Student in Komsomolsk-na-Amure.

'My grandmother came to Komsomolsk-na-Amure in 1940 at the age of 16 to work in the arms factory. There she met my grandfather and they got married. He went in the army and was killed in 1944.' – Student in Komsomolsk-na-Amure, pointing to her grandfather's name on the war memorial.

'I came here with a Komsomol building crew. I worked on all the buildings in Khani. You know the hill behind Khani with the monument? After work we would run up there. We were never tired!' – *Provodnitsa* on the Tynda–Komsomolsk-na-Amure train.

'My father was a mullah in a Tatar village. In 1932 he was imprisoned in a work-camp as a *kulak* (rich peasant). I was born in the camp. When I grew up I became a railway worker, and later I entered Moscow Institute

---

❏ **Evenki (Tungus) and related tribes**

● **Evenki (Tungus)**  (40,000 in total, including populations in Mongolia and China - 28,000 in the former Soviet Union.) Their lands are bounded by the Yenisei River to the west, the tundra between the Yenisei and Lena rivers to the north, the Sea of Okhotsk to the east and the Amur River to the south.

● **Even (Lamut)**  (12,800) East of the Lena River.

● **Negidais**  (400-500) Along the Amgun and Amur rivers between Komsomolsk-na-Amure and Nikolaevsk-na-Amure.

● **Nanais (Goldy)**  (13,100) Along the lower reaches of the Amur River and right tributaries of the Ussuri River.

● **Ulchas (Manguny)**  (923) On the lower reaches of the Amur River.

● **Oroki**  (190) On the eastern side of the Sakhalin Island.

● **Oroch**  (1,200) Two areas near Sovetskaya Gavan and Komsomolsk-na-Amure.

● **Udehes**  (1,902) Along the Kungari and Aniui rivers.

of Railway Engineers. In 1978 I came to Severobaikalsk working on the railway.' – Rashit Yahin, Editorial Consultant of this guide

But even with a long history of exile and imprisonment, the north-easterners are cheerful people – energetic, open, generous and given to joking and partying. (Don't believe Muscovites, who, perhaps burdened with historical guilt, talk of the easterners as thugs and savages – an attitude that the Siberians do not entirely discourage.)

## Indigenous people

There are only 800,000 indigenous people in the whole of Siberia, making up just 3 per cent of the region's total population. 300,000 live in the Republic of Sakha (Yakutiya), where they make up 33 per cent of the population. Some 15,000 still lead a nomadic lifestyle with the rest living in collective farms and fisheries, or working in Russian cities and villages.

Siberian indigenous people can be divided into several main groups: The Yakuts and the Buryats were part of Genghis Khan's great empire. 300,000 Yakuts live in the Republic of Sakha (Yakutiya) and speak a Turkic language; 353,000 Buryats live in the southern part of the Buryatiya Republic. They were a people of grass lands who led a nomadic life based on horse and cattle breeding, but following Russian colonisation have been integrated into mainstream Russian society.

The next largest group is the Tunguso-Manchurian tribes, which arose from a mixing of aboriginal tribes from Northern Siberia with tribes from Southern Siberia and Manchuria. The first Tungus people appeared in the Lake Baikal area and migrated north and east sometime after AD1,000. Their constituent tribes, numbers and locations are shown in the box opposite.

The smallest group is the Nivkhi (Gilyaks). Four thousand four hundred live on the lower Amur River and Sakhalin Island. They have a separate language and culture and are believed to be the original inhabitants of the area. They are a maritime people living mainly on fishing and seal hunting. They cremated their dead unlike their neighbours who usually used air burials, which involved putting corpses in trees. The Nivkhi share many characteristics with the North American Inuit people.

Exhibits of the culture and way of life of indigenous peoples can be seen in regional museums at Yakutsk, Komsomolsk-na-Amure, Nikolaevsk-na-Amure and Yuzhno-Sakhalinsk.

## Shamanism

While both Lamaism (Tibetan-style Buddhism) and Christianity are widespread in eastern Siberia, Shamanism is the religion most widely associated with the region. Shamanism takes many forms with each tribe and clan having different traditions and practices. However, all forms are based on the belief in a universe consisting of three worlds linked by a river. The upper world is inhabited by gods, the middle by people and the

A *massi* idol which sits in the corner of a house protecting the occupants. The shaman invests the massi with a guardian spirit from the lower world and by feeding the spirit through the hole in the idol's stomach or mouth, the occupants believe that it will keep the spirit's strength up while purifying the food. *Massis* are produced by an idol maker to the shaman's orders and are not considered art but practical items.

lower by the spirits of the dead. In the human world, nature is dominated by occult forces from the other two worlds.

A shaman is not a priest and does not officiate at ceremonies but is a person who has been blessed with the sacred power of spirit contact. The shaman's work is mostly to do with healing, divination, clairvoyance, magical bodyguard creation and guiding the dead into the underworld.

Shamanism is an aggressive discipline involving constant combat with occult forces, demons and evil spirits. The contact and battles are achieved during an ecstatic state induced by dancing, drum-beating and occasionally by eating hallucinogenic Fly Agaric mushrooms.

## Life for indigenous people

Like many indigenous people around the world, the eastern peoples have suffered from the colonists – their lands overrun, their way of life disrupted, a new culture imposed, children removed to boarding schools, perceived as poor, dirty, idle and drunken. On the other hand, many have taken advantage of the egalitarian opportunities of the developing society, particularly in the Republic of Sakha (Yakutiya).

A positive aspect of the collapse of communism for the indigenous people has been the ability to protest. Recent protests have stopped environmental logging and dredging practices, stopped logging of certain habitats that disrupt the food chain and won back sovereignty over traditional hunting and fishing grounds. With the decentralisation of power from Moscow to the provinces, now is the best and possibly last chance many indigenous communities will have to make changes that for once will benefit them.

## TOWNS (Города)

This section describes types of town and the elements common in every town, which will help you to orient yourself in the north-east towns and also in virtually any town in Russia.

### Types of town

There are three main types of towns in Russia – rural settlements, urban settlements and cities. All have the same elements, which is hardly surprising as every Soviet town was built according to Moscow's universal civic blueprint.

**Rural settlement** Rural settlement (населенный пункт сельского типа) is a broad term for any collection of houses whose inhabitants' main occupation is farming, hunting or fishing. The vast majority of towns in the north-east that existed before the railway are of this type. These settlements are normally made up of single-storey wooden houses with no running water. Romantically they could be referred to as 'rustic villages', but this camouflages the tough life of the inhabitants.

Offerings to local deities, near Lake Baikal on the road to Baikalskoe. (Photo © Nicholas Zvegintzov).

Rural settlements have a variety of historical names in Russian with most carrying connotations of backwardness. The more common names include *selo* (село) meaning village, *derevnya* (деревня) meaning hamlet, or *khutor* (хутор), meaning a few dwellings in a forest. Examples of these sorts of settlements include Kholodnoe near Severobaikalsk, Ust-Nyukzha near Yuktali, and Ust-Muya near Taksimo.

Pre-BAM villages are usually located near river junctions and in valleys protected from the wind. While this was excellent for the villagers, the location of most villages was inconvenient for the railway builders and consequently the BAM bypassed many of these places. Instead, new towns were built on the railway just a few kilometres away from the existing towns. Examples of these pairs of towns include Staraya Chara and Novaya Chara, Urgal 1 and Novy Urgal, and Fevralskoe and Fevralsk.

Rural settlements are also found around a kolkhoz or collective farm. These farms were created from collectivising private farms or, more commonly in the BAM Zone, by creating new farm land. They are sometimes fancifully known as agricultural towns (агрогород) and, being relatively recent, have more concrete and brick buildings than older villages.

**Urban settlements** Urban settlements (посёлок городского типа) are the most common on the BAM. Technically an urban settlement is defined as a settlement with a minimum population of 3,000 of which over 85 per cent are employed in non-agricultural work. They are really miniature cities and most are designed with plenty of space to expand into full blown cities. The vast majority of urban settlements were built as the BAM was being constructed and they are dominated by 1970s pre-fabricated concrete buildings. Notable exceptions are Nizhneangarsk, Ekimchan and Chegdomyn, which still have many wooden buildings.

**Cities** There are only a few cities (город) in the north-east. A city is defined as having a minimum population of 12,000 of which over 85 per cent are employed in non-agricultural work. These include the small cities

---

❏ **Some BAM towns and their sponsors**

| BAM town | Sponsor | BAM town | Sponsor |
|---|---|---|---|
| Niya | Georgia | Dipkun | Moscow region |
| Severobaikalsk | St Petersburg | Tutaul | Moscow region |
| Kichera | Estonia | Verkhnezeisk | Ufa |
| Angoya | Armenia | Ogoron | Ulyanovsk |
| Taksimo | Byelorussia, Latvia | Tungala | Novosibirsk |
| | | Dugda | Moldova |
| Kuanda | Uzbekistan | Fevralsk | Moldova |
| Tynda | Moscow region | Soloni | Tadzhikistan |
| Marevaya | Moscow region | Suluk | Khabarovsk |
| | | Postyshevo | Novosibirsk |

of Severobaikalsk, Vanino, Tynda, Lensk, Mirny and Magadan, and the big cities of Bratsk, Yakutsk and Komsomolsk-na-Amure.

## Town planning and layout

As most of the towns in the north-east were built according to Moscow's Russia-wide town-planning regulations, they all share a similar city centre layout of a central square bordered by a town administration building, a hotel and often the railway administration building. If the town is pre-BAM, then the square probably has a statue of Lenin on it. Nearly all towns have a memorial to those who died in the Great Patriotic War, though these memorials are considerably larger in towns that actually existed during the War. Pre-BAM towns often name their streets after Lenin, peace, or the Great Patriotic War, while new towns named them after communist heroes, BAM builders and the place where the builders came from.

Outside the centre, the towns' layout and development are haphazard. The reason for this is that each settlement was made up of different organisations, such as steel works, forestry mills and construction enterprises, each of which cared firstly for the needs of their organisation and workers. This meant that each organisation built its own premises with its own independent power and water supplies, sideline farms to feed its workers and even worker settlements.

The new towns on the BAM were an ideal opportunity for new town architecture. These apartments are on the plaza in Tynda. (Photo © Nicholas Zvegintzov).

Most towns have substantial reserved areas for parks and fairgrounds and room to expand. While some towns have left these as simple cleared areas, others have developed their parks – Komsomolsk-na-Amure, for example, has several elegant parks with meadows, woods, avenues and playgrounds.

The new BAM towns have noteworthy, sometimes astonishing, architecture, as if, for once, architects were given freedom to rethink conventions and to adapt to sites. The buildings and town plans of the new BAM towns are bold and original. Several towns – Tynda, Novy Urgal and Neryungri, for example – are sited as 'shining cities on the hill'. While much Russian architecture (and much Western architecture too) is standardised and stereotyped – the pedimented palace of culture, the 'country mansion' railway station, for example – even the standard buildings are freshly rethought in many of the towns. The government centre, the shopping centre, the railway station, the palace of culture, the sports centre, the residential blocks – whole towns are built in a harmonious style.

Since the BAM was a national project, all the constituent regions of the USSR sponsored towns, and sent their own architects and construction teams, as the box 'Some BAM towns and their sponsors' shows. These teams used distinct regional styles.

## Town buildings

The following describes the major elements to be found in virtually all towns in the BAM Zone.

**Railway station (Железнодорожный вокзал)**  This is the central focus and rationale of most BAM towns. There is a marked difference between the stations, depending on their year of construction. The 1930s and 1940s stations are either wooden, such as Chuna and Vysokogornaya, or classic Stalinesque buildings with imposing steps and stairways, tall columns, massive lintels and energy inefficient high ceilings, such as Komsomolsk-na-Amure and Vanino. The stations along the newest sections of the BAM are built to harmonise with the town and include majestic concrete and glass stations as at Severobaikalsk and Tynda.

The larger stations are equipped with a waiting room, buffet, a room for mothers and children, ticket windows, baggage rooms, an enquiries office, a bookstall, a first-aid point and a railway police office. The stations sometimes have an overnight transit hotel attached to them providing basic facilities. The waiting rooms are crowded, stuffy and scented with the odours of pickled cucumber, dried fish, sunflower seeds and water melon.

Most of the stations have railway yards for exchanging locomotives and filling freight wagons, while the larger ones also have several hectares of repair yards. Strangely, some stations use old steam engines to generate hot water. It is interesting to note that most stations have inefficiently large equipment, such as overhead cranes rather than more useful forklifts, but this probably reflects the inability of State workers to maintain small machines.

## Town administration building (Административное управление)
It is easy to locate the town administration building as it is invariably on the main square, flies the Russian flag and stands behind the statue of Lenin. This building runs the town's social and administrative services. If the town is a rural or urban settlement, it is called a *possovet* (посёлковый совет), if it is a city it is called a *gorsovet* (городской совет), or if it is the largest settlement in the region and controls the surrounding area, it is called a *raionsovet* (районный совет). (The word sovet, from which 'Soviet' comes, means 'council').

## Railway administration (Железнодорожное управление)
Invariably, this building is larger than the town's administration building, which reflects its greater power.

## Hotel (Гостиница)
The hotel normally faces the city square although at smaller stations it can be at the station. If the accommodation is primarily for railway workers, it may be beside the station, as it is at Verkhnezeisk and Ust-Kut.

## Shops, market (Магазины, рынок)
In large towns, shops are dispersed around the town. In small settlements, almost everything is located in one large complex called a TOTs (Торговый Общественный Центр). TOTs have the big advantage of protecting shoppers from the winter temperatures. In some towns, such as Kunerma, even the cinema and library are located in the TOTs.

Shops are a mixture of the spacious Soviet-era planned stores and private enterprise concessions, usually much smaller and more crowded. Every town has a market of free enterprise stalls where home-grown food, car parts, imported clothes etc are sold, organised by types of product. These markets are often in the open air, outside the shopping centre.

## Post office (Почта)
Post offices have three sections. One part is for letters and telegrams, another for parcels and the third for telephone calls. While in most towns, all three sections are in the one building, in some towns all three are frustratingly located in separate buildings, as is the case in Komsomolsk-na-Amure, while in towns like Tynda and Sovetskaya Gavan just the post and telephone sections are separate. See Post and telecommunications, pp50-3.

## Bus station (Автовокзал)
In small towns, the bus station is just a shelter at the railway station or on the main square, while in large towns, it is a building with cafés and shops such as at Aldan and Komsomolsk-na-Amure.

**Housing (Жильё)** Most BAM towns have the bland Soviet, box-shaped multi-storey flats arranged in pentagons. This layout provides a wind sheltered, snow drift free area for children. Most buildings are either five storeys, which is the maximum height before elevators are required, or 10 storeys. On the ground floor of the flats are grocery stores.

Russia has the lowest per capita housing allotments in Europe. In 1988, Moscow had an average allocation of 14 sq metres of living space per person while in the BAM Zone it was just 6.4 sq metres. This may have been tolerable for young, single, short-term workers but is a major problem for BAM families.

By the early 1990s, only 310,000 sq metres out of a planned 1.4 million sq metres of permanent housing had been built in the BAM Zone with many of the original inhabitants still living in run-down hostels, caravans and ramshackle buildings in temporary settlements.

**Worker settlement (Рабочий посёлок)** Worker settlements are self-contained satellite suburbs for employees of particularly large enterprises and consequently are only found in large towns, such as Komsomolsk-na-Amure, Bratsk and Neryungri. As the enterprise provides most of the civic services and stocks the local stores, the lifestyle of the residents is very dependent on the profitability of the enterprise.

**Temporary settlement (Временный посёлок)** Hidden away on the outskirts of most BAM towns are temporary settlements. These were hurriedly constructed before work started on the town, as they were for the initial builders of the railway and town. The houses are normally single-storey wooden hostels, shared houses, or transportable buildings.

Theoretically the residents of the temporary settlements build the permanent town and then move into the new apartments or depart for the next job. The temporary settlement is then demolished. However, due to the shortage of apartments, many people still live in them and consequently few have been demolished. This situation is best illustrated at Novaya Chara (see p124) and Verkhnezeisk (see p143).

It is interesting to note that a few of the BAM towns were designated as temporary towns and the whole town was actually demolished. These include the tunnel construction towns of Dzelinga and Kodar.

**Military settlement (Военный городок)** In the BAM Zone there are only a few towns, such as Sovetskaya Gavan, Vanino and Komsomolsk-na-Amure, that have major military bases. However, there are a number of towns where small military garrisons are based to guard important bridges. The garrison compounds are normally at one end of the bridge and can be seen from the train. It is not advisable to photograph them.

**Library (Библиотека)** Most towns have a library run by the town administration, but there are a number of towns that have another library run by the railways. The railway library contains technical railway journals and books as well as many of the same books as the local library. Everyone is allowed into both libraries.

**Palace of Culture (Дворец культуры)** Every town's cultural activity is focused around the Palace of Culture. This building normally has a large hall for films, theatre, musical performances, or school performances. If there is a national holiday, you can be guaranteed that something will be on here. The best and most active Palace of Culture on the BAM is at Severobaikalsk which boasts an excellent indoor garden.

**Central-heating plant (жилищно эксплуатационное управление)** Hot water and heating for apartments come from the town's central-heating plant. The water is distributed by above-ground pipes which should be covered with insulating material and a galvanised tin protective skin. As most pipes are in poor repair with sections of insulation fallen off, plumes of steam rising from the pipes during winter are common sights. The pipes are clearly visible in all towns and are quite an eyesore. The plants do not generate electricity as this is supplied by high-voltage long-distance power lines from Bratsk, Zeya, or Komsomolsk-na-Amure.

**Museum (Музей)** There are two sorts of museums – regional and special interest. The former normally includes information on the life of past generations, indigenous people, town history and local industry, while the latter includes the BAM, local geology, industry and the military. The best way to see which business, military, or government delegations have recently visited any town is to check the museum's visitors book.

**Bookshop (Дом Книги)** In the past, these shops were an excellent source of books, calendars and maps. Nowadays they principally sell Western adventure and crime novels translated into Russian. A few book shops also sell old Russian and Soviet notes, coins, medals and stamps.

**Bakery (Булочная)** Bakeries are absolutely essential; a small bakery produces about 300 loaves a day and employs one baker and a number of assistants to lug the ingredients and chop the wood for the ovens.

**Bank (Банк)** Each town has a branch of the national savings bank, Sberbany Bank (Сбербаный Банк). This normally has a large queue as it pays pensions. It will buy and sell foreign currency.

**Dacha village (Дачный посёлок)** This is an area outside town, often near a river or lake, with individual holiday cottages and, equally important, individual gardens. For more on dacha life, see p339.

**Police (Милиция)** See Security and police, pp53-6.

**Hospital (Больница)** See Health, p22.

**Banya (Баня)**  A banya is a Russian wet sauna but the word is also used to mean a Russian bath-house, which can include a banya, Swedish dry sauna, a scrubbing area and a cold pool. Visiting a bath-house starts with a number of friends sitting in the sauna and lightly hitting each other with branches of dried birch leaves dipped in water, which leave the skin tingling. After a few minutes you leave and scrub yourself down on a washing table. If you are so inclined you can jump into a cold-water pool, before returning to the banya. This process is normally repeated three times. If there is no pool, people often roll outside in the snow. Avoid getting your hair wet between bouts in the sauna as this can give you a cold (Russians believe). After the banya you normally have something to eat, which could be a meal or more likely just a snack of dried fish and beer. Banyas normally have session times so make sure you know when you have to be out before you enter. Birch branches, beer and even fish are on sale at the best of the banyas.

Some Russians like to pour beer, birchwood essence, or eucalyptus oil onto the banya's hot rocks as this creates delightful aromas. By the end of your banya trip, you will feel clean, weary and wonderful. Make sure you are bundled up when you leave, as it is really easy to get a chill.

## THE MISUNDERSTOOD CLIMATE (Непонятный климат)

Snow and Siberia are often mistakenly thought of as synonymous. Therefore it is surprising for many to learn that eastern Siberia is one of the driest climates in the world with almost no precipitation in winter and little during summer. This dryness is mostly due to the fact that Siberia is a long way from the source of most precipitation – the sea. Moist air from the east (Pacific Ocean) and south (North-East Asia) is cut off by high mountains, while winds from the west (Atlantic Ocean) lose all their moisture by the time they reach eastern Siberia after travelling across Europe and most of Russia. To the north (Arctic Ocean), rain-bearing winds are never generated.

Another result of being far from the sea is that the air temperature fluctuates wildly due to the absence of the regulatory effect of oceans. In some places, the temperature can vary by 30°C between day and night.

During winter, the rapidly cooling land leads to the formation of a permanent high-pressure zone, known as the Siberian High. This high-pressure zone is stationary over Sakha for the whole winter and results in cloudless skies, no wind and little precipitation. The effect is further accentuated by the basin shape of the region, which traps the cold air near the ground. During summer, the Siberian High breaks up and remoteness from the sea becomes the major climatic influence on precipitation. The annual rainfall ranges from 700mm at the coast to just 350mm in Tynda. Along most of the BAM, the snow depth rarely exceeds 30cm but stays on the ground for an average of 190 days a year.

The dryness also means that forest fires are a major problem throughout eastern Siberia. Due to the short growing season and therefore slow growth rate of vegetation, fire damage is visible for decades. Along the Komsomolsk-na-Amure–Sovetskaya Gavan line, the evidence of the 1976 Khabarovsk Krai forest fire was still obvious until overlaid by the 1998 fires.

## Permafrost

Permafrost is ground that is frozen throughout the year. Permafrost has an active layer of about 2m, which thaws every spring and freezes each winter. The soil or rock below this active layer never melts and has a constant temperature of -4°C.

The greatest depth of permafrost in eastern Siberia is 1.5km but the greatest depth in the BAM Zone is 600m at Udokan near Chara. Permafrost is a relic of the last ice age, formed between 800,000 and 2.5 million years ago. The modern climate, while extreme, is no longer cold enough to create permafrost. However, its aridity is enough to prevent the existing permafrost from melting.

Surprisingly, permafrost supports forest growth in the dry climate because it traps the precipitation in the soil against the underlying ice.

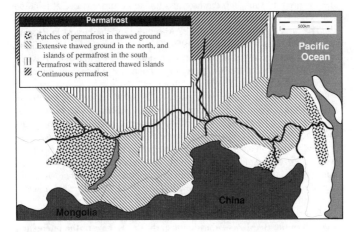

## Glaciers

There are 18 places in the former Soviet Union where glaciers are found and three of these are in the BAM Zone. It is surprising that glaciers exist in the Zone, considering its low altitude and that it is over 1,000km south of the next closest glacier.

One glacier site is just south of Severobaikalsk at Mt Cherski (see pp97-99). This 1.5 sq km glacier is at a height of just 2,588m.

The second glacier site is in the Kodar mountain range. There are 40 known glaciers here, with a total area of 15 sq km and more to be discovered. Each glacier is relatively small, with the longest just under 2km. The Kodar range peaks at 2,999m. The majority of Kodar range glaciers are mountain ones that slowly flow down the slopes or through valleys in winter and melt slightly in summer. The glaciers are 80m thick on average and move at a maximum speed of several metres a year for smaller ones to several hundred metres a year for large ones. There are also a few valley glaciers, which trundle along at three to six metres a year and some mountain glaciers that don't grow or shrink. For information on how to get to these glaciers see pp121-3. The third glacier site is very small and is near Neryungri.

## Earthquakes

Seismic activity is common in the western part of the BAM and up to 802,000 minor tremors a year are felt. There have been three major earthquakes in the region since recording started.

In 1930-31, the earth's crust subsided at the northern end of Lake Baikal near the mouth of the Kichera river and the settlement of Nizhneangarsk. The town partly sank into the lake and had to be moved several hundred metres north towards the hills.

The largest earthquake in the BAM region, and the largest in Russian history, was recorded on 27 June 1957. This quake was so big that it is the only Russian one listed in the world's catalogue of earthquake disasters. The epicentre was in the Northern Muya mountains which is now the site of the 15.7km Severomuisk BAM tunnel.

A few years after that earthquake, on 29 August 1959, inhabitants in a Lake Baikal town on the shores of the Proval Strait woke to find that some of their houses had rotated 35-40 degrees clockwise due to a massive land slip. Luckily few houses were destroyed due to the extensive use of wood which can easily withstand earthquakes measuring nine points on the Richter scale. Scientists went to the earthquake's epicentre and found that in places the lake had sunk by up to 15 metres. These subsidences are part of Lake Baikal's continual growth of five to eight kilometres in width every million years.

Over 15 million roubles ($30 million) were allocated to seismic research of the BAM Zone during the early 1970s. One of the interesting discoveries was that permafrost significantly reduced the severity of earthquakes by absorbing their energy through the tens and hundreds of metres of frozen sand, water and rock. Research has found that the removal of the permafrost layer leads to an increase in seismicity by two to three points on the Richter scale. For this reason, it was essential that as much of the permafrost ground as possible was not disturbed when the BAM was built.

## Rock rivers

Rock avalanches, called rock rivers, are common in some parts of the BAM, particularly in the section from Novaya Chara to Khani. The avalanches are caused by a combination of frost, which shatters rocks, and earth tremors. The avalanches are so common in some sections that vegetation does not have time to take root so hills and even entire mountains are completely bare.

## FLORA (Флора)

The types of vegetation along the BAM Zone vary enormously and include tundra, taiga, broad-leaved forests, meadows, swamps and drunken forests.

## Tundra

Tundra is a treeless, frozen land where only primitive plants such as lichen and moss can survive. In the Siberian tundra, it rains less than 200 mm a year and daylight length varies from 24 hours in summer to complete darkness for a whole month in the middle of winter. Technically, tundra is defined as an area when the mean monthly temperature never exceeds 10°C.

There are two sorts of tundra, arctic tundra and mountain tundra.

Arctic tundra is usually flat as most of it was levelled by the great glaciers of the Quaternary ice age. These glaciers scraped and crushed rocks on their advance and dropped boulders and stones haphazardly on their retreat. Since the departure of the glaciers the landscape has changed little as erosion from running water, the major cause of landscaping, has had insufficient time to act. Frost weathering (where water permeates a rock, the frost freezes the water, and the rock is shattered as ice takes up more space than the water) is the greatest agent for change and its actions level any remaining features. The net result of frost weathering is that it has produced tonnes of debris that surrounds summits, litters plateaux and clutters up valley floors.

While arctic tundra is now confined to the north of Yakutsk, it once descended into the BAM Zone and its effects can still be seen in the flat land with numerous creeks meandering through in it.

Mountain tundra is confined to above 1,700m and has the same barren appearance as arctic tundra. Mountain tundra occurs on the BAM between Novy Chara and Tynda and on the AYaM railway between Tynda and Aldan and in the Kolyma region.

## Taiga

The taiga forests of Russia are the largest contiguous forest in the world. Essentially all the BAM railway and the Lena river region as far north as

Yakutsk and east into the Kolyma region, is in the taiga. Taiga is conifer-ous forest (also known as boreal forest) made up of spruce and larch trees with cones and needle-like leaves. Common taiga trees are Dahurian larch, Yeddo spruce, Erman's birch, Khingan fir, Norway spruce, Scots pine, Siberian larch, Siberian fir, Siberian spruce, Ayan spruce and the Siberian Silver Fir.

While both spruce and larch are varieties of conifers, there is a con-siderable difference between the two.

Spruces are evergreen, meaning that their leaves do not fall off during winter. Spruces have leaves that are borne singly on peg-like projections that remain attached to the twig when the leaves fall. The cones develop at the tips of the branches and hang downwards when they are ripe. Spruces have evolved a unique evolutionary mechanism that allows them to retain their foliage all year. In the autumn, the leaves enter a dormant state in which photosynthesis ceases and respiration falls to an extremely low level enabling their leaves to endure the very low winter temperatures. At the start of spring, when the day starts to lengthen, they quickly reac-tivate. There are about 34 types of spruce.

Spruces can endure shade but require moist, nutrient rich soil. For this reason, the best spruce stands are along river valleys with good drainage. The location of these stands was used by the first settlers to locate good arable land. The spruces are ideally adapted for growing in permanently frozen subsoil as they have a superficial root system, which means that they can spread in the thawed top soil.

Larches are a light-loving species and can tolerate various soil types and moisture contents. They can grow in sandy soils, in swamps and on granite ledges. Larches have soft leaves in tufts that fall off in winter. There are about nine species of larch trees. The undergrowth of the taiga includes heathers such as *Ericaceae vaccinium* and *Ericaceae arc-tostaphylos*, and flowering herbs such as twinflower, wintergreen and creeping orchid. Mosses are usually abundant, but in the driest taiga only lichens grows. During the winter most of the herbs die down to their roots while small shrubs are covered by snow which insulates them from extremes of cold.

Taiga covers the landscape to a height of 1,500m on most northern slopes and to 1,700m on the southern slopes.

## Broad-leaved forests

Despite the predominance of conifers, there are a large variety of other trees along the BAM including the Korean cedar (a light and beautifully-hued wood used to produce turpentine oil, rosin, pine oil and plywood), ash (used as a decorative material and in engineering and shipbuilding), aspens (used for match sticks), the Amur cork tree (a good substitute for the classic Algerian cork tree), the Brazilian oak (used as an insulating

material in ships, aircraft and refrigerators), Japanese stone pine, rhodo-
dendron and Asiatic white birch.

## Other types of terrain

There are three other main types of terrain you will pass through in the
BAM Zone – meadows, swamps and drunken forests. Meadows exist in
isolated regions and their small size is one of the major limiting factors for
local agriculture. There are two types of meadows – flood plain meadows
which are located in river valleys and flood regularly, and dry valley
meadows which are located in floodless regions or on hillsides and only
exist temporarily following forest fires or logging.

Natural swamps are not that common in the BAM Zone due to the
scant precipitation, dry air and good drainage of eastern Siberia. Although
there are several hundred kilometres of swamp, most of this is a result of
destruction of the natural ecosystem during the BAM's construction.
Before construction, the forests evaporated the water that lay in the
thawed soil above the permafrost.

However, following the removal of the absorption layer, the water
forms a swamp as it cannot penetrate the permafrost, thereby killing the
trees. If the area is not further disturbed, the swamp will eventually silt up
over hundreds of years, thereby creating a new absorption layer, and the
forests will eventually reclaim the area.

Drunken forests are a product of the annual freezing and thawing of
the soil which causes the earth to swell and shrink, resulting in the soil
pushing out stones to the edge of the thaw area. This action often results
in regular stone patterns, which on flat ground are usually polygons, and
on sloping ground are lines. The churning of soil tilts over trees and hence
their name of 'drunken' forests.

## ANIMALS (Животные)

There is a large variety of animals in the north-east, as it encompasses the
vastly different habitats of taiga, broad-leaved forests, meadows, swamps
and mountain tundra.

The taiga is a harsh environment for animals with an abundance of
food in summer and very little in winter. Consequently, the animal density is quite small. For example, in the Bodaibo *zakaznik* there are only 10
sables and 50 squirrels for every 10,000 square kilometres. Animal variety is greatest in the taiga of the east and decreases as you move westward.
Broad-leaved forests contain the greatest variety of native animals of all
habitats while meadows are inhabited by many introduced species from
European Russia. Mountain tundra supports only a small number of
species due to the vegetation's lack of protection and food.

The largest cats in the world still roam the coastal mountain ranges of
Khabarovski krai and Primorski krai south of Vanino and north of

Vladivostok – The Siberian tiger, Panthera tigris altaica, called the Amur tiger in Russian (Амурский тигр). For more on these tigers, see p204.

## THE FRAGILE ENVIRONMENT (Хрупкая окружающая среда)

The BAM Zone's ecosystems have evolved over tens of thousands of years but can easily be destroyed in months. Due to the long months of icy win-

❏ **Some animals of the BAM Zone**

**Bears** (медведь): Every year bears kill one or two people in the BAM Zone and the Russian Far East. Attacks invariably happen at the end of winter when the bears awake from their hibernation and are very hungry. Most deaths occur in areas far from human settlement so you are perfectly safe in a town. If you go trekking in remote areas, a guide with a rifle is normally only essential when the bears are hungry. But remember, it's better to be safe than sorry.

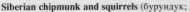

**Siberian chipmunk and squirrels** (бурундук; белка): The chipmunk, squirrel and flying squirrel are ideally suited to the vast *taiga* as they can eat the conifers' bark and cones. The best squirrel pelts in Russia come from the Barguzin area where local pride in the animal is shown by the heraldic symbol of a squirrel sitting on a silver ground.

**Sables** (соболь): While sables are still hunted in Siberia, over 75% of them come from farms. Despite years of scientific breeding, raising sables in captivity is still very difficult due to rapid transfers of disease. In the BAM Zone there are about 10 sable farms; these are worth a visit. The most precious sable is the Vitim or Barguzin black sable. This animal only lives in Russia and was saved from extinction when hunting was prohibited in 1912 for three years and again from 1935 to 1941. These animals cannot be raised in captivity and are extremely rare outside the Barguzin *Zapovednik* on the Lake Baikal eastern shore, and small areas of the Urals where they have been introduced.

**Musk-rat** (ондатра): Also known as musquash, these animals have been used for centuries to make the popular Russian musk-rat fur cap. Due to over hunting, these hats haven't been available for several years in Russian shops. In addition, musk-rats are used by fishermen to make lures for the taimen fish.

**KEY**

1. hare (заяц)
2. marmot, Mongolian bobak (сурок, тарбаган)
3. musk deer (кабарга)
4. wolf (волк)
5. reindeer (олень)
6. roe deer (косуля)
7. pine marten (куница)
8. Ussuri wild boar (Уссурийский кабан)

ter and the short growing season, Siberian ecosystems are biologically very slow. This means that any environmental disturbance will be felt for years, if not decades. For example, following a forest fire, vegetation reaches equilibrium (climax vegetation) within 50 years in the southern republics of the former Soviet Union while it takes 200 years in the BAM Zone.

The first article published in a National Soviet newspaper criticising the BAM's environmental record appeared in 1984 in *Izvestiya*. It wrote of the environmental blueprint for the BAM Zone. 'We became acquainted with a project...known as the Territorial Comprehensive Plan for Environmental Protection along the BAM. Its many volumes provide a comprehensive analysis of the territories and resource potential of the BAM Zone and forecast potential pollution and environmental damage. But we failed to find in the plan specific proposals as to how to protect primary topographical features and basic ecosystems...and what kind of organisational measures are needed to protect the environment. Yet such proposals are essential.'

The authors were justified in their concerns about the BAM as it caused and still causes considerable environmental damage. The problems can be divided into five categories – the railway line, the daily operation, construction debris, industrial development and population pressures.

● The railway line's very presence has dramatically altered the ecosystems through which it passes. Not only has it affected much of the landscape by diverting rivers, creating new swamps and disturbing the permafrost, it has also divided the migration path of animals and introduced new species in the permanently cleared reserves alongside the line.

● The daily operation of the railway is a continual cause of large-scale environmental pollution. Locomotives drip about one litre of oil per 100km onto the rails while raw effluent from the train's toilets falls directly onto the tracks. Both of these pollutants find their way into the waterways. In addition, tens of thousands of tonnes of diesel soot and unburned diesel fuel are pumped into the atmosphere each year by the trains.

● Construction debris, such as discarded equipment, rotting camps and left-over construction materials, litters the BAM route and continues to cause pollution as it decays. The biggest construction debris polluters are oil, petrol and chemical drums. As there were no refuelling points along the route when it was being constructed, all vehicles had to carry their own fuel needs. This resulted in a large number of spills and abandoned oil drums along the route.

● Industrial pollution is a major problem due to a combination of poor environmental standards in factories and the climate. Inadequate standards tolerate higher levels of pollution than are internationally accepted and the practice of storming (a last minute work frenzy) to meet the monthly target frequently creates a surge of pollution that is high even by lax Russian laws.

● The region's expanding population also causes various forms of pollution such as river silting due to the clearing of forests for pastures, raw sewage overflowing into rivers and mountains of garbage which never seem to decompose.

## THE CONTINUAL STRUGGLE FOR FOOD
### (Непрерывная борьба за пищу)

Since the start of the BAM until the mid-1980s and again in the early 1990s, the BAM Zone dwellers have suffered continual food shortages with fresh milk being restricted to children and the sick, choices of vegetables limited to cabbages and potatoes, and meat always scarce.

This is despite a massive self-sufficiency programme since the early 1970s that was formalised into Brezhnev's 1978 announcement that, 'The newly developed economic regions should be provided with their own agricultural base and should be in a position to supply themselves with their own animal products and vegetables'. In the media, the programme was justified using a combination of ideology and warped scientific rationalism.

Ideological support came from Lenin himself when he wrote that new enterprises should be built near raw resources rather than carting the resources to be processed hundreds of miles away. In the case of the BAM, this was interpreted to mean that farms should be established near the human resources that they needed to feed.

The theories of scientific rationalism, where science could always triumph over nature, also justified the ideas of self-sufficiency in areas not farmed before. Although the last major Soviet attempt to apply science to farming, in Khrushchev's 1950s Virgin Lands campaign, was a massive failure, Soviet technocrats believed that it was simply a matter of fine tuning. The BAM offered a second chance, admittedly a much harder one considering the land's poor potential for agriculture. To ensure that the nation's best minds were working on this project, in 1976 the Research Council on Agricultural Development in the BAM Zone was formed and slightly later the Scientific Council on the Problems of the BAM was created.

However, the real reason for the self-sufficiency programme was pragmatism. Regardless of the Soviet Union's propaganda of massive technological advances, continual plan overfulfilment and improving living standards, the government realised that virtually all Russian regions barely produced enough to feed themselves, let alone provided a surplus for other areas. In addition, the transport system was so chaotic that surplus food could not be guaranteed to reach its consumer in a fit state. Railway reports of the early 1980s stated that about 35 per cent of rail freighted vegetables were spoiled during shipment over 2,000-3,000km.

To achieve self-sufficiency in the BAM Zone was an overly ambitious and unrealistic target. In 1978 there were only 27 farms in the entire area which met only 25 per cent of local needs in five of the seven BAM administrative regions and contributed nothing at all in the other two.

The magnitude of this problem is illustrated by one directive emanating from the central planning headquarters in Moscow that declared that the BAM Zone should be 65 per cent self sufficient in milk. Using the figures from another government department that stated that each citizen was to receive 185 litres a year of fresh milk, this meant that the 10,600 cows in the region in 1978 had to increase to 144,500 by the late 1980s. Providing fodder for the anticipated number of animals required a massive programme of deforestation, reclamation, redirecting water courses and damming. Before the self-sufficiency was stopped, 96,600ha of hay land and 33,000ha of range land were created at the cost of the destruction of numerous river ecosystems.

Increasing vegetable cultivation was just as difficult. There is only an average of 94 frost-free days per year, which is just sufficient for cold-resistant varieties of cabbage, red beets and carrots. To grow other vegetables requires expensive heated and artificially lit greenhouses. In addition, the new farms would require farmers but few were attracted to work in the BAM Zone with its harsh climate, unworked land and limited potential for farm machinery due to the hilly terrain.

Despite the best efforts of economists, scientists and politicians, the Agricultural Academy of the Siberian Division of the Soviet Academy of Agricultural Sciences finally admitted the defeat of the self-sufficiency policy in 1985. The Academy reluctantly admitted that while technically all the food could be grown locally, it would be too expensive and it was recommended that the BAM Zone import 80 per cent of its butter, cheese and grain needs from West Siberia.

Following this announcement, food supply increased until the economic downturn in the early 1990s, when inhabi-

Some local people supplement their incomes by selling food and other goods on the platforms at railway stations. (Photo © Nicholas Zvegintzov).

❏ **Dacha**

While people living in houses have a garden, most high-rise dwellers have a small plot on the outskirts of town to grow vegetables. This land is normally rented from the government for a minimal amount. Over time, the owner often builds a small shed which invariably gets enlarged into a little weekend cottage.

A growing number of people, particularly the unemployed and pensioners, are living permanently in their *dachas* all year-round. The advantages include more space than apartments and a source of food, while the disadvantages include being a long way from shops and no running water or electricity.

Typical of the move from city to *dacha village* are Nikolai and Erena Ushakov of Komsomolsk. Both have retired and they have slowly built their *dacha* over the last 10 years from bought and scavenged material. Despite its lack of electricity and running water, they are immensely proud of their two-storey house. The principal source of cooking is natural gas and their tanks are filled every three months by a delivery truck.

The garden produces their entire year's supply of potatoes, cucumbers, eggplant, strawberries, sunflower, beans, radish, cabbage, lettuce, corn, onions and tomatoes. A small greenhouse is heated with a wood fire.

The short summer is an exceptionally busy time for Nikolai and Elena with gardening, *kolbasa* making, pickling, jam making, *kvas* and vodka brewing, mushroom collecting and continuing the construction of their *dacha*. In winter, the cold is too much for Elena and she returns to the city to live in their flat which now houses her son's family. Nikolai prefers to live in the *dacha* where he can ice fish and hunt for wild sheep and deer. The long winter evenings are spent making things out of the pelts and eating sunflower seeds by the light of candles.

In many ways, *dacha* life is remarkably similar to Siberian life of a hundred years ago.

tants of the BAM Zone had to survive on their own resources. The food shortage peaked in 1991 and 1992. Nowadays food is readily available just as it is anywhere in Russia.

## Farming and gardening

Locally produced food comes from four sources – collective farms, state farms, industrial sideline farms and private garden plots.

Collective farms are farming enterprises technically owned by the members, in reality simply large commercial farms owned by the government.

Industrial sideline farms are small farms owned by large industrial enterprises that provide food for their workers. These farms are important in attracting and retaining workers in a region where food shortages are common. Examples include the Osetrovo River Port Industrial Farm at Ust-Kut, the Aircraft Plant Farm at Komsomolsk-na-Amure and the Tin Concentrator Farm at Solnechny. Sideline farms create a number of problems. Firstly, the operation of a sideline farm distracts the management of the industrial enterprise from its principal task. Secondly, the more self-sufficient an enterprise becomes, the more insular it becomes. Thirdly, as the free market forces started to take effect in the late 1980s and early 1990s, some enterprises realised that they could make more money with their sideline farms than their principal business. This resulted in resources being directed to the farms with a corresponding fall in industrial output.

Private garden plots are essential in supplementing the limited quantities and varieties of fresh food available. Most people keep a small garden around their houses while flat dwellers were entitled in the 1980s to a 600 square metre plot of land on the outskirts of the town. In the late 1980s, about 40 per cent of all of Moscow's food was produced in small garden plots and in the BAM region there can be no doubt that it would have been even higher. To extend the short growing season, most gardens have a greenhouse maintained at an optimal 28°C. These extend the growing season to mid-September and, if it is heated by a slow burning stove or by a hot water pipe, to mid-October. Although in the past, some enterprise-owned glasshouses were heated and lit all year-round, the price of electricity and hot water has risen astronomically in the last few years and this is no longer practical.

## What do the locals eat?

The meals eaten by locals in the BAM Zone are classically Russian. This means that they are of limited variety, mostly fried and noted for their absence of spices. In the summer months there is an abundance of home-grown vegetables but in winter the choice is reduced to a few staples such as potatoes, cabbages and onions.

Despite the fact that the residents of the BAM came from all over the former Soviet Union, the food is fairly uniform, particularly the commercially available bread and cakes. This is an interesting comment on the food imperialism of Russia.

The basis of all Russian meals is bread and tea. There are many types of bread, but the commonest are black and white. The black is a heavy rye bread that lasts for over a week without going stale. The white is delicious when fresh but goes bland and stale within a few hours.

Tea is made by pouring hot water onto leaves in a small container. This concentrated tea is kept for the day and, when needed, small amounts of it are poured into a cup and boiling water is added. The tea is different from the common Indian or Ceylonese varieties, as it does not go bitter when stewed. At most meals there will be sweets which can be a substitute for sugar in tea.

A typical traditional worker's lunch will be a slab of bread, an onion, tea and *salo* or *kolbasa*. Salo is salt or smoke cured bacon. Kolbasa is a sausage that can be eaten without cooking. It has many varieties ranging from a bland bologna to a chewy smoked hunter's sausage.

Wild food: a fisherman with a taimen, north of Yakutsk.

Typical snack food is beer, dried fish and sunflower seeds. The dried fish consists of a whole fish and to eat it you rip off the skin and tear off the chewy dried fish flesh. Sunflower seeds are bought by the cupful at the market or still attached to the giant flower head which is more fun eating.

A typical dinner includes shallow fried potato chips and a slab of meat. Common variations include fried macaroni with meat, boiled fish and fried slices of kolbasa. During winter most vegetables are pickled, while in summer the vegetables will be fresh.

As well as tea and coffee (made from powder), a popular drink is *kompot* (компот), which is made from stewed fruit. Vodka is the most common alcoholic drink, as beer is frowned upon as a workers' drink. However, this attitude is changing with the increasing popularity of imported beer. Milk is hardly ever drunk by healthy adults.

## Preserving food

Once food is grown, it has to be preserved so that there is something to eat over the long winter.

Vegetables are normally pickled in a mixture of vinegar, sugar, blackcurrant leaves and dill. Fish is salted which simply involves gutting the fish and tossing lots of salt on it. The salt sucks the fluid out of the fish and the salt slurry is regularly drained off and replaced by fresh salt. After 24 hours, the fish can be hung out in the open and after two weeks, the breeze and sun produces long-life dried, salted fish. Another option is to leave the fish in salt for a few days and then eat it raw like salty sushi. A third option is to fillet the fish, cover it with salt and keep replacing the salt until no more moisture comes out. The fish is then packed with salt and sealed in a barrel. Fish can also be smoked but this will not keep for as long. Smoking is done by filling the bottom of a metal container with green leaves and wood chips and laying the fish on a metal grill above this. A lid is then placed on the container and a fire lit underneath it. It takes about one hour to smoke a fish.

Red meat can be either frozen or smoked. In houses that do not have refrigerators or electricity, the meat is kept in an underground coolstore. This coolstore is kept cold all summer long by blocks of ice cut from frozen lakes and rivers in winter. Smoking is normally reserved for salami-like kolbasa and, as most people prefer to buy it rather than make it, kolbasa smoking is a dying art.

Kolbasa is usually made from pork and is made as the weather cools in late autumn. The process starts with slitting the throat of the pig and catching the drained blood. The skin on the pig is then singed with a blow torch, which removes the hair. The animal is then gutted and the intestines are cleaned out to be used as the kolbasa skins. Meanwhile the flesh of the pig is minced and stuffed into the cleaned intestines. Salt, pepper and paprika are added to give flavour and help preservation. The kolbasa are then hung up in a smoking shed with the salo and after 24 to 48 hours are ready to be eaten. Kolbasa can be stored for over a year without going off. Some people use the remaining organs and the blood by boiling them, mincing them up, mixing them with rice and finally stuffing them into the intestines to make a rice-based black pudding. Kolbasa is not made from reindeer or rabbit as their meat has too little fat and their intestines are too large.

### Wild food (Дикая пища)

Collecting wild food is a major social event as well as providing an important dietary supplement. Going to the forests or fields collecting berries, mushrooms, nuts and roots is not just limited to rural folk but is also an activity city dwellers love.

A number of native foods in eastern Siberia are not found in European Russia and for the initial explorers many had an unpleasant taste. An example of this is *cheremsha* (черемша), a wild onion with a leafy stem and a hot garlic taste, called ramps or ramsons in English. Back in 1850, the Eastern Siberian Governor General N. Muravev-Amurski, on one of his explorations of the Amur, noted that 'I bravely ate cheremsha to prevent scurvy' as an example for his men. At that time, spring onions was unheard of in Russia. Nowadays, most Russians in the BAM Zone eat cheremsha and Westerners will enjoy it.

Collecting mushrooms (грибы) is probably Russia's most popular outdoor activity. There are 3,000 varieties of mushrooms in the former Soviet Union, but there are only a few hundred which are edible with the most common being the white mushroom (белый), rough stemmed boletus (подберёзовик) and orange capped boletus (подосиновик). Mushrooms can be eaten raw, salted, pickled, or fried. Mushrooms pop up from June to September depending on the rain. As with other native food, if you don't know if it is edible, don't eat it.

The Wild foods table lists foods found along the BAM Zone. The picking time is for the western section of the BAM between Severobaikalsk and Novy Urgal. At the eastern end of the BAM, the picking time may be a month earlier. Participating in a picking expedition with Russians is a highly recommended, enjoyable and educational experience.

## THE FISHING WONDERLAND (Рыбалка)

The BAM Zone contains some of the best fishing places in Russia and in most places the fish stocks are increasing. This is partly due to the decrease in fishing following the collapse of government subsidised fishing enterprises and partly because of the increase in breeding following a reduction in pollution as industrial enterprises shut down.

Virtually everyone in the BAM Zone fishes as it provides both a recreation and an important source of food. However, there are only a small number who are truly fanatical fishermen and have an excellent knowledge of all the fish in their region. These people are introducing foreigners to the delights of Russian fishing and, in return, foreigners have spread the concept of throwing back rare fish so they can continue to breed.

---

❏ **Caviar (икра)**
There are three sorts of caviar, roe, or fish eggs – black sturgeon caviar (kaluga sturgeon, Siberian sturgeon, beluga sturgeon), soft red salmon caviar (dog-salmon, taimen, red sockeye salmon, humpback salmon) and other fish caviar (black carp, black Amur bream, whitefish, Amur pike, grayling, silver carp, sea urchin, Amur pike).

The first two types of caviar are commercially produced by pasteurising, pressing and salting eggs taken from live fish. Many fishermen make their own caviar by scooping out the fish eggs from the fish and pouring them into a container. A stick with a nail through it is then rotated like a beater in the container to break up the membrane between the eggs. After a few minutes, salt is added and the caviar is ready to eat. However, it is best to leave it for a few days as it improves with age.

In August and September, fish are spawning and locals sell fresh caviar for $3 a glass jar at the BAM stations. The sight of hundreds of dead fish following the spawning is disconcerting for some.

**Wild foods**

1. Amur barberry
2. blueberry
3. woodbine
4. wild strawberry
5. cowberry
6. raspberry
7. sea buckthorn
8. blackcurrant
9. small cranberry
10. redcurrant
11. Mongolian dandelion
12. wild onion
13. Siberian cedar
14. bracken fern
15. hazelnut
16. rowan tree, mountain ash
17. wild rose, dog rose
18. hawthorn

## ❑ Wild foods

**Siberian cedar/сибирский кедр** (September to October) Needles boiled to make a stomach-soothing tea and vitamin C drink. Pine nuts (from cones) are eaten raw or crushed for oil. This tree lies down in winter parallel with the ground and springs upright when it thaws. Found in the taiga.

**Amur barberry/амурский барбарис** (September to snowfall) Used in jam or as meat seasoning. Found in broad-leaved forests along the upper Amur.

**Bird cherry tree/черёмуха** (mid-July to August) Eaten raw and the seeds ground for cooking spice or coffee. The grounds are also used for a stomach-soothing drink. Found in light taiga and along rivers. The beautiful trees have white flowers and black berries.

**Blackcurrant/чёрная смородина** (mid-June to mid-July) Eaten raw or used in jam. Found in light taiga and along rivers.

**Blueberry/голубика** (mid-July to August) Eaten raw or used in jam.

**Bracken fern/папоротник** (May to mid-June) Boil the shoots and fry with garlic and egg. Found in light taiga and around swamps. Beware of the rhizome (roots) which are poisonous and will give you stomach, liver and bowel problems.

**Cowberry, red whortleberry, red bilberry, mountain cranberry/брусника** (September to snowfall) Eaten raw or used in jam or in kompot fruit drink. Found in taiga. The red berry survives all winter under the snow and last year's crop can be eaten just after the thaw. Popular with the Chinese and Japanese.

**Hawthorn/боярышник** (September to October) Eaten raw or used in jam. A red fruit with pink or white blossoms.

**Hazelnut/лесной орех** (September) Roasted. Found in broad-leaved forest.

**Mongolian dandelion/монгольский одуванчик** (from late May) The leaves are eaten raw in salads. Found in meadows. Yellow flowers.

**Raspberry/малина** (early August) Eaten raw or used in jam or in tea. Found in meadows, light taiga and along rivers.

**Redcurrant/красная смородина** (mid-July to August) Eaten raw or used in jam. Found in meadows, light taiga and along rivers.

**Rowan tree, mountain ash/рябина** (September to October) Eaten raw or used in jam. Found in broad-leafed forests.

**Sea buckthorn/облепиха June** Used to make kompot fruit drink. Seeds pressed for medicinal oil. Found in water meadows or by creeks.

**Sedge/осока** (Summer) Eaten raw or cooked like shallots. Found in marshes.

**Siberian apple/сибирская яблоня** (tree) **сибирское яблоко** (fruit) (August) Eaten raw. Very small.

**Small cranberry/болотная клюква** (August) Eaten raw or used in jam or kompot fruit drink. Found near waterways. The red berry survives all winter under snow and last year's crop can be eaten just after the thaw.

**Ussurian pear/уссурийская груша** (August) Eaten raw/used in jam.

**Water chestnut/водяной орех** Raw, boiled, or roasted. Found near waterways.

**Wild onion/черемша** (mid-June to mid-July) Eaten raw or pickled. Eat both bulb and leaves. Tastes like garlic. Very pungent. Milder when cooked.

**Wild rose, dog rose/шиповник** (August to September) Eaten raw or used to make rose tea and rose-flavoured liqueur. Found light taiga and along rivers.

**Wild strawberry/земляника** (end June to July) Eaten raw. Found in meadows, light taiga and along rivers. Not as large as commercial strawberries.

**Woodbine/жимолость** (late June to August) Eaten raw or used in jam.

During summer, locals use a combination of bait, lures and fly fishing to catch fish. In winter, there is only one method, which is to cut a hole in the ice and dangle a line. The fanatical fishermen have several prepared camps along rivers, which they use depending on the weather and season. During winter they often built a shelter over their hole cut in the ice so they can stay there for several days at a time.

## Places to fish

The best places to fish on the BAM are around Kuanda, Verkhnezeisk, Postyshevo and Komsomolsk-na-Amure. A brief summary of the fish in these areas follows with detailed information on how to organise a fishing trip listed under the respective towns in the BAM Mainline Route Description chapter. The laws governing fishing vary from region to region and fishing is prohibited at some places at certain times of year. However, generally a licence is not needed unless you catch over 50kg of fish or use a net.

Kuanda is surrounded by over 30 lakes and numerous rivers that flow into the long Vitim river. It is one of the few places left in Russia where you can find the mighty taimen, but even there you will have to travel several hundred kilometres up the Vitim to be guaranteed a catch. In the surrounding lakes and rivers are grayling, Amur pike, whitefish, Soldatov's catfish and the endemic targun.

Verkhnezeisk is on the Zeya Reservoir, which is becoming a rich fishing area. Fish include Amur pike, Soldatov's catfish, taimen, Amur id, grayling and Brachymystax salmon.

Postyshevo is a 10-minute walk from the Amgun river which is famous as one of the best fishing rivers in eastern Siberia. In late summer and autumn, you can flyfish for dog salmon and hunchback salmon, while in winter you can icefish for Brachymystax salmon, taimen and grayling.

Komsomolsk-na-Amure is on the Amur river which is fed by 120,000 big and little rivers. The Amur is populated with 99 different species of fish, which is the greatest variety in any Russian river. The main fish caught are the dog salmon and humpback salmon. Other fish caught include silver carp, kaluga, skygazer, Erythroculter Mongolicus and Siberian sturgeon. While the fish stocks in the river are dwindling due to overfishing and pollution, there is still a great deal of fish in its tributaries.

The rivers of the BAM region, and the mountain tributaries of the Lena north of Yakutsk, are the places to catch taimen (таймень), a native Siberian carnivorous fish that can grow to 50kg in weight and 2m long.

# Appendix C: Russian-language guide
Путеводитель по Русскому языку

## THE RUSSIAN ALPHABET (Русский алфабит)

It is wise to learn the Russian alphabet; with that you can read station names, timetables, street-signs and addresses.

The following table shows the Russian letters in alphabetic order, with the corresponding English letter as used in this guide and the pronunciation.

| Russian | English | Pronunciation |
|---|---|---|
| А а | a | far |
| Б б | b | bet |
| В в | v | vodka |
| Г г | g | get |
| Д д | d | dog |
| Е е | e | yet |
| Ё ё | e | yoghurt |
| Ж ж | zh | treasure |
| З з | z | zebra |
| И и | i | seek |
| Й й | i | boy |
| К к | k | Kiev |
| Л л | l | Lenin |
| М м | m | Moscow |
| Н н | n | never |
| О о | o | over |
| П п | p | Peter |
| Р р | r | Russia |
| С с | s | Samarkand |
| Т т | t | train |
| У у | u | move |
| Ф ф | f | frost |
| Х х | kh | loch |
| Ц ц | ts | lots |
| Ч ч | ch | chilly |
| Ш ш | sh | show |
| Щ щ | shch | fish |
| Ъ ъ | Omitted (no English equivalent) | hardens the preceding letter |

| Russian | English | Pronunciation |
|---------|---------|---------------|
| Ы ы | y | did |
| Ь ь | Omitted (no English equivalent) | softens the preceding letter |
| Э э | e | let |
| Ю ю | yu | union |
| Я я | ya | yak |

Russian words are transliterated according to the table, with the following simplification rules: ый = y, ий = i. In addition, a few Russian words, notably well-known place names, have not been transliterated but use the common English spelling.

You may notice that some of the stations have a different spelling than the nearby town, eg Kholodny station but Kholodnoe village and Kholodnaya river. This is because Russian has different spellings for adjectival endings.

## BASIC ENGLISH/RUSSIAN PHRASES (Основные выражения)

The following is the bare minimum needed for non-Russian speakers to get around. The first part is a small basic dictionary and pronunciation guide. The second part consists of specialised dictionaries of words and phrases not covered in phrasebooks. Rather than trying to pronounce these phrases, it is better to simply point to them.

| English | Pronunciation | Russian |
|---------|---------------|---------|
| yes | da | да |
| no | nyet | нет |
| please | pazhalista | пожалуйста |
| good day | zdravstvuite | здравствуйте |
| hi | zdravstvui | здравствуй |
| thank you | spasiba | спасибо |
| goodbye | dasvidaniya | до свидания |
| bye | paka | пока |
| please give me | daite pazhalista | Дайте, пожалуйста |
| call me a doctor | pazavite vracha | позовите врача |
| do you have ... ? | u vas yest ...? | у вас есть ...? |
| Cheers! | za vashe zdarove | за ваше здоровье |
| good | kharasho | хорошо |

## RAILWAY DICTIONARY (Словарь железнодорожных терминов)

| | |
|---|---|
| **касса** | **ticket window** |
| предварительная касса | for tickets after 24 hours |
| в день отправления касса | for tickets within 24 hours |
| текущая продажа билетов | for tickets within 24 hours |

часы работы с 8 до 20
working from 08.00 to 20.00

круглосуточная касса
open 24 hours

перерыв 13 до 14
break from 13.00 to 14.00

технический перерыв 10.15 до 10.45
technical break from 10.15 to 10.45

**расписание**
**timetable**

Чет. (четным числам)
even days (ie 2, 4, 6, ... of May)

Неч. (по нечетным числам)
odd days (ie 1, 3, 5, . of May)

вых (по выходным)
weekends and public holidays

раб (по рабочим дням)
weekdays

От. (отправление)
departure

Пр. (прибытие)
arrival

Пл. (платформа)
platform

станция назначения
station of destination

**поезд**
**train**

скорый поезд
fast train

транзитный поезд
transit train

пассажирский поезд
passenger train

пригородный поезд
suburban train

фирменный поезд
deluxe express train

поезд опаздывает
train is late

поезд не останавливается
train does not stop

поезд не заходит на станцию
train does not stop at the station

**вокзал, станция**
**station**

начальник вокзала
station master

дежурный по станции
station attendant

справка
information

**вагон**
**carriage**

СВ (спальный вагон)
2-berth compartment carriage

мягкий вагон
2-berth compartment carriage

купейный вагон
4-berth compartment carriage

плацкартный вагон
open sleeping carriage

общий вагон
open sitting carriage

безпересадочный вагон или отцепной вагон
wagon which separates and joins another train part way through the journey

**билет**
**ticket**

туда
one way

обратно
return

полный
adult

детский
child

| | |
|---|---|
| место | berth number |
| верхнее место | upper berth |
| нижнее место | lower berth |
| проездной билет | pass such as a monthly pass |
| льготный билет | discount ticket for pensioners, students etc |
| зона | price zones |

**время** — **time**

| | |
|---|---|
| московское время | Moscow time |
| местное время | local time |

**на поезде** — **on the train**

| | |
|---|---|
| начальник поезда, начальник бригады проводников | Train Captain (head conductor) |
| проводник, проводница | conductor |
| стоп-кран | emergency stop handle |
| багажная полка | baggage rack |
| одеяло | blankets |
| белье | sheets |
| постельные принадлежности | rolled-up mattress and pillow |

**Полезные железнодорожные выражения** — **Useful railway expressions**

| | |
|---|---|
| Вот мой билет. | Here is my ticket. |
| Покажите, пожалуйста, мое место. | Please show me my place. |
| Разбудите меня в ...... часов | Please wake me at ....... |
| Разбудите меня, пожалуйста, за час до прибытия в ....... | Please wake me an hour before we arrive at ....... |
| Где находится вагон-ресторан или буфет? | Where is the restaurant car or buffet car? |
| Где находится туалет? | Where is the toilet? |
| Здесь можно курить? | May I smoke here? |
| Принесите, пожалуйста, (еще одно) одеяло. | Please bring me a (another) blanket. |
| Какая следующая станция? | What is the next station? |
| Сколько минут стоянка поезда? | How many minutes will the train stop here? |
| Я опоздал на поезд. | I am late for the train. |

# Appendix D: Glossary
## Толковый словарь

These words are the main foreign words and abbreviations used in the text.

**AYaAD (АЯАД)** The initials of the Amur Yakutsk Highway (Амуро-Якутская Автомобильная Дорога) which technically starts at the Amur river and finishes at Yakutsk. However, in this book the popular definition of the AYaAD is used, which means the highway from Tynda to Yakutsk.

**AYaM (АЯМ)** The initials of the Amur-Yakutsk Mainline (Амуро-Якутская Магистраль) the railway that technically starts at the Amur river and finishes at Yakutsk. However, in this book the popular definition of the AYaM is used, which means the railway from Tynda to Yakutsk.

**BAM (БАМ)** The initials of the Baikal-Amur Mainline (Байкало-Амурская Магистраль) railway which technically starts near Lake Baikal and finishes at the Amur river. However, in this book the popular definition of the BAM is used, which encompasses the BAM mainline from Taishet on the Trans-Siberian to Sovetskaya Gavan on the Pacific Ocean coast, plus the BAM branch lines.

**BAM mainline** The backbone of the BAM which stretches from Taishet to Sovetskaya Gavan.

**BAM Zone (Зона БАМа)** The development area around the BAM which is up to several hundred kilometres wide.

**banya (баня)** Russian sauna.

**blin, bliny (блин, блины)** Pancake, pancakes – light crêpes served with butter, roe, or jam.

**bolota (болота)** A swamp.

**borscht (борщ)** Soup based on beets, potatoes, onions and cabbage, sometimes with chunks of meat added.

**CCCP (СССР)** See SSSR.

**coupé (купе)** A carriage with four berths per cabin. The most common carriages for foreigners.

**dacha (дача)** Usually a small cottage on a small farm plot owned by city dwellers.

**dacha village (дачный посёлок)** A suburb on the outskirts of most towns where most dachas are located.

**Decembrist (Декабрист)** A revolutionary who took part in the 14 December 1825 uprising in St Petersburg, demanding a constitutional monarch rather than an autocratic Tsar.

**derevnya (деревня)** A village or hamlet. There are numerous other words for village, but with the exception of derevnya and *selo* these words are only of historical significance.

**dezhurnaya (дежурная)** Hotel floor attendant. Also sometimes the shift station manager at a railway station.

**elektrovoz (электровоз)** An electric locomotive.

**firmenny train (фирменный поезд)** Private, as in 'private train', a fast train leased to a private company.

**GES (ГЭС)** A hydro-electric station.

**glasnost (гласность)** A Gorbachev-era buzzword meaning political and media openness.

**glazunya (глазунья)** Fried eggs.

**GOELRO (ГОЭЛРО)** From the initials of the 1920s Government Plan for the Electrification of Russia (Государственный план электрификации России) which shaped and still shapes the electrification policy in Russia today.

**gorod (город)** A city with a minimum population of 12,000 and at least 85 per cent of its employed population engaged in non-agricultural work.

**Great Patriotic War (Великая Отечественная война)** The Soviet Union fought in World War Two (1941-45); this is their term for this war.

**gulag (ГУЛаг)** From the initials of the organisation that ran prison camps, the Main Department of Corrective Labour Camps (Главное Управление Исправительных Лагерей). The word is now used to mean a prison camp of the Stalin era.

**homestay (остановиться в семье)** Accommodation in a Russian family home.

**Intourist (Интурист)** Russia's formerly state-owned travel company. It still has the nation's largest network of hotels.

**izba (изба)** A wooden rural house.

**kasha (каша)** cooked grain or porridge

**kassa (касса)** A ticket window.

**KGB (КГБ)** The initials of the Soviet secret police (Комитет Государственной Безопасности) which operated from 1956 to 1991. It is now called the FSK or Federal Counter-Intelligence Service (Федеральная Служба Контразведки).

**khutor (хутор)** Isolated farm in a forest

**kladbishche paravozov (кладбище паравозов)** A steam-engine graveyard.

**kolkhoz (колхоз)** A collective farm.

**kombinat (комбинат)** A large industrial complex.

**kompot (компот)** A fruit drink made of berries.

**Komsomol (Комсомол)** Abbreviation for the Communist Youth League (Коммунистисческий Союз Молодёжи) which represented 14 to 27 year olds.

**Komsomol Shock Project** (Всесоюзная ударная Комсомольская стройка) A nationally significant project managed by the Komsomol.

**Krai (Край)** A territory.

**KSO (КСО)** Abbreviation for the search and rescue teams for people lost in the wild (Контрольно-Спасательный отряд).

**kurort (курорт)** A health resort or a town of sanatoriums.

**kvas (квас)** Fermented drink made with brown bread and herbs. Sometimes written 'kvass' in English.

**Little BAM (Маленький БАМ)** The railway connecting the Trans-Siberian at Bamovskaya to the BAM at Tynda.

**lyuks (люкс)** A deluxe hotel room.

**manevrovy (маневровый)** A shunting locomotive.

**mikroraion (микрорайон)** A satellite town or suburb.

**militsiya (милиция)** Police.

**myagky (мягкий)** A first-class sleeping carriage with two beds only in the compartment. Synonym for SV.

**novy (новый)** New.

**oblast (область)** A region.

**obshchi (общий)** An open carriage with no reserved seating or sleeping benches.

**Oktyabrenok (Октябрёнок)** The communist-era national youth organisation for young children from seven to nine years of age.

**OViR (ОВиР (Отдел Виз и Регистраций))** Former name of the agency that issues visas for foreigners and passports for Russians. See PVS.

**parokhod (пароход)** A steamship.

**parovoz (паровоз)** A railway steam engine.

**perestroika (перестройка)** A Gorbachev-era buzzword meaning restructuring.

**pereval (перевал)** A mountain pass.

**permafrost (вечная мерзлота)** Ground that is permanently frozen.

**Pioneers (Пионер)** The communist-era national youth organisation for children from nine to 14 years.

**pirozhok, pirozhki (пирожок, пирожки)** Patty, patties ('little pie'). Fried dough with a filling of meat, curd, or jam.

**ploshchad (площадь)** A city square.

**poezd (поезд)** A train.

**poselok (посёлок)** An urban settlement with a minimum population of 3,000 and at least 85 per cent employed in non-agricultural work.

**pr. or pr-t (пр. или пр-т)** Abbreviation for prospekt (проспект), meaning avenue.

**provodnik, provodnitsa (проводник, проводница)** A train conductor (male and female) (plural - provodniki)

**PVS (ПВС (паспортно-визовая служба))** The agency that issues visas for foreigners and passports for Russians. Formerly OViR.

**raion (район)** A district.

**raketa (ракета)** Type of hydrofoil, sometimes generically used for any hydrofoil.

**raz. (раз.)** Abbreviation for razezd (разъезд), meaning a railway siding.

**rechnoi vokzal (речной вокзал)** River Station, stopping place of river passenger craft.

**salo (сало)** Smoked, cured or salted bacon still attached to the rind, eaten in thin slices.

**samovar (самовар)** A hot-water urn.

**sanatorium (санаторий)** A health resort often built near mineral springs or mud pools.

**selo (село)** A rural village.

**shapka (шапка)** Winter fur hat

**shashlik (шашлык)** Cubes of meat grilled over coals, shish kebab.

**sortirovka (сортировка)** A marshalling yard where passenger trains join, separate, or wait.

**Soviet (Совет)** A council.

**sovkhoz (совхоз)** A state-owned collective farm.

**SSSR (СССР)** Abbreviation for Union of Soviet Socialist Republics (Союз Советских Социалистических Республик).

**stary (старый)** Old.

**SV (СВ)** Abbreviation for a first-class sleeping carriage with two beds only in the compartment (спальный вагон). Synonym for myagky.

**taiga (тайга)** Coniferous boreal forest of Siberia and the Far East

**teplokhod (теплоход)** A motorised ship.

**teplovoz (тепловоз)** A diesel locomotive.

**tonnel or tunnel (тоннель** or **туннель)** A tunnel.

**TOTs (ТОЦ)** The Russian equivalent to a mall where a number of shops are all located in one place (Торговый Общественный Центр).

**Trans-Siberian Railway (Транс-Сиб)** The 7,200km railway stretching from Moscow to Vladivostok.

**trassa (трасса)** Line, route as in Kolymskaya trassa - Kolyma route.

**turist (турист)** The Russian word 'turist' traditionally meant adventure travel such as mountaineering and camping, while the English word 'tourist' usually referred to a traveller on a packaged holiday or one who stayed for a short time in a city. However, the Russian word turist is now commonly used to mean the same as the English tourist.

**ul. (ул.)** Abbreviation for *ulitsa* (улица), meaning street.

**vetka (ветка)** A railway branch line.

**vokzal (вокзал)** A railway station.

**yurt (юрта)** Mongolian tent house

**zakaznik (заказник)** A nature sanctuary.

**zapovednik (заповедник)** A nature reserve.

**zheleznaya doroga (железная дорога)** A railway.

# Appendix E: Further study
## Что ещё можно узнать

The following are books, maps, videos and other resources to learn about the regions of the north-east.

## BOOKS

### The BAM (О БАМе)

Over the years, the BAM construction has generated its share of glossy albums, hero-constructor novels and technical books.

*Trailblazing Through the Taiga* and *Working for Present and Future Generations* by Yuri Kazmin. These enjoyable socialist realist novels were written in the 1930s during the first stage of the BAM.

*The Mainline of My Youth* by Nikola Nikolarov, 1932. The story recounts the author's experiences working on the first stage of the BAM. Nikolarov was the son of the famous Bulgarian revolutionary and general secretary of Comintern, Vasili Kalarov.

*The Second Trans-Siberian Railroad: The new stage in the development of the USSR's eastern region* by Leonid Shinkarev, 1977, and *The Great Baikal-Amur Railway* by V I Malashenko, 1977, are interesting Soviet propaganda.

During the 1970s and 1980s photographers and artists covered the BAM construction. They produced many evocative picture books that you can find in Russian bookstores and libraries and occasionally in foreign libraries (*BAM Mainline*, 1976; *BAM goes forward*, 1990; *The road that they did not choose*, 1993, about the railway troops). Here you can see the young men and women working in the wilderness, the trucks and lifts and helicopters, the hard hats and work jackets with brigade lettering, the bell bottoms and knee-length skirts and sideburns, the woodland camps, the first settlements, the first weddings in the mud, the first children.

*Gateway to Siberian resources (The BAM)*, by Theodore Shabad and Victor L. Mote, Scripta Publishing Co, A Halsted Press Book, John Wiley & Sons, 1977, ISBN 0-470-99040-6, is the only Western analysis of the BAM. It includes a chapter 'Siberian resource development in the Soviet period' by Shabad, a long chapter 'The Baykal-Amur Mainline: Catalyst for the development of Pacific Siberia' by Mote, including extensive economic analysis and several chapters reprinted from Russian sources.

*Soviet Locomotive Types: The Union Legacy* by A J Heywood and I D C Button, 1995, Luddenden Press, UK, ISBN 0-9525202-0-6.

## Guidebooks (Путеводители)

The following are good guidebooks to Russia and include at least a mention of the BAM or the north-east:

*Russia by Rail with Belarus and Ukraine* by Athol Yates (first author of this guide), Bradt Publications, 1996, ISBN 1-898323-32-1.

*Trans-Siberian Handbook* by Bryn Thomas and others, Trailblazer Publications, 5th edition, 1997, ISBN 1-873756-42-9.

*The Russian Far East* by Erik Azulay and Allegra Harris Azulay, Hippocrene Books, 1995, ISBN 0-7818-0325-X.

*Russia, Ukraine and Belarus* – Lonely Planet Travel Survival Kit by John Noble, Andrew Humphreys, Richard Nebesky, Nick Selby, George Wesely and John King, Lonely Planet, 1996, ISBN 0-86442-320-9.

*The Trans-Siberian Rail Guide* by Robert Strauss and Tamsin Turnbull, Hunter Pub, 4th edition, 1996, ISBN 0-9520900-1-5.

*Trekking in Russia and Central Asia: A Traveler's Guide* by Frith Maier, The Mountaineers, 1994, ISBN 0-89886-355-4.

*Russia and Central Asia by Road: 4WD Motorbike Bicycle* by Hazel Barker and David Thurlow, Bradt Publications, 1997, ISBN: 1-898323-61-5.

## Travellers' tales (Рассказы путешественников)

*Off the Map: Bicycling across Siberia* by Mark Jenkins, 1991. A memoir with photos about the author's bike ride along the Trans-Siberian route from the Pacific Coast in 1989.

If you intend to drive yourself, have a look at the website ⌨ www.turtleexpedition.com. Gary and Monika Wescott, also known as Turtle Expedition Unlimited, drove their 4WD van, towing a travel trailer, in late winter 1996 from Magadan to Yakutsk on the Kolyma Highway, then down the Lena river to Ust-Kut, west to Bratsk and south to Irkutsk, then up and down Lake Baikal (and on around the world).

In *Reeling in Russia* (St Martin's Press, 1998, ISBN 0-312-18595-2) Fen Montaigne fly fishes across Russia (sort of). He explores the north-east of Lake Baikal, takes the BAM to Tynda, the AYaAD highway to Yakutsk and the Kolyma Highway to Magadan – and doesn't seem to like much of it.

In *Siberian dawn: A journey across the new Russia* (Hungry Mind Press, 1999, ISBN 1-886913-26-9) Jeffrey Tayler travelled by truck in late winter from Magadan to Yakutsk and Yakutsk to Berkakit, and then by train to Tynda and Chernyshevsk. He was obsessed by drunks and didn't like the journey much either.

*The Big Red Train Ride* by Eric Newby, *The Great Railway Bazaar* by Paul Theroux and *The Trans-Siberian Railway: A Traveller's Anthology* by Deborah Manley are about or include the Trans-Siberian.

## Nature (О природе)

*Russian National Parks*, an article in *Surviving Together*, Spring 1993, covers the problems facing managers of Russian national parks.

*A Field Guide to Birds of the USSR* by V E Flint, R L Boehme, Y V
Kostin, and A A Kuznetsov, 1984, is the best book on birds of Siberia.

## History (Об истории)
*Guide to the Great Siberian Railway*, edited by A I Dmitriev-Mamonov
and A F Zdziarski, was published in English in 1900 by the Russian
Ministry of Ways of Communication and reprinted in 1972 by Drake
Publishers Inc, ISBN 87749-147-X. It is a comprehensive guidebook to
the Trans-Siberian, with excellent maps and illustrations. For a govern-
ment-sponsored book it is unexpectedly rich in those titbits that attract the
seasoned traveller, and also shows an interest in the future territory of the
BAM and the AYaM, with photogravures of *skoptsy* (скопцы, castrated
cultists) in the Vilyuisk district, lepers in Yakutsk, remarks on the difficulties of populating the territory with exiled felons ('the age of the convicts ... is not suitable for marriage and for a fresh start in family life'),
and the winter mail schedule to Sakhalin Island (1st and 15th of the month
by dog-sled across the Nevelskoi strait).

*Red Planes Fly East* by Piotr Pavlenko (1899-1951) is a communist novel
about the settlement of Siberia in the 1930s that captures the enthusiasm
of opening up a brave new world. The book served to encourage people to
live in eastern Siberia and advocated the Khetagurova movement.
Pavlenko's other books include *In the East*, which became a film in 1937
called *In the Far East*.

*The Soviet Far East in Antiquity* by A P Okladnikov, 1963, is an excellent
overview of Siberia's ancient people by Russia's greatest ethnographer.

*Farewell to Matyora*, a novel by Valentin Rasputin, is the tragic story of
the flooding of the Ust-Ilimsk region which necessitated 249 settlements
being moved and resulted in serious social problems. Rasputin also wrote
a number of other stories about his local area, Lake Baikal and Irkutsk,
including *You Live and Love*, *Going Downstream*, *Unexpected Trouble*,
*Borrowed Time* and *Money for Maria*.

*Behind the Urals: An American Worker in Russia's City of Steel* by John
Scott. This 1942 book is the autobiography of an American who volunteered
to work in the newly developed city of Magnitogorsk. Although this city is
thousands of miles from Komsomolsk-na-Amure, the two cities were
founded about the same time and experiences parallel each other.

*How the Steel Was Tempered* by Nikolai Ostrovsky. This 1952 book portrays the enthusiasm of the early years of Communist power. The anti-
hero of this novel was so popular that a future BAM town will be named
after him. This book is great and don't let any literary critic tell you it's a
worthless piece of socialist realism.

*A Dance with Death: Soviet Airwomen in World War II* by Anne Noggle.
This excellent 1994 book covers in detail the life of air navigator Marina
Raskova, her place in aviation history and her crash in the BAM Zone.

*Arctic Mirrors: Russia* and *the Small Peoples of the North* by Yuri Slezkine, 1994, is an excellent review of the past and present policies of the Russians towards the indigenous people of eastern and north Siberia.

Other important books on indigenous people include:

● *A History of the Peoples of Siberia: Russia's North Asian Colony 1581-1990* by J Forsyth, 1992.

● *Popular Beliefs and Folklore Traditions in Siberia*, ed V Dioszegi, 1968.

● *The People of Siberia*, edited by M G Levin and L P Polapov, 1964.

● *Crossroads of Continents: Cultures of Siberia and Alaska* by William W. Fitzhugh and Aron Crowell.

● *Shamanism: Soviet Studies of Traditional Religion in Siberia and Central Asia*, edited by M Mandelstam Balzer.

● *Shamanism: Archaic Techniques of Ecstasy* by M Eliade, 1974.

● *Karl Marx Collective: Economy, Society and Religion in a Siberian Collective Farm* by C Humphrey, 1983.

## About gulags (О ГУЛагах)

Aleksandr Solzhenitsyn's masterly six-volume *The Gulag Archipelago*, 1974, describes the history, politics, geographic extent, hierarchies and life of the camps, and the path of the prisoner from arrest to death or release. His *One Day in the Life of Ivan Denisovich*, 1963, first published in the Khrushchev thaw, describes daily life in a camp. Solzhenitsyn had little direct experience of the camps of the far east and defers to Shalamov's accounts.

Varlam Shalamov's *Kolyma Tales*, 1980, is one of the best-known memoirs of the gulags and is admired by Solzhenitsyn. In Chekhovian tales, Shalamov describes life in the camps along the highway and in the hinterlands. He was a prisoner in the Kolyma camps from 1937 to 1951 and an exile until 1953.

Michael Solomon (*Magadan*, 1971) was a Rumanian-born journalist who fought with the British during World War II and was arrested in post-war Rumania and sent to the camps. He gives a vivid picture of the great transit camps of Vanino and Magadan, the Kolyma mines and construction sites, and the gulag characters – gallant, tragic and monstrous.

*Kolyma: The Arctic Death Camps* by Robert Conquest, 1978, pulls together published and unpublished accounts and a few sources known in the west, including the tonnage of the prisoner transport fleet taken from Lloyd's Register of Shipping and the grotesque visit by Owen Lattimore to Kolyma in 1943, when NKVD soldiers dressed up as husky miners and jolly swineherds (*National Geographic*, December 1944).

*A World Apart* by Gustav Herling, 1951, *Forever Flowing* by Vasili Grossman, 1972, and *Forced Labours in Soviet Russia* by David Dallin and Boris I Nicolaevsky, 1974, also describe the camps, sometimes mentioning the BAM and the Kolyma.

## MAPS (Карты)

The General-Geographical Maps of the Russian Federation (Общегеографические карты российской федерации), published by the Federal Service of Geodesy and Cartography of Russia (Федеральная служба геодезии и картографии России) show places, buildings (including individual buildings such as winter cabins and meteorological stations), roads, railways, topography and spot elevations.

The maps are available for all the political divisions through which the BAM, the AYaM and the AYaAD, the Lena river and the Kolyma highway go. These are, roughly from west to east: Irkutskaya Oblast (Иркутская область), Republic of Buryatiya (Республика Бурятия), Chitinskaya Oblast (Читинская область), Republic of Sakha (Yakutiya) (Республика Саха (Якутия)), Amurskaya Oblast (Амурская область), Jewish Autonomous Oblast (Еврейская автономная область), Khabarovski Krai (Хабаровский край), Magadanskaya Oblast (Магаданская область).

Russian military topographic maps in scales of 1:500,000 and larger are sporadically available..

The following are sources of these and other Russian maps:

● FOUR ONE Co Ltd, 523 Hamilton Rd, London, Ont N5Z 1S3, Canada ☎ +1-519-433-1351, 📠 +1-519-433-5903, 📧 maps@fourone.com, 🖥 www.fourone.com

● Victor Kamkin Inc., 4956 Boiling Brook Parkway, Rockville MD 20852 USA, ☎ +1-301-881-4905, 📠 +1-301-881-1637, 📧 kamkin@igc.apc.org, www.kamkin.com.

In Yakutsk, the Federal Service of Geodesy and Cartography of Russia operates an excellent and friendly map shop, which may be able to supply all the above maps and others. Globus, Pr. Lenina, 16, ☎ 42-30-72 (677892, г. Якутск, пр. Ленина, 16, «Глобус»).

You may find maps randomly in bookstores or even on the street. The usual rule for buying in Russia applies: if you want it and can afford it, buy it now, because you may never find it again.

The US Government Tactical Pilotage Charts (TPCs) at 1:500,000 show places, rivers and reservoirs, roads, railways, electricity transmission lines, pipelines, aerodromes and radio facilities, topography (with both contours and colour shading) and spot elevations. Being for pilots, they are more detailed on 'vertical obstructions' than on political details. They are lettered in Latin letters and show heights in feet. TPCs are indexed on Standard Index Chart #4. There are also Operational Navigation Charts (ONCs) at 1:1,000,000, indexed on Standard Index Chart #3. NOAA Distribution Division, N/ACC3, National Ocean Service, Riverdale MD 20737-1199 USA, ☎ +1-800-638-8972 or +1-301-436-8301, 📠 +1-301-436-6829, 📧 Distribution@noaa.gov.

## VIDEOS (Видео)

*Road to the Ocean*  A 1945 black-and-white film on the construction of the Komsomolsk-na-Amure to Sovetskaya Gavan line.

*Iron Road*  A 1992 film revealing the truth of the 1945 construction of the Komsomolsk-na-Amure to Sovetskaya Gavan line.

*BAM 20th Anniversary*  A 1994 film commemorating the construction of the BAM.

The above films are available from Marina Aleksandrovna Kuzmina, Editorial Consultant of this guide. For details about how to contact her see Getting assistance under Komsomolsk-na-Amure (p176).

Tele Rail (9a New Street, Carnforth, Lancs, LA5 9BX UK, ☎ +44 1524 735774, 🖹 +44 1524 736386, 🖳 orders@telerail.co.uk) offers documentary Russian railway videos including the BAM line, the Trans Siberian, and the Caucasus, featuring steam and modern traction. The BAM video covers the BAM as well as the Trans-Siberian, with steam locomotives on the pre-1974 sections. L-class locomotives haul on the western section and Lend-Lease Yeas on the eastern section, with a crossing of the Sikhote Alin range on the 55th anniversary of the first train on the Komsomolsk-na-Amure to Sovetskaya Gavan line. Videos are supplied in all formats.

*Aerograd* by Alexander Dovzhenko (Аэроград, Александр Довженко). This masterly 1935 Mosfilm concerns the construction of a new city at the mouth of the Amur (think Komsomolsk-na-Amure). With musical numbers, intrepid Muscovite aviators in leather flightsuits, gallant *kolkhozniki* (Russian and Evenk) who battle Japanese saboteurs and benighted Russian Old Believers in the taiga, and breathtaking aerial photography of a mass parachute drop – all in all, it doesn't teach much about the building of Komsomolsk-na-Amure, but it does reflect its mythical impact and it is contemporary.

*Baikal: The Blue Eye of Siberia*, Cicada Films, 1990, is a 107-minute video in Russian with English subtitles. It portrays a year-long journey around the lake – rugged cliffs and isolated villages, the birds, endemic fish and below-surface organisms that inhabit the lake, the winter and spring hunts for Baikal seals and the effect of pollutants on the lake's food-chain balance. Local inhabitants describe the present and past condition of the lake; their respect for nature and the spiritual force of the lake is a powerful element of this production. Rashit Yahin, Editorial Consultant of this guide, worked as an interpreter for this production.

# Appendix F: BAM mainline timetables
## Расписание

Russian train timetables change three times a year but not usually by much.

**MOSCOW–TYNDA** (Москва–Тында)

| Place | Станция | Km east of Taishet | Eastbound train 76Zh Arrive, MT (stop) | Westbound train 75E Arrive, MT (stop) |
|---|---|---|---|---|
| MT = Moscow Time | | | | |
| Moscow, Kazan Station | Москва, Казанский вокзал | | 20:27 depart | 10.58 |
| Kazan | Казань-пасс. | | 08.54 (15) | 21.50 (15) |
| Sverdlovsk | Свердловск-пасс. | | 00.29 (15) | 06.44 (16) |
| Novosibirsk | Новосибирск | | 22.43 (30) | 09.32 (28) |
| Taishet | Тайшет | 0 | 19.03 (30) | 12.04 (30) |
| Sosnovye Rodniki | Сосновые Родники | 129 | 21.31 (2) | 10.05 (2) |
| Chuna | Чуна | 142 | 21.49 (2) | 09.47 (2) |
| Vikhorevka | Вихоревка | 269 | 23.59 (20) | 07.26 (20) |
| Anzebi | Анзёби | 292 | 00.49 (5) | 06.54 (3) |
| Padunskie Porogi | Падунские Пороги | 325 | 01.30 (2) | 06.18 (3) |
| Gidrostroitel | Гидростроитель | 339 | 01.50 (2) | 05.58 (3) |
| Korshunikha-Angarskaya | Коршуниха-Ангарская | 554 | 05.11 (10) | 02.18 (10) |
| Lena | Лена | 722 | 08.07 (20) | 23.16 (20) |
| Zvezdnaya | Звёздная | 786 | 09.45 (2) | 21.55 (2) |
| Kirenga | Киренга | 890 | 11.41 (5) | 19.49 (10) |
| Ulkan | Улькан | 931 | 12.30 (2) | 19.02 (2) |
| Severobaikalsk | Северобайкальск | 1,064 | 14.49 (35) | 16.08 (39) |
| Nizhneangarsk | Нижнеангарск | 1,104 | 15.53 (1) | 15.26 (2) |
| Kholodny | Холодный | 1,120 | 16.12 | 14.57 (13) |
| Kichera | Кичера | 1,141 | 16.26 (1) | 14.34 (3) |
| Angoya | Ангоя | 1,196 | 17.14 (1) | 13.44 (1) |
| Novy Uoyan | Новый Уоян | 1,257 | 18.15 (15) | 12.30 (15) |
| Kyukhel-bekerskaya | Кюхельбекерская | 1,330 | 19.39 (4) | 11.19 (3) |
| Taksimo | Таксимо | 1,484 | 23.35 (20) | 07.15 (30) |
| Kuanda | Куанда | 1,577 | 01.31 (5) | 05.33 (7) |
| Novaya Chara | Новая Чара | 1,734 | 04.24 (20) | 01.48 (27) |
| Ikabya | Икабья | 1,772 | 05.17 (5) | 01.07 (3) |
| Khani | Хани | 1,879 | 07.40 (35) | 22.23 (40) |
| Olekma | Олёкма | 1,934 | 09.11 (2) | 21.22 (2) |
| Yuktali | Юктали | 2,028 | 10.53 (15) | 19.26 (15) |

## Moscow–Tynda (Москва–Тында) cont'd

| Place | Станция | Km east of Taishet | Eastbound train 76Zh Arrive, MT (stop) | Westbound train 75E Arrive, MT (stop) |
|---|---|---|---|---|
| Chilchi | Чильчи | 2,137 | 12.55 (2) | 17.37 (2) |
| Lopcha | Лопча | 2,185 | 13.54 (2) | 16.37 (2) |
| Larba | Ларба | 2,232 | 14.45 (2) | 15.46 (2) |
| Khorogochi | Хорогочи | 2,284 | 15.39 (2) | 14.20 (12) |
| Kuvykta | Кувыкта | 2,334 | 16.22 (2) | 13.36 (2) |
| Tynda | Тында | 2,364 | 17.07 | 12.50 depart |

## TYNDA–KOMSOMOLSK-NA-AMURE (Тында–Комсомольск-на-Амуре)

| Place | Станция | Km east of Taishet | Eastbound train 204E Arrive, MT (stop) | Westbound train 203E Arrive, MT (stop) |
|---|---|---|---|---|
| Tynda | Тында | 2,364 | 11.05 depart | 02.55 |
| Marevaya | Маревая | 2,452 | 12.46 (5) | 01.00 (3) |
| Unakha | Унаха | 2,511 | 14.04 (1) | 23.46 (2) |
| Dipkun | Дипкун | 2,527 | 14.27 (10) | 23.15 (10) |
| Dess | Дёсс | 2,541 | 14.55 (1) | |
| Tutaul | Тутаул | 2,582 | 15.52 (2) | 22.04 (3) |
| Verkhnezeisk | Верхнезейск | 2,707 | 18.34 (40) | 18.21 (68) |
| Ogoron | Огорон | 2,796 | 21.10 (2) | 16.17 (2) |
| Tungala | Тунгала | 2,863 | 22.40 (15) | 14.32 (15) |
| Dugda | Дугда | 2,912 | 00.02 (2) | 13.21 (2) |
| Nora | Нора | 2,932 | 00.37 (1) | 12.46 (2) |
| Fevralsk | Февральск | 3,033 | 02.50 (40) | 09.50 (40) |
| Zvonkoe | Звонкое | 3,040 | 04.00 (1) | 09.22 (1) |
| Demchenko | Демченко | 3,065 | 04.32 (1) | 08.51 (1) |
| Ulma | Ульма | 3,149 | 06.40 (15) | 06.48 (2) |
| Etyrken | Етыркэн | 3,179 | 07.20 (3) | 06.23 (2) |
| Alonka | Алонка | 3,264 | 09.43 (3) | 04.10 (2) |
| Bureinski | Буреинский | 3,305 | 10.56 (1) | 03.00 (1) |
| Novy Urgal | Новый Ургал | 3,315 | 11.20 (40) | 02.15 (25) |
| Urgal-1 | Ургал-1 | 3,330 | 12.22 (6) | 01.38 (12) |
| Soloni | Солони | 3,383 | 13.42 (3) | 00.23 (3) |
| Dusse-Alin | Дуссе-Алинь | 3,403 | 14.15 (1) | 23.52 (1) |
| Suluk | Сулук | 3,421 | 14.45 (3) | 23.23 (3) |
| Gerbi | Герби | 3,475 | 16.10 (3) | 21.54 (3) |
| Urkaltu | Уркальту | 3,500 | 16.44 (1) | 21.22 (1) |
| Amgun | Амгунь | 3,581 | 18.35 (3) | 19.27 (3) |
| Postyshevo | Постышево | 3,633 | 19.51 (25) | 17.40 (25) |
| Evoron | Еворон | 3,697 | 21.54 (3) | 16.06 (3) |
| Gorin | Горин | 3,733 | 22.46 (3) | 15.16 (3) |
| Khurmuli | Хурмули | 3,769 | 23.36 (15) | 14.25 (5) |
| Khalgaso | Хальгасо | 3,808 | 00.45 (7) | 13.31 (3) |
| Komsomolsk-na-Amure | Комсомольск-на-Амуре | 3,837 | 01.40 | 12.45 depart |

## KOMSOMOLSK-NA-AMURE–SOVETSKAYA GAVAN (Комсомольск-на-Амуре–Советская Гавань)

Note: The numbering of the following trains may seem to violate the rule stated on p37: 'The train number indicates which way it is heading. If the number is even it means that it is going to the east, if odd to the west towards Moscow.' Train 252E starts at Vladivostok and heads west toward Moscow until turning north at Khabarovsk and then east again at Komsomolsk-na-Amure. Vice versa for Train 251E.

| Place | Станция | Km east of Pivan | Eastbound train 251E Arrive, MT (stop) | Westbound train 252E Arrive, MT (stop) |
|---|---|---|---|---|
| Khabarovsk | Хабаровск | | 02.05 depart | 13.31 (59) |
| Komsomolsk-na-Amure | Комсомольск-на-Амуре | -19 | 12.15 (65) | 02.15 (45) |
| Pivan | Пивань | 0 | 14.09 (3) | 01.19 (3) |
| Gaiter | Гайтер | 29 | 14.47 (2) | 00.43 (2) |
| Kartel | Картель | 41 | 15.04 (4) | 00.25 (3) |
| Selikhin | Селихин | 51 | 15.23 (5) | 00.06 (4) |
| Kun | Кун | 95 | 16.35 (5) | 23.00 (3) |
| Gurskaya | Гурская | 112 | 17.03 (5) | 22.32 (5) |
| Oune | Оунэ | 182 | 18.46 (2) | 20.56 (2) |
| Kuznetsovski | Кузнецовский | 203 | 19.36 (4) | 20.12 (2) |
| Vysokogornaya | Высокогорная | 220 | 20.08 (27) | 18.54 (36) |
| Datta | Датта | 240 | 21.01 (2) | 18.18 (8) |
| Kenada | Кенада | 260 | 21.25 (4) | 17.51 (4) |
| Tuluchi | Тулучи | 303 | 22.22 (4) | 16.53 (4) |
| Tumnin | Тумнин | 340 | 23.16 (7) | 15.57 (8) |
| Ust-Orochi | Усть-Орочи | 380 | 00.17 (5) | 15.00 (5) |
| Mongokhto | Монгохто | 403 | 00.56 (2) | 14.24 (1) |
| Vanino-Vokzal | Ванино-Вокзал | 441 | 02.05 (10) | 13.05 (10) |
| Sovgavan-Sortirovka | Совгавань-Сортировка | 449 | 02.35 | 12.45 depart |

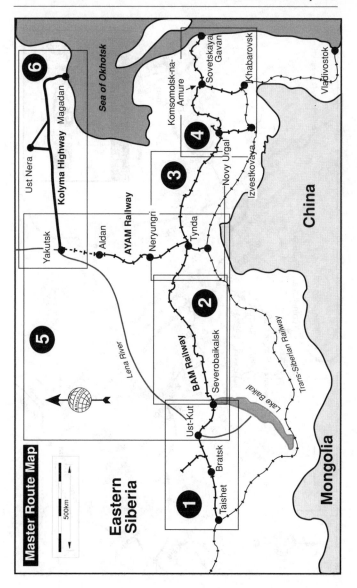

Master Route Map

500km

Eastern
Siberia

① ② ③ ④ ⑤ ⑥

Taishet
Bratsk
Ust-Kut
Severobaikalsk
Lena River
Yakutsk
Aldan
Neryungri
Tynda
Novy Urgal
Izvestkovaya
Komsomolsk-na-Amure
Sovetskaya Gavan
Khabarovsk
Vladivostok
Ust Nera
Magadan

BAM Railway
AYAM Railway
Kolyma Highway
Trans-Siberian Railway
Lake Baikal
Sea of Okhotsk
China
Mongolia

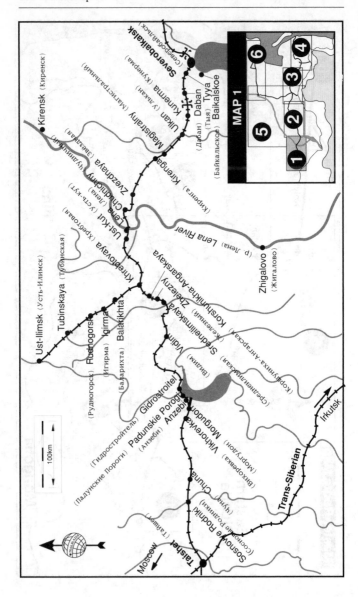

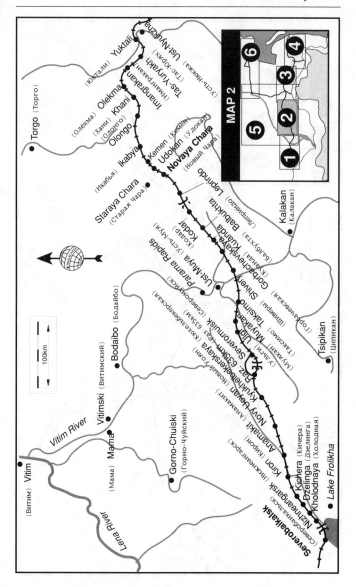

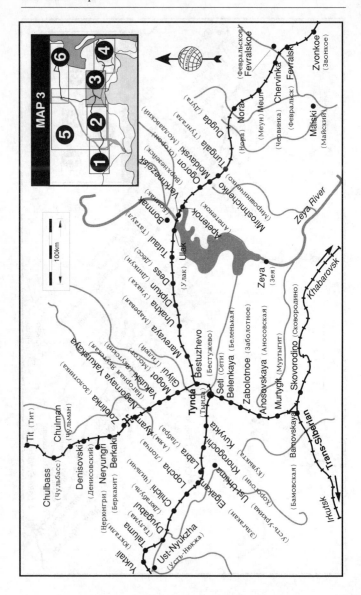

MAP 3

100km

Zvonkoe
(Звонкое)

Fevralsk
(Февральск)

Fevralskoe
(Февральское)

Chervinka
(Червинка)

Meun
(Меун)

Maiski
(Майский)

Nora
(Нора)

Dugda
(Дугда)

Tungala
(Тунгала)

Miroshnichenko
(Мирошниченко)

Zeya River

Zeya
(Зея)

Moldavski
(Молдавский)

Ogoron
(Огорон)

Verkhnezeisk
(Верхнезейск)

Arbalenok
(Арбаленок)

Bomnak
(Бомнак)

Verkhnezeisk

Ulak
(улак)

Tutaul
(Татаул)

Unakha
(Унаха)

Dess
(Десс)

Dipkun
(Дипкун)

Mateveaya
(Маревая)

Mogot
(Могот)

Giljui
(Гилюй)

Yakutsk-Tynda
(Нагорная Якутская)

Zolotinka
(Золотинка)

Nagornaya Yakutskaya

Bestuzhevo
(Бестужево)

Seti
(Сети)

Belenkaya
(Беленькая)

Zabolotnoe
(Заболотное)

Anosovskaya
(Аносовская)

Murtygit
(Муртыгит)

Skovorodino
(Сковородино)

Khabarovsk

Tit
(Тит)

Chulman
(Чульман)

Chulbass
(Чульбасс)

Denisovski
(Денисовский)

Neryungri
(Нерюнгри)

Berkakit
(Беркакит)

Chilchi
(Чильчи)

Lopcha
(Лопча)

Larba
(Ларба)

Tynda
(Тында)

Kuvykta
(Кувыкта)

Khorogochi
(Хорогочи)

Ust-Urkima
(Усть-уркима)

Elgakan
(Эльгакан)

Bamovskaya
(Бамовская)

Trans-Siberian

Yuktali
(Юктали)

Taluma
(Талума)

Dyugabul
(Дюгабуль)

Ust-Nyukzha
(Усть-Нюкжа)

Irkutsk

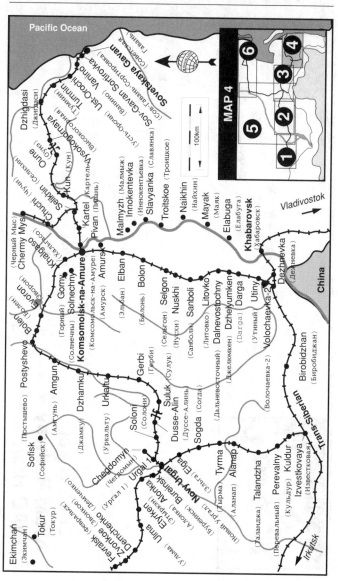

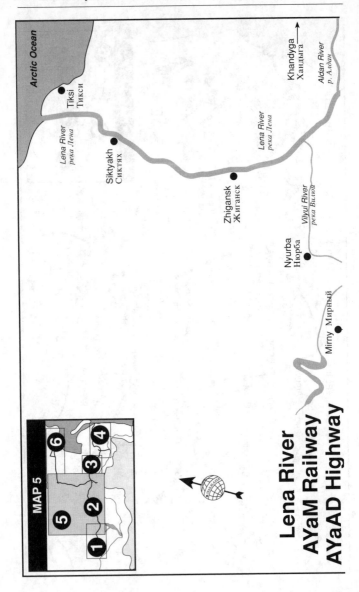

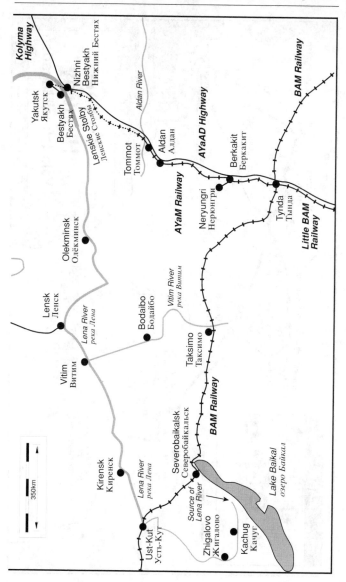

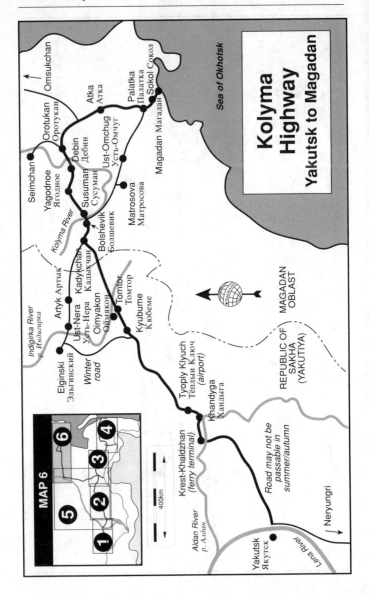

Kolyma
Highway
Yakutsk to Magadan

MAP 6

380  Index

## ❏ OTHER GUIDES FROM TRAILBLAZER PUBLICATIONS

For more information about Trailblazer and our expanding range of guides,
for where to find your nearest stockist, for guidebook updates
or for credit card mail order sales (post free worldwide) visit our Web site:

**www.trailblazer-guides.com**

**ROUTE GUIDES FOR THE ADVENTUROUS TRAVELLER**

### Trekking in the Moroccan Atlas  *Richard Knight*
256 pages, 53 maps, 30 colour photos
ISBN 1 873756 35 6, *1st edition*, £11.99, US$17.95
The Atlas mountains in southern Morocco provide one of the most
spectacular hiking destinations in Africa. This new guide includes
route descriptions and detailed maps for the best Atlas treks in
the Toubkal, M'goun, Sirwa and Jbel Sahro regions. Places to
stay, walking times and points of interest are all included, plus
town guides to Marrakesh and Ouarzazate.

### The Inca Trail, Cuzco & Machu Picchu  *Richard Danbury*
256 pages, 32 maps, 24 colour photos
ISBN 1 873756 29 1, *1st edition*, £9.99, US$16.95
The Inca Trail from Cuzco to Machu Picchu is South America's most
popular hike. This practical guide includes 20 detailed trail maps,
plans of eight Inca sites, plus guides to Cuzco and Machu Picchu.
*'Danbury's research is thorough...you need this one'.* **The Sunday
Times**   *'...difficult to put down...This book is essential.'* **ITN (USA)**

### Trekking in the Dolomites  *Henry Stedman*
256 pages, 52 trail maps, 13 town plans, 30 colour photos
ISBN 1 873756 34 8, *1st edition*, £11.99, US$17.95
The Dolomites region of northern Italy encompasses some of the
most beautiful mountain scenery in Europe. This new guide features selected routes including Alta Via II, a West-East traverse
and other trails. Places to stay, walking times and points of interest are included, plus detailed guides to Cortina, Bolzano,
Bressanone and 10 other towns.

### Trekking in the Pyrenees  *Douglas Streatfeild-James*
320 pages, 95 maps, 30 colour photos
ISBN 1 873756 50 X, *2nd edition*, £11.99, US$18.95
All the main trails along the France-Spain border from the famous
GR10 coast to coast hike and the most scenic sections of the GR11,
to many shorter routes. 95 route maps include walking times and
places to stay. This new edition has extended coverage of Spain.
*'Readily accessible, well-written and most readable...'* **John Cleare**

### Trekking in Ladakh  *Charlie Loram*
288 pages, 70 maps, 24 colour photos
ISBN 1 873756 30 5, *2nd edition*, £10.99, US$18.95
Since Kashmir became off-limits, foreign visitors to India have
been coming to this spectacular Himalayan region in ever-
increasing numbers. Fully revised and extended 2nd edition of
Charlie Loram's practical guide. Includes 70 detailed walking
maps, a Leh city guide plus information on getting to Ladakh.
*'Extensive...and well researched'.* **Climber Magazine**

### Trekking in the Everest Region  *Jamie McGuinness*
256 pages, 38 maps, 20 colour photos
ISBN 1 873756 17 8, *3rd edition*, £9.95, US$15.95
Third edition of the guide to the world's most famous trekking
region. Includes route guides, Kathmandu and getting to Nepal.
Written by a professional trek leader.
*'The pick of the guides to the area.'* **Adventure Travel**

**Japan by Rail** *Ramsey Zarifeh*
432 pages, 60 maps, 30 colour photos
ISBN 1 873756 23 2, *1st edition,* £12.99, US$18.95
The cheapest and most efficient way to travel around Japan is by train with a Japan Rail pass. This guide includes detailed route and planning information, where to stay, where to eat and the most interesting places to stop off along the way. Includes more than 60 rail maps and town plans.

**China by Rail** *Douglas Streatfeild-James*
384 pages, 54 maps, 30 colour photos
ISBN 1 873756 15 1, *1st edition,* £11.95, US$17.95
ISBN 1 873756 62 3, *2nd edition,* £12.99 due early 2002
The guide to China for rail travellers. Most visitors use the comprehensive rail system to get around. This guide takes in all the main attractions, with full details of where to stay and where to eat – for all budgets. Beijing, Hong Kong and 32 towns covered in detail.

**Australia by Rail** *Colin Taylor*
288 pages, 50 maps, 30 colour photos
ISBN 1 873756 40 2, *4th edition,* £11.99, US$19.95
Re-researched and expanded to include 50 strip maps covering all rail routes in Australia plus new information for rail travellers. Includes 14 town plans and six city guides: where to stay, where to eat and the most interesting places to stop off along the way.

**Silk Route by Rail** *Dominic Streatfeild-James*
320 pages, 37 maps, 30 colour photos
ISBN 1 873756 14 3, *2nd edition,* £10.95, US$17.95
First edition short-listed for the **Thomas Cook Guidebook Awards**. Covers the railway line which follows the old Silk Route. It's possible to travel by rail from Moscow via the Central Asian cities of Samarkand and Tashkent across western China to Beijing. Includes guides to 17 cities along the way.

**Trans-Canada Rail Guide** *Melissa Graham*
240 pages, 31 maps, 24 colour photos
ISBN 1 873756 39 9, *2nd edition,* £10.99, US$16.95
Expanded 2nd edition now includes Calgary city guide. Comprehensive guide to Canada's trans-continental railroad. Covers the entire route from coast to coast. What to see and where to stay in the cities along the line, with information for all budgets.
*Invaluable – **The Daily Telegraph***

**Vietnam by Rail** *Tess Read*
320 pages, 45 maps, 30 colour photos
ISBN 1 873756 44 5, *1st edition,* £11.99, US$18.95
The 'Reunification Express' railway links the north and south and is the most popular way to travel the country. Includes a history of Vietnam's railways, a blow by blow account of the war, and a detailed route guide with 12 strip maps. Plus comprehensive guides to 24 towns and cities.

**Trans-Siberian Handbook** *Bryn Thomas*
432 pages, 50 maps, 32 colour photos
ISBN 1 873756 42 9, *5th edition*, £12.99, US$19.95
First edition short-listed for the **Thomas Cook Guidebook Awards**. Fifth edition of the most popular guide to the world's longest rail journey. How to arrange a trip, plus a km-by-km guide to the Trans-Siberian, Trans-Manchurian and Trans-Mongolian routes. Fully updated and expanded to include extra information on travelling independently in Russia.
'The Trans-Siberian Handbook is a must.' *The Sunday Times*
'Definitive guide' *Condé Nast Traveler*

**Tuva & Southern Siberia** *Neil McGowan*
256 pages, 20 maps, 32 colour photos
ISBN 1 873756 61 5, *1st edition*, £12.99, US$19.95
To be **released in early 2003**. Once famously written up as unvisitable, Tuva remains a destination for the determinedly dedicated. For those few who go, the region offers not only shamanic cults, Buddhist centres, world-famous throat-singing and a living nomadic culture but also outdoor activities such as river rafting and riding that can also be enjoyed in neighbouring Altay – one of the most beautiful parts of Siberia. The whole area is archaelogically rich; it was here that the fabulously-wealthy Kurgan warlords flourished and cannibal cults once practised their extreme cuisine in the region.

# Map legend

| | | | |
|---|---|---|---|
| ♟ | Government building (town administration, sports complex or police) | ♈ | Chemist/drugstore |
| 🚢 | Railway station | ⚓ | Port for passengers |
| 🚌 | Bus station | 🎓 | School |
| 🅴🅻 | Hotel | ⬭ | Stadium |
| 📷 | TOTs (shopping complex) | ♣ | Park |
| ☕ | Cafe or restaurant | ⊕ | Hospital |
| 🏠 | Food shop | 📕 | Book shop or library |
| 🄰 | Market | ♫ | Memorial |
| 🎁 | Speciality shop | ✈ | Aeroflot/airline office |
| ✉ | Post office | 🎬 | Cinema |
| ☎ | Telephone office | ★ | Special feature |
| ☎✉ | Combined post/phone office | 🏛 | Historic building |
| ✈ | Airport | ✝ | Russian Orthodox Church |
| | | 🎿 | Downhill ski run |